RITUALS AND RITUAL THEORY IN ANCIENT ISRAEL

THE BRILL REFERENCE LIBRARY OF JUDAISM

VOLUME 10

RITUALS AND RITUAL THEORY
IN ANCIENT ISRAEL

BY

ITHAMAR GRUENWALD

BRILL
LEIDEN · BOSTON
2003

This book is printed on acid-free paper.

Library of Congress Cataloging-in-Publication Data

Gruenwald, Ithamar
  Rituals and Ritual Theory in Ancient Israel / by Ithamar Gruenwald.
  p. cm. — (The Brill reference library of ancient Judaism, ISSN 1556-1237 ; v. 10)
  Includes bibliographical references and index.
  ISBN 9004126279 (alk. paper)
  1. Bible—Criticism, interpretation, etc. 2. Judaism—Liturgy—Philosophy. 3. Ritual. 4. Judaism—
    History—To 70 A.D.   I. Title   II. Series

BM660 .G78 2003
296.4/9 21   2002033038

ISSN   1566-1237
ISBN   90 04 12627 9

PRINTED IN THE NETHERLANDS

CONTENTS

The study of rituals in the context of an anthropological approach. A definition of rituals as behaviourally autonomous expressions of the human mind. Focussing attention on what is done, how it is done, and what it brings into effect. The need to separate the discussion of rituals from the context of theology and symbolic acts. The meaning of rituals is embedded in the process of doing. The inner logic that makes the individual segments of the ritual acts work. The ritual theory of every ritual is embedded in the logic of the ritual process. Jewish law and Halakhah as rituals. The ritual "cosmos", or attitudinal space. The labelling-approach to rituals as opposed to a detailed discussion of ritual processes.

The Book of Genesis and the ethos stage in the religion of ancient Israel. Ethos as a way of life (in our case, an economic system) that shapes culture at a stage that precedes the one in which a full-scale religion unfolds. In the case of ancient Israel two rival kinds of economic ethos compete for hegemony: Sheep herding, nomadism, tribal organisation *versus* agriculture, cattle breeding, urbanisation, and monarchic organisation. What brings economics and religious ethos together? Ethos and rituals. The story of Cain and Abel. The cursed *Adamah*. Abraham, the shepherd. Jacob and his sons. The ethos-duality in the case of Isaac. John the Baptist. The two Enochs. The ritual notion of walking in the Book of Genesis.

Myth is the shaping story behind ritual. Mythology comprises of myths that lost their connectedness to rituals. Myth and rituals in the history of their scholarly perception. The mythic status of philosophical explanations given to rituals. The case of Maimonides. Suggestions for a psychoanalytic approach to myth. The creation of Man in the *Tselem* of Elohim. Ritual and mythopoesis. Eliade's discussion of myth. Myth, temple, and ritual purity. The mythic status of the Exodus story. The various processes of ritualising the Pessach-event. The mythic status of the concept of the written/oral Torah.

PREFACE

Let me briefly explain what this book wishes to accomplish, with an example. Eating to satisfy one's feeling of hunger obeys natural needs. Eating addresses life-preserving instincts. When we eat every hour or so, we demonstrate a habit that belongs to a particular repetitive pattern or rule. When we say that we require a specific mixture of ingredients in order to satisfy our hunger, our habits reflect a personal preference or predilection. Paying special attention to such matters as hygienic rules, a specific recipe, establishing a repetitive pattern of repetition and even the manner in which we serve the food, upgrades the eating process to the sphere of ritual behaviour. We may even have an vegetarian ideology that bears upon the choices we make with regard to the kind of food we prefer.

I believe there is no need to show how the example works in the case of rituals. On a personal level, rituals imply a fixed order to the act and, even more importantly, the conviction that any deviation from the "protocol" is likely to create counter effects, or cause damage to one's wellbeing. Rituals easily cross the borderline between the personal and the communal. When the event is shared by a community, the ritual is upgraded in function: it creates a sense of participation in the community, as well as its identity. On the communal level, the prevailing notion holds that any deviation from the "protocol" annuls the function of the ritual. In such a case, the ritual fails to connect to the situation for which it is intended. In many cases, not doing a ritual means that an element that could preserve the wholesomeness of the community is not enacted.

An important principle of rituals is that the components of the ritual act require an orderly performance. This order establishes the inner logic of the ritual acts. The essential factors, therefore, that are active in shaping rituals, are the detailed prescriptions that should be followed and the notion that not following the prescription means failure, with all the consequences that such a failure entails. In any event, all rituals are conducive to creating desired changes, technically called 'transformations'.

These introductory comments are designed to make the reader see the starting point of my discussion. At this point, it addresses one major issue, namely, what differentiates simple human activity from ritual behaviour. One may go a step further and ask, "Why does the eating according to a fixed protocol have the desired effects, which a normal meal lacks?" The initial answer would be, "This is how rituals work, and we do not really know why". Although a specific ideology may account for the doing of the ritual, it does not explain what makes rituals work the way they do. In fact, no intrinsic meaning or self-explanatory reason is normally attached to the manner in which we do the various parts of a specific ritual. In the example given above, a chemist may add an explanation: The components work chemically on the digestive system and on the metabolism, only when the ingredients are put together in a specific order and in the right quantities. This explanation makes matters look logical. So would the explanation given by a brain physiologist, although, at best he would simply locate the zone or nerve-centre in the brain, that control digestion and make one feel satisfied. In the realm of religion, a theological stance will offer an explanation. However, from the point of view of the doing of rituals, there is a limit to what explanations can achieve *in the very doing of rituals*. Explanations cannot explain how an explanation works in the ritual act itself, that is to say, an explanation may stimulate the doing of rituals, but the explanation itself has no effect on how the rituals work to achieve their specific results. In a religious context, explanations set the framework for the cause and result, but the rituals, which link the two ends, operate by a logic that an explanation does not necessarily possess or address. In brief, explanations do not function in the ritual act itself.

To make my point as clear as possible, the degree to which eating satisfies hunger does not depend on any explanation. The act of eating does it all, regardless of the explanation. What the explanation does is to convince people to persist in what they are doing, and to point to the logic implied by the order that is essential to the act. Practically speaking, though, the explanation says, "this is the order," but it fails to account for what it accomplishes and how. Thus, knowing the general explanation of why we cook this meal and for what purposes is not as essential as we may think to the very

preparations we make, the process of cooking, and, finally, the protocol involved in eating it. As we shall see, the same principle applies to most of the rituals that we shall examine here. That is to
say, the degree to which the doing of rituals requires an ideology or
theology is not self evident. It is one of the major questions to be
discussed in this book.

A further point needs to be mentioned here. When we say, "This
is the only way to do it, because my father and grandfather did it
the same way," we introduce the notion of (family) *tradition*. This adds
a new factor to the study of rituals. In religions, this constitutes a
"theological" dimension, but significant as this may be in the eyes
of the people doing the ritual, it does not explain the ritual itself. If,
furthermore, people are told that they have always to do the same
thing in the same manner, one introduces the factor of *authority*. Both,
the notion of tradition and the factor of authority, have sociological
significance and relevance, but they do not explain how rituals work.
Nonetheless, rituals function as constitutive acts in what may be the
basis of a social structure. In religion, telling people to behave or to
do things in a certain manner has an additional relevance. It helps
to shape a community that is bound together by factors such as the
belief in a divine being, a hierarchy of authorities, and textbooks that
contain regulations on which rituals to do, when, how, and to what
purpose. Rituals make a community live by agreement on the centrality of a certain set of actions and signs. In the final resort, though,
all these factors have little to say on which kind of ritual is done and
how it is done.

II

It is important to note that, in my discussion of rituals, I refer to
rituals as (a) a form of human behaviour that primarily reflects the
mind that generates them, rather than any ideology or symbolic
structures; (b) not specifically religious forms of behaviour, unless,
of course, they are included in a religious structure or context; (c) a
mode of behaviour that represents a significant departure from instinct and custom; (d) promoting the preservation, regeneration, and
reconstitution of conditions that people consider essential to their
vital life processes; (e) addressing the issue of survival, whether biological or other. In rituals, the mind demonstrates its reaction to
existence. When existence is at stake, the mind reacts in structured

actions, namely, in rituals. In trying to understand a ritual, it is important to focus on the very manner in which it relates (= "*how*") to a specific reality or form of existence. The questions "*why*" and "*what for*" enter at later stage, and mark the introduction of an ideology or theology. In my view, then, rituals are neither expressive of any ideology or theology. Rituals are what they are by the force of the mind that generates them, as an independent, autonomous, indigenous—that is, *sui generis*—form of reaction, or expression, to a specific condition or form of existence. In other words, they are not a behavioural expression of symbols.

I am aware that this way of treating the subject of rituals is something of a novelty in religious studies. It stems from recent research in anthropological studies, in which the human mind is seen as the major factor that explains and accounts, among other things, for rituals. In this respect, the social setting of rituals comes next in line. The theory of rituals, developed in this book, derives from the consequences of this way of looking at rituals. I am fully aware of the fact that viewing rituals as behavioural expressions of the human mind, regardless of any ideology or pre-existing symbolism, is likely to elicit criticism. I am equally aware of the risk I take in placing social settings and motivations second in line. My primary concern is to focus on rituals in their own performative content. In this manner, I hope to be able to reposition the understanding of rituals in the framework of religious studies. In fact, the present work seeks to place the study of rituals at the centre of interest in religious studies. Paradoxically, I do this by discussing rituals in a broader context than simply the religious one.

The field of religious studies has shown interest in many issues, but not sufficient interest in the detailed study of rituals. Consequently, a repositioning of rituals in religious studies is, to my mind, a scholarly desideratum. Understanding rituals from a behavioural perspective, rather than from the usual textual, historical, or theological perspective, is likely to bring about a transformation of the prevalent conventions in the field of religious studies. This is indeed an ambitious project, but I believe that I am not alone in attempting to address, in a new way, the subject of rituals in religion in general, and in the religion of ancient Israel, including, for that matter, aspects of Judaic Halakhah in particular. Consequently, I reposition certain issues in Judaic studies, as well.

III

The ideas contained in the present book first crystallised in a graduate seminar on rituals (1996), which I gave in the framework of Tel Aviv University's Program in Religious Studies. What I said then came as an utter surprise, even shock, to many of my students. They knew me as a practising, orthodox, Jew whose scholarly interests were mainly Apocalypticism, mysticism and religious ideas in the early centuries of the Christian era. In short, in the students' eyes, my academic image was primarily connected to the exploration of religious ideas. The methodological rigour, with which I persisted in the pursuit of a completely different scholarly path, caused a cognitive dissonance that was difficult to overcome. This was not something they had expected of me.

This marked the beginning of my venture into the field of rituals and ritual theory. Ultimately, I reached new conclusions with regard to the methodological approach needed for the study of rituals in a program of religious studies. By the end of the academic year, my students admitted that they had been fully rewarded and enlightened. Their questions and comments offered critical support and were a mark of their unreserved, intellectual participation. For this, they deserve many words of praise and sincere appreciation. They consistently urged me to work harder, they made me think more clearly, and they helped me reach a point at which I was able to express myself more convincingly. In the terms used in this book, I was transformed.

The new stage in my study of rituals evolved, when a year later I was asked to write a proposal for an international research group on "Narratives of Rituals" at the Institute of Advanced Studies, at the Hebrew University of Jerusalem. The intensive work executed in connection with the various drafts of that proposal were my first venture in putting into writing what had been conveyed only orally till then. However, no tinge of originality could have emerged without the invaluable help, benevolently extended to me by Professors Don Handelman and David Shulman. Together, we hammered out something that was new to me and to us. The proposal and the work of the group itself (February to August, 1999) are reflected in almost every page of this book.

I hope that the reader will have the patience to discover the reasons why and in what sense I consider it a ritual act to thank my colleagues at the Institute. I shall list them alphabetically: Professors Hans Dieter Betz (University of Chicago), Cristiano Grottanelli (University of Pisa), Don Handelman (The Hebrew University of Jerusalem), Bruce Kapferer (now at the University of Bergen), Jadran Mimica (University of Sydney), Simo Parpola (University of Helsinki), Uri Rubin (Tel Aviv University), David Shulman (The Hebrew University of Jerusalem), and Margaret Trawick (Massey University, New Zealand). We all felt "transformed" by the discussions and seminars at the Institute. In this connection, special thanks are also due to the staff of the Institute and to its then Head, Professor Alexander Levitzki. When the Institute's electric system was rewired in January 1999, the work ritually anticipated the process we were to undergo on the intellectual plane. Finally, the workers who took from my room a volume of the Hebrew Scripture and a clock must have wanted to give me a real-to-life intimation of a sacrificial parting-with. They convinced me, and the reader is invited to follow suit, that sacrifices are the core of rituals.

Words of deep collegial appreciation are also due to Professors Jacob Neusner and Alan Avery-Peck, who graciously opened for me scholarly venues of various kinds. Several chapters of the present book thus found a stage for their dress rehearsal. If encouragement is part of the ritual process, then Professors Neusner and Avery-Peck enabled it in a model-setting manner. The chapters, published here, constitute substantially revised versions of earlier publications (the titles are mainly the same). They reflect the progress my work has made over the years. I hope that the many good friends and colleagues, who graciously offered comments and suggestions, will find that I have taken them at their word. In this respect, I would like to thank Professor Philip Wexler, who read a draft of this book and made valuable suggestions.

On behalf of Brill Academic Publishers, Ivo Romein showed that handling the production of a book can be a matter of friendly concern.

Finally, a word is due to and about my family. My wife, Rachel, had to suffer from the fact that when she needed my attention, I insisted on practising my personal ritual of devotion to academic work. Now, she is likely to go through yet another ordeal. She will have to read the book to understand what I mean when I say that I 'sacrifice' the book to her. Our daughter, Na`amah, and her husband, Benny, helped provide the setting in which the connections

between my study and their profession, clinical psychology, began
to make sense and to reap the first fruits. Our daughter, Efrat, and
her husband, Kuki (Ya`acov), watched from a distance, but were
intimately involved through their love and good spirits. Both families gave Rachel and me wonderful grandchildren. They are all the
proof that is needed for a positive answer to the question: is there
life beyond the academic world?

We all remember our beloved son, Eviathar, who was taken from
us before he had a chance to fulfil himself.

*****

A few technical comments are in order here.

(1) I wish to alert the reader to fact that the book contains a certain
amount of repetitive material. In planning the overall structure of
the book, I decided to devote individual chapters to specific issues,
within the larger framework of the theory of rituals. In order to
accomplish this goal, some material had to be repeated whenever
the case required. This material remains the same, though sometimes slightly altered, in the course of the discussion. Instead of
referring the reader to other locations in the book, each chapter
provides an independent and closed unit of discussion. At times, the
reader will come across something he has already read in a different context, though worded differently. A new context always allows
for variations, revisions, and changes to take place. Ultimately, this
enables the discussion to broaden and deepen.

(2) The bibliographical references follow the form in which they were
published. In most cases, the name of the publisher is given first,
followed by the location and date of publication. When the order is
different, I have made the necessary technical adjustments. When
there are more than two editors or places of publications, only the
first is given, followed by three dots (...).

CHAPTER ONE

RITUALS AND RITUAL THEORY—
INTRODUCTORY REMARKS

I

This book on rituals and ritual theory addresses four questions.

(1) How do I define rituals and which factors differentiate them from other forms of human behaviour and action?[1]
(2) How do rituals work and what makes them work?
(3) What is the ritual theory, which is embedded or embodied, in each ritual?
(4) What are the terms of reference, or methodological procedures, which are most suited to the discussion of the subject?

With regard to the last question, I wish to clarify two points: I conduct the present study in the framework of terms of reference related to structured human behaviour. I do *not* use terms of reference that relate to theology, ideology or symbolism. Further on, in this chapter, I shall explain the reasons for proceeding in this way. In essence, I make use of advanced research methods in anthropological studies, many of which came to my attention through my colleagues mentioned in the Preface, but philosophical and experientially phenomenological considerations also substantially influence the way I present the materials. Thus, the subject of religious studies, in general, will gain from these vantage points. The specifics of the discussion, though, will focus

---

[1] This question should not be confused with another one, frequently asked in the study of anthropology and religion. Scholars usually view rituals as a religious phenomenon. Consequently, many of them (Frazer, Durkheim and Malinowski are notable examples, in this respect) asked the question: what is the difference between a religious rite and *magic*? Since the present book maintains a completely different approach to the study of ritual behaviour, I have judged it unnecessary to deal with this question.

on the study and understanding of rituals in Judaism. To my re-
gret, Judaic studies have, so far, had little to offer, in this respect.

The overall premise, which gives the discussion an integrating
orientation, is that rituals are an unmediated mode of expression.
The human mind is the direct source of ritual behaviour. Rituals
are one of the major ways in which the human mind expresses
itself and it does this without first creating the ideas or the symbols, to which, according to the prevalent view, rituals give expression. Rituals do not translate ideas into actions, nor do symbols enter the behavioural context of rituals. The present study
will offer a systematic examination of the compositional and operational structure of rituals. It will do this by demonstrating that the
ritual theory of each ritual is its embedded logic. This logic endows each ritual with an inner coherency that binds the segmented
details into a functioning Gestalt. This logic works like a genetic
code, which determines and shapes the rituals. This logic also
represents the imprint that the human mind leaves on rituals. In
other words, rituals express, by themselves, the ritual theory
embedded in them. Ritual theory relates to the coherent logic that
makes rituals do what the mind wishes them to do. Since humans—
whether acting individually or in socially integrated groups—are
the ones who do the rituals,[2] the perspectives, from which I examine the subject of rituals, are connected with behavioural anthropology. In this context, issues related to scholarly methodology and research ontology, too, will also receive close attention.

In line with the above, the shortest definition of rituals that
I can suggest at this point is the following: rituals are behaviourally
autonomous (that is, intrinsically independent) expressions of the
human mind. The notion of the mind, here and elsewhere in this
book, presupposes the operation of special modes of interaction
between various mental, human faculties. Feelings, and to some
extent sensational perceptions, are part of these faculties. In the
first place, therefore, rituals operate as behavioural entities. Rituals
are structured as specifically purposive, and targeted, forms of
behaviour. Of course, if one considers the issue of religious rituals, contextualizing traits constitute a dominant presence. Religion

---

[2] I wish to make a terminological point. I speak of 'doing' rituals, rather than
of performing them, for performance indicates that something is being done in order
to show that it is done. I wish to emphasise doing for its own sake.

configures a special context in which rituals have specific forms, reasons, and purposes. However, on a general epistemological level, I consider rituals to be structured forms of human behaviour which, initially, have no specific links to religious issues, that is, issues that are grounded in and shaped by theological notions and motivation. Understanding rituals in their almost universal context may prove helpful in understanding rituals in their specifically religious context. *Mutatis mutandis*, religious rituals may tell us a lot about rituals in general. Almost every chapter in this book illustrates, in one way or another, the extent to which these two streams, rituals and religious rituals, create a beneficial venue for mutual fructification.

The study of rituals primarily deals with the particulars of what is done, how it is done, and, when specified, the reason and purpose for doing it. All these factors are embedded in the very act of the doing. However, as indicated, they do not necessarily constitute an issue that has religious consequences—neither in essence nor in their specific configurations.[3] More specifically expressed, in my understanding of rituals and their ritual theory, there is no room for the inevitable inclusion of theological considerations. I wish to stress this point as clearly as possible. People doing rituals, in their specifically religious configuration, do not necessarily have a theology that creates for them a required context.[4] Many rituals are done by religious people who have nei-

---

[3] A brief comment on verbal utterances and prayers, however, is due. Linguistic—and, for that matter, artistic—activity involves a more intellective process of the human mind than my definition appears to allow. Unless a meditative stance accompanies the prayers, most people tend to recite the texts almost automatically. When the prayers are recited with a special purpose in mind (for instance, praying for the health of a person), the words, in many cases, weigh as much as does the very act of praying. I admit that spontaneous prayer, in which the person chooses his/her own words, defies this observation. Furthermore, I would argue that the introduction of *nomina barbara* ("foreign names") in magical incantations aims at making people aware of what they say. If the magician mispronounces these "foreign names," the magical act is likely to fail.

[4] The question of meaning in rituals is one of the most hotly debated issues in recent scholarship. As will be seen, I side with those who say that rituals create their own meaning. Rituals do not represent a meaning or truth, outside of their own performative dimensions. The ritual process, done according to its own embedded logic, is the only telling factor, in this respect. Demonstrating the implications of this point is one of the major goals of this work. For a full reference illustrating the opposite view, here is a quote from A. R. Radcliffe-Brown, *Structure and Function in Primitive Society*, The Free Press: New York, 1965 (originally published in 1952), p.

ther the language nor the mental capacity to create, or engage in, theological activity. Admittedly, theology contributes to shaping the essential factors that are vital for maintaining identity and an overall systemic structure. However, rituals do what they do, even without having an ancillary theological basis. Among other things it does, theology postulates the divine as the ultimate authority present in ritual activity; but, in the final resort, it does not explain the intrinsic modes of doing, which characterise rituals.

There are additional questions that demand scholarly attention: (1) How should one proceed in decoding ritual theory in practised rituals, when the rituals themselves make no explicit statement about it? (2) What are the terms of reference that should be utilised in decoding ritual theory? (3) What does ritual theory do to our understanding of practised rituals? For the time being, I shall attempt to give a general answer to these questions. I assume that every ritual operates on a series of systemic principles that make rituals what they are. These principles are the inner logic of rituals.[5] Exploring the method involved in decoding these principles, rather than discussing the theological framework in which rituals are done and do their work, is one of major tasks of the present book. In short, this book focuses on general modes of ritual behaviour and their respective modes of ritual theory. Furthermore, I suggest viewing rituals and ritual theory from an epistemological point of view. That is to say, the approach adopted here examines questions of intrinsic essence and their relationship to the doing of rituals and the ritual theory reflected in the rituals.

143: "A second approach to the study of ritual is therefore by a consideration not of their purpose or reason but of their meaning. I am here using the words symbol and meaning as coincident. Whatever has a meaning is a symbol and the meaning is whatever is expressed by the symbol." In many ways, this statement and my approach go in opposite directions.

[5] Very few scholars disengage the discussion of rituals from the assumption that they express symbolic content. In this respect, it is worth quoting Pierre Bourdieu, *Outline of a Theory of Practice*, Cambridge University Press: Cambridge, 1977. Bourdieu writes: "Understanding ritual practice is not a question of decoding the internal logic of a symbolism but of restoring practical necessity by relating it to the real conditions of its genesis, that is, to the conditions in which it functions, and the means it uses to attain them, are defined" (p. 114). In many ways, Bourdieu's general exposition and mine have a few things in common. However, it differs from mine in one essential respect. Bourdieu does not engage in systematic analysis or discussion of detailed rituals. That is to say, he refers to rituals rather than discusses them.

An important point needs to be made. Many studies of rituals contain sentences such as this: In order to achieve certain results in a particular context or setting, people offer sacrifices. However, very few scholars show real interest in the specifics of the ritual acts, as they are done in their programmed sequence. At best, scholars will state generally that, in a given setting, a specific ritual has special functions or specific purposes.[6] In remarkably rare cases, the detailed ritual process is viewed as crucial for the study of rituals, in the context of ritual theory. I, therefore, consider it a matter of utmost importance to change this tendency in the study of rituals. I believe that the unfolding of rituals in their processual modes is the major issue in the study of rituals.[7] In each case, I shall seek ways of identifying, in the sequential segmentation, the principles that give shape to the embedded ritual theory. The only way to do this is by exploring the details of each ritual action, and by following the traces that reflect its inner processual logic.

II

Having made these introductory comments, I believe it best to alert the reader, who has some knowledge of the modern study of rituals, as to what he or she should *not* expect this book to do: (1) Although I do not avoid making generalisations, I am not seeking to define an overall theory of rituals. What I state about individual rituals may be applied to other cases, but the differences are emphasised as clearly as possible; (2) As indicated above, it is my opinion that, in the phase that I cover, theology and ideology have no place in the discussion of rituals. Theology and ideology belong to the periphery of rituals as they are done and practised. Nonetheless, in cases where I consider theology to be relevant to the discussion, I refer to it without hesitation; (3) I do

---

[6] In order to illustrate this, I shall refer, in the terms of the present book, to a remote location, China: "In addition to literally feeding and clothing ghosts, the ceremony attempts to obtain salvation from them." This quote comes from P. Steven Sangren, *History and Magical Power in Chinese Community*, Stanford University Press: Stanford, 1987, p. 147. However, no details are given with regard to what is done, how it is done, and what makes the efficacy of the ritual achieve its goals. I give this example to illustrate the extent to which I examined scholarly studies that could inform my work. Further examples of this kind will follow.

[7] I shall return to this point later, in this Introduction, and particularly in Chapter Five and Six, where specific rituals are discussed in detail.

not consider rituals as symbolic expressions of ideas or as concrete expressions of symbolic entities. I accept that rituals are symbolic forms in their own right (like language, the arts, and historical thinking), but, to my mind, they do not translate symbols into
actions. What can be said is that, in certain cases, rituals help to
create or maintain icons and symbols. These points will be elab-
orated on, in the course of this book. It is, however, only fair to
inform the reader, from the outset, which direction, in the discussion of rituals, this book does not follow.

Having outlined the general points of departure, the question
now is: what *does* this study attempt to do? This study wishes to
explore the different aspects of ritual theory, as they are embodied in the performative context of rituals. The basic premise, which
this book puts forward, is that each ritual has its own, embedded, or embodied, ritual theory. I shall also explore the ways in
which the specific conclusions that are reached apply to other
aspects of research. I have, particularly, in mind points of convergence and integration that help to throw light on the manner
in which people interact with their immediate environments. In
this respect, "environments" encompass a rather rich phenomenological spectrum. They are not necessarily physical or spatial. They
include social, psychological, and metaphysical factors—to name
but a few.

A crucial question, which has already been addressed in the
"Preface," is: what makes rituals different from any other form of
human action or behaviour?[8] The full answer will become clear
in the course of the book. Indeed, its exploration constitutes the
major part of this study. To begin with, it is important to point
out the structured and specifically purposive nature of rituals. In
this connection, I wish to draw the reader's attention to the fact
that I use ritual in its plural mode, 'rituals.' Each ritual has its
own structure and its own embodied ritual theory. Depending on
its specific structure, each ritual achieves its purposive goals in a

---

[8] A similar question, though phrased in different terms, is also the starting point
in the discussion of rituals in E. Thomas Lawson and Robert N. McCauley, *Rethinking
Religion: Connecting Cognition and Culture*, Cambridge University Press: Cambridge and
New York, 1990. The authors write: "It is noncontroversial that rituals are actions.
So, one thing any theory of participants' representations of religious rituals had better
be able to do is to say what the relation of religious rituals is to other sorts of
actions" (p. 84). While the authors speak of a basic analogy between actions and
religious rituals, I strive to show the difference.

manner that differs from other rituals. Since I refer to rituals in a
rather broad sense, that is, as a term covering both religious and
non-religious forms of structured behaviour, the goals change
substantially from case to case. I concur with the view that human activity, in general, exhibits similar traits to those found in
ritual forms of behaviour. People may not always be aware of this
fact. On closer examination, one can see that human actions have
discernable features and, more important still, an inner structure.
Structure is a key word here.[9] It should translate into notions of
functional commensurability, which are individually applicable to
specific cases. The manner in which this comes into effect is hard
to explain. In some mysterious ways, a certain act brings about
results that, without any explicit logic, create a link between the
action and the specific result. In terms of behavioural stances, there
is no abstract notion of "ritual," only various rituals. Each ritual
is done in a special manner; otherwise, it cannot achieve its specifically designated goal. Since each ritual is unique, it embodies
its own, uniquely modelled, ritual theory.

Rituals often have a ceremonial presence, that is to say, they
require preparation and a display of various accompanying elements (special garments, colours, olfactory materials, etc.) Ceremonies aim at drawing people's attention to something that is
worth noticing, something that is extraordinary in some way. They
do not necessarily aim, as rituals do, at signalling to people that
there are certain practices, which they should consider crucial to
their life or existence.[10] Rituals, like ceremonies, are repeatable
events; people can do them for the same purposes, in the same
orderly manner, and with the expectation of the same results. Some
rituals have a more localised character, which means that they
represent a specific function or identity. In these cases, the specific place and time chosen for the doing of the rituals indicates
functional specificity.

---

[9] Since I examine rituals in their endless configurations, I distance myself from
the kind of universal structuralism sought by Claude Levi-Strauss.

[10] Here, I fully agree with A. R. Radcliffe-Brown, *Op. Cit.*, pp. 134-5: "A ritual
prohibition is a rule of behaviour which is associated with a belief that an infraction will result in an undesirable change in the ritual status of the person who fails
to keep to the rule. This change of ritual status is conceived in many different ways
in different societies, but everywhere there is the idea that it involves the likelihood
of some minor or major misfortune which will befall the person concerned." We shall
return to this characterisation of rituals at different points in this study.

Indeed, many rituals are done, when the fixed occasion, to do them, comes. This brings up the question: what comes first, the date (the occasion) or the ritual? In a way, this is the same question as that about the chicken and the egg. Nonetheless, the relativisation of the problem is a first step in suggesting an answer that is different from that usually given. Briefly, dates create ritual opportunities. However, without the rituals, the date remains a neutral sign on the calendar, a mere day. Rituals activate the date, transforming it into an event that carries significance. In this respect, rituals configure the mechanical time sequence into a potentially meaningful process. Furthermore, rituals break up the mechanical time-flow into significant units. Usually, they are cyclically repeatable. Rituals shape time into structurally recognisable patterns: days, weeks, months, and years.[11] In this respect, it is true to say, that rituals (mostly sacrificial ones and prayers) endow the time units with their specifically functional character. Often, though, people are ignorant of the significance of a particular date and its accompanying rituals. They do not know why they celebrate a specific date with a specific sequence of rituals. How many people know the significance of Halloween, and particularly why they celebrate this day by this or that practice? I wish to argue that a particular date has to wait, so to speak, for its particular ritual(s) to activate, and then fix its potential qualities into a ritually meaningful date. The meaning in this case comes into being through the fact that the date, or day, is passed in a ritual mode. In religious language, one uses terms such as sacred or holy. For reasons that must be clear, by now, I do not consider it essential to use these terms here. In short, unless people do the relevant rituals, the particular day does not become a ritually meaningful date.

The repetitive potential of rituals is an essential factor in establishing cyclic time patterns. Here, ritual makes the pattern and consolidates it. Scholars often argue that rituals work both ways:

---

[11] This is the essence of the idea of creating the luminaries in *Gen.* 1: 14: "And God said: 'Let there be lights in the dome of the sky to separate the day from the night; and let them be for signs and for seasons and for days and years.'" The specific rituals connected with the delimitation of "times" for ritual purposes are still missing from this text. They are mentioned in other parts of the Pentateuch. Since my theoretical discussion of rituals does not deal with their specifically religious, that is, theological, configuration, I intentionally avoid using the notion of "holy times."

they single out time and place, and then time and place cause the enactment of specific rituals. I wish to add that time and place continue to preserve their special status, as long as the relevant rituals are done. The manner in which observant Jews keep the holiness of the Sabbath Day is telling, in this respect. From the candle lighting on the eve of the Sabbath Day (on Friday afternoon before sunset) until the candle lighting at the end of the Sabbath Day (on Saturday evening after nightfall), a highly detailed protocol of practices, that should or should not be done, preserves the special character of the day. As long as people observe the protocol, the Sabbath Day prevails. For any person to annul the validity of the Sabbath Day ("desecrating the Sabaath Day," is the technical term used) means that the Sabbath Day has no ritually binding protocol. In short, a ritual act marks the beginning of the Sabbath Day, and another marks the termination of the Day. Between the two events, many ritual practices mark the length, character, and nature of the day.

Time, in connection with place, provides a more complex setting for the enactment of certain rituals. Thus, entering into the land of Cana'an was an occasion (the time factor) for the enactment of certain rituals, particularly those connected with the land and its vegetation.[12] According to Jewish Halakhah, there are many ritual acts (many of them connected with the land) that are binding as long as people are settling the Land. When people leave the Land of Israel, these rituals cease to maintain their religious validity. More specifically, the Jerusalem Temple is considered the only place in which sacrificial rites could take place. When these rites are done outside of the Temple territory, they count as a religious desecration. There are also special rites that affirm the designated functions of the Temple. In religious terms, we would speak of the sanctification of the Temple. Since, as already

---

[12] Jacob Neusner discussed this issue in several connections. See, for instance, "The Religious Meaning of Halakhah," in: *The Halakhah: Historical and Religious Perspectives*, Brill: Leiden...2002, pp. 3-28. For Neusner, "religion" is the platform that calls forth category formation, whether Halakhic or theological. In the paper mentioned above, he speaks of the category of "enlandisement," that is the meaning which the settlement of the Land of Cana'an had for the ancient Israelites from the point of view of enforcing upon them certain *rules*. Neusner uses the term religious "rules" where I use the term "rituals." "Rules" is a term that has Halakhic— *i.e.*, theological and jurisdictional—significance, while "rituals" is a term, which encompasses a practising-behavioural setting.

indicated, I view rituals in a broader context than the religious one, I avoid using, whenever this makes sense, religious terminology and categories. In neutral terms, then, the Temple is the place that houses the rituals that preserve its existence and proper functioning.

This fact requires an explanation. For instance, reading the Hebrew Scripture gives the impression that specific dates in the annual calendar call for the doing of specific rituals. Thus, the late afternoon of the fourteenth day of the first month of the year (= "Nissan") is the appointed time for the Pessach (Passover) sacrifice. The ritual of "sitting" in a Succah (= booth) is one of the ways of marking the Feast of Booths, which begins on the eve of the fifteenth day of the seventh month (= "Tishri"). However, nothing significant, from a ritual point of view, can happen unless these two events are carefully prepared, in a ritual way. The preparation of the lamb for the Pessach sacrifice and the building of the booths, before these respective feasts begin, are two important examples. Those, who do not care, will not prepare anything for these events. A non-event does not require any preparatory ritual to enact it. I wish, therefore, to reiterate that the date creates the "temporal space," or occasion, for rituals to exercise their function. Nothing of significance happens without the rituals that are done to mark the beginning (and then the end) of the event. Furthermore, no ritual status is given to any action that is done at the wrong time. In other words, a circumstantial connection has to be established between a particular date and its relevant rituals, before the date is established as one of the Appointed Times (in Hebrew: *Mo'adim*). Once the Appointed Time (*Mo'ed*) has been ritually established, it calls for the doing of other rituals. The special character of the Appointed Time is sustained as long as these rituals are done. When the appointed time is over, no ritual status is given to its termination, before a ritual act is done to mark this fact. The same holds true with regard to the spatial delimitation of a place or space such as the Temple.

As indicated, once the special qualities of the calendric event are ritually established (for example, by lighting candles on the eve of the Sabbath), a series of other rituals are due. Their role is to keep the status of the event for as long as its legal regulations prescribe ("from evening to evening..."—*Lev.* 23: 32). Once the time comes to terminate the ritual activity, another special ritual is done to mark the termination. In other words, the "enter" and "exit" directions have a ritual formatting. The transition, in the annual cycle, from a plain calendric date to the complementary status of an "Appointed Event" takes place in the context of a ritual activity. The fact that people often act in a routine manner, without paying too much attention to what the prescribed rituals do for them or bring into effect, does not contradict the main argument proposed here. On the contrary, it shows that, initially, rituals can take place almost as an automatic reaction to a date or place. In light of our forthcoming discussion of the factor of intention in rituals, one should note that a minimal degree of attention (and, hence, of intention to do the ritual) already comes into effect in the very decision to do the ritual at an appointed time. In general, rituals are structured and composite entities. Consequently, their practice always requires at least a minimal degree of attention; otherwise, everything gets mixed up and the effects easily turn into counter-effects.

Speaking of the composite nature of rituals, an essential feature of rituals is their inner segmentation. Ensuring the right sequence that is necessary for each part of the ritual underlines the fact that conscious attention must be given to what is done. Similarly, when several rituals are done in a line, their orderly sequence is all that matters. I shall say more on these issues in due course.[13] However, it is worth referring to them, at this point, since they help us to view rituals in a framework that transcends instinctual reactions and utter meaninglessness. Instinctual reaction and utter meaninglessness are the trademarks of the radical views in the modern study of rituals. As close as this study may come to these views, it still wishes to maintain an essential point of difference. My argument is that rituals create meaning in the very act of doing. Paying attention to the right sequencing of the details is a paramount consideration in maintaining an elementary degree of order, hence meaning, in this respect.

As we have noted, the human mind is a key factor in making rituals what they are. We should note, though, that before it be-

---

[13] In this context, it is interesting to quote the definition of rituals given by Roy A. Rappaport in, *Ritual and Religion in the Making of Humanity*, Cambridge University Press: Cambridge, 1999, p. 24: "I take the term 'ritual' to denote *the performance of more or less invariant sequences of formal acts and utterances not entirely encoded by the performers*."

gins a process of conceptualisation (*i.e.*, in a formalised theology), the human mind expresses itself in structured actions (*alias*, rituals). Connected to this is the fact that rituals are usually structured in such a manner that requires or facilitates their being shared with others. Sharing, too, begins a socially-behavioural activity. The accompanying element of ideological considerations enters the scene at a more advanced stage. It is conceivable that these facts alert people to the need to synchronise and unify their participation in the communal acts. This is yet another illustration of the importance of giving attention to matters of protocol, which are the predominant characteristics of a mind set on doing rituals.[14]

Finally, in this respect, one should note that in spite of the fact that rituals initially emanate freely from the human mind, it does not necessarily follow that all rituals are spontaneous reactions to given situations. On the contrary, rituals are often prescribed to fulfil a specific mission. In life, they are prescribed in manuals or protocols of behaviour. In religion, we find them prescribed in a context that seeks meaning in the framework of the holy. In moments of danger and emergency people seek rescue in life-saving protocols. This is true of rituals in life and religion alike. Evidently, people believe that they can fully trust their chosen protocol. People are advised that, if they do not follow the protocol "by the letter of the law", they are likely to expose themselves to misfortune. Every manual affirms that success is guaranteed, only by following the written text in the right manner and order. Technical manuals specify that certain things must be done, at this or that time, in this or that order, etc., for a machine to work properly. Everything is clearly laid out, in this respect. In principle, the trust people show in manuals and the confidence they have in recipes,

---

[14] It should be remarked that the factor of intentionality comes close, but is not identical with, the factor of intention (in Hebrew: *kavanah*) which is a debated issue in Halakhah. The question is, whether in doing the *mitzwot*, the religious precepts, one should be fully aware of what one does, and for what reason and purpose. Indeed, the Halakhic ruling is that, in most cases, no "intention" is required. The factor of intentionality introduces a different aspect. It will be discussed in Chapter 4. In using the term "intentionality" I mean, an awareness of the mind that is vital to creating a ritual situation. The examples that will be discussed in Chapter 4 concern the mind's orientation with respect to edibles becoming wet—a condition that makes them susceptible to being impure. The fact of being wet counts, in matters of impurity, only when the owner of the edibles is pleased with the fact that they are wet.

for instance, is as strong as the trust religious people have in the efficacy of ritual prescriptions, as defined in their scriptures (and by God).

III

More needs to be said, at this point, about the subject of the mind and rituals. As indicated above, I consider rituals to be autonomous expressions of the human mind. The mind creates various forms of reactions to the phenomenal world, or existence, and the kind of behaviour, which we call 'ritual', is one of the principle forms, in this respect. The mind creates rituals, just as it creates linguistic forms of expression. Semiotically expressed, rituals are performative "signs." In due course, I intend to carry this analogy between ritual and language a little further, not without noting some of the more common confusions that it causes. One of the essential arguments, here, is that the human mind expresses itself directly in rituals. No intermediary stages, such as symbols and ideas, necessarily come between the mind and its ritual form of expression. The manner in which the mind expresses itself in rituals, both physiologically and psychologically speaking, is far from being clear to us. We can, however, say that rituals emanate from the human mind in a manner that reflects the mind's predisposition to relate to situations in structured patterns of expression and behaviour.

Generally, the human mind relates to perceptual, conceptual, and cognitive information in various ways. I limit myself, here, to ways that can be defined as autonomous. By autonomous, I mean forms of relatedness that do not depend on other forms. Mathematics quantifies reality; language makes verbal communication possible; historical perceptions connect times and events; and myths give expression to images that do not necessarily obey the laws of the physical world. These are all examples of autonomous expressions of the human mind. I view behavioural actions and rituals, also, as autonomous functions of the mind. Indeed, behavioural actions, and hence rituals, belong to the most immediate forms of relating to the environment—whether physical, social, cosmological, or metaphysical.

In many respects, behavioural actions do not reflect consciously cognitive processes. Behavioural actions are the bedrock of ritu-

als. I see the difference, between the two, in the fact that rituals
are purposely *structured, transformative* actions. They have to achieve
something very specific though not always consciously formulated,
whereas behavioural reactions, in general, are not necessarily
targeted towards a particular end. In other words, rituals follow
a certain plan that the mind sets up, with regard to specific aspects of reality and the desired change. What singles out rituals
from other forms of behaviour is that their being set to do something very specific that cannot be done in any other way. Indeed,
rituals have an inner logic that sustains their processual coherence.
Their various components function in a manner that coherently
contributes to bringing about the desired result. True, people
doing rituals are not always aware of the existence of this logic.
The internally binding consistency of the components is, nevertheless, an intrinsic factor in rituals. It fixes the functionality, or
efficacy, of rituals.

   The autonomous character of rituals also means that they do
not *translate* other forms of expression into behavioural utterances.
Basic forms of expression of the human mind—like language,
mathematics, and the arts—do not render themselves to translation. One cannot translate music into pictures or words. Since
rituals are independent phenomena, they are not intended to translate anything, including for that matter ideas, into actions. Those,
who believe in their efficacy, know that nothing can replace the
actual doing of rituals. Unless speaking about rituals is a ritual in
its own right,[15] the process of describing rituals cannot come instead of the actual doing. Rituals are believed to have the power
to change things: a specific life condition, one's status, and, to some
extent, even the very reality of things (for instance, creating, in a
religious context, a sacred time and place). This is the transformative power of rituals. As already noted, talking about rituals
cannot bring into effect what the act of doing a ritual can achieve.
Of course, one can study the history of the rituals, in their specific religious setting or in a comparative manner. One may even
learn how to do them. However, only in doing them, one can
achieve what they are supposed to achieve. Even a Talmudic dis-

---

[15] For instance, in the Passover ritual, described in Mishnah Tractate *Pesahim*
10: 5 of the Mishnah, one finds: "Rabban Gamliel used to say: Whoever has not
said these three things at the Passover [sacrifice] has not fulfilled his obligation: And
they are Passover, unleavened bread (*Matsah*), and bitter herbs (*Maror*)."

course about a Halakhic issue cannot replace the doing of the religious obligation itself.[16]

Rituals can be seen as patterns of behaviour that give expression to relational attitudes. Every ritual crystallises in relation to a certain reality or form of existence. The fact that rituals develop in, or as, a variety of mental attitudes towards various configurations of reality, makes rituals a mode of purposeful reaction in which the human mind expresses itself in structured and targeted patterns of behaviour. More important still, in the final resort, rituals aim at preserving, or putting, the various aspects of existence, to which they relate, in an orderly and liveable form. In many cases, rituals organise human behaviour in such a way, as to enable people to assume control over the forms of existence to which they relate. In this respect, magic is a good, albeit extreme, example. The mind strives to gain control, particularly in situations when the "cosmos" (the totality of a particular type of existence), in which people live, is likely to undergo a deteriorative change.

In religious terms, any change that is likely to bring about deterioration or damage (Radcliffe-Roper uses the word "infraction" for such situations) is designated in negative terms: sin, impurity, desacralisation or profanation, etc. A concept, such as sin, requires explanation. In general, sin is associated with "guilt" or "transgression" and connotes that an authoritative (often divine) law has been infringed. After a sinful condition has been created, consciously or unconsciously, something then needs to be done. In religious terms, this is functionally designated as a corrective act.[17] In anthropological language, mostly associated with James Frazer, the Polynesian notion of "Tabu" (usually spelt as "Taboo"), replaces the notion of transgression in its religious context.[18] To my mind, however, this change in terminological

---

[16] Which of the two—"*Talmud*" ("Study") or "*Ma'aseh*" ("Rituals")—should receive precedence is a hotly debated subject in Tannaitic circles. There are conflicting views on the subject and, consequently, the preferred stance is Talmud that leads to *Ma'aseh*. See, Bavli *Qiddushin* 40/b. However, there is a consensus that *Talmud* cannot come instead of *Ma'aseh*

[17] The notion of atonement is a common religious term for such cases. In chapter 5, we shall see what the term implies and whether it adequately translates the Hebrew *le-khapper*.

[18] A. R. Radcliffe-Brown, *Structure and Function in Primitive Society*, The Free Press: New York, 1965, pp. 133-152, elaborates on this change in terminological usage.

usage suggests a comparative setting but it does not really exhaust significant scholarly possibilities. "Sin" generally implies that an individual or a group has done something wrong in relation to a religious system, a specific "cosmos." Without going into the details, this is not what "Tabu" implies. With the term "cosmos," on the other hand, one contextualises the study of rituals and ritual theory in broader and more inclusive terms of reference than generally addressed in religious study. Cosmos implies existence in a very broad, structured (or systemic), and profound sense. Indeed, the disrupting of an existing order has metaphysical implications. I view cosmos as a metaphysical entity, as encompassing all levels of existence which people consider relevant to sustaining life. In this respect, the notion of cosmos includes non-physical components. Restoring the original conditions of this cosmos, therefore, has similar implications. Thus, the process of reacting behaviourally (= doing a ritual), in such cases, not only has a technical, or formal, effect on the situation, it restores an infracted metaphysical condition.

In most cases, the purpose of rituals is to restore the initial order or existential equilibrium of a cosmos that has been endangered or badly affected. This being the case, it is not an overstatement to say that the relational structure that is established, between the rituals and the cosmos which they address, has existential qualities. To argue, as many do, that rituals are or enact symbolic representations of reality, misses an important point. Any approach that treats rituals in a symbolic context undermines the ontological reality, or essence, of ritual behaviour.

Any change that rituals bring about, in whatever manner and direction, is referred to, here, as transformative.[19] Rituals have the power to transform reality. Making a day on the calendar "holy" entails more than dressing up the day with ceremonial features. It changes the essence of the day. People are told to live the event in a ritual manner. Special practices, as well as public processions,

---

[19] I would like to add that the notion of transformation is not new in the study of rituals. Several scholars, in the past, used it in various ways. However, my approach differs from previous ones, in two ways: (1) I try to avoid the specifically theological and ideological notions in the context of which transformation is often discussed; (2) I shall try to show what transformation is or entails in every case that is studied. Arguably, there is a universal notion of transformation but, according to the context and the need it takes on different forms and purposes.

sacrifices, and special meals are part of the protocol that establishes the special character of the day. In religious language, rituals
keep the event holy, for as long as the rituals prescribe. Events,
which the non-religious view as routine sequences of time, are
viewed, by the religious, as deserving to be ritually institutionalised
as public events.[20] In short, rituals are empowered to create and
establish changes in both realities, physical and spiritual alike. As
noted, there is no other way to accomplish such change. Rituals
do what they are expected to do in a manner that is essentially
different to any other form of human expression. It is also important to note, in this connection, that the transformation, brought
about by ritual behaviour, also affects the people who do them.
In this respect, rituals have a reflexive effect on those doing them.
This point will be given further attention in the ensuing discussions.

Human actions are sometimes viewed as a unique performative
language, both in terms of their structure and communicative
functionality. This does not mean that linguistic paradigms can
explain every aspect of rituals. The modern scholarly trend, associated with structuralism, encouraged analogies in which linguistic
patterns include aspects of human behaviour, such as myths and
rituals. Every ritual would thus have a subject, a predicate, and
an object. The same would apply to myth. In this respect, ceremonial embellishments would function, in the same way as ad-
jectives and adverbs do in language, increasing the inner volume
of the ritual, or mythic, statement. At times, these statements are
qualified with highly specific details. To my mind, this seems like
some formal procedure: it reduces everything to the same essential components and divests the study of myths and rituals of
whatever engenders curiosity in what is unique and stimulates the
imagination through confrontation with diversity.

Where language can suggest interesting points of analogy, is
in its compositional dynamics. Language creates the purposive links
between vocabulary, grammar and syntax.[21] Here, linguistic co-

---

[20] I wish to mention, here, Don Handelman, *Models and Mirrors: Towards an
Anthropology of Public Events*, Cambridge University Press: Cambridge, 1990, a book
that has influenced this work.

[21] Caroline Humphrey and James Laidlaw, *The Archetypal Actions of Rituals: A theory
of Ritual Illustrated by the Jain Rite of Worship*, Clarendon Press: Oxford, 1994, discuss at length the notion of communication, in relation to rituals. I agree with the

herence and order parallel the inner logic, which imparts similar traits to the details, which make up the ritual act. Initially, a linguistic utterance has to make sense in its own terms of reference. Only when one utterance is joined to another, does a coherent context emerge. The same holds true of rituals. To begin with, rituals have to make sense in their own terms of reference. Then, they begin to create clusters of rituals that follow specific contextualising paradigms. At this point, ideas and theology may enter the scene. In addition, just as a coherent statement often transcends its intrinsic frame of reference, a ritual may, in the context of a ritual cluster, transcend its own purposive goals. In this sense, it is true to say that a cluster of rituals is more than the arithmetic sum total of its composing elements. Indeed, one may argue that context becomes an essential factor in shaping the ritual event. In my view, the question, as to whether context is of primary importance in the understanding of rituals or not, can have various answers. There may be cases in which context is not an essential factor, although in most cases, context plays an important role in making rituals what they are.

One example will suffice to illustrate this point. A number of ritual events mark the Feast of Booths (*Succoth*), which is celebrated at the end of the summer. An extremely rich variety of rituals

---

authors that the ultimate purpose of rituals is not exhausted in such notions as communication, signalling, and setting boundaries. However, the sense in which I use the notion of communication is different. Communication creates a communion or a community which is bound together by force of the rituals to which it adheres. Epistemologically speaking, the notion of participation, which is ritually enacted in a specific community, makes it possible for those sharing in the relevant rituals to speak, as it were, the same performative language. Viewed as a language, ritual accomplishes something that transcends ordinary forms of action and verbal communication. The key notions, here, are change and transformation. Further on, in the book, I shall discuss the metaphysics of transformation. In any event, the metaphysics of this change have to be outlined more precisely than is the case in *The Archetypal Actions of Rituals*. One further point must be made, in this connection. We have already mentioned the fact that scholars refer to rituals as labels and omit paying attention to the segmented details of the rituals that build the whole. Humphrey and Laidlaw's book is no exception to this rule. When they ask, "So how is the daily *puja* performed?" (p. 24), the descriptions that follow briefly discuss each part of the ritual, without referring to the embedded ritual theory or the contribution of each part to the whole. Chapters 5 and 6, in which I analyse *Leviticus* 16 and the "Lord's Supper" respectively, clearly illustrate what I have in mind, in this respect. The three levels or stages of my analysis are: (1) an in-depth analysis of each detail; (2) an examination of each detail in light of its embedded ritual theory; (3) an overall assessment of the details and of the embedded ritual theory which integrates the parts into the whole.

characterises the feast. Each ritual addresses a different issue connected with the feast: the building of the *Succah*; following the rules for the four kinds of vegetation (*arba'ah minim*); offering in the Temple various kinds of sacrifices; doing certain rituals (and later, saying special prayers) for the rain to come. These are just some of the rituals done in connection with the feast. However, the feast of Succoth is not complete, in the ritual sense of the word, unless all its rituals are done at their specified time and order. In this respect, the organised chain of rituals creates the ritual status of the period of the feast. Furthermore, the very building of the Succah, done in anticipation of the feast, demands close attention to many details: choosing the building materials, adhering to a certain structure and size, selecting materials for the roof, and preparing the internal decorations. Hence, a statement such as, "people (subject) build (predicate) *Succoth* (object)," tells us almost nothing in terms of assessing this particular ritual from the point of view of ritual detail and theory. The same can be said in respect of any other ritual that is done during the Feast of Tabernacles. As noted, nearly every ritual is a composite entity. It contains many parts, each of which contributes significantly to making the whole into a powerful and efficacious Gestalt. In terms of studying rituals and their corresponding ritual theory, little can be accomplished by simply labelling, as is often the scholarly practice, the ritual act and making general statements about it. In a Judaic context, highlighting detailed structures is the business of Halakhic deliberations and expositions, and, in as much as space allows and the arguments require, we shall depart from the short-hand reference-style in the discussion of rituals.

IV

I hope that, by now, the reader is acquainted with the special manner in which the subject of rituals is discussed in the present book. To the best of my knowledge, this is the first book of its kind that discusses rituals in ancient Israel in a systematic manner, (a) from the perspective of ritual theory, and (b) in a context linked to an epistemological assessment of the subject matter.[22]

---

[22] A book that one would expect to have done the job, at least in reference to the scriptural materials is, *Transformations, Passages, and Processes: Ritual Approaches to Biblical Texts* [*Semeia* 67] (Guest Editor: Mark McVann), Scholars Press: Atlanta,

I wish to offer a systematic study of Judaic forms of ritual practice, including Halakhah, from these vantage points. I am aware of the need to make the Judaic materials at hand and their discussion available to those studying rituals in other cultures and religions. Thus, I expect the reader to simultaneously consider two aspects in my study. The Israelite materials supply the case studies, while the views and theories of modern ritual studies create the scholarly background of the discussion. The bridges that link the two domains endow the discussion with a wide range of perspectives, many of which are new in this context.

In the preceding pages, the reader's attention was directed to certain aspects of study that highlight, in my view, the essential characteristics of rituals vis-à-vis other forms of human behaviour. Briefly, rituals help people create constituting effects on life-processes or realities, which have been exposed to instability or undergone deterioration. Responding in a ritual mode is a unique way of creating a situation that is expected to be operative in averting these situations or in redressing their destructive thrust. More specifically, almost every ritual creates a certain transformative state, the implicit purpose of which is to change the course of the adverse conditions. When rituals are done to establish something positive (for instance, marking time and place), there is danger, too. By not doing the right rituals, the individual or community may bring upon themselves what they view as punitive measures. Inevitably, these measures have catastrophic consequences. Rituals—mostly of a sacrificial nature—can bring about a reversal of adverse conditions. In enacting a catastrophic event (the death of the sacrificial victim), they bring about an existence-saving transformation. Sacrifices, done as "penalties", either repair a previously damaged reality or avert a calamity that is likely to befall the individual or the community. This subject will receive full attention in Chapter 5.

It is very common to find scholars of religious studies referring to sacrificial rites with sentences such as, "people bring sacrifices

---

1995. Almost all the papers published in that volume show the authors' acute awareness of the fact that the study of biblical rituals is a desideratum and must be given first priority. However, ideology, symbolism, and theology are the frameworks in which the various authors operate. The anthropological-behavioural approach and the epistemological emphasis found in the present study are clearly absent from their work.

to the temple to appease the gods and, thus, guarantee atonement."
We shall see that, for the purposes of ritual theory, a different
kind of language has to be applied to the sacrificial act (or event).
To begin with, it avoids using the terms "gods, "temple," and
"atonement."[23] As indicated, it will discuss rituals as processual
events that unfold in a way that shows their inner logic. As suggested above, the discussion of rituals in behavioural terms requires a change in terms of reference. Theological terms of reference hardly apply. Thus, as we are going to see, one can argue
that sacrificial acts make the people concerned participants in a
ritual event that involves a process of annihilation. Something that
belongs to the person/community offering the sacrifice (it is not
insignificant that it is part of their life-sustaining property) is an-
nihilated to keep the other parts of the community whole and safe.
Since the process of annihilation takes place on a ritual level—
which, in a deep sense, is a mimetic act—the enactors can emerge
from it safe and with their "cosmos" reconstituted.

Often, scholars view the sacrificial process in terms of substitution, with the animal victim taking upon itself the fate of the human
being who wishes to redeem himself through the animal victim.
But this is only partly correct. I would suggest that, apart from
the substitution factor, there is an additional act of painful participation. The person who brings the offering inflicts an act of
destruction upon the animal victim. In other words, he side-tracks
something he had to suffer himself. In this respect, it is the very
enactment of annihilation that matters, not the victim. Thus, all
the attention is directed to the act of slaughtering, and the handling of the blood, rather than to the role the helpless and innocent victim takes upon himself.[24] The person bringing the offering mimetically accomplishes, through the animal victim, the act
of destruction that he deserves. The ritual event makes it possible
to act out the destruction and still emerge re-constituted. Ritual
actions operate on the premise of an existing symbiosis between

---

[23] For present purposes, I would even prefer any term that by-passes "sacrifice."
In regular forms of speech, the term is also used in a non-religious context.

[24] It should be noted, though, that the person who brings the sacrifice to the
temple confesses his sins. He does so laying his hands on the head of the animal.
In this manner, the animal is made to carry the sin(s). Consequently, when the
animal victim is killed, these sins are simultaneously annulled in the very act destruction that slaughtering the victim brings about.

humans and the reality that concerns them. Thus, the cosmos that has been shattered by a misdeed is put right again by mimetically enacting another act of shattering, this time on another level, or in the framework of another event. The sacrifice, conceived as a holocaust, brings this into effect. It leads a death event to a corrective "resurrection." In a deep sense, then, the person undergoes a process of annihilation, though this time it moves in a different direction—not to dissolution but to reparation. In short, the mimetic essence of sacrificial rituals makes them act as cathartic events.

Involvement with reality on a ritual level is a unique human experience. It creates modes of participation with life processes through forms of behaviour that have a unique intrinsic logic. The manner in which this logic works is not always clear to us. It is remarkable, though, how people view those forms of behaviour to be effective in reversing processes or in engendering them. This is the unique feature of rituals. Behaviour is the major mode of getting involved with reality and interacting with it. Mental perception is another. Rituals combine behaviour with a sense of purposive involvement and interaction with reality. Like language, rituals are a vehicle of communication with reality. Mental processes conceptualise reality into ordered, cross-referential patterns. Language conceptualises and articulates reality. Changes in linguistic expression are tantamount to changes in the respective configurations of reality. Thus, rituals can attempt to establish modes of interacting with reality with a view on changing certain aspects in it.

In a wider sense, rituals create a relational provenance that facilitates establishing a circular linkage between the persons doing the rituals, the rituals themselves, and their targeted outcome. People then become existentially involved in the processes generated by their own ritual activity. Thus, for instance, in ritually setting the Sabbath Day apart from regular weekdays, people doing the rituals create a temporal reality, I would even say, a metaphysical reality. The day is accorded an almost unlimited status amongst those who accept the reality created by these rituals. Thus, any deviation from what the rituals of the Sabbath Day bring into effect, from a ritual (= Halakhic) point of view, is punishable. In Judaism, the Sabbath Day commemorates foundational events (the creation of the world and the exodus from Egypt, respectively).[25] Consequently, any break from the many forms of differentiation and setting apart which begin with the Sabbath Day, triggers a process that represents the opposite of what these foundational events stand for. The opposite signifies destruction and the loss of the right to continue one's free life. In religious terms, a person, who deliberately desecrates the Sabbath Day, becomes liable to capital punishment. It can be said that, as a time unit that ritually commemorates foundational events, the Sabbath Day extends a sense of a sustaining coherence to the cosmos in which people live. In sharing its rituals, it offers protection to the community. Not taking part in those rituals—that is, disrespecting their constitutive status—is likely to destroy the binding coherence which the day aims at establishing.

To make my point clear I shall, for a moment, use the theological notion of 'holiness.' Holiness is the usual translation of *Qedushah*, the Hebrew word for ritual separation, or separatedness. In religious language, rituals engender modes of holiness, whether in time or in space. We shall see (in Chapter 5, which deals with the rituals prescribed in *Leviticus* 16) the various procedures involved in entering a holy space (and, for that matter, also a "timespace"), sojourning in it, and then leaving it again in peace. They all entail a special ritual that is aimed at guaranteeing the peaceful beginning and completion of these actions. Rituals, then, reflect the state of mind, or attitude, crystallising in relation to the time and the place which they establish and then seek to preserve or observe. The Sabbath Day begins with lighting candles (including a blessing following the lighting), reciting special prayers in synagogue, and then, at home again, reciting blessings over wine and bread. The Sabbath Day terminates in almost a reverse order: The evening prayer is recited with a special section concluding the Sabbath. Then, a blessing is said over wine and over a newly lit candle. Significantly, this candle has a different shape to the Sabbath candles and the blessing is accompanied by a special movement of the fingers.[26] These are simple descriptions of two

---

[25] The Ten Commandments, in *Exodus* 20: 11, mention the creation of the world in six days as the reason for doing the Sabbath rituals, while those in *Deuteronomy* 5: 15 mention the slavery in Egypt and the ensuing exodus.

[26] It is interesting to note that the Sabbath candles are lit with the palms of both hands covering the eyes. This gesture is usually explained by the fact that the blessing

obverse sets of rituals. Interestingly, two different words are used
to mark these events—*Qiddush* (for the beginning of the Sabbath)
and *Havdalah* (for its conclusion)—although both involve the same
semantic field of separation and setting apart.

In short, viewed from their time/space angle, rituals establish
and enact differences that are vital for establishing uniqueness,
as that of specific events or territorial entities. Thus, we may say
that rituals create boundaries. Rituals are intensely functional in
crystallising what is special and extraordinary. Rituals also regulate the modes, or conditions, of passing in and out of the boundaries. In doing so, rituals are effective in modelling graded forms
of existence, such as are created when climbing the stairs of a
temple or passing an interim period of time before the beginning
of a holiday. We have referred to these modes of existence in terms
of a cosmos. In as much as relating to a cosmos involves a specific attitude, every cosmos, or part of it, constitutes an "attitudinal space." This term signifies an existential space that generates
an attitude and facilitates its unfolding in behavioural patterns.

I have referred to rituals in connection with the notion of existence. More succinctly expressed, people do rituals to define and
maintain existence. Existence is used, here, in the wide sense of
the term. I suggest this definition: existence is everything that the
people concerned consider (a) vital for their life and (b) likely to
undergo processes of disintegration, deterioration or annihilation.
In short, conditions, in which being and non-being are the two
likely possibilities the separation between which is ritually activated. In being aware of what it perceives and how it conceptualises
experience, human consciousness defines, in practical terms, what
existence is at every instance. In this sense, it is true to say, as we
did above, that the human mind does not only generate rituals,
it also generates the very existence to which the rituals relate.
People make their choices with regard to what life, existence, is
and means in each case. Rituals are intensely functional in this

---

is said *after* lighting the candles. In other cases, blessings are said *before* doing the
act. However, there are other cases in which the blessing is said after the doing of
the ritual (for instance, the blessing said *after* washing the hands before meals). Thus,
from a phenomenological point of view, it makes sense to say that using the hands
(a symbolic act of craftsmanship or its reverse) marks the beginning and the termination of the Sabbath Day which (temporarily) marks the cessation of creative
processes.

process. To put it somewhat differently, if the mind is a vital factor in defining existence, then rituals give a complementary expression to the kind of energy the mind invests in, in order to safeguard existence against possible decay or entropy.[27]

It follows from the above that it is essential to the doing of rituals to establish adequate connecting lines that link them to the particular modes of existence to which they relate. A mode of purposive adequacy permeates rituals. Adequacy, here, means avoiding shortcuts that disrupt the efficacy of the rituals. Furthermore, by establishing wrong connections between a ritual and its corresponding mode of transformation, counter-effective results can be caused and aggravate the situation. The manner, in which specific rituals become effective in a given situation, or in relation to a specific mode of existence, is still their enigmatic part. In our discussion of the subject, we shall try to approach, as closely as possible, an assessment of these issues. However, the riddle will stay with us, unless we assume that belief in the efficacy of rituals is the key factor in any explanation of this problem. Speaking of belief brings us close to theology. However, the theological track is problematic in this connection. If we follow it, it will distract us from our ultimate goal—referring to their behavioural essence as the major explanation of rituals. Of course, one can argue that, under the circumstances, theological discourse is inevitable or that it is even an integral part of the scholarly discourse. However, we view matters differently and shall proceed accordingly.

V

In our view, then, rituals emerge as purposive acts that have constitutive functions in a given reality or form of existence. With regard to the purposive components, we have already mentioned that transformation is a central component in the doing of rituals. By transformation, I mean any change that rituals bring about in a manner that is vital to sustaining existence, whether of the

---

[27] This brings us to Bruce Lincoln's definition of sacrifice in *Death, War, and Sacrifice: Studies in Ideology and Practice*, The University of Chicago Press: Chicago & London, 1991. Lincoln writes: "I have spoken of Sacrifice as a ritual which effectively repeats the cosmogony, shifting matter from a victim's body to the alloformic parts of the universe, in order to sustain the latter against decay and ultimate collapse" (p. 170).

person doing the ritual(s) or the issues addressed by the rituals (the persistence of time-events, the endurance of places, the benevolence of divine entities, and the well-being of humans). In a more specific manner, rituals bring about generative (constitutive), preservative, and regenerative (re-constitutive) processes. In this respect, repeating the rituals at pre-defined intervals reactivates processes that are vital for maintaining existences that are constantly undergoing change. Many rituals have daily, weekly, monthly, or yearly schedules. We can say that rituals energise the pulse rate of existence in order to preserve its functional stableness. This guarantees existence. The conditions that give rise to rituals can be called moments of crisis.[28] Something bad may happen unless the rituals in question come into play.

There is clearly a danger/risk/anxiety factor behind many rituals. People have expectations, as well as concerns, regarding the kind of normality and regularity that sustains existence. Will there be rain or drought? Will the eclipse pass without leaving behind a trail of bad luck and destruction? Will the sick person overcome the crisis? Will the night pass without a calamity that will stop the sun from rising the next morning? These are extreme concerns but they all point to the same fact, namely, that existential anxiety looms behind many rituals. Mental stress is the trigger that lets loose a chain reaction of bio-chemical processes in the human organism. Rituals are another form of reacting to states of stress and tension. In a religious context, people fear that their

---

[28] The element of life crises is very much in focus in Arnold van Gennep, *The Rites of Passage*, The University of Chicago Press: Chicago, 1960. As the reader can see for himself, I consider the notion of crisis to be a vital component of many rituals. In this connection, P. Steven Sangren's definition of ritual makes good sense: "Ritual here is usefully defined as behavior formally and explicitly concerned with the restoration and reproduction of order. Any notion of order implies a notion of disorder and chaos…"—*Op. Cit.*, p. 167. A constant in the work of several scholars is the notion of disorder, and complementarily, that of danger and crisis. This is a major factor in generating ritual activity. The names of W. Robertson Smith, René Girard, and Walter Burkert come first to mind, in this connection. Recently, Rene Girard, *I See Satan Fall Like Lightning*, Orbis Books: Maryknoll (New York), 2001, re-emphasised these factors. He writes (p. 63): "It may be a matter also of more ordinary disasters: famines, floods, destructive droughts, and other natural catastrophes. In all cases, the initial mythic situation can be summarized in terms of a crisis that threatens the community and its cultural system with total destruction." Girard also emphasizes mimetic and cathartic factors, in connection with violence. In Chapter 5, I shall discuss these issues, but from a different viewpoint to that suggested by Girard.

failure to consecrate a certain time will result in God bringing about the collapse of the whole system—the "cosmos" in which they live. In other cases, disobeying the word of God is believed to cause havoc and death. In states of crises, expressions such as, "God is punishing you," are often heard.

We have already noted an essential factor that characterizes rituals, namely, internal segmentation. Every ritual consists in several sub-acts that configure rituals into sequentially structured events. These are spread out in time and in space. In other words, doing a ritual creates a dynamic that transforms a complex structure into a process. There is no need to qualify the notion of rituals spreading out in *time*. However, rituals spreading out in *space* calls for an explanation. Examples easily come to mind. When pilgrims walk towards their destination, the way itself and what the pilgrims do as they walk, is of great importance. In some cases, as in the Muslim Hajj, special ritual preparations have to be done before one sets out on the pilgrimage. These preparations are concerned primarily with abstinence from defiling things.[29] Visiting a shrine or a temple is a ritual event. Thus, walking through the various areas (gate-door, inner court, various rooms, and seat of the deity) is a protracted experience in ["holy"] space.[30] The donations boxes, at the gate, ensure continuity in the "collecting process" and, like the altars, ritually enable sacrificial gestures on a number of parallel levels. Walking down the Via Dolorosa, in Jerusalem, is another example of a ritual procession that is spread out in space (and time). A different ritual marks each of the seven "Stations" on the Via Dolorosa. However, accomplishing the totality of the "walk-ritual," called Via Dolorosa, requires stopping at all seven Stations. In short, rituals work when their segmented parts become a whole, a Gestalt. In this respect, a ritual that is broken off, before it is completed, is like an unfinished sentence.

---

[29] In this respect, heavenly ascensions, of the type associated with apocalypticism and Merkavah mysticism, constitute another aspect of a pilgrimage that requires a long string of preparatory rituals. Essentially, these rituals centre on various forms of abstinence, particularly from certain foods and sexual intercourse. See, Ithamar Gruenwald, *Apocalyptic and Merkavah Mysticism*, Brill: Leiden and Koeln, 1980, pp.98-123.

[30] Entering and exiting sacred space is the starting point of the discussion in Arnold van Gennep, *The Rites of Passage*: "The Territorial Passage."

In the context of the shorthand mode, which scholars all too
often use when referring to rituals, it is important to stress that
ritual behaviour always involves a processual factor. Scholars will
often refer to the ritual of "the washing of hands" (*netilat yadayim*)
in such terms: "Before taking their meals, religious Jews engage
in a ritual of washing their hands."[31] As we shall immediately see,
such a sentence misses everything that is essential to the understanding of rituals and their inner mechanism. The ritual of washing one's hands before a meal, that includes bread, involves several things. To begin with, one needs a special vessel filled with
clean water. The right hand holds the vessel while it is filled. The
vessel is then held by the left hand, so that the water is poured
first onto the right hand. The water is then poured three times
on each hand (the palm). The hands are raised, a biblical phrase
is said and the hands are dried with a towel. Finally, a blessing is
recited to indicate the completion of the ritual.[32] An additional
element is the injunction not to speak between the blessing said
over the washing of the hands and the blessing said before breaking or cutting the bread. Thus, we see how one ritual leads to
another. Interestingly, a ritually enacted silence constitutes part
of the attitudinal space mentioned above. It marks the time gap
between two interlinked rituals—the washing of the hands in
preparation for the cutting and eating of the bread. This is a simple
procedure, but it shows the importance of the sequencing-factor
in rituals, whether in a single (segmented) ritual or in a series of
rituals. Nothing is accomplished before the whole process is
brought to completion.[33]

One of the goals of the present study is to extricate the study
of rituals from the labelling paradigm that scholars commonly
apply. Noting the fact that all rituals are composed of structured
details is important also for another reason. The detail-structure

---

[31] Arnold van Gennep, *Op. Cit.*, p. 42, refers to the ceremonial pregnancy rites
of the Indian Todas. He uses a shorthand kind of description: "She burns her hands
in two places."

[32] I should remark that, for those familiar with the details of the Halakhic
procedure, this description would look more like a heading than reflecting a process.

[33] We have already mentioned the factors of intention and intentionality. In this
connection see, for instance, Tosefta *Yadayim* 2: 3: "He who washes his hands—if
he intended to fulfil a religious obligation, his hands are pure; if he did not [intend
to do so], his hands are impure." This is the essence of *Kavanah*, intention.

of rituals causes the mind to engage in a process of thought, what to do, how to do it, and in what sequence, which enhances the factors of intention and intentionality. The more one pays attention to matters of detail, the more one engages one's conscious awareness of, or relatedness to, the ritual process. One should not only do the ritual correctly, but also remember the right order of its details. "The entire rite of the Day of Atonement stated in accord with its proper order; if he did one part of the rite before its fellow, he has done nothing whatsoever."[34] Thus, what the High Priest has to know, step after step, cannot be reduced to a general statement. Shorthand descriptions in the study of rituals leave us with nothing real in our hands.

One may argue, though, that admitting the presence of intentionality in rituals ushers in, through the main door, a theological aspect. The scholarly discussion of rituals is thus tied, by an umbilical cord, to theology. In the course of the book, I shall address this issue extensively. However, by way of anticipating the forthcoming discussion, I admit that intentionality brings us close to the point where theological stances begin to matter. Once the human mind engages in a conscious reflection on what it generates, the contextualising factor of "God" easily moves to the centre of the discussion. Notwithstanding this observation, I hasten to add that theological positions usually do not bear directly on the manner in which the details make rituals do what they are expected to do. Furthermore, theology has little to say on the technique which people use to do their rituals. Theology creates the context for, but not the essence of, the practice of rituals.[35] At best, theology is a mentally supportive factor. It gives people an overall motivation or reason for doing what they do. It also introduces factors of retribution and reward. However, it does not easily translate into the ritual behaviour itself.

---

[34] The *Mishnah*, Tractate *Yoma* 5: 7. The English translation is by Jacob Neusner, *The Mishnah: A New Translation*, Yale University Press: New Haven and London, 1988.

[35] In this respect, I disagree with (the rather unclear wording of) the definition given by Lawson and Cauley, *Op. Cit.* p.88-89: "… religious actions and religious ritual actions in particular are distinguished by a religious conceptual scheme's penetration of the formation system for the purpose of specifying the action elements."

VI

At the beginning of this introductory chapter, we asked what differentiates a ritual from a non-ritual act. How do we distinguish between an ordinary act, such as washing hands for hygienic purposes and a similar act that is done for ritual purposes? The answer focussed on three elements: (1) the logic that shapes the internal structuring of a ritual action; (2) the mental processes that accompany the right sequencing of the ritual actions; (3) the behavioural dynamics that emerge from the sequencing of ritual actions. We have spoken of an inner logic that constitutes the structure of every ritual, and without which the ritual statement becomes redundant. The specific manner in which the various parts become a coherent whole illustrates the way in which every ritual becomes a uniquely shaped compositional argument. Whatever its shape, every ritual is always a statement that exists in its own right. Doing the ritual in the right manner allocates to it, as well as to its various components, processual coherence. In this respect, rituals are analogous to verbal arguments. Reverse or displace any part of a certain argument, or drop it altogether, and the whole argument changes or loses its communicative power.

The analogy with language entails the factor of communication, mentioned above. Scholars often speak of the communicative potentials of rituals. I would like to fine-tune this observation. Doing rituals within a community, and in the framework of a long tradition, gives people the opportunity of interacting at a level that transcends that of the individual. The rituals acquire a social setting and sociological significance. This means that rituals are functional in ways that often transcend their immediate, performative, frame of reference. For instance, they may bring about—as a by product—social integration. This integration is accomplished on two levels: (1) within the group of people themselves; (2) in relation to the way the people view their historical and social past. Here, tradition has a bearing on the subject. When rituals connect to the past, the notion of tradition becomes a relevant factor. Rituals that are embedded in tradition project a form of guarantee, enabled by the presence of their ongoing existential stability. This stability is essential to the management of the cosmos that constitutes the life of the people. It also helps to hold the ritual community together and prevent its disintegration.

We have mentioned the importance of the correct order for both the macro and micro levels of rituals. Sequencing the various details of a ritual and its respective sub-parts is an issue that matters more than we think. For instance, the question of fixing a ritual sequence is a crucial issue, which can lead to sectarian splitting and denominational conflicts. Indeed, numerous examples attest to the fact that the issue of sequencing the details of a particular ritual led to denominational, even sectarian, fractionation. A different sequence for the same prayers, which to an outsider may seem of trivial significance, divided the Judaic world into East and West European liturgies: "*nusach sefarad*" and "*nusach ashkenaz*," respectively. The two prayer books cannot be used in the same synagogues. The fact that one "*nusach*" is used in a synagogue makes it impossible for a person using a different one to join as a liturgical leader ("*chazzan*") in a common session of prayer ("*minyan*"). One is expected to use the same prayer book that was used by one's father. Jews from Islamic countries have yet another form ("*nusach*") of prayer book.

The phenomenon of communities splitting up into denominational synagogues goes back to the first centuries after the destruction of the Second Temple. Among other things, this is an interesting subject for those studying the sociology of religion. Rituals are a dominant feature in creating sociologically meaningful differences. If we keep to the example of prayer books, we can see that Judaism is not alone in this phenomenon. In the early years of its activities, the Church of England printed an enormous number of editions of prayer books, as a way of establishing its denominational independence. This practice persisted and was also used by the mainstream in order to establish its hegemony over rival groups in the same church.

Another interesting example, in this respect, is the split between the Sadducees and the Pharisees over whether the high priest had to place fire on the incense before he entered the Holy of Holies (the view of the Sadducees) or after he entered it (the view of the Pharisees). This was not the only difference between the two "parties." However, in the historical consciousness of the people, this was the crucial issue that caused the split between the two groups. We should not take the easy line and say that rituals are instrumental in engineering power games. However, one can find power games manipulating, in a dramatic setting, rituals for sectarian purposes.

In this connection, I wish to add that the factor of authority, whether divine or other, that is often part of the discussion of rituals, does not explain what rituals are or how they are made to work.[36] At best, it accounts for the degree of motivation and the commitment shown by the people doing the rituals. But it tells us nothing with regard to the essence of ritual structure. I have already referred to the need to exclude theological matters, including the notion of the divine, from any scholarly discussion of rituals. This said, the belief that rituals claim to have a divine, or other, authority may make people behave in a certain way and authority may be relevant to the manner in which they do their rituals. On a more general level, any attempt to make a certain factor bear upon the discussion of rituals should be made subject to a functional examination: does it, or does it not, bear on their inner structure, logic, and efficacy. I consider the issue as of limited relevance to our discussion. It is essential to give the doing of rituals and their inner structuring the attention they require and deserve. Once the divine becomes part of the scholarly discussion, attention moves in a completely different direction. Paradoxically, the divine explains the context rather than the operative mechanism that makes rituals work.

VII

A word is now due on Judaic Law (commonly referred to as Halakhah) and ritual studies. The subject of Halakhah is studied in many disciplines, among them, history, law and jurisprudence, sociology, theology, and folklore. Generally, Halakhah stipulates and regulates what individuals and communities should do or avoid doing. Halakhah presents itself as the only factor that has the

---

[36] See, for instance, E. Thomas Lawson and Robert N. McCauley, *Op. Cit.* p. 113. Referring to the ritual of making the sign of the cross after dipping one's fingers in a receptacle containing water in the vestibule of the church, the authors write: "Of course, the cross is a conventional symbol for Jesus Christ, who on this representation, is ultimately responsible for this ritual's efficacy" (p. 113). Other notions that the authors use, in this connection, are "superhuman agency" and "superhuman qualities." The focus here is the ultimate empowering of rituals in order for them to have and exercise efficacy. For Lawson and McCauley, and for many other scholars, the superhuman factor is the default condition, namely, it makes religious rituals what they are. This is a completely different position to the one I take, which posits that the human mind is accountable for generating rituals.

authority to organise Jewish life as a continuum that depends on, and fulfils, the will of God. Viewed from the angle that interests us here, its rulings function as rituals, that is, their study can be divorced from the theological context. The laws of Halakhah sustain the life of the people (or their existence) and contain everything that is needed to restore disturbed conditions to their normal state. Halakhah is an applied philosophy of life. It organizes in a ritual manner every aspect of life in systemic categories that create ritual clusters. Halakhah develops and is practised in the framework of certain presuppositions, which are primarily based on the principle that doing, rather than critical thinking, shapes and preserves life and the social order.

However, in spite of its enormous wealth of materials, and their seminal importance for the study of rituals, in general, Halakhah is completely ignored in the modern study of rituals. Furthermore, it seldom occurs to those studying Halakhah that the inclusion of ritual studies in their spectrum of scholarly considerations would produce interesting results, in terms of understanding and assessing their subject matter. Indeed, Halakhah constitutes one of the richest treasure houses of ritual practices. Thus, if the present study is to claim any degree of innovation, it has to bring about substantial changes in this domain.

The question to be asked is: what kind of discourse can accord Halakhic rituals the justice that they deserve, as a scholarly area of studies? I use the term "justice," because there are cases where Halakhic rituals, in particular, are looked down upon as mannered and outdated forms of behaviour. For the same reason, they are viewed as undermining true religiousness and, worse still, a serious intellectual approach. Such views developed, not only in circles that were highly critical of religion, but also in certain theological circles, which profess what I refer to as a Protestant frame of mind. Protestantism is known for its criticism of, what it considered to be, excessive indulgence in cultic and ritual practice. Reform Judaism is also known for its criticism of the Halakhic stances of orthodox Rabbinism. Evidently, denominational interests often play a role in such matters. There is no need to identify who voiced these views, it is sufficient to note that these views had a strong impact on the field of study that the present book wishes to advance. Also of note is that, in the Christian world, Paul's criticism of Judaism as a religion that was practised "in the flesh" had a decisive role in establishing the critical position that was identified as rejection of Judaic Law.

These comments explain why, in the present book, I present rituals as the major component of religion that often emerges long before theological positions acquire normative formulation. As much as it is possible, I wish to study rituals in their original terms of reference, that is to say, before they became involved in theological issues, discussions, or value judgments. As noted above, my aim is to undertake an epistemological assessment of rituals and their embedded ritual theory. Epistemology, in this case, entails a close analysis of the manifestational aspects, that is, the phenomenological, experiential, configurations of rituals in their own context and terms of reference. In the first place, I assume that the meaning of rituals is found in the manner in which people do them, and in the mode of transformation that they expect will evolve as a result.[37] The point at which the infusion of theological element begins is always, to my mind, secondary if necessary at all. The ritual action itself comes first, then any further element that boosts its doing. I admit that the extent to which an intellective process (a theological or ideological position) is, or is not, involved in the doing of rituals is a debatable question. In my view, this question does not necessarily enhance the understanding of the nature of rituals or the various ways in which they are done.

In many cases, in order to examine the manner in which rituals inform us about the ritual theory that sustains them, a close reading of the texts that prescribe them is required. Texts usually force the reader to take a hermeneutic approach. This is particularly true in the case of ancient texts. Apart from the linguistic issues that their remote style raises the question of semantic fields and contextual meaning have to be taken into consideration. In other words, hermeneutics, or the inclusion of a private kind of "theology," is an inevitable part of the scholarly process. The crucial question is: whose theology should prevail? In my view, it is reasonable to argue that any "theology" that is maintained, in the context of a critical, scholarly work, makes more sense than

---

[37] Here, I take a different view from that expressed by Frits Staal, *Rules Without Meaning: Ritual, Mantras, and the Human Sciences*, Peter Lang: New York..., 1990. The reasons for my criticism of Staal's views will be given in the course of the forthcoming discussions.

that of a devout believer or someone who speaks on his behalf. Scholarly "theology" obeys one essential criterion: it changes in face of new knowledge and better understanding. It is open to criticism and to comparison, without falling into the pitfalls of heresy and blasphemy. Furthermore, it applies critical standards of investigation and does not obey a divine authority. This argument has one proviso, namely, that the "theology" of the scholar is restricted to understanding the ritual at hand, in its performative, rather than ideological, context. The scholar does not attempt, in any way, to persuade people to do the ritual as a religiously meaningful act. No sides are taken, and all forms of propaganda are shunned. The "theology" which the researcher brings to the subject of his research is examined according to one criterion, only: whether it intends to make people do the rituals and believe in their religious efficacy, or not? If the answer is negative, the scholar is on the safe side.

It follows that the present book will not discuss sporadic and spontaneous expressions of reverence, respect or, for that matter, aversion and antagonism.[38] These, and other mental and emotional stances, often accompany ritual activity in its religious configuration. Indeed, these stances may ostensibly be present in, and even explain, the enthusiasm and intensity that often accompanies the ritual act. Evidently, one may see certain outbursts of emotions reflecting the intensity of the ritual act, *per se*. However, the ritual act is not directly *explained* by the emotional or theological stances that are infused into its behavioural space.

In this connection, I wish to emphasise another factor that accords with this epistemological approach. This is the sharing aspect of rituals. The practice of rituals is not only shared by people, in a formal manner. As we shall see, the very act of sharing is a constitutive factor in rituals and in the modes that make them work. There are also rituals, which are specifically configured to be functional in the creation of a community. The "Lord's Supper" is an interesting example worth exploring, in this respect (see, below, Chapter 6). I prefer to highlight the community, rather than the social order, because, in daily life, rituals have a stronger impact on the immediate community than on the more detached grid of the social structure/order. Furthermore, commu-

---

[38] Rituals which enact hatred constitute an interesting subject in their own right.

nities are flexible and, hence, dynamic entities. After sharing in
a certain ritual in one place (synagogue or church), the community disperses and its members engage in sharing other ritual activities in other groups, such as the family, friends, and the work-
place. In this respect, a community—indeed any community,
including non-religious ones—engenders processes that are functional in the constant process of renewal of its self-constitutive,
or reconstitutive, rituals. In the terms developed above, this is the
transformative essence of rituals.

VIII

In the twentieth century, the study of religions followed, for a long
time, two principle directions, which, in a general sense, can be
described as theological and historical. Text-critical hermeneutics
and philosophical questions created focussed centres of study and
discussion. Consequently, areas of religious life and study that did
not come under these headings received little attention in religious studies. Important aspects of religious life were consigned
to anthropological studies and there was almost no ongoing dialogue and cooperation between these areas of study. Although they
were dealing practically with the same materials, scholars of religious (mostly theological) studies and scholars of anthropological
(mostly behavioural) studies were often ignorant of the other side's
work. Furthermore, scholars of Judaic studies showed little interest in the work done in either of the above fields.

In recent years, there has been a significant change, in this
respect, reflecting not only new interest in rituals but also an
important concession regarding the inclusion of anthropological
perspectives in religious studies. This statement requires explanation. Anthropology was the academic discipline *per se* for the
study of non-European cultures and societies. Anthropological
knowledge grew with time and its methods underwent considerable change and fine-tuning. At the beginning, however, a somewhat disturbing value judgment prevailed in this discipline. Anthropology often referred to the human or social objects of its
research in terms, which underlined their primitive, savage, aboriginal, rudimentary, or elementary, character. The domain of
the religious was relegated to the realms of magic and superstition. In respect of religious studies, the discipline confined itself

to the study of the three great monotheistic religions, while archaeology focused, among other things, on the study of religion
in the ancient civilizations of the East (Egypt, Babylonia, Assyria,
Mesopotamia, Ugarit, etc.). Classical studies dealt with the religions of Greece and Rome and Biblical scholars studied the world
of the religion of ancient Israel. Comparative religion tried to create
some kind of universal integration, but the outcome was, quite
often, a rather anecdotal collection of observations. If it had any
aspirations of being a science in own right, its potentials were
limited from the start.

Clearly, the situation described above creates a rather confus-
ing picture. Religious experience, as epitomised in rituals, has
rarely found an independent focal location of scholarly discussion. Scholars specialising in one area of discussion often do not
know what the other disciplines can offer. As noted above, one
area of studies that suffered from this confusion was rituals and
ritual theory. As noted, rituals and their theory were believed to
be the major point of interest of the anthropologist. Consequently,
scholars of religious studies had, for a long time, an excuse to abandon the systematic study of this field. On the other hand, anthropologists did not possess the kind of expert knowledge needed
for the study of rituals in their specifically religious configuration.
Culture and magic were the two ends of the axis that marked the
anthropological interest in religion. I believe that we have finally
outgrown this segmentation in the study of religions, and left
behind the value judgments that often accompanied it.

This said, in studying the religious rites of society, anthropology was able to draw on a wider range of perspectives than religious studies. The latter was mostly oriented on the theology,
history, and textual status of the texts and societies that came under
their study. From a socio-cultural point of view, anthropology
offered a more diversified mode of study than religious studies.
Understandably, there was widespread fascination, among those
interested in religious studies, with what the anthropologists had
to offer in this field. Several of these studies also strengthened
Western notions of identity. They affirmed the culturally oriented
distinction between "we here" and "they there," with all the
implications that such a distinction had. Comparative religion,
however, pointed in a different direction. Under the aegis of this
discipline, the world was reduced to a small range of common

denominators, and the illusion of alleged converging similarities pushed aside important local diversities. But the time soon came to establish factors that emphasised diversification. The illusion created by comparative religion of a global farm, in which every house practised one variation or another of the same, proved to be delusive.

The above may help to explain the fact that, in many studies, ritual is used in the singular, as if there was one universal entity, ritual, from which spread off all other sub-forms of rituals. If we keep in mind that rituals are intensely functional in consolidating differences, such a view can barely hold water. Furthermore, if the individually structured performative aspects of rituals are consistently assessed, it becomes obvious, very quickly, that a universal concept of ritual is yet another scholarly illusion. Rituals vary from place to place, from epoch to epoch, and from one religion and society to another. More important still, people use different rituals to achieve different goals within the same system. Consequently, rituals have to be studied in their individual forms of occurrence and performed configurations. The phenomenology of religions, in its philosophical essence and existential variability, should therefore consider rituals in their almost inexhaustible diversity. In other words, there is nothing more challenging in the study of rituals than to examine them in the context of their ever-changing features and characteristics. Ultimately, though, some of the scholarly observations regarding individual rituals will repeat themselves. When this happens, a structured theory may emerge, but it will have taken into account the differences resulting from phenomenological diversity.

The notion of the changeable nature of rituals, in their development, is included in this concept of variable diversity. This is what tradition means when applied to rituals. It does not necessarily follow that the student of rituals has no firm ground on which to stand. It simply means that one cannot discuss rituals as an abstract notion or universal concept. Rituals cannot be detached from the various forms of their crystallisation, in the course of their respective embedding traditions. A Pentateuchal ritual will have a different structure when it re-crystallizes as part of the Halakhic setting in the Mishnah. With the change of circumstances, later developments of the same ritual will look different to preceding ones. The examples are too numerous to be quoted here.

However, one principle prevails throughout. Whether newly-shaped rituals incorporate elements from previous stages or not, is a question worth noting in each case. However, at every stage of its development, every ritual has to be studied in its own performative context. The historical context is also an important factor, but, like any other peripheral explanation, its explanatory efficacy in showing how rituals work is limited. Thus, for instance, the study of the Passover sacrifice in the Book of Exodus (chapter 12) is not exhaustive, unless it includes the study of the Passover rituals as described other parts of Scripture, in Mishnah and Talmud, and later in the Passover Haggadah. We shall return to this example further on. Changing historical circumstances clearly had their impact on the development of the rituals at hand. Their intrinsic explanation, though, has hardly anything to do with the changing historical conditions. In this respect, adding a new link in one chain of rituals may change the nature of the whole chain. It does not only make it longer but also more variegated.

The various texts that recount the same ritual and its change in the course of history create the essentials of what the context, in this case tradition, means in each case. Tradition creates an extended time-span in which various aspects of the same rituals and their evolutionary changeability comes into effect. These aspects of rituals will receive only sporadic attention in this book. The factor of tradition is significant from another point of view. Some scholars refer to popular culture as factors that demonstrate no conscious sense of tradition. We need not discuss this point at length here. However, if rituals are transmitted from one generation to the other, then their persistence in the social structure creates cultural constants. In this sense, one can argue that the human mind learns how to act ritually. The learning process, in this case, takes place in the culturally set ambience of tradition. It is worth examining whether this learning process involves ideological stances or not. In my view, it is not an essential issue in formulating the epistemology of rituals, although it again demonstrates the prevalence of the mind-factor in rituals.

CHAPTER TWO

ECONOMIC ETHOS AND RITUALS IN THE RELIGION OF ANCIENT ISRAEL

I

Since this book focuses on rituals in the religion of ancient Israel, I find it also necessary to make my point clear with regard to what I mean by "the religion of ancient Israel". It is incorporated in the multi-facetted forms of expression that unfold in two complementary Scriptures: the Hebrew Tanakh and Mishnah. Both corpuses supply the major source of information in the present study. It is important to note that a close reading of these Scriptures shows that the religion of ancient Israel is not a uniform, or homogeneous, cultural phenomenon, but a unique convergence of a number of layers. In this chapter, we shall investigate two layers, or stages, in biblical religion. The materials that we shall discuss, as well as the perspectives from which we view them, are not altogether new. However, those familiar with the subject will soon realise that in many respects the present discussion adds new dimensions to existing scholarly knowledge. Furthermore, the connection to rituals studies is new, and amounts, in my view, to a revision of the prevalent discussion of the subject.

It is a commonplace observation in biblical scholarship that nomadism and urbanism are the two ends that mark the line of progression in the history of ancient Israel. This chapter will demonstrate that this picture of historical development is a simplified version of the case studied. In fact, rather than signifying the two ends of a historical development, nomadism and urbanism are dichotomic entities that were often enacted simultaneously, as two sides of a dialectic process. In short, this chapter explores two opposing lifestyles in the history of ancient Israel: (1) nomadism, sheep herding, and tribal organisation, versus (2) urbanisation, agriculture, cattle breeding, and monarchic organisation. These lifestyles had an impact on ritual practice. *Mutatis mutandis*, ritual practice contributed to establishing these lifestyles as foundational factors in a cultural process. This process is described here in terms of an "ethos." The Greek word "ethos" means 'custom,' 'habit.' In modern usage, however, it often designates the guiding principles in people's lives. In this book, I use the notion of ethos in a more general sense, as indicating *practices and ways of life that shape a culture at a stage that precedes the one in which a full-scale religion unfolds.*[1] Ethos epitomises, for the people concerned, the vital principles that sustain existence. In due course, ethos becomes a full-fledged, structured, religion.

I am aware of the fact that similar traits and processes marked the cultural life of ancient Mesopotamia.[2] However, a major difference, in this respect, is the fact that, in the historical narrative that prevailed in ancient Israel, these traits and processes constituted a consistent ideological structure. In fact, they constituted the cultural infrastructure of what became a canonical Scripture. Furthermore, these lifestyles did not only shape opposing forms of cultural identity, and concepts of "otherness," as they did in ancient Mesopotamia, but they also defined ritual preferences. In the present analysis, a great deal of attention is given to the scrip-

---

[1] By way of establishing connecting points with other studies that show similar interests, "ethos" is used, here, in a similar sense to "form," as defined by H. Frankfort, *The Birth of Civilization in the Near East*, Doubleday Anchor Books: Garden City (NY), 1956, p. 25. Frankfort writes: "... the 'form' of a civilization... is implicit in the preoccupations and evaluations of the people. It imparts to their achievements— to their arts and institutions, their literature, their theology—something distinct and final, something that has its own peculiar perfection. Thus, a discussion of the emergence of form entails a knowledge of a civilization in its maturity, a familiarity with its classical expression in every field." I would like to point out, though, that my views here differ from those of Frankfort in two respects. To begin with, I am using the term "ethos" in relation to scriptural views that established themselves as the normative version of the history of the culture of ancient Israel in its allegedly pre-mature phases. Then, I include in the term "ethos" material aspects of existence, such as the economics of the people concerned.

[2] A number of important scholarly works discuss these features and their prevalence in ancient Mesopotamia. See, most recently, Beate Pongratz-Leisten "The Other and the Enemy in the Mesopotamian Conception of the World," in: R.M. Whiting (ed.), *Mythology and Mythologies: Methodological Approaches to Intercultural Influences* [Melammu Symposia II], The Neo-Assyrian Text Corpus Project: Helsinki, 2001, pp. 195-231. There are interesting parallels between this substantial paper and the present chapter, though the respective perspectives are somewhat different.

tural narratives, at least until the revelation on Mount Sinai. Later
phases of these processes show that the cultural dichotomy, as
manifested in both lifestyles, continued to shape central modes
of historical perception and ideational structuring. In short, these
opposing lifestyles create the grid of the literary and thematic structure of the historical narrative of ancient Israel. As indicated above,
I shall discuss this stage in the history of ancient Israel in terms
of an "ethos"-phase. Later phases crystallised in structured forms
of religion and ideology.

I refer to the history that unfolds in these narratives as paradigmatic history. My reason for doing so is this: the narratives that
unfold in Scripture, from the beginning of the Book of Genesis
until the revelation on Mount Sinai and even later, are not historical in the usual sense of the term. One may characterise the
nature of these stories in a variety of ways. One may even raise
the question, whether these stories are at all relevant to any attempt at historical reconstruction. In my opinion, the answer to
this question is positive: they are vital to a process of reconstruction that, primarily, is cultural in essence. Initially, though, the
reconstruction focuses on the information, which the writers believed constituted the historical narrative of the people concerned.
However, it is not always clear what sense of historical development these writers had. It was certainly different from the modern sense in which the term is used. Much has been written on
this subject, and there is no need to dwell upon it here. History
started with the creation of the world, and led to the stage where
the Israelites became "a holy people," as told in Ex. 19-20. We
do not know of any other, external, sources that tell a different
story. However, in Scripture itself, one may find variations of the
major narratival themes. In this respect, reconstruction, here, means
the unearthing of those principles, which, in all likelihood, guided
the scriptural writers in their respective accounts of the historical
reality of the people they were writing about.

Although the parameters of the discussion focus on material
processes, it is particularly in relation to the cultural and religious
reality of these people that I find the reconstruction so challenging. The materials at hand are those that Scripture offers us. As
indicated, they are our principal source of information. There is
no other, in this sense, alternative source at our disposal. In this
respect, I believe that the information that Scripture contains about

these events and processes is also paradigmatically relevant to scholarly arguments regarding specific cultural situations. If the question is, whether this represents historical or mythological fiction, my answer is that it is neither. It is paradigmatic history, that is to say, its verisimilitude is paradigmatically established.[3] It deserves being studied within its own terms of reference and for its own worth, for it provides valid information about what the writers thought was a historical reality that sustained the culture.

We can of course take advantage of what the various schools of biblical scholarship have taught us regarding methods of reading the scriptural texts. However, it is valid to ask whether the scriptural materials necessarily have to be confronted with this particular kind of knowledge (Form-Criticism and the sources-theory), or whether they can tolerate other modes of reading. In other words, the question must be asked, to what extent do we have to, for the purposes of this study, abide by the conclusions of the historical and text-critical approaches and their respective influence on the manner in which Scripture is read critically? Since it is irrelevant to our line of argumentation to investigate which school of scribes was responsible for this ritual or that, the prevalent considerations and methods of study in biblical scholarship need not concern us here. After all, we are interested in questions that relate to the epistemology of rituals and their corresponding theory of ritual. The question as to who wrote the texts that inform us has no bearing upon the issue raised here. We have to allow the rituals described in these texts to tell their own story, regardless of their compositional origins. If this approach produces interesting results that do not defy common sense or negate what the texts themselves say, then the procedure adopted here may be valid.

I do not wish to claim that the approach used, here, should be the norm in biblical studies, or replace the accepted rules of scholarly studies on the history of ancient Israel. Some readers may argue that if I accepted these rules, I would be able to discover more in the materials that I explore. This may well be the case. However, the conclusions that are reached, here, have not

---

[3] In the next chapter, I discuss the question of whether these stories fall under the category of myth. Briefly, in as much as they link to a ritual, the answer is "yes". However, the reasons for this particular understanding of myth will be given in that chapter.

emerged in any regular, previously written, study of the scriptural
texts. Thus, in confining myself to the scriptural materials as they
present themselves to those reading them, whether in the past or
in the present, I show my interest in what people had to say about
their ethos and rituals rather than anything else. History is conceived, here, as a by-product of ethos stances rather than as the
crucible forging these stances. This is also relevant to understanding
the manner in which the people concerned shaped their own
identity. Furthermore, I consider their own reports to be as methodologically important to religious studies as any other materials
or theories that are imported from outside of these texts.

This chapter thus focuses on, and then wishes to assess, the
identification and definition of basic lifestyles that developed before
religion became normatively established. It must be clear by now
that, in defining the nature of these lifestyles, it is vital to note
the ritualised forms of behaviour that played a central role in them.
The general context in which the specific lifestyles, to which I refer
in the present chapter, developed consists of two economic systems that are strong enough to create dialectics of social conflict.
The social conflict is underlined by factors that are typical of
cultural tension. In fact, the relevant scriptural narratives reflect
two rival forms of economic practice that shaped Jewish history
beyond the limits of these narratives.

Eventually, these forms of economic practice established themselves as two cultures. I have already referred to them above: they
are sheep breeding and agriculture, with their respective lines of
development—nomadism and tribalism, on the one hand, and cattle
breeding,[4] urbanisation and monarchy, on the other. It is important to note, however, that in both lifestyles, economics and ritual
practice were firmly intertwined. Furthermore, preferential choices
had a religio-cultural significance, even if they seemed purely
economic. Indeed, at times, it is difficult to tell which came first—

---

[4] Beate Pongratz-Leisten writes: "Animal husbandry is a feature of sedentary
culture. However, under special circumstances, as for example climatic or envi-
ronmental conditions, it may turn into nomadism, too" (p. 204). This is a good
example of how the discussion here differs from that of Beate Pongranz-Leisten. I
distinguish between cattle breeding in general, and sheep herding in particular.
The difference is essential to the understanding the cultural ethos of ancient Israel.
I also attribute greater cultural weight to the shift from sheep herding to cattle
breeding. In the ethos of ancient Israel, the shift is not simply a matter of climate
and environment.

the economic decision or the cultural preference. However, what makes religio-cultural preferences existentially relevant is not the technical labelling of the phenomena in question as economic, but the cultural, and hence ritual, assessment of their basic values.

All this happens in the context of modes of living that are typical of pre-institutionalised religion. Just as, in the history of ancient Israel, I view the biblical period that precedes the Exodus from Egypt and the revelation on Mount Sinai as constituting such a pre-religious stage, so, in Christianity, the life story of Jesus, as told in the Gospels (allegedly, before Paul became historically and theologically involved), constitutes a similar stage. In comparison to later stages of these religions, such modes of religious life have a unique character. Religious behaviour is part of the natural life-process, the *res gestae*. At this early stage, no person acts in a certain manner because he is authoritatively told to do so. No normatively binding code of written laws yet regulates the lives of the people.[5] It must be clear by now that I see this stage in the life of people as deserving a characterization that uses special terms of reference. I shall suggest one in as clear and precise terms as possible. This requires a somewhat complex line of argumentation—both methodologically and phenomenologically speaking. To repeat, these stages of development correspond to religion in its pre-institutionalised stages. Even without constituting religion in the full sense of the term, these stages of development, or features, are still recognisable by their unique forms of lifestyle and social behaviour. Retrospectively, however, they emerge more noticeably when considered in a framework that crystallises in later forms of religiousness.

II

Notwithstanding the above, we do not know much about the manner in which the materials incorporated in Scripture crystallised into structured narratives. It is conceivable that, in writing these narratives, the scriptural writers or their editors wished to high-

---

[5] I intentionally avoid using, here, the rather philosophically-loaded term, "natural law." The "natural" laws by which people live are orally instituted, their origins being in the natural will to survive.

light certain considerations, which had not necessarily been part
of the historical development to which they refer. In this sense,
alluding to early and late in these documents requires caution.
As indicated above, biblical scholars have worked hard to establish research methods that enable one to make such a distinction.
For the present purposes, I generally assume that, to these writers,
history was what mattered to them in the past that they described.
What they came up with genuinely reflected what they thought
their historical past was. Whether the texts hide anything that a
specific research tool may help to uncover with more precision
and certainty than is granted to it here is an interesting question.
In any event, there can be no single answer to it. I therefore believe that biblical scholars and archaeologists should show toler-
ance and listen to a different voice, one that paves alleys to
uncovering ritual theories in the biblical theories at hand. Whether
this voice makes sense or not, should be discussed, not in light
of a preliminary theory or hypothesis, but on its own merits and
in light of the question, whether it facilitates a new reading of the
texts in question.

Accordingly, I suggest seeing in this "pre-religious" setting of
the Genesis stories more than just a fictional allusion to what comes
later, following the revelation at Sinai (which some may consider
fiction, too). It constitutes a cultural milieu in its own right and
manifests principles of a coherent lifestyle that deserve full scholarly attention. I want to view in the kind of coherence that the
texts display the essence of the culture of ancient Israel in what
we call pre-Sinaitic times. Things and events draw our attention
not because they are there or because they happen but because,
culturally speaking, they make sense and project a sense of cogency that transcends their own narratival terms of reference. Thus,
in spite of their superimposed theological garments, something
shines through that is not specifically characteristic of the later,
more theologically minded, periods. In speaking the language of
economics it is more mundane However, its terms of reference
are markedly relevant from a cultural point of view.

At times, however, it is necessary to decode certain aspects of
the relevant texts. In fact, decoding is essential, if one wishes to
separate the early materials from the newer fabric into which they
were embroidered. This process of decoding produces results that
are also of special interest to the historian of religion. It uncovers

phases in the history of religion in ancient Israel that an untrained eye would not notice. Above all, these phases are of particular interest to those studying rituals and their ritual theory.

As mentioned above, we shall focus, here, on economic factors, as they seem to address more basic life-needs than administrative and political organisations. The main questions, in this respect, are: How do people manage property, trade, and their material welfare? How does the tribe manage its economy? How does an economic system regulate the relationships between individuals and the tribe? Finally, and most importantly, what kind of socio-economic grid does support these processes? The answers to these questions, even when taking into account the cultural context of a certain people, usually focus on technical issues, such as organization and administration. Seldom do the answers highlight issues that reflect a wider range of interests and considerations. In our case, the answer pursues a line of argumentation that considers the role that an economy plays in the structuring of a culture and the manner in which a culture shapes the values that are particularly reflected in its economy.

In this respect, my approach suggests viewing economics as part of a larger range of considerations than is usually the norm. In the cases studied here, the economic system emits cultural signals. Furthermore, it is connected to the structuring of a cultural dichotomy. In this dichotomy, the economic system shapes the moral code of good and evil. In most cases, though, it works the other way round, namely, notions of good and evil shape the standards of the economic system by which people are supposed to abide. In the modern world, Marxist communism is a good example of a socio-ethical code of values that shaped economic and political systems. In the scriptural context, that is, in the narratives up to the Exodus and the revelation on Mount Sinai, economics is a major factor in making the daily lifestyle of the people culturally and, for that matter, religiously meaningful. More succinctly expressed, in the pre-religion stage, as maintained in these narratives, the economic system *is* an important factor in people's culture.

What brings economics and religious ethos together? I wish to suggest that a religious ethos creates the conditions in which an economic order becomes an integrating *cultural* factor. Because an economic order makes sense when it reflects the spirit of an overall structure or system, it can easily serve as the trajectory of a cultural or religious ethos. It is possible to see, in rituals, interesting aspects of experiencing religion. When these rituals regulate the economic behaviour of individuals and society, they become a major constitutive factor in shaping ethos and religion. In other words, since economy often functions as a building block in religion, it represents one of the most common and accessible ways of experiencing religion. It is obvious that I use the qualifier "experiential" in a broader sense than is usually the case in the study of religions, where experiential notions usually indicate various psychic experiences, such as mysticism, trances, alternate (or better, expanded) states of consciousness, and states of being possessed. Thus, in including rituals in the major modes of experiencing religion, one substantially widens the range of the notion of religious experience. Briefly stated, rituals belong to the realm of religious experiences.

Since rituals are shareable and communicative, they create formative experiences in structuring the community and maintaining its identity. Although rituals are expected to enforce unanimity, they do not always fulfil this expectation. Rituals do not have the same effect on all people. However, people *are* shaped by their actions as individuals or groups, often vis-à-vis "the other". Their institutions, too, evolve from their, mostly ritualised, actions. With regard to the economic system, its ethos-context helps to make it more than just a financial factor. *Mutatis mutandis*, the economic system assists the ethos in establishing its values in daily-life. In either case, the cultural identity of the people concerned receives its status through practice. Since the economy is one of the most important factors in people's lives, its presence as a culture-shaping factor is highly prominent. In this respect, when the economy is linked to rituals, it helps us to see the importance of rituals in religion.

Scholars have often discussed economics in the framework of religion, and religion in the framework of economics. However, the subject that we examine in the present chapter concerns the various forms of interaction that make economics and cultural ethos the two sides of the same coin. This transcends the question of the impact that the economic order has on the creation of social structures. Indeed, very few studies that I am aware of, if any at all, examine this subject from the vantage points explored here.

To give one example, several scholars have observed that Protestantism and the economic order (especially capitalism) were closely connected, and influenced each other. However, very little is known or has been investigated regarding the function that ritual behaviour exercised in creating a cultural symbiosis between the religion of ancient Israel and the economic order that was a part of it.[6]

III

In the preceding discussion, I presented the subject matter in a rather quintessential manner. The basic issues that this chapter wishes to explore, however, require extensive elaboration. To begin with, I shall expand the discussion of the subject of ethos and its various shades of meaning. As indicated above, I associate ethos with a people's culture before it is shaped into an established order, that is, a religion. By established religion, I mean the omnipresence of a text or a corpus—whether oral or written—which the people concerned universally accept as establishing normative guidance. I have already mentioned the fact that, in my view, the ethos stage in the scriptural narrative corresponds to everything that unfolds, from the creation of the world to the revelation on Mount Sinai. In this narrative, the revelation on Mount Sinai constituted a turning point. From this moment, the word of God shaped a normative religion. As indicated above, in a comparative setting, the life story of Jesus from birth to the crucifixion marks an ethos stage. Paul represents the turning point, in the direction of formulating and theologically formalising the normative creed.[7]

---

[6] Jacob Neusner touches upon these matters in several of his writings. For a compact outline of his ideas see Jacob Neusner, "The Transformation of Economic Thinking in Classical Judaism: When a Religious System Incorporates an Economics and Then Changes Its Mind", in: Jacob Neusner (ed.), *Religious Belief and Economic Bahavior*, Scholars Press: Atlanta, 1999, pp. 241-291. Neusner sees in the economic order a major feature in the philosophical (!) programme that underlies the religious system of *Mishnah*. To wit, his main concern is with theological issues. My concerns, however, are formulated in relation to a framework that I define as pre-philosophical, at least in the way it is described in the documents used for the purposes of this study.

[7] The Gospels recount the life story of Jesus, in all likelihood, in response to Paul, who provides all the theology and rituals that the early Christians needed in order to establish themselves as communities, but very little that concerns the life of Jesus.

In the scholarly discussion of the monotheistic religions, 'ethos' is not a frequently used term. When it is used, it may signify different things that generally relate to various aspects of the cultural context. However, to the best of my knowledge, the specifically technical sense, suggested here, is rather infrequent.[8] It precedes the degree of mental sophistication that is required for a systematic theology to crystallise as a religion *par excellence*. In the framework of theology, everything that is scriptural is, by definition, religion. No distinctions are made between "pre-history" and "history".

In the type of ethos discussed here, the kind of livestock that people own is an expression of their lifestyle, whether nomadic or urban. We shall see that sheep and the nomadic lifestyle create a different ethos from that connected with agriculture, cattle, and urbanisation. In each case, one finds a different type of social structuring and leadership. In the first case, one finds tribal organisations with chiefs as leaders; in the second, one finds monarchs and kings. In short, property and lifestyle crystallise as an ethos in which different modes of ritual behaviour prevail. A quick example is found in the dramatic story of Cain and Abel. God shows a ritual preference for the firstlings of the herd and rejects the fruit of the earth offered by Cain. In its own context, this story does not contain anything that reflects an established form of religion. However, it sets a pattern, a cultic paradigm, which can be expressed as religious.[9]

---

[8] The famous discussion of ethos in the work of Clifford Geertz has no direct relevance to the kind of analysis offered here. See Clifford Geertz, *The Interpretation Of Cultures*, Basic Books: New York, 1973, pp. 126-141: "Ethos, World View, and the Analysis of Sacred Symbols." The title of the chapter makes clear the direction that Geertz's discussion takes. The reader who has followed my line of argumentation, in the previous chapter, will be aware of the fact that I reverse the order: Ethos creates symbols rather than represents them. Geertz writes (p. 127): "A people's ethos is the tone, character, and quality of their life, its moral and aesthetic style and mood; it is the underlying attitude toward themselves and their world that life reflects. Their worldview is their picture of the way things in sheer actuality are, their concept of nature, of self, of society. It contains their most comprehensive ideas of order." I shall stop at this point, though Geertz has more to say on these matters. The reader may check for himself what Geertz's actual characterisation of ethos, *in extenso*, entails. One thing remains clear, though: Geertz puts great emphasis on ideas, concepts, and moral values. My approach concerns the more material and behavioural aspects of ethos and the manner in which they shape a specific lifestyle.

[9] In modern usage, the term "secular" often represents the notion of not belonging to a religious framework or simply not having faith in the religious order. Other

To show the reader where and how the present discussion marks a new turn in scholarship, I shall give two examples of scholarly discussions of the materials at hand. In his study of society and economy in ancient Mesopotamia, J. N. Postgate discusses the role that sheep, shepherds, and cattle had in that world. Postgate rightly distinguishes between sheep and cattle. For him the issue is entirely an economic one and he fails to see that it reflects certain patterns of cultural ethos that have a bearing on the formation a normative, state, and religion.[10]

Evidently, if we have any claim to go beyond scholarly simplification, then we clearly have to find a more sophisticated pattern. We have already seen that economic factors such as livestock (sheep *versus* cattle), create distinctions that have a cultural impact. Similarly, agriculture is not only an economic marker; it also makes a cultural statement over against nomadic sheep herding. A detailed discussion of these issues will follow soon. In the framework of the history of religions, I have suggested using the term ethos for these issues. Ethos, to be more specific than before, is the term that holds together the intertwining patterns that link purely economic conditions and cultural practices, which eventually receive religious configuration. When Scripture tells us that God favoured the sheep sacrifice of Abel over against the fruits of the ground offered by Cain, we are expected, in my view, to see in this, neither an expression of sympathy vis-à-vis Abel nor a token of God's wish to inform future generations of his sacrificial preferences. At this early stage, the preference constituted an *in situ* statement with regard to several issues: sacrifices, good and evil, and retribution. It also showed the power of authority of the one who was in charge. More than it followed a religious norm it defined it. It set the constants of civilisation as the writer of the book of Genesis saw them.

Thus, the fact that, sheep and cattle were depicted on temples and personal seals, as noted by Postgate, represents, in my view,

---

usages include the notion of the profane and the de-sacralised. In principle, I concur with Sara Yaphet, "Some Biblical Concepts of Sacral Place", in: Benjamin Z. Kedar and R. J. Zwi Werblowsky (eds.), *Sacred Space: Shrine, City, Land*, Macmillan and The Israel Academy of Sciences and Humanities: Houndmills, London, and Jerusalem, 1998, pp. 55-72, who criticises Eliade on this issue.

[10] See J. N. Postgate, *Early Mesopotamia: Society and Economy at the Dawn of History*, Routledge: London and New York, 1992, pp. 159-164.

much more than is observed by Postgate. Of course, people may
carve, in stone or clay, or paint devotional images that are to-
kens of trust and thankfulness towards their gods. Depicting household animals and trees expresses, in all likelihood, the wish that
they should be healthy and produce good fruits, milk and meat.
However, in my opinion, these depictions indicate a broader range
of "interests." What, then, do these depictions reflect? In my view,
they functioned at an iconic level. They tell us about a people's
cultural and religious ethos. By placing pictures on the walls of
their temples, they were stating cultic expectations and preferences:
God will give life only to those people who reciprocate by declaring—in public depictions—their trust in the kind of the economic order allegedly sanctioned by their god. Thus, this kind
of depiction of an economic order corresponded to a religio-cultural statement that was mirrored in the economy of the people.
One may even argue that it functioned in the context of a totem
structure or gesture. Sacrificing this totem was the highest ritual
gesture that these people could make. The sacrificial gesture meant
giving back to their god something, which belonged to him, in
the first place. Culturally speaking, this was part of the ethos, which
shaped people's lives. At this early stage, God did not yet ask the
people, as he did in the Book of Leviticus (and in other prescriptive texts), to bring sacrifices. In the ethos stage, people did so
spontaneously. Whether the totem was chosen from sheep, cattle,
or the land was intensely relevant—the only thing that deeply
mattered.

   The second example comes from Thorkild Jacobsen's study of
the religions of Mesopotamia. He reports about the Sumerian
Goddess, Inanna,: "As younger sister she appears in a story in
which her brother Utu, the sun god, has found a suitable husband for her, the shepherd god Dumuzi, only to discover that
Inanna could never dream of marrying a shepherd; it has to be a
farmer, and so a farmer it is."[11] Inanna's exact words, in translation, are indeed very powerful: "Inanna spoke: 'The Shepherd! I
will not marry the shepherd! His clothes are coarse; his wool is
rough. I will marry the farmer. The farmer grows flax for my

---

[11] Thorkild Jacobsen, *The Treasures of Darkness: A History of Mesopotamian Religion*,
Yale University Press: New Haven and London, 1976, p. 142.

clothes. The farmer grows barley for my table.'"[12] The marital preference, in the manner expressed here, is certainly noteworthy, although, to an outsider, it may look somewhat capricious. Interestingly, Jacobsen adds no comment that could place the story in a specific cultural context. In other words, for Jacobsen this is yet another specimen deserving the section title "Myths." However, the materials presented in the present chapter clearly shed light on the nature of the marital preference of the goddess. The preference is normative, not incidental. Like the story of Cain and Abel to which we referred above, it shows—in a reverse type of preference—where the conflict between shepherding and agriculture could lead.

It is possible to take this point a step further. If, as we argue, here, Inanna expressed, in what she said, more than scholars have noted so far, then, her determination represents an ethos diametrically opposed to that voiced by the scriptural narrator, who favoured the shepherds. She prefers the flax plant for her garments rather than the wool of the sheep. More significantly, she shows a culinary predilection for barley. The barley and table, in this respect, epitomise a Cainite type of sacrificial meal. The portrayal of this meal shows that Inanna and the God of Abel could not dine together. Can we, then, say that Cain represented, in the story, the cult of Inanna? In other words, can we say that there are traces, polemical as they seem to be, hitherto unidentified, of the Inanna cult in the scriptural story? Evidently, if these traces exist, they create the antithetical pole of the ethos that Scripture wishes to establish. For the time being, there is no clear answer to this question, but a positive answer cannot be ruled out.

IV

At this point, I would like to raise a few issues that may be helpful in understanding the methodological framework in which the present book intends to operate. I have already referred to the fact that I do not consider historical sequencing as the first methodological prerequisite. Still, it is only natural to expect a reason-

---

[12] See, Diane Wolkstein and Samuel Noah Kramer, *Inanna, Queen of Heaven and Earth: Her Stories and Hymns from Sumer*, Harper and Row: New York, 1983, p. 33.

able degree of historical sequencing, when establishing factors of coherent continuity and linear development. Travelling back in time certainly defies the laws of reason. However, if the aim is to endow ancient realities with notions of a realistic presence, travelling back in time may be the preferred option. We have first to show a capacity of understanding ourselves, before we can turn to understanding the beliefs of those who lived in ancient times. For the modern person, religion can easily be separated from other spheres of life. However, for the people who lived in the ancient world, such a separation was less conceivable. People in antiquity lived in a world in which spirits, deities, demons, and ghosts were likely to manifest themselves at any time and in every place. Consequently, the immediate existential choices, which people in the ancient world faced, were connected to questions such as, which god(s) to worship and how. The "why" was dictated and shaped by practical considerations and needs. Questions of theological belief and non-belief were not a primary concern of the people at that time. There was belief. The question was, who was worthy of this belief and who was not? Decisions, in these cases, were mostly determined by personal inclinations, local interests, and existential needs.[13] For our purposes, though it is important to note that the decision was expressed in ritual. Ritual, in turn, made the decision a pivotal event in the life of the people.

In later rabbinic hermeneutics, the Patriarchs lived according to the scriptural norms that developed in post-Sinaitic times. In reality, though, this was not the case.[14] We should be aware of the fact that, in practice, the patriarchs followed standards of morality and cultic behaviour that had their own rules. Set against a larger scriptural setting, some of these rules had a more, others had a less, normative-fitting configuration. The life-stories of the Patriarchs contained everything needed to make them the sub-

---

[13] This point comes through clearly in E. R. Dodds, *Pagans and Christians in an Age of Anxiety*, Cambridge: University Press, 1968; and Robin Lane Fox, *Pagans and Christians*, Alfred A. Knopf: New York, 1987. Although these studies deal with religious phenomena typical of the times of early Christianity, some of their major conclusions are easily applicable to the topics studied in the present chapter.

[14] One should keep in mind the fact that Jacob married two sisters and that Joseph married an Egyptian. Abraham, in a different context (Gen. 18: 7-8) served meat and dairy together, contrary to what became the norm of separating meat and milk (Ex. 23: 19; 34: 26).

stance of scriptural materials. Once again, the question of whether the biography of the Patriarchs matches historical verisimilitude or only constitutes a mythic construct is a side issue, in my view. What really mattered was the intrinsic purpose of telling these stories. It is probable that the scriptural writers aimed at setting standards of behaviour and paradigmatic models of lifestyle. Once the lives of the Patriarchs became models of imitation, the first links between myth and ritual were created. As we shall see in chapter 3, myth is a unique kind of reality that the human mind conceives and shapes *in relation to a ritual*. The specific links between the various myths and rituals have to be assessed individually. Each myth has its corresponding ritual and each ritual adopts a myth that sustains it.[15] Thus, each link entails a *sui generis* mode of perception and corresponding mode of human behaviour.

People are inclined to see, in myth and ritual alike, symbolic expressions of something that is neither the myth nor the ritual. However, in my view, myth and ritual are autonomous expressions of the human mind. They speak their own "language" in their own formative terms of reference. In both, respectively, the connection to normal modes of perception and behaviour has a rather unique nature. Myths, we shall see, do not necessarily mirror realities that are historically grounded. Rather, they seek to shape reality in their own manner. The kind of the change and its depth that reality undergoes in each case varies from myth to myth and from one ritual to another.

Myth and ritual entail a special kind of statement about reality. In the first place, they bring to life a reality that invites people to join in and participate. In this respect, they epitomise what cults and religion wish to achieve. When people begin to join in, a community comes into being. In turn, this community requires the doing of certain rituals that sustain and regularly regenerate the communal reality. We have noted that the ultimate goal that activates modes of ritual behaviour is usually one that produces a certain kind of transformation. Thus, when a crisis erupts, a substantial change is needed. We shall try to show that the place to enact such changes, or transformations, is in the cosmos where rituals are behaviourally defined. This cosmos draws, into its realm,

---

[15] In due course, I shall explain, in what sense, my views on the connection between myth and ritual differ from those of the "Myth and Ritual School".

mental powers that have no other ways of accomplishing what is needed, except in and through rituals. Rituals are effective, because they operate in a kind of reality that allows myth and behavioural practices to interact. Together they bring into effect changes that are inconceivable in normal modes of existence. Rituals imply special modes of existence. This existence generates behavioural practices that are likely to bring about types of transformation, the metaphysical essence of which is conceived as strikingly different from what people commonly think of when they speak of change. Thus, rituals cannot be assessed properly outside the realm of this kind of metaphysical essence. The reality, in which rituals unfold, is more than just the sum total of its physical components.

However, in mentioning metaphysics, in connection with rituals, I do not wish to usher in theology. We have already noted that people are likely to do rituals without necessarily involving theological considerations. In this respect, rituals are an almost instinctive response. By doing rituals, people become involved in the metaphysics of a transformable reality. In more mythic terms, rituals redress something that was evil, a damage done, or something that involved a fatal departure from normative forms of behaviour.

It is repeatedly argued, in the present book, that the prevalence of theological considerations in the rituals of people who lived in the ancient world is an open question. It is reasonable to argue, however, that the degree of mental sophistication that is required to formulate theological positions is not a negligent factor. Acting, too, at the behavioural level and attempting to make behaviour effective, requires "planning," but it is not necessarily theological. In this case, planning is tantamount to structuring and the structure, here, is ritual. Even when rituals use verbal expressions, they do not speak about a certain situation. They relate to it at the behavioural level. People who are used to see, in words, a sophisticated mode through which they give expression to the mind, may consider rituals an inferior mode of expression. However, the degree of sophistication that rituals imply should not be dismissed offhand. I, nonetheless, believe that the people in antiquity could not fully envision the degree of symbolic representation that modern scholars claim to find in their study of rituals.

For people in the ancient world (and for some, even today), representation meant creating a space for the physical embodiment of entities (gods, goddesses, angels, Jesus). I view icons as a tool created by humans to make these entities present. These entities may also make present life-factors, such as economic preferences and objects. They are not symbols. Carving or sculpting meant that the carved object was given a chance to become present.[16] The material image contained the object made present. Smashing idols, thus, always means annulling the objects, which their images incorporate. Notwithstanding the attempts made in ancient Israel to forbid by the word of the law the worshipping of iconic images of the God of Israel, the popular inclination, severely criticised by the prophets, was to worship idols. Almost everywhere, gods were worshipped in their immediate presence, that is, as fetishes. In drawing the picture of a god or a goddess, or in telling a story about him or her, the people concerned expressed their desire to give their god or goddess a manifestational presence. In other words, the aim of creating a presentation, or a re-presentation, of any divine being was to create its manifestational presence. In a sense, making God present is the ultimate aim of religious rituals. God is made to watch and receive, then help and protect. That is to say, he is ritually seduced to be present. This is what people do in order to guarantee their existence. This is where artistic presentation links to ritual.

A further comment is in place to make clear our position in the discussion of comparative work in religious studies. A key factor, in the study of rituals, is the setting or the framework in which they are done. Every religion creates its own context. If context means anything—and it certainly does in rival religions such as that of ancient Israel and the other religions of the ancient Near East—then its function as a factor that creates and maintains differences and boundaries substantially limits any comparative work. I do not intend to enter too deeply into questions of theological meaning. However, I would like to give one example to reinforce the limits of comparison. Take the injunction:

---

[16] I prefer the wording "to become present" to "to be present," because I think that a process is involved. The act of carving prepares a space for the gods to appear. The icon is, thus, a theophanic cosmos. If the icon is in a room, the whole room is affected by the presence of the being whose representational image is in the icon.

"Say to all the congregation of the people of Israel, You shall be separated (this is the correct translation of *qedoshim*, usually translated as "holy")[17]; for I the Lord your God am *qadosh*, separated" (Lev. 19: 1). This verse contains three essential elements: God, the Israelites, and—the connecting link—ritual separation or self-segregation. These elements set the terms of reference that define the vital nature of the rituals, whose aim is to ensure the existence of the community. The inherent 'separation' aspect is the factor that limits comparative work.

V

Let me briefly recapitulate the discussion. Reading the scriptural narratives in the Book of Genesis, one cannot fail to notice that the narrative dramatically unfolds in settings that are completely different from the ones that prevail in post-Sinai times. Some of the questions that we have asked are, how can we assess the information that these narratives impart, in terms that are also of interest to those studying religio-cultural phenomena? What do the texts in question say about the cultural history of the people? What kind of ideas and ideological messages do the texts convey? These are important questions, which are central to the study and understanding of almost every religion. In general, the relevant answers do not derive from perspectives that focus on religion—or, for that matter, on ethos—as it is practised. Textual, historical and theological perspectives constitute the major concerns of religious studies. The approach I take differs, in that it draws the answers to these questions from the ritual behaviour of the people who are at the centre of the narratives in question. The assumption, taken here, is that people practise, rather than think about, their religion. This assumption directs us in the formulation of the answers, suggested in this chapter, as well as in the rest of this book. In short, in order to know what a particular religion is about, one has to consider what it tells people to do.

I have suggested viewing the two settings, ethos and religion,

---

[17] See Norman H. Snaith, *The Distinctive Ideas of the Old Testament*, Schocken Books: New York, 1964, pp. 21-50. Midrashic literature, too, attests to the notions of separation and self-segregation implied by the term *qadosh*.

as two distinct phases or stages in the development of the religious history of the ancient Israelites. I have noted that, in the ethos stage, the religious attitudes of the people are spontaneously expressed in their daily transactions. No special ideology is applied, at this stage, to contextualise these forms of activity in a systemic structure. The narrative is the structure. Experiencing divine revelations is presented as a matter-of-fact occurrence. Even Hagar could see an angel, though she wondered why this had happened while she was away from her master's home (Gen. 16: 13). In later phases of development, though, God's revelations established general standards and the norm that concerned the creation of nationhood. The revelation at Sinai established the special status of normative Law. In comparison, the ethos phase was characterised by personal messages, although in several cases (e.g., God's punishment of Adam and Eve and the promises given to Abraham), these had far reaching implications. In principle, though, they were mostly sporadic revelations. They did not raise doctrinal issues. In addition, as mentioned, they did not aim to build a systemic ritual edifice.

As indicated above, the present chapter will demonstrate how two apparently casual forms of livelihood, emerge as two economic lifestyles. These lifestyles had cultural, even religious, implications. In this respect, they were shaped as conflictual entities. The two entities were sheep herding and agriculture. In a wider context, these two ways of life were respectively connected to processes of nomadic and urban lifestyles. In yet a wider context, urbanisation was connected to establishing the monarchic rule of ancient Israel, and nomadism declared its absolute opposition to it.[18] Although processes of decision-making of real economic importance seem to underline the scriptural narrative, what was really at stake was something altogether different—namely a cultural dichotomy. The scriptural narrative makes God part of these events and processes. Thus, every decision or preference makes a point that has religious significance. More precisely expressed, in the story of Cain and Abel God is setting life principles that define religiously engaging norms that are equally binding in their manifestation

---

[18] See Samuel's speech against the appointment of a king in 1 Sam. 8. It is interesting to note that Samuel functioned as a wandering, that is nomadic, judge: 1 Sam. 7: 15-16. We shall come back to this point later on.

as economic preferences. The economic options between which people could make their choices with regard to their lifestyle made a cultural difference. We view the unique combination between economics and culture in the life of the people as the ethos of ancient Israel. In turn, this ethos developed into the basis of religious attitudes and behaviour of the people.

In rejecting the fruit sacrifices offered by Cain and in destroying the city of Bavel and its "tower" [evidently, a *ziggurat*], God made his preferences resonate clearly, in a logically progressive sequence. First, agriculture is rejected and, then, the city. The city and the surrounding agricultural environment create a convergence of economic interests. In fact, they create a marketing-community in which the boundaries between the surrounding agricultural villages and the township are crossed. The agricultural countryside and the urban administration form an interesting economic symbiosis. Naturally, when this implies making a certain statement concerning the crossing of boundaries, certain administrative practices are enforced. They come into effect in various forms, the main one being the payment of dues to those in charge. Depending on whether people pay money (taxes) or hand over tithes of their animals or crops, I suggest considering these practices as sacrificial. Indeed, people accompany these crossings of boundaries with rituals or ritual gestures.[19] We shall see, further on, that sacrificial acts aim to guarantee normal life-conditions for the people concerned. People, who have a full-fledged system of rituals, consciously use sacrifices for these ends.

Taking a closer look at the scriptural narratives, one is struck by the manner in which the rival lifestyles mentioned above create the drama, not to mention the basic dialectic structure. Adam was placed in the "Garden of Eden," as the narrative in the Book of Genesis 2 puts it, "to till it and to keep it." Interestingly, the Garden of Eden is the epitome of agricultural work. The word *Adamah* (ground, land), and the name Adam, which appear several times in this context, are of particular interest to us. In this respect, farming is the context in which the scriptural ethos views Adam as fulfilling his vocation as Adam/man, and it is here that

---

[19] See the interesting discussion of this phenomenon in China (and Taiwan) in P. Steven Sangren, *History and Magical Power in a Chinese Community*, Stanford University Press: Stanford, 1987, pp. 105-126: "Local Ritual, Economic, and Administrative Systems".

misbehaviour is counted as sin. Adam, who was made from *Adamah,* fulfils himself in tilling the land/*Adamah.* This is his ethos and one in which biological survival depends on a specifically structured economic system. When this is the case, man's actions bear directly on the axis linking physical survival with the economic structure, namely, existence. The ethos-structure holds all these factors together. Consequently, any break up of this axis or disturbance of its pivotal functioning ushers in disaster. It represents a significant infringement of the correct order of a specific "cosmos" and is, therefore, punishable. As we shall immediately see, the expulsion from the Garden of Eden marks the point at which *Adamah* becomes a cursed entity. Adam, too, is cursed. God tells him that the land will never again yield its fruits unless hard labour is invested in tilling it. Briefly, then, Eden and farming are the two ends of the same axis, linked by a straight line. In a way, this explains the change towards the ethos of sheep herding. Since the order that Eden signified, and that originally meant stability, collapsed, the opposite—shepherding—was introduced. Almost by deterministic programming, the character representing evil in the ensuing story, Cain, could not but become a farmer. This is economic predestination with cultural consequences. They are well known: Cain killed his brother, the one who God favoured because he made the right choice and lived differently. Apparently, Abel drew all the needed conclusions from the curse of *Adamah,* as proclaimed to his father. As we see matters here, what he did involved, not only a different type of economy, sheep herding, but also a different ethos. This ethos had cultic consequences. They were acted out on the sacrificial scene. It tuned in a case demonstrating irony of fate that sacrifice was not stopped where it was enacted mimetically. Evil desperation on the part of his brother brought about Abel's destruction.

In terms taken from gangster economics, we could say that Cain eliminated his competition by assassinating the chief of his rival gang. Here, and elsewhere, God cannot prevent the crime from happening. Apparently, omniscience has its own limitations. However, God easily functions as the law-enforcing authority on the scene. He immediately makes clear what is right and what is wrong. He is ready to enact his decision with no hesitation: Cain had to bear the punishment of roaming the earth, that is, he was prevented from settling down and forming an agricultural base

again. Capital punishment was not yet in force. On the contrary,
Cain was given a chance to change. However, as we shall see,
his conduct only worsened. He was not the kind of person to
succumb easily, to depart from his ethos. Instead, he built a city.
Evidently, this entailed a graver sin. If farming is the economic
structure that culminates in urbanisation, as even modern economic
theory has it, then in building a city, Cain was simply stepping
up his rebellious behaviour or reinforcing his ethos. The intensification of his rebellious ethos brought about his ultimate destruction. Lemech inadvertently killed him.

What does this story depict? It depicts a negative curve, which
is referred to in the notion of *Adamah*. Adam was carved out of
Adamah (Gen. 2: 7). *Adamah* is cursed because of Adam's sin in
the Garden (Gen. 3: 17). *Adamah* is blamed for participating in
the killing of Abel: it is described as having opened its mouth to
swallow the blood of the murdered brother, thus becoming an
active accomplice in the murder. Cain is then declared cursed,
even more than the *Adamah* that had already been cursed in the
days of his father (Gen. 4: 10-12). When, later on, Noah's par-
ents gave their son his name, they too mentioned the *Adamah* that
God had cursed (Gen. 5: 29). Finally, in this respect, God decided to wipe out the living creatures that inhabited the *Adamah*
(Gen. 7: 4). All these instances create an interesting and recur-
rent pattern. It is worth following the other instances in which
Adamah is mentioned in a negative sense, or context, in the Book
of Genesis and elsewhere in Scripture.[20] One thing is clear, however: in many cases, *Adamah* is the negative counterpart of *Eretz*
or *Ha-Aretz*. *Eretz* is the more neutral term. It often signifies the
"world" as opposed to the heavens, and more significantly, the
Promised, agricultural, Land.

VI

To many people, in the modern world, religion and economics
still signify two polarised ends. Religion is expected to give people
a chance to express their confidence in rewards that are stored in
the heavenly treasure houses. Economics means investing in some-

---

[20] A significant change, though, occurs when God tells Abraham that "all the
families of the Adamah" will be blessed in him (Gen. 12: 3).

thing solid, in treasure houses that provide material gains and security. It is often argued that when religion and economics interact, this can only mean that religion exploits economics, or, else, that the economic system inevitably corrupts religion. A fashionable approach, oriented by the type of criticism that philosophical materialism directs against the religious order, sarcastically claims that religious institutions have an almost inbred greed for capital. It allegedly disguises under the mantle of ideals of sacred poverty. Religion also preaches austerity in material matters, but does so in order to rob the masses of their basic material possessions. Finally, it allegedly keeps the masses in conditions of poverty. Doing so, it wishes to secure the religious order from a much-feared opposition that threatens to gain power and establish an alternative order. Evidently, these arguments reflect fashionable prejudices, which, among other things, are functional in power games.

Religion is, indeed, an easy target for criticism from all flanks. The religious order was often criticised for its hypocritical attitudes in matters of wealth, material possessions and money. "Mammon," the Aramaic/Greek word for money, is used in many European languages to indicate that not everything that shines is morally justifiable, sterling silver. By definition, almost, Mammon is the evil chieftain who leads corrupt financial systems. Using another kind of imagery, Mammon is a currency that emits a bad smell. Money, allegedly, unsettles the social order and introduces inequality and injustice. Preferably, then, a religious person should show no interest in the material world, including, for that matter, the needs of his own body.[21] It is argued that, if economics is the science that regulates the material interests of people, religion is expected to be its diametrically opposed counterpart.

---

[21] It is pertinent to mention, here, Peter Brown, *The Body and Society*, Columbia University Press: New York, 1985. Brown is aware of the attitude of the Qumran community to bodily defilement. In line with the sub-title of his book, "Men, Women and Sexual Renunciation in Early Christianity," Brown (p. 38) underlines the austere sexual codes of the Qumran community. However, in "Body and City," the subject of the first chapter of Brown's book, a stronger case could be made in favour of the argument made by Brown. The Qumran community condemns "Israel" (=Jerusalem) because of three vices of Beliya'al: prostitution, capital (in Hebrew: *hon*) and temple defilement. *Hon*, or mammon, has a corrupting effect, no less than prostitution and temple defilement. All three, in the eyes of the Qumran community, are characteristic of the then capital city.

Thus, the manner in which the religious order should handle money ideally is to encourage donations rather than savings. Tithing is one institutional means whereby working people donate, by the dictate of the scriptural law, part of their profits. Even when the priestly beneficiaries were forbidden, by the word of the law, from possessing land of their own (Deut. 18: 1), the priesthood was never the poor sector of the population. The image of a priesthood that is wealthy, greedy, and corrupt runs through the criticism of the prophets, the accusations voiced by the Qumran community, and the words of Jesus ("blessed are the poor in spirit"). Indeed, this is a constant theme in the social criticism articulated by religions. Ideally, of course, religion should support the system in which deposits are made into spiritual accounts. Security safes, where mundane wealth is safely stored, quickly become superfluous, since they cannot be taken to the grave.

As noted above, historical materialism attempts to expose the weak points of religion, those that cherish money, rather than saintliness. *Mutatis mutandis*, religion sees in materialism the major corrupting force that deflects interest from the real, sublime, and divine towards the earthly, seductive and corrupt. At one end, there are those who say that religion should be banned from the state, because it promotes hypocrisy in matters pertaining to social and material justice and welfare. At the other end, there are the professional preachers, who demand distance from all that is material and worldly, namely, money. One group (the Marxists) claims that religion is the opium of the masses. Another urges people to wash their hands after holding money (this is not only a hygienic precaution) and completing financial transactions.

Many reasons could probably be given to justify the opposite of what this chapter aims at, which is the depolarisation of religion and economics. The premise, here, is that religion and economics may be viewed as interacting in order to create a venue in which specific patterns of ethos and religious ritual develop. By highlighting the cultural, rather than the material and financial aspects of economics, I have tried to illustrate this kind of interaction. I hope that I have succeeded in showing that, in the culture of ancient Israel, religion and economics are not rival systems. Indeed, cultural entities can be shown as moving in and out of economics. Economics, too, will be shown as moving in and out of culture. Accordingly, the interest that Scripture shows in economics is not simply concerned in convincing people of the profits they can make, if they follow the preferences suggested to them: Scripture has goals that are different to those of modern-day financial experts. To be more precise, the economic system that Scripture prefers, is not socially more just, financially more profitable, or even just. Rather, it is an economic preference that articulates a unique cultural statement. In short, in the sources that we discuss here, money itself does not smell. Indeed, wealth is accepted as a token of the blessings of the gods. What matters is where the capital comes from—whether it come from this rather than that type of economic system.[22]

The economic system, therefore, is one of the ways in which religion formulates the essential components of its scale of values—whether social, political or material. If assessed systematically, it will very likely reveal the "philosophy" behind it. I have already pointed to the fact that the role played by economics in a religious context has an intrinsic structure and systemic mechanism, which override material concerns.[23] It fulfils certain cultural (or religious) functions. More specifically, various forms of economic style and behaviour constitute an integral part of culture, in general, and of religion, in particular.

VII

One essential feature of the ethos stage is that its ritual expressions have no repetitive patterns. People do rituals mostly on a one-time basis, as one-time events. In this phase, cyclic patterns

---

[22] It is interesting to refer to the Zionist ethos of settling the land of Israel in the twentieth century. The Zionist ethos represents an interesting change, in this respect. It emphasises the return to the land. The celebrated pictures of the early pioneers show farmers ploughing the land and reaping crops.

[23] These aspects of economics have been extensively studied by Jacob Neusner, *The Economics of the Mishnah*, Chicago University Press: Chicago and London, 1990. As indicated above, the systemic nature of economics, as presented in *Mishnah*, justifies, in Neusner's eyes, referring to them as a philosophic system. This chapter takes a different path. We are not looking, as Neusner does, for the system of Mishnaic economics, or of any other kind of religious economics. We are exploring the cultural implications of the choice certain people made between two economic systems. We focus on the manner in which economics shape a cultural ethos, rather than the other way around, namely, the way culture uses economics to strengthen marks of identity.

neither shape nor measure time. As noted, the cyclic pattern is essential to the recurrence of ritually enacted events. In the religion phase, weekly, monthly, and annual events serve as building factors that give ritual form to timely events. They do this beyond the immediate, or spontaneous, needs and concerns of the people.[24] Rituals impose on people an agenda the purpose of which is to draw people out of their routine, out of the ordinary. I consider it reasonable to argue that any process of formalisation of religious behaviour begins with the establishment of repetitive patterns, as the structural grid of issues that have crystallised in the ethos phase.

Another feature, that formalises an ethos into a religion, is the crystallisation of ritual events as an enactment of certain "archetypal" events in the past. The process of ritualising such events is a foundational factor in the life of the people concerned. In this respect, rituals are instrumental in keeping historical memory alive. They are an ongoing factor in the life of the people.[25] Rituals are intensely functional in any cultural setting that wishes to preserve the past. Memory builds the bridges between the past and the present while rituals activate the incorporation of the past into the present. Rituals are also functional in preventing past events from becoming amorphous entities that disappear into forgetfulness and cultural redundancy. With these comments in mind, I wish to direct attention to the role that rituals are playing in upholding the past and preventing forgetfulness. Repeating the past in a ritual mode is not only a way of preserving its relevance to the present, it is also a way of preserving the present on historically solid foundations. Liturgical phrases, such as "do this in my memory" or "in memory of the Exodus from Egypt," are packed with intensely meaningful functions.

This issue has another aspect of interest. Scholars often argue

---

[24] See Mircea Eliade, *The Sacred and the Profane: The Nature of Religion*, Harcourt Brace: San Diego..., 1959, pp. 68-69: "Every religious festival, any liturgical time, represents the reactualization of a sacred event that took place in a mythical past, "in the beginning." Religious participation in a festival implies emerging from ordinary temporal duration and reintegration of the mythical time reactualized by the festival itself. Hence sacred time is indefinitely recoverable, indefinitely repeatable." In the next chapter, we shall discuss Eliade's views on myth and ritual at some length.

[25] Full attention to this issue is given in the next chapter.

that, in the religion of ancient Israel, the memory of historical events was somehow superimposed on existing seasonal festivals and celebrations, which were mainly connected to the agricultural cycle of events. Scripture then created additional connections between these festivals and specific historical events marking the days in the desert. It should be noted, however, that Scripture does not mention any ritual events that are celebrated in connection with sheep herding. In this respect, the dominating infrastructure of ritual life, in ancient Israel, was primarily agricultural. It is reasonable to argue, then, that the transition from the ethos stage to that of the religion of ancient Israel took place in and through the creation of agricultural feasts and ceremonies. This fact underscores the special character of the ethos stage: it established neither time patterns, nor their corresponding rituals. The new religion-stage, however, is connected to the formalisation of cyclic time patterns, corresponding rituals, a temple, a hierarchical priesthood, and a centralised governing system (the monarchy). In short, an ethos becomes a religious system, when incidental rituals are formalised by repetitive patterns. Furthermore, tradition creates ritualised modes of enacting the memory of the events of the past, if not the events themselves.

Finally, and on a completely different level of consideration, rituals play an important role in creating the notion of "otherness." The modern study of ethnicity has amply shown how concepts of otherness shape boundaries that are essential to maintaining self-identity. This is also the point where the concepts of other gods and their worship enter the scene. Once a theology is added to the ritual process, these concepts of "otherness" are conceptually formalised and easily translate into hate and misanthropy. However, at the ethos stage, no otherness is established, in the strict and exclusive sense of the term. On the contrary, Abraham is told that his blessing will extend to all the nations of the earth (Gen. 12:3). When God changed Avram's name to Avraham, He said that the new name represents the universal fathership of Abraham (Gen. 17: 5).

In short, in the history of ancient Israel, the transition from ethos to religion is connected to the passage from a nomadic lifestyle to an urban one. No clear answer has yet been given to the question posed above—whether it is possible to reconstruct, with a reasonable degree of verisimilitude, the historical process that underlies the scriptural narratives. We have to rely on the texts we read. In this respect, what we have is what we know. There is almost nothing, in this case, that can adequately serve as an informative substitute. I therefore suggested reading the texts paradigmatically, that is to say, as texts that establish paradigms of historical knowledge and understanding. This is how people, writing the texts in question, came to trust, and believe in, the value and validity of what they were writing. These writers usually had a unique concept of historiography:[26] it expressed, in particular, modes of ancestral lifestyles that had a cultural status. Culture, in this respect, meant everything that played a formative role in the early stages of nationhood. We should be reminded of the fact that, cognitively speaking, history is what people believe it to be. Historical memory is selective. It retains or disposes of information on principles that are not necessarily showing a preference to reporting of what really happened. Being aware of this has become a commonplace observation in modern historiography. I think that in this respect some biblical scholars have still a lesson to learn. Literary theories that sustain the documentary hypothesis should be subjected to the scrutiny of theories of historical reconstruction. My approach focuses on a certain mode of reading the story of ancient Israel. I find in this story the economic paradigms that were then fixed as the guidelines of a specific cultural behaviour. We may also read the last sentence in reverse order, that is, a specific cultural behaviour paradigmatically set the dialectics of the norms that set the economic order.

Thus, when I suggest viewing economics as a test case for the manner in which common forms of a particular lifestyle became culturally relevant and meaningful, I do so in the context of what I call a myth. Myth, as we shall see in more detail in the next chapter, is the reality configured to establish a functional relation to ritual.[27] In this reality, the practice of an economic system easily becomes the source of narratives that are connected to ritualised forms of behaviour. In the context of the discussion of ethos,

---

[26] For a clear and stimulating discussion of "Paradigmatic Time" see Jacob Neusner, *The Presence of the Past, and the Past of the Presence: History, Time, and Paradigm in Rabbinic Judaism*, CDL Press: Bethseda, Maryland, 1966, particularly p. 59, where Neusner defines the notion.

[27] More will be said about the connection between myth and ritual in the next chapter.

I view economics as constituting such an attitude. In this respect, an economic order is more than just a system of measuring, planning and organizing products and methods of marketing. It is a compelling way of enacting certain attitudes, which, in turn, establish preferences of cultural values and ritual behaviour. These preferences sustain a particular lifestyle. They do this in various ways, although what interests us, here, is the manner in which rituals reciprocally institutionalise these preferences at the ethos level.

In the preceding chapter, I drew attention to the fact that rituals are all too often viewed as material substitutes for things that are, in principle, more spiritual. The doing of rituals is often thought to be referentially reflecting a previously conceived idea. Accordingly, rituals are viewed as enacting symbolic entities. In contrast, I argue that rituals are attitudinal expressions of the mind and that they should be understood by what they aim to accomplish, rather than by what they stand for. Thus, what primarily matters in doing rituals is the doing, not the idea behind the doing. It is customary to refer to rituals as a means of attaining states of transformation. As explained in the previous chapter, rituals create special links between the person doing the ritual, the ritual act itself, and its transformative outcome. The extent, to which the outcome is a product of the imagination, a belief-dependent construct, or a real event, does not concern us here. People doing the rituals always maintain that the reality of the ritual and its outcome are epistemologically verifiable. The fact that they speak the language of behavioural gestures gives rituals their special status and strength. Involving the body in the doing of rituals "materialises", or reifies, the ritual act.

If this line of argumentation is accepted, then the main issue, in the study of rituals, must be the assessment of how rituals bring about the respective transformative effects. Transformation entails a certain change in the prevalent conditions or status. I have suggested viewing these conditions or status in the framework of a "cosmos." Among other things, the notion of "cosmos" indicates that what is happening in one part affects the whole. Rituals do not work before people begin to view them in terms of functioning in a coherent system, whatever its nature. Even when this "cosmos" is composed of different parts, in the final resort, these parts converge together in the ritual process. The economic lifestyle of the Patriarchs constituted such an ethos-cosmos. In as much as it offered people, living also in a different time and in another place, a practicable system that could sustain their existence and livelihood, conditions had to prevail (the "lifestyle" factor) to make the specific rituals relevant and commensurate to the kind of transformation that they were expected to bring about.

Of course, existence meant for these people more than survival, in its essentially material sense. Without clearly specifying its limits and extensions, existence (the "cosmos" factor) for these people included notions of the predominance of something that also had spiritual implications. In this respect, one may argue that rituals define boundaries of "a different kind". They outline a cosmos that includes the supernatural. One may even argue, as I did above, that the physical aspects of that cosmos entail something unique that amounts to a metaphysical essence. In a sense, it is an existential type of totality, very different from what people experience, living with the materials concepts of the modern world. For such a metaphysical totality to endure, a specific kind of systemic order and organisation must prevail. The alternative, in this case, is chaos the apocalyptic expression of which is the collapse of the universal order. This explains the vital role played by rituals in a society that maintains its beliefs with regard to a ritual-bound order and existence.

This brings us back to our main subject—the ritualised modes of life in the pre-religious stage. Initially, these are daily practices believed to guarantee physical survival. These practices were ritually enacted in a most natural way, without necessarily involving a written, institutionalised, or constitutional code of social and moral values. At this stage, too, religious life was not separated, in any respect, from other forms and aspects of life. Religion was integrated into daily life, with no theology to justify its place and role in people's lives. People moved in and out of the domains of the religious with no specific timetable or normative obligation. If one may refer to religion as a biological necessity, people worshipped their gods, at this stage, almost as a natural instinct.[28]

---

[28] Saying this, I do not wish to express my opinion on the debate about the question of the origins of religion. See the recently published study of Walter Burkert, *Creation of the Sacred: Tracks of Biology in Early Religions*, Harvard University Press: Cambridge, Mass. & London, 1996. As the subtitle of the book clearly states, Burkert argues that the explanation of the origins of religion lies chiefly in the biological

While this may sound somewhat mechanistic and deterministic, it seems to me that it adequately reflects the phenomenological realities of this kind of lifestyle. Thus, I argue, that, when a special ideology, albeit practically-oriented, sustained this kind of lifestyle, spontaneous principles aimed at sustaining life shaped it into a modular "ethos." I use the word modular, because it can take on various, even antagonistic, forms. Religion is the next stage. To begin with, people lived by their modes of religiousness, as a spontaneous extension of their daily lifestyle.[29] Ethos, therefore, entails a form of life in which basic institutions, values, laws, and other norms have not yet reached a stage that is analogous or identical to religion.

There is yet another question, which requires consideration, with regard to rituals in their ethos stage. Are these rituals as vital to existence as we describe them to be? We have noted what "ethos" entails in terms of lifestyle. There are good reasons to view this kind of lifestyle as a rather accidental aggregate of practice-related decisions. However, I wish to argue that once a specific system—here economics—sets preferences that obligate people on a wide existential scale, it transcends the stage of the accidental, and becomes intensely functional in the lives of people. I would also argue that the principles that shape the economic ethos and their links to ritual modes of behaviour are powerful cultural entities. The pre-religion stage and religion can thus be seen as constituting a continuum.

More specifically, the stories that describe the voluntary offerings that were brought to special places make a particular point. They tell of the primordial status of these places, in light of future claims to their demographic, political, and religious centrality. There are several instances of this kind, in the stories of the

---

behaviour of animals and the human species. One should be reminded of the fact that, in his famous essay, published in 1907, "Zwangshandlungen und Religions-uebungen" [ET "Obsessive Actions and Religious Practices," in *Complete Psychological Works* IX (London: Hogarth, 1962), pp. 115-127], Sigmund Freud stressed the role of instincts in religious behaviour.

[29] This is not to say that religious people, who profess their religion in institutional modes, always express themselves in theological terms. In the ethos mode, this works somewhat differently. People make no distinction between the religious and the non-religious and theology is not carved in stone. Religion drifts in and out of the lives of the people, according to prevalent needs and aspirations.

Book of Genesis.[30] Often, these legends have a function in creating, establishing, and preserving a certain mood or attitude. Indeed, they create a venue for the (re-)appearance of the deity
connected with place. Abraham goes from place to place, calling
the name of his God at each place. People may show their respect for a certain place, and even venerate its sanctity, because
of a divine revelation or a miracle that occurred there. The place
may also carry the memory of certain (venerable) people who were
buried there.[31] In any event, by its very nature the persistence of
a particular tradition dictates the choice of locations to be held
in venerable esteem. The same holds true of the notion of specific times or dates. These characteristics become factually evident,
when reading the relevant stories about the Patriarchs in the Book
of Genesis.

VIII

One advantage of using the term "ethos" to designate the early
stages of a religion is that it liberates pre-structured religion from
the designation "primitive."[32] The term "ethos" allows one to focus
on the early stages of religion, in the context of *cultural* factors that
significantly lack negative evaluative overtones. "Ethos" also enables us to refer, in a religious framework, to people who do not
theologically define themselves as religious, but who occasionally
move in and out of the religious domain. This happens, for instance, when people participate in religious ceremonies on a non-
regular basis. These people need not proclaim principles of faith,
as is customary in a full-fledged religion.

Furthermore, viewing economics in terms of an ethos, defines
the values by which certain kinds of property are measured posi-

---

[30] See Gen., 12: 7-8, 18; 21: 33; 22: 14; 28: 19-22.

[31] See Jonathan Z. Smith, *To Take Place: Toward Theory in Ritual*, the University of Chicago Press: Chicago and London, 1987. My approach to this subject
differs from that of Smith. See also Jane Hubert, "Sacred Beliefs and Beliefs of
Sacredness," in: David L. Charmichael, Jane Hubert, Brian Reeves and Audhild
Schanche, *Sacred Sites, Sacred Places*, Routledge: London and New York, 1994, pp.
9-19.

[32] It is indeed amazing to note how often the term "primitive" is used in such
a highly acclaimed study of religions as Bronislaw Malinowski, *Magic, Science and
Religion and Other Essays*, reissued by Waveland Press: Prospect Heights, IL, 1992.

tively, as a factor that establishes a relationship with the divine. As observed above, it is quite unusual to find "ethos" used in this special connection.[33] In this setting, the material gains of economics easily become an extension of the religious, with no serious distortions incurred on either side.[34] After all, a prosperous economy is in the interest of the gods: it is instrumental in providing the gods with housing (temples), nutrition (sacrifices), and decoration (icons, sacred vestments, and ornaments). Fertile crops are also in the interest of the priesthood (and the Levites) whose income derives from a structured system of tithing. The amount of crops yielded would seem to depend on what humans had offered their gods. All this entails something to which I would here refer to as a cyclic pattern of seduction. The rules of the game are found entirely in the economic system.

Speaking in terms of cultic seduction, two rival economic systems compete, in this respect, in the Book of Genesis. They involve, as we have seen, sheep herding and agriculture. In their attempt to draw the attention of God, the two systems create a fatal conflict, which culminates in fratricide. Not less significant, in this respect, is the dichotomy between the economic lifestyle of the Patriarchs, before the descent of Jacob's family to Egypt, and that promised to them by God who led the People to the *land* of "milk and honey" (Ex. 3: 8, and numerous other references). Milk comes mainly from sheep and cows, but the honey, in this case, from date trees. In other words, the return to the land partly implies a fusion of two lifestyles that in the ethos stage were strictly held apart. In any event, the introduction of cattle breed-

---

[33] The socio-religious functions of economics have often been discussed, albeit mostly in an anthropological context. An early and still stimulating discussion can be found in Bronislaw Malinowski, *Argonauts of the Western Pacific*, reissued by Waveland Press: Prospects Heights, Il., 1984, pp. 146-194. Other aspects of the same problem are discussed in Marcel Mauss, *The Gift: The Form and Reason for Exchange in Archaic Societies*, [English Translation by W. D. Halls], W. W. Norton: New York and London, 1990. Of interest to the present discussion are the two chapters "Historians and Economists" [I & II] in Eric Hobsbawm, *On History*, The New Press: New York, 1997, pp. 94-123. See, further, Morris Silver, *Economic Structures of Antiquity*, Greenwood Press: Westport CT, 1995, especially Chapter 1: "Gods as Inputs and Outputs of Ancient Economics." Silver's discussion bears upon our subject but takes a different direction.

[34] Of course, one may argue the opposite, namely, that religion can easily become the extension of the economic order. However, this aspect does not concern us here.

ing and agriculture as the two flagships of the promised economic prosperity connected with them landmarks a drastic change from previous preferences. The economic system of the Patriarchs persisted, though in a somewhat submerged form, until the beginning of the monarchy. Representing the ethos of the nomadic lifestyle, Samuel warns the people that the king, whom they wish to enthrone, will appropriate their real-estate property and everything that it—including slaves and soldiers—requires for its management and protection. Sheep can be mentioned in passing, with no comment.[35]

In this connection, we may explore yet another direction. The ancient Egyptians reportedly considered sheep herding an abomination. The Israelites, therefore, had to be given separate grazing land, Goshen (Gen. 46: 34). Whether this has been corroborated by archaeological findings is a question that need not be discussed here. We know that the Egyptians, as other peoples in the ancient world, considered shepherds a symbol of political leadership. Scripture presents the Egyptians as a people of the city.[36] What matters, then, is what the biblical narrator views as the cultural differentiating line between the Egyptians and the Israelites. Furthermore, in referring to this differentiation in terms of a *"to'evah"*, a ritual abomination,[37] the scriptural writer enhances the ritual status of this differentiation.

In short, I suggest viewing the economic system as a systemic structure that also defines and enables basic forms of interaction between humans and the divine. God's refusal to accept Cain's sacrifices indicated that seduction failed the one who tilled the land. In other words, the rules by which Cain tried to operate his cosmos completely failed him. God's acceptance of Abel's sheep offering was indicative of, in the scriptural framework, the right kind of seduction commensurately applied with the kind of (economic) "cosmos" that God favoured. The progression here is from the economic order to cultural ethos and, then, to cultic

---

[35] See 1 Sam. 8: 11-18. It is worth noting that the essence of the "rule of the king," as Samuel puts it to the people, is completely different to its counterpart in Deut. 17: 14-20. Deuteronomy does not mention the land and its complex forms of administration.

[36] See Gen. 47: 21; Ex. 1: 11.

[37] See Gen. 46: 34. The reference is to sheep herds, not to sheep themselves. That the Egyptians owned sheep is clearly stated in the same cycle of Josheph-stories: see, Gen. 47: 16-17. See also, Ex. 8: 22.

preferences. The order can be reversed, though, without substantially diminishing the thrust of the argument. Since, as we have argued, rituals create, maintain, and preserve the cosmos in which they are done, they are functional in sustaining order and stability, in general. Consequently, they facilitate a mechanism in which predictability plays an important role. However, the argument can equally go in the opposite direction. Where there is confidence in predictability, there is belief in a stable cosmos. A stable cosmos, for the people concerned, means the right application of the adequate rituals. Rituals, in this respect, reflect the ethos of the people, and the economic order is the foundational factor around which the system is built.

Briefly, the dialectics of these dichotomic lifestyles shaped the narratives of the history of the ancient Israelites, before and after they entered the Land of Canaan. Whether this was history as it happened or history as conceived in the minds of certain writers, is irrelevant to the discussion of *what* the documents in question wish to convey. These documents present a certain type of memory. This is what, so people were told, was relevant to their religious ethos, and this was what their memory was expected to retain. It retained notions of patterned lifestyles that represented significant lines of development—sheepherding, tribalism, and nomadism, on the one hand, and agriculture, cattle breeding, urbanisation, and the monarchic system.[38] If it needs mentioning here, urbanisation entailed a real-estate type of economy.[39] In the ancient world, and not only there, it ultimately sustained and was sus-

---

[38] It is difficult to decide whether Samuel's objection to the election of a king reflected the pervasive spirit of tribalism, or whether other matters—such as the attempt to preserve a charismatic leadership *per se*—were involved. In any event, Samuel warns the people that the king will demand services that are typical of a society that lives mainly in cities and depends for its sustenance on agriculture. Sheep are mentioned only at the end, in two words. The king "will tithe the sheep" (1 Sam. 8: 17).

[39] Two recent publications that discuss processes of urbanisation in the ancient world are: W. E. Affricate et al. (eds.), *Urbanism in Antiquity: From Mesopotamia to Crete*, Sheffield: Academic Press, 1996; and Marc Van de Mieroop, *The Ancient Mesopotamian City*, Clarendon Press: Oxford, 1997. See also, A. I. Baumgarten, "Urbanization and Sectarianism in Hasmonaean Jerusalem," in: M. Poorthuis & Ch. Safrai (eds.), *The Centrality of Jerusalem: Historical Perspectives*, Kampen: Kok Pharos, 1996, pp. 50-64. In this connection, I would mention the factor of water supply and irrigation. An irrigation system had to be built and, ultimately, it supplied the needs of the city, too.

tained by monarchic regimes.[40] Monarchs often exercised their power on the inner political scene manipulating agrarian management. They were the lords of the *land*, in the strict sense of the term. They used to distribute lands to their faithful gentry and to farmers thus ensuring loyalty and a constant supply of food. As the story of Joseph in Egypt shows, they could in turn buy off the land in exchange of a supply of needed products which they kept in the storehouses of the monarchy (Gen. 47: 18-26).

IX

In elaborating upon the first kind of lifestyle that is discussed here, sheep breeding and herding, I wish to point to the ample iconographic materials that existed in the Ancient Near East and Greece showing the monarch in the symbolic function of a shepherd. We also find the appellation, the "Faithful Herd" (in Aramaic, *Ra'eya Mehemna*), attributed to Moses. We find this, primarily, in midrashic sources and in medieval Jewish mysticism. In the second case, the Christological notions of the Good Shepherd (John 10: 11) and the Lamb of God (John 1: 29) are attributed to Jesus. Numerous studies have been devoted to these terms and their significance, from all aspects of religious thought and practice. It is commonly said that, in his capacity as the "Lamb of God," Jesus expresses human compassion, meekness, and sacrificial submissiveness. The notion of "Good Shepherd" may indeed derive from the ancient Near Eastern and the Hellenic depictions of royalty, as mentioned above. However, on a more profound level, the notions of "Faithful Herd" and "Lamb of God" convey something that is more theme engaging and complex than is generally assumed. These appellations were not given accidentally. They refer back to a basic ethos that was adopted from the culture of ancient Israel.

If we keep in mind the fact that the scriptural writer(s) distinguished between two types of economic systems *Tson*-herding—that is, sheep, goat, and lamb herding—and (2) agriculture, which was linked to *Baqar*-herding, that is, cow/oxen-herding, then the

---

[40] The Book of Joshu'a clearly shows that every city in Canaan had its own "king." However, the kind of monarchy that Saul, David and their followers represented was equal to the Pharaoh in Egypt and the Emperor of Assur or Babylonia. It was a more centralised form of government.

symbolic representation of the monarchic order in the terms of reference of the sheep-ethos is all the more telling. *Baqar*, oxen, was commonly used for ploughing fields.[41] Thus, it primarily represented settling down in established farms.[42] Ultimately, it signified urbanisation and a monarchic regime.[43] In this sense it, and not the *Tson*, would be the more suitable symbol to use in the case of the monarchy. *Tson*-herding represented, as it still does today, the economic system of nomadic people, and therefore, from a monarchic point of view, it stood for instability. The city, which is the place of the monarch, is at the same time the economic centre of the farmers who go there to sell the produce of the land. The city is also expected to provide military protection to the neighbouring farms. The city cannot survive without the food supplies that the surrounding farms provide, nor can the farms survive without the city-markets and the protection that the city affords. Thus, if, contrary to logical expectation, the choice fell on the symbolic depiction of the shepherd, this was a telling fact in the cultural history of the people.

In this respect, the symbolic depiction of the monarchic system in patriarchal signs revives an ancient, archetypal, ethos. The Patriarchs, Abraham and Jacob, were shepherds. *Tson*-herding receives full attention in the patriarchal narratives.[44] Isaac's story,

---

[41] The term *Miqneh*, cattle (literally, "owned [or live] property"), is often used in this connection. However, it is not always clear when it refers only to *Tson* or also to *Baqar*.

[42] This raises an interesting issue. The cow, bull and goat were all cultic animals in different parts of the ancient world. In some cases, they figured as idols who were worshipped in temples. The subject is too wide-ranging to be discussed here, but it cannot be bypassed without mention. There is a vast literature on the subject, the most recent work, which I am aware of, is, Michael Rice, *The Power of the Bull*, Routledge: London and New York, 1998. Interestingly, Rice has a separate chapter on "Settlement, Domestication and Urbanization." Also relevant to the subject matter—though not mentioned in Rice's book—is, L. Bodson, *Hiera Zoia: Contribution à l'étude de la place de l'animal dans la religion grecque ancienne*, Brussels: Academie Royale de Belgique, 1975.

[43] For the ritual context of agriculture, see Gerhard Baudy, "Ackerbau und Initiation: Der Kult der Artemis Triklaria und des Dionysos Aisymnetes in Patrai", in: Fritz Graf (ed.), *Ansichten Griechischer Rituale: Geburtstags-Symposium fuer Walter Burkert*, B. G. Teubner: Stuttgart und Leipzig, 1998, pp. 143-167.

[44] It should be pointed out that Abraham also owned *Baqar*: Gen. 21:27, 24: 35. Furthermore, in spite of the fact that Jacob, and then his sons, lived, primarily, on sheep herding, Jacob's livestock was richer in its forms of economic diversification. See Gen. 32: 5, 14-15. However, the nomadic way of life characterises both, Abraham and Jacob.

however, is more complicated. Besides herding sheep, he also
sowed the land. Isaac, in this respect, marks a cultural exception,
a deviation from the prevailing socio-economic norms. Indeed,
he represents a dramatic change in the family-ethos. Situated in
the middle of the patriarchal stories, he is a reminder of everything that can go wrong, when a break with the central ethos occurs.

Looking closer at what Scripture tells us about Isaac, one is likely
to discover either a wavering of tones in the biblical story or else
a dialectic preparation of the ensuing complications that the Jacob-
stories entail. Although Isaac, also, "had possession of flocks and
herds" (*Gen.* 26: 14), he was principally a man of the field. Of
the three Patriarchs, Isaac was the only one who "sowed in that
land" (Gen. 26: 12). Furthermore, it may not be accidental that
the scriptural narrator tells us that Isaac met Rebecca in a field
(Gen. 24: 63). Later on, we hear the now blind Isaac ask his son,
Esau, "to go out to the field and hunt game for me" (*Gen.* 27: 3).
We may venture an interpretation here. Isaac's blindness was more
than a physical disability. It symbolised his ethos-blindness with
regard to the root-lifestyle of the family. It was Rebecca, his wife,
who insisted that Jacob should prepare another kind of meal,
reminding of the real ethos of the family: "Go to the flock, and
fetch me two kids" (27: 9). The blessing that Jacob received from
his father was, once again, a remarkable expression of Isaac's
"ethos-preference," which—in the context of the family ethos—
marked his utter cultural blindness: "May God give you... the
fatness of the earth, and plenty of grain and wine" (27: 28).

It should also be noted that, when Rebecca dressed Jacob with
"the best garments of Esau, her older son... and the skins of the
kids she put upon his hands and the smooth part of his neck" (Gen.
27: 15-16), she actually dressed him in the guise of a live sheep-
totem. When blind Isaac touched and smelt Jacob, he made a fatal
decision. He ignored the kids' skin—the token of the family ethos—
and preferred the smell of the field of Esau's garments. Thus, the
rivalry between Jacob and Esau had an additional dimension: it
indicated the rivalry between flock herding and agriculture (or even
the wild life of rural areas).

If this analysis makes sense, then one may read the story of the
binding of Isaac, too, in the context of a dramatic disapproval on
the part of the father [Abraham] of his son's future lifestyle. Apparently, Isaac rejected, or even was predestined not to become,

the kind of shepherd that family tradition required. In this case, the *'Aqedah* [his binding as a sacrificial lamb!] is intended to represent him as the victim of his rejection of the family ethos. He himself was turned into the sacrificial lamb: Gen. 22: 7-8. The fact that God reportedly changed his mind can be interpreted in various ways. It probably represented an attempt to keep the story, with all its conflicts, in a "humanistic" framework. In any event, it did not entail a substantial shift in emphasis regarding the cultural concerns of the specific *Tson*-ethos. After all, it was a wild ram, which was offered instead of the lamb/Isaac.

In short, the scriptural writer most probably wanted his readers to conclude that any break with the prevailing ethos would engender trouble. The ensuing narratives make clear the nature of these problems, and the fact that they could not be easily solved. Indeed, they resulted in a series of events that led to the Egyptian exile. Interestingly, Moses, the man who redeemed the people from Egypt, was a *Tson*-herder himself. He had no property of his own, but herded the *Tson* of Jethro, his father-in-law.[45] God revealed himself to Moses in the desert (Ex. 3: 1), while the Israelites were building "store-cities" (Ex. 1: 11). The building of cities was the epitome of slavery, in the kind of ethos that characterised the mind of the ancient Israelites. As we have seen, the Egyptians were city-dwellers, at least in the eyes of the scriptural writers. A little later in Israelite history, the desert functions as the opposite of the city. Interestingly, too, the culmination of the

---

[45] One may see in the fact that Jacob and Moses were the shepherds of their respective fathers-in-law a literary motif that eventually developed into an interesting sub-ethos. The respective stories about their first meeting with their future wives at water-wells are another literary motif in the same vein. The transition from literary motif to cultural ethos presents itself in the fact that these details are viewed as fitting into a certain marital ethos. The future son-in-law is tested by his ability to assist—even rescue [in the case of Moses the term "redeem" is used: Ex. 2: 17]—the shepherdess who was to become his wife. In both cases, Jacob and Moses alike, showed the same kind of integrity, strength, and determination. The moral determinants and strength of both men underline the ethos. Giving water to the flocks of a stranger-shepherdess is more telling in the context of this ethos than its expression of practical resourcefulness and chivalrous help. An interesting example of a scholarly ethos that involves, what I would refer to as the hermeneutics of prejudice, is described with regard to the figure of Moses, in Jan Assmann, *Moses the Egyptian: The Memory of Egypt in Western Monotheism*, Harvard University Press: Cambridge, Mass., and London, 1997. Among other issues, Assmann traces the various ways in which the Egyptian origin of Moses was handled in pagan and Christian writings. However, all this has rather little to do with our subject matter.

history of the Israelites in Egypt—their redemption from slavery—
began, when they were told to slaughter a lamb (Ex. 12). The
blood of the lamb marked their rescue. Evidently, when viewed
in a redemptive context, such an act prefigured—as it eventually
did in Christian eyes—everything that Jesus, the Christ, stood for.
Do we have to revert to the emblematic "Lamb of God"?

Looking back on the materials just described, one becomes
aware how complex the culture is that goes with the two rival
lifestyles. It is significant to mention, in this connection, that Scripture describes the ultimately rejected king Saul as a *Baqar*-herder
(1 Sam. 11: 5), while David, the *Tson*-herder, was chosen to begin the lineage that replaced him.[46] David was the king who also
established what, *post factum*, was known as the House of David,
the epitome of the messianic lineage. In other words, personal
character and historical significance are established by either making
them fit into, or depart from, the prevailing ethos. It is interesting to note that, although David built a city (Jerusalem), he was
prevented from building the Temple. The religious layout was
still on the "ethos-side," in which a wandering sanctuary was temporarily to remain the cultic ideal. Israeli culture, throughout the
ages, vacillated between these two types of cultures and cultic
structures. In many respects, exile also represents nomadism, while
the messianic hopes for the return to the Land of Israel represent
the re-institution of urbanisation (the re-building of Jerusalem) and
the monarchy.[47]

---

[46] This is the place to mention the negative connotations associated with *Baqar*
in connection with the Bull-Ba'al of the Canaanite pantheon. This is also reflected
in the sinful episode of the *'Egel*-worship by the Israelites, both in the Sinai Desert
and in the days of King Jeroboam. See Michael Rice, *The Power of the Bull*, mentioned above in footnote 31.

[47] H. Frankfurt (*Op. Cit.* above, footnote 1) rightly points out that primitive
agriculture was also somewhat nomadic. After a while, the land spent its fertile
resources and people had to move and search for more fruit-lending soil. However, after the conquest and the settling on the land in clearly allotted tribal ter-
ritories, the ancient Israelites were told to observe the *Shemitah* rest-year. Every
seventh year, the people had to abstain from any work that was connected with
vegetable and fruit farming. After a cycle of seven such *Shemitah*-years, came the
jubilee year. See Lev., chapter 25. In all likelihood, the *Shemitah* saw to it that the
people kept to their legally owned land, without having to wander about and search
for new land, thus upsetting the entire agrarian system. Apparently, this is also
the idea behind the rule stipulating that the Jubilee year causes sold lands and
houses to be returned to their original owners. This is the nature of a real-estate
economy when, as in ancient times, it creates a cultural ethos.

X

We have already referred to the fact that it is quite difficult to reconstruct the original settings to which the scriptural materials refer. I do not believe that every piece of information contained in Scripture serves, by definition, a religious purpose. In several cases, a hermeneutic approach has to be applied to activate the desired connections to the religious. There is no scholarly consensus, however, on how to view scriptural materials in terms of reference that are relevant to religious studies, proper. Biblical studies are often part of religious studies. This fact, though, is a matter of academic organisation and administration, not a matter that has methodological consequences. What does the area of religious studies entail for scholars of biblical studies? In many cases, people assume that religious studies are automatically activated, whenever religious materials are studied even in their historical setting, including for that matter, biblical studies.

One result of this state of affairs is that the existential and experiential aspects of biblical religion are nowadays less at the centre of scholarly interest than they deserve to be. At best, they are viewed as belonging to the spheres of theology and historical archaeology. However, if scholars of religious studies were to direct their attention to the more experiential aspects of biblical religion, rituals would also receive the kind of prominence they deserve. At present, exegetical, text-critical and editorial questions take precedence over the phenomenological, that is, experiential, aspects of biblical religions.[48] Briefly, then, biblical studies should

---

[48] In this respect, Rudolph Otto's famous book, *The Idea of the Holy*, illustrates the point made here. The title of the English translation reflects the ideological framework of the book in an even more pronounced manner than the German original, *Das Heilige*. Otto's book is often considered as the master example of religious phenomenology. Its basic focus, however, is theological. In my view, the book lacks substantive discussions of such essential aspects of the holy and rituals, purity, as well as sacred places. In short, what the book does is to present religious psychology as a theological issue. Even when Otto addresses a phenomenological or psychological issue, he does so in theological terms of reference. See Lynn Poland, "The Idea of the Holy and the History of the Sublime," *The Journal of Religion*, vol. 72 (2), 1992, pp. 175-197. Another example, though not accessible to the English reader, is Joseph Dan, *'Al Ha-Qedushah*. The English title reads, "On Sanctity...". The interest the book shows in the subject is, primarily, historical and philological. The experiential and existential aspects of the subject are only randomly referred to. Finally, it is interesting to note that the writings of Mircea Eliade on the "the Holy" and "Rites" are mostly concerned with issues of meaning. Having

show greater interest than they did, in the past, in factors that shape
the life of the individual and the community. Here, the existential and experiential aspects matter most. In this respect, rituals,
even those practised at the ethos-stage, can serve as good examples.

The extent to which rituals at the ethos stage have contributed
to the formation of a coherent cultic system can be determined,
in retrospect, only at the religion-stage. This does not mean,
however, that the rituals done in the context of "ethos" are less
rigidly professed than those prescribed in the context of religion.
Although ethos implies a mental attitude that is spontaneously
configured, on the personal level, it is no less compelling, for it
relates to vital aspects, and norms, of life that concern people and
call for respect. As indicated above, at the ethos stage life is shaped
more spontaneously than it is in the religious phase. However,
the needs and the choices at the ethos stage are as a compelling
as they are in any other phase of life and culture.

One of the many differences between ethos, as described here,
and religion is that ethos has no central moment of revelation.
Cain was not told to till the land, nor was Abel ordered to do
the opposite, namely, to raise sheep: they simply established or
represented two conflicting lifestyles. Thus, in doing wrong to his
brother, Cain displayed, at a primary level, bad character. At a
more advanced level, his conduct demonstrated a wrongful im-
pulse propelled by his ethos. God entered the scene only *post
factum*. There is nothing in the story, as we read it, which indicates that in the respective choices as displayed by the two brothers
there was a normatively established right or wrong. It is the manner in which the biblical drama unfolds that highlights the real
issue. The God that mattered in the eyes of the scriptural narrator preferred sheep. He is the same God that declares the killing
to be a sinful act. True, the Patriarchs experienced moments of
divine revelation. However, in the course of these revelations,
nothing was conveyed that concerned the praxis of a full-fledged
religion. More precisely expressed, ethos transforms the segmented
particles of the "natural law," or the "law of nature," into a systemic cultural ethos. It organises people's lives in a meaningful
manner in what is, retrospectively, the pre-history of religion.

---

re-read Eliade for the purposes of this study, I cannot avoid remarking that it is
always easier to speculate on meaning and symbolism than it is to investigate—
and then assess—the manner in which rituals work in the framework of the sacred.

Normative decisions regarding what is right or wrong are not explicitly stated, but are set in a narratival form. The narrative, in this respect, is an *exemplum*. As the scriptural story evolves, it also becomes clear what will be included in future preferences and what will come under criticism.

XI

We now move to a different locale and time, that of John the Baptist. It is my opinion that, in telling the story of John the Baptist, the Gospels spontaneously re-enact the ethos of ancient Israel. Ancient Christianity revived the spirit of the prophets and, in particular, their anti-urban and anti-monarchic ethos.[49] This holds true for Jesus and his teachings. Special attention is given to the fact that everything began in the "desert." The baptismal act did not take place in the Temple or its environment, but in the River Jordan,[50] a place that had special significance in the days of the conquest of the Land of Canaan (Jos. 3: 1-4: 24) and at the death of Elijah (2 Kings 2: 1-11). In this respect, it represents, even constitutes, a transitional territory. In a sense, it is an initiatory locale. The Gospel writers themselves did not hold unanimous view regarding the question of whether Jesus was baptised by John or not. The Gospel of Luke reports that John the Baptist was arrested by King Herod before could have baptised Jesus (Lk. 3: 10-20). However, all the Gospels agree over the fact that John led an intensely modest lifestyle, and that the desert was his home. In many respects, this lifestyle served as a model for Christian hermitic life and for the rusticity preached by the monastic orders.

What does the "desert" imply in this context? In many respects, it is more than simply a geographical designation of a desolate and uninhabited land, which is the lexical meaning of the Hebrew word *Midbar*. As a cultural notion, the desert is a "topos." It

---

[49] It is interesting, with regard to this discussion, to refer to Chapters 1 and 3 of Gerd Theissen, *Social Reality and the Early Christians*, Fortress Press: Minneapolis, 1992.

[50] As will be pointed out later on, the "desert" became a topos of Christian theology. The most recent study I am aware of is D. Burton-Christie, *The Word in the Desert: Scripture and the Quest for Holiness in Early Christian Monasticism*, Oxford University Press: New York & Oxford, 1993.

may even be said to entail an ethos. Historically and culturally speaking, it represented a unique ethos in the life of ancient Israel. The redemption from Egypt and the conquest of the Land of Canaan were the two ends that allocated to the desert a transitional role. Closer to early Christianity, we find that the "desert-ethos" or motif represented the unique lifestyle depicted in the writings of the Qumran community. As many studies have shown, *Midbar*, (more precisely, "the desert of Damascus"), in the writings of the Qumran community, represented the opposite of Jerusalem and its Temple. In all likelihood, this is also what the Gospel writers wanted the story of John the Baptist to convey. It represents a critical view of the social corruption of the monarchy and the moral defilement of the priesthood. In this respect, the fact that Jesus drove the merchants out of the Temple has more than an emblematic significance.[51]

It should be noted that, if the sources at our disposal can be historically trusted, John the Baptist did not only opt for the desert as a dwelling place, he also accompanied his choice with certain practices. He dressed as a hermit, he lived on a special diet and, above all, he baptised people as an act marking a radical change in their lifestyle. This change, implying a "return" (this is the original sense of the Hebrew word for "repentance," *Tshuvah*), allegedly prepared the way for their redemption through Jesus, the "Lamb of God." In doing these things, John the Baptist advocated a lifestyle that had a ritual aspect. He believed that this ritual would lead to redemption. Thus everything, that John the Baptist did, had a transformative function and value. Transformation, as we have seen, is the most essential aspect of ritual. In the case of Jesus, it marked redemption through the "Lamb of God", thus introducing a new element into the ancient ethos. In short, Christianity infused the ethos of ancient Israel with a redemptive element, thus transforming the rather limited sense in which we have previously viewed ethos.

With regard to rituals, one cannot avoid mentioning, once again, the notion of myth. We have defined myth as the context-endowing narrative of ritual. In fact, myth and ritual mutually contextualise

---

[51] See H. D. Betz, "Jesus and the Purity of the Temple (Mark 11:15-18): A Comparative Religion Approach", in: *Antike und Christentum: Gesammelte Aufsaetze IV*, Mohr Siebeck: Tuebingen, 1998, pp. 57-77.

each other. At times, in according a mythic status to a certain narrative, a number of hermeneutic approaches come into play; that is to say, a hermeneutic stance can endow the event to which it refers with the desired mythic-character. This happens, when the event becomes—through the hermeneutic that is attached to it—the mythic basis of a ritual. In the case of John the Baptist, we find that he is identified, in the words of the Book of *Isaiah*, as the "voice calling in the desert." In other words, a verse in The Book of Isaiah (40: 3) creates a hermeneutic condition in which the Gospel-narrative receives, in the newly born religion, a mythic function. Living in the desert, as John the Baptist did, does not fulfil itself in an austere stance taken over against "civilisation". It has created a "topos," this time for Christian believers, and received a cultic context that spread beyond the event itself. The book of Isaiah, Chapter 40 played a formative role in this process. In other words, John the Baptist is the living Midrash of the Book of Isaiah 40.[52] The Midrash crystallises in a ritual performance, rather than in the more regularly known setting of a theoretical hermeneutic stance.

I, therefore, suggest viewing the desert-centred negation of the Jerusalem-type of lifestyle as a cultural statement that is enacted on a ritual plane, implying a specific social and religious ethos. In this respect, ethos functions as the mental disposition that, culturally speaking, lends structure and context to the ideas, acts, and forms of behaviour, which belong to the pre-religion (= Pre-Christian) stage. In my usage of the term "ethos," I have pointed to the systemic, long-term, principles that shaped and organised the life of certain groups of people in relation to their own history, memory, and identity without erecting a full-fledged religious ideology or theology. This is true of what the Gospels tell us about John the Baptist and it still holds true, in spite of the fact that there are significant literary divergences from the core

---

[52] Elsewhere, I have dealt with this phenomenon in the context of the "Midrashic Condition." See Ithamar Gruenwald, "Midrash and the 'Midrashic Condition': Preliminary Considerations," in: Michael Fishbane (ed.), *The Midrashic Imagination: Jewish Exegesis, Thought, and History*, State University of New York Press: Albany, N. Y., 1993, pp. 6-22 (printed without proof reading!). The notion of midrashic exposition in the framework of a live experience is discussed in Ithamar Gruenwald, "The Midrashic Condition: From the Midrash of the Talmudic Sages to that of the Qabbalists" [in Hebrew], *Jerusalem Studies in Jewish Thought*, Vol. 8 (1989), pp. 255-298.

story, as reconstructed from the various versions that recount it. Obviously, the opposite pole of a foundational ethos is cultural redundancy. Forgetfulness, oblivion, and loss of identity are the usual marks of such a state of redundancy. If people are inclined to forget, or are expected to do so, their forgetfulness itself becomes part of an ethos or counter-ethos, as the case may be.

Dialectically speaking, historical development went in the opposite direction to that, which is described here, namely, the "sheep-desert" ethos that was initially invented to criticise urbanisation and the corruption it involved. Thus, the process we have described, in terms of development from ethos to religion, may be viewed as a dialectic process, in which the ethos aims to criticise the established religion. This is the sense in which we read the story of John the Baptist and, in many respects, also that of Jesus: they criticised the Jerusalem urban-lifestyle. In similar way, scholars have suggested a different mode of reading the scriptural narratives of the Pentateuch. Instead of reading them in progressive succession, they argued that the texts make better sense when read regressively. Thus, the standard historical sequence, as presented in Scripture, had to be inverted. The Temple-centred religion came first, then, in the form of a different ethos, its wandering-sanctuary criticism. Although, in my opinion, it is not certain that this was the case in ancient Israel, biblical scholars have often argued that the wandering desert-sanctuary functioned initially as a critical reaction to the Jerusalem Temple. Thus, in many ways, it corresponded to the main message of the Qumran writings and the Gospels.

XII

We are approaching the end of this discussion. Let us, therefore, take yet another look at the Garden of Eden story, as told in the Book of Genesis. It sets the model for the type of paradigmatic history that is discussed in the present chapter. When enfranchised from its regular hermeneutic context, the story entails more than is usually realised. By destroying their prospect of an idealised type of rural life, as symbolised by the Garden of Eden, Adam and Eve prepared the way for the ensuing drama in which their offspring were to play a pivotal role. In this drama, the norms of good and evil, righteousness and sin, are delineated in a unique manner. They are not stated as an ethical code, but in the form of an "economic narrative." In this narrative, good and bad and the parameters of obedience and disobedience are defined in terms of their functional effect, in their respective lifestyles. The ethical norms that set the respective distinctions are not theoretically defined, but there is a tacit assumption that they should be implemented. The relevant conclusions that one is expected to draw for himself are assumed, but are not normatively stated. The moral basis of what happens is found in the story as it develops, and what evolves accords with patterns of behaviour that reflect a particular norm. In other words, ethos and exempla interchange.

The post-diluvial covenant with Noah begins a new phase in the story under discussion. The turn that the events now take openly reflects urbanisation and culminates in the building of the "Tower of Bavel." We have already referred to the fact that, if one follows the scriptural text closely, it becomes clear that the Tower was a temple, a *ziggurat*, which was built in the middle of the city that the people had founded. As the scriptural narrative presents matters, God was displeased with what these people were doing. Their punishment involved a process of decentralisation, or de-urbanisation. They were forced to scatter all over "the earth." On a wider cultural scale, they were no longer able to speak one language, which had enabled them to create a community sharing a common ethnic identity. In other words, they were forced into migration or ethnic nomadism. In a way, they were collectively doomed to the same kind of punishment as Cain. Abraham's migration to the Land of Cana'an can be seen in light of these processes. His righteousness, though, is underlined by the fact that he established shepherding as the economic identity of the clan. Seen from this point of view, Abraham signalled the biblically favoured kind of criticism that shunned urbanisation.

A few more observations about the story of Cain and Abel are in place, for it still requires additional fine-tuning. In killing Abel, Cain is viewed as committing a crime or sin. Since the story is linked to a ritual, or to making a statement about certain sacrificial preferences, I view it as a myth. Cain's story informs us about the wrong kind of ritual worship. His punishment signifies an attempt to impose on him the kind of cultural ethos—nomadism—which he had tried to avoid. Since this latter lifestyle was enforced upon him, it met with opposition. Cain could not but rebel. Indeed, he went to the extreme: he built a city. Significantly, he called the city after his son's name, Hanoch.

We now enter a new phase in the narrative as well as a new stage in the deployment of the cultural ethos discussed here. Hanoch, or Enoch, is a key name in ancient Apocalypticism. However, it should be noted that there are two Enoch-figures in the *Genesis*-story. One is the son of Cain and the other—the son of Yered. The "apocalyptic" Enoch is the son of Yered (Gen. 5: 18). A significant cultural drama unfolds between these two Enoch-figures. Only the second one is viewed as a righteous figure, being highly praised and valued in both apocalyptic circles and in the New Testament.[53] Gen. 4: 16-17 says about the first Enoch: "Then Cain went away from the presence of the Lord, and dwelt in the land of Nod, east of Eden. Cain knew his wife, and she conceived and bore Enoch, and he built a city and called the name of the city after the name of his son, Enoch." The information, contained in these verses, refers to something that, to the best of my knowledge, has been ignored by scholars. Apparently, the writer of this passage wished to indicate that, in spite of the fact that Cain was sentenced to wander without settling down in any specific place ["*Eretz Nod*," in all likelihood, reflects the *n'a va-nad* aspect of his punishment], he built a city. Furthermore, he called it after his son's name, Hanoch.

If I understand the ethos implied in the story correctly, the name of Cain's son entails more than what is usually attributed to it. The name is connected to the root, הנך which is used, in Scriptural Hebrew, to indicate the inauguration or consecration, of a house (Deut. 20: 5), of the Temple (Num. 7: 10; 1 Kings 8: 63; and more), and of the city walls (Neh. 12: 27). The Book Proverbs 22: 6, however, poses a problem. The standard translations of the verse agree on "Train [in Hebrew: *hanoch*] the child according to his 'way.'" However, the question remains: does the imperative mode of the verb, "*hanoch*," refer, in this case, to the upbringing and education of the boy or to his final maturation? In line with the other occurrences of the verb, it makes sense, in my

---

[53] Scholars have noted more than a trace of ambivalence in the rabbinic discussions about Enoch, the son of Yered. One view sees in the "second" Enoch a negative figure that does not deserve the high esteem that apocalyptic tradition accords him. The debate over the figure of Enoch seems to include anti-apocalyptic and anti-Christian trends. See *Bereshit Rabba* on Gen. 5: 22.

opinion, to argue that the verse in Book of Proverbs also refers to the final stage of the boy's upbringing. Since the first occurrence of the name, Hanoch, in Scripture occurs in connection with the founding and consecration of a city (calling the name of the city Hanoch is tantamount to consecrating it), the linguistic linkage between the event and the name cannot be accidental. In terms of the cultural ethos discussed above, Hanoch gives his name to the completion of one phase in the process of urbanisation. Cain founded a city and consecrated it as a cultural factor, as an ethos. Giving children their names is a ritual act in its own right, here and elsewhere in scripture and many cultures. Thus, the immediate sense in which we may view this event is as another attempt on Cain's part to resist nomadism. First, Cain killed his shepherd-brother, Abel; then, he founded a city. In both cases, he broke away from the life-patterns that he was expected to follow. When he repeated his wrong-doing, he suffered death. This is how the narrator gave expression to his cultural preferences and norms. He told a story, an *exemplum*, in which the details reflected, at every stage, the relevant ethos. An exemplary story puts on display the moral code that is normatively binding.

As indicated, something more profound than is usually assumed in the scholarly discussion can be found here, by way of a coded insinuation. One of the results of building a city is the laying of the groundwork for the monarchic rule. When it was established, monarchy inferentially implied the renunciation of the tribal-nomadic lifestyle for the sake of "Hebron" or "Jerusalem," the symbol-markers in the biblical story of the later Davidic monarchy![54] The official biography of David, as told in Scripture, typically and dramatically implies such a transition or transformation. Whether this biography is historically correct or not is an issue hotly debated in recent scholarship. For present purposes, we consider it as the foundational myth in the history of the monarchy of ancient Israel, and in this respect, it is "mythically true." Is it too far fetched, then, to argue that the difficulties that David faced, or the dramatic confusions in his life, reflected the change

---

[54] We need not enter here into the dispute between archaeologists and biblical historians as to whether the historiography of the Davidic rule, as told in Scripture, fits the prevalent views of archaeological chronology or not. See recent views expressed on the subject in *Biblical Archaeology Review*, Vol. 24/4, July/August 1998.

of roles (from *Tson*-herding to kingship) that was forced upon him? We cannot but notice how powerful and dramatic the relevant narrative is, and how fatal are the consequences of this change! We all know the story: kingship is described in Scripture as engendering—even in the case of David—moral corruption. Later on, in the days of King Solomon, idolatry was introduced at the monarchic level and, in all likelihood, served as a paradigm for the people. Eventually, the nation was split in two, and the process spiralled into the abyss of destruction.

Returning to the story of Enoch, the son of Yered, the question of how to understand God's decision "to take him" (the literal translation of the Hebrew root לקח) requires our attention. In line with the above, I would suggest—on intralinguistic grounds—that the second Enoch "was taken" simply because he *was* a righteous person. However, Scripture does not specifically state what his righteousness consisted of. Indeed, Scripture enigmatically says: ויתהלך חנוך את האלהים ("Enoch walked with God.) It is valid, therefore, to ask, what does walking imply here? What does the verb הלך imply, in the present context?

I believe that the clue lies in what God tells Abraham: קום התהלך בארץ (Gen. 13: 17; "go and walk through the land…" In accordance with the above, one can argue that, when God told Abraham to walk through the land, what was intended was an ethos or lifestyle rather than an *ad hoc* commandment to tour the land. This lifestyle had—and, to many, it still has—ritual significance and status (the Hebrew word for Halakhah derives from it). Only towards the end of his "narratival career" did Abraham settle down permanently, planting, as Scripture tells us, "a Tamarisk tree (אשל)" (Gen. 21: 32-33). However, he then had to undergo the most trying of his ordeals, the binding of Isaac. Was this ordeal intended to show dissatisfaction with the change that Isaac brought into Abraham's way of life? We shall never know the exact answer to this question, and the way the scriptural writer presented the sequence of events certainly camouflaged this possibility. It would seem that the sequential concurrence of these two events is not accidental. In essence, Abraham used to live in tents. When he settled down in Be'er Shev'a for a longer period (ימים רבים), all that Scripture tells us, by way of commenting on this change, was that Abraham planted a tree. Furthermore, the writer tells us that this took place in the land of the Philistines, the longstanding enemies of the Israelites. Obviously, the reader is expected to draw his own conclusions from the fact that Abraham seems to have radically moved away from the nomadic life that he had led, and settled down in the land of Israel's enemies. Planting a tree, which no one would have noticed (unless it was a grove), added another layer that constituted shameful behaviour: it had symbolic significance as an ethos icon and clearly represented using the land. It is interesting to note, in this connection, that the scriptural narrator explains the name of the place by the "seven ewe sheep of the flock" which Abraham set aside, as a ritual gesture marking the covenant that he and Abimelech had pledged to each other.[55] He had made a covenant that accorded with his ethos. However, he gave part of it away (the sacrifice factor) to a person whose name was, significantly, Avimelech, "the father king"!

In a different context, Lot, who was a shepherd, is also described as making a wrong decision. He settled in the territorial vicinity of Sodom. This city eventually became the notorious symbol of abomination and corruption. Were it not for the "angels," Lot would have perished there. His wife, who looked back, meaning she persisted in favouring city life, perished. She became part of the surrounding natural environment of the Judean Desert.

With regard to the second Enoch, one may argue, that it is not accidental that his righteousness is expressed by the introduction of a unique verb, "and he walked", ויתהלך, which again belongs to the same semantic field of the verb used in connection with Abraham. In all likelihood, this word implied that he abstained from taking part in the process of urbanisation that was well under way in those days. In this context, the verb used to describe Enoch's righteousness resonates louder than usual. Indeed, it seems to me to function as a code. Walking is the real issue, here, as opposed to settling on the land, engaging in agriculture and, ultimately, building a city. If this interpretation is correct, it means that, despite his name, the second Enoch epitomises the negation of city-life. This dialectically increases his righteousness, and explains his elevation to the realm of the divine. Thus, one phase

---

[55] Gen. 21: 25-34. Clearly, the Hebrew writer plays on the pun, *shev'a*, seven, and *shevu'ah*, oath. It is also interesting to note that Abraham took oxen. He probably singled them out for the monarch, Abimelech. The reader may, once again, be reminded at this point, of the sequence agriculture>cattle> urbanisation>monarchy, as discussed above.

of the ethos of Ancient Israel, the one that is expressly depicted
in the Book of Genesis and was later transferred, with some modifications, to Early Christianity, is basically anti-urban and, by
implication, politically anti-monarchic.

Another point is worth making here, particularly in relation to
Christianity. The verb התהלך deserves a full-scale semantic study.
Interestingly, it is used in connection with Enoch, Noah (Gen. 6:
9), and Abraham and is intended to indicate their respective phases
of righteousness. Thus, it may not be altogether accidental that
the writer of the *Epistle to the Hebrews* (chapter 11) mentions the
righteousness of the three Sages. Most significantly, he says of
Abraham (verses 9 and 10): "By faith he [Abraham] sojourned
in the land in tents... For he looked forward to the city that has
foundations, whose builder and maker is God." We need not
quote the rest of the chapter. The statement makes its point clear.
It hardly needs to be compared to the obvious, namely, Paul's
utterances about the earthly and heavenly Jerusalem.

One can argue that three, different, anti-urban channels present
themselves here. They are somehow interconnected, but should
not be confused with one another. One strand maintains an anti-
urban ethos, *per se*. Another makes a link between anti-urbanisation
and anti-monarchism. The third displays a more radical type of
anti-urbanisation, which is more eschatological or messianic in
nature, and is, in a sense, the most spiritual of all of them. From
the outset of the *Genesis*-stories, this type of anti-monarchism ideally
fitted Christianity (Gal. 4: 26).

In conclusion, the aim of this chapter was to show how, by
focusing on the subject of rituals, new perspectives can be gained
in our understanding of the way Scripture recounts the story of
ancient Israel. Particular emphasis was placed on the cycle of
narratives about the Patriarchs. These stories clearly idealise the
tribal-nomadic lifestyle. This chapter attempted to show how this
lifestyle represents an ethos and, in historical terms, the prehis-
tory of the religion of Israel. In all likelihood, the tribal lifestyle
prevailed throughout the period of the Judges. Gradually, it
changed its character and was transformed into agricultural farming. However, the transition to full-scale urbanisation and monarchy did not take place without outbursts of tension. Typically,
Samuel employed all his persuasive powers to convince the people
that kingship would bring them only economic and social hard-

ship.[56] Opposition to the city and the monarchy was also part of
the *prophetic* ethos. In the prophetic literature, this ethos became
a theology and, in later times, it played a major part in the ideology of the Qumran community. The predilection for what the
Qumranites called the "Desert of Damascus" is the epitome of
their cultural and political ethos. It is of no surprise, then, that
both John the Baptist and Jesus lived, and proclaimed, a nomadic
lifestyle. Significantly, too, both were executed in the city, which
to them figured as the symbol of city life and cultic abomination.
Finally, it may not be completely accidental that pastoral leadership is the basic Christian institution. "Pastor," or herd, in this
respect, is a reflection of the ancient ethos, which is our subject
here. Viewing the members of a congregation as "the pastor's
sheep" accords with this kind of ethos, or world picture.

Evidently, more can be said on these issues. They entail a wider
range of implications and require more extensive forms of documentation than can be described here. However, I hope that the
broad lines, drawn in this chapter, illustrate the point I have been
trying to make.

---

[56] See 1 Sam. 8. See also, significantly, 12: 3, where Samuel already speaks
the language of the farmers: "ox and ass" are the principal tools of the "industry."

CHAPTER THREE

THE RELEVANCE OF MYTH FOR THE UNDERSTANDING OF RITUAL IN ANCIENT JUDAISM

I

It is no exaggeration to say that a certain amount of uneasiness used to accompany the scholarly discussion of myth.[1] This uneasiness was reflected in various apologetic stances, and in the downgrading of myth as a minor tint in the palette of human experience and culture. Attempts at finding a more "central" or respectable place for myth can be seen, however, in more recent studies. Scholars now realise that myth is not a stepchild of culture. It is a mode of cognition and form of expression in its own right. Furthermore, there is no longer any reason to measure it against scientific knowledge, nor is any philosophical-allegorical interpretation required to justify its cognitive validity. This is certainly true of myth as a religious phenomenon in general, and it is all the more true of myth in Judaism and monotheistic religions in particular. In the past, however, the presence of myth in various manifestations of the Judaic religion was almost, by definition, predestined to create problems. In the minds of many, myth and mythology were synonymous for strange or fantastic materials. More important even, myths were viewed as futile and misconceived notions, completely worthless from a ritual point of view. They were deriving from the ancient pagan world, and this world was totally rejected by what has become known as Judaic monotheism and its derivatives in Christianity and Western culture. Myth and mythology posed an existential threat to the very existence

---

[1] See the recent survey of these views in Robert A Segal, *Theorizing about Myth*, University of Massachusetts Press: Amherst, 1999. Hebrew readers can refer to my articles on myth published [in Hebrew] in *Eshel Be'er Sheva*, 4 (1996), pp. 1-14, and *Jewish Studies*, Vol. 38 (1998) pp. 178 -210.

of Judaism. Indeed, myth and mythology were usually connected to notions of belief in idols and in the efficacy of their worship.

The above attitudes were motivated by theological stances that, eventually, found their way into scholarly circles, Christian and Jewish alike. The study of myth underwent considerable changes since the second half of the nineteenth century. Tylor, Robertson-Smith and Frazer were justifiably associated with these changes. Two major centres of discussion then emerged. The first focussed on the relationship between myth and rituals: myth being either the background of ritual or its hermeneutic consequence. The second centre of discussion focussed on myth, magic and science and their inter-relationships. Scholars argued that myth and magic constitute pre-scientific—and also pre-philosophical—modes of cognition and human activity. In the discussion, presented here, I shall leave these debates behind, and attempt to present myth in a new, cognitive context. For reasons that shall be explained in this chapter, I suggest viewing myth and rituals as interconnected and interrelated entities. Consequently, the repositioning of ritual, as promoted in this book, allows for a reconsideration of the interaction between myth and ritual and, correspondingly, for new insights into our understanding of myth. More precisely, I shall show how the discussion of myth and ritual, in a mutually conceptualising framework, can enhance our understanding of both phenomena.

I believe that the manner in which myth and mythology are handled in Judaic studies is greatly influenced by the manner in which they are handled in religious studies, in general. For this, and other reasons, I shall give at the outset a rather extensive outline of how I view myth and mythology in the larger context of religious and ritual studies. Thus, the first part of this chapter will focus on the general problems of assessing the cognitive and epistemological status of myth and ritual, particularly with regard to the monotheistic religions, while the second part will focus on the more specific aspects of the problem, in a Judaic context.

I shall begin the discussion by clarifying my position with regard to the longstanding debate over the question of whether myth precedes ritual or ritual generates myth.[2] My interest, in this book,

---

[2] See the discussion of this issue in Wendy Doniger O'Flaherty, *Other Peoples' Myths*, Macmillan Publishing Company, New York, 1988, pp.25-43.

follows a completely different direction than the one generated
by prevalent discussions of this debate. Since no story defines itself as myth, the question has to be asked: what are the factors
that confer the status of myth on a particular story or fact. In many
respects, this question repeats the one asked earlier in this book
with regard to the factors that differentiate between a normal,
everyday act and ritual. I take the position that a story that is
connected to a ritual, whether in its original or later stage, is a
myth. I say this because, in Greek, the word "myth" simply means
"a story," without attaching to it any functional qualifications. In
the more technical sense, to which I shall refer here, the word
functions in the context of its relationship to ritual. Once again,
I view myth as a story that is connected to a ritual—whether in a
referential, explanatory or circumstantially historical manner. The
reader should be reminded that, since I view rituals in a broader
context than the specifically religious, myth, too, may evolve in
a nonreligious context. More will be said on this issue later on.
Now, stories that are no longer connected to a specific ritual are
likely to lose their mythic status and function. They may become
part of an inventory that houses out dated myths, to which I suggest referring as mythology, or mythological stories. These stories have become part of materials that once had the status of an
active myth. In the strict sense of the term, as I use it, they cease
to be myth. Mythology may serve as the inventory from which
stories are taken to serve as active myths again. But mythic features may attach themselves to stories and facts that have never
before enjoyed this status.

  I would like to state, from the outset, that my position makes
myth an omnipresent factor. The human mind creates attitudes
that, in one way or another, acquire the form of stories. When
one of these is connected to a specific mode of behaviour—a
ritual—it takes on the status of a myth. Since myths often crystallise
as fantastic narratives, including content about supernatural beings, many people, guided by rationalistic thinking, consider them
eccentric or irrational, from the outset. This attitude, almost by
definition, downgrades myth and calls into question its cognitive
functions and epistemological reliability. My discussion of the
subject will refer to myth as a vitally creative expression of the
human mind. I would like to state the following point as emphatically as possible: myth is a natural and normal factor in human

life and culture. As we shall see, myth is as essential to the health of cultural life as any other creative factor of the human mind or inner self that does not succumb to suppressing its natural, instinctive, urge to relate to the outside, experiential, world. Indeed, I would dare to say that myth is an existentially indispensable factor in making human life liveable. In a sense, myths function like dreams: they have a regulating effect on the psychic life of people. Myths also have a social function. They present constitutive stories that build the substance of culture. They sustain structured and socially applicable modes of behaviour, namely, rituals. What people wish to say about their origins and their basic modes of organising life is often enacted on a ritual plane. Thus, public myths and public rituals go hand in hand, as do myths and rituals for individual people.

We have already referred to the fact that myths are not specifically limited to, and characteristic of, ancient pre-scientific cultures. Myth and myth-making are part of the modern world, too. Without referring to specific examples, every reader, I am sure, can think of stories that are connected to specific modes of behaviour. This is particularly true of political leaders (Yosef Stalin = "Man of Steel"), guerrilla fighters (Ernesto Che Guevara), and popular artists (Elvis Presley). These are a few examples that illustrate the extent to which a particular mythic attitude inspired millions of people to an idealised way of life—social and economic in the case of Stalin, aggressive idealism in the case of Ernesto Che Guevara, and stylised and eccentric manners in the case of the Elvis Presley. The list is a partial one and could be extended in many directions. These forms of ritual behaviour were accompanied by an entire industry of story telling. They clearly belong, in my opinion, to a mythic framework. One essential part of the mythmaking process, in this respect, is the production and preservation of memory. In the three cases mentioned above, memory was feeding a complex industry.

II

Storytelling engages the domain of creative imagination and this is certainly true of the mythic "story." To begin with, it consists in subjective data that seek ways of coming to life as objective realities. More important still, myth is the space created for a

certain reality to acquire a unique narratival form and shape. In
many ways, myth is an organisational manifestation in which
psychic and mental entities seek a mode of imaging the self and
the world. Psychologically expressed, myth making is functional
in imaging the relational stances between self and world. Myth
organises the imaged world into structures, whose chief qualities
are self-sustained (or self-sustaining) cogency and coherency. Myth
creates modes of understanding for those who make use of them.
It is possible, also, to look at myth from a slightly different angle. In the ancient world, mythic stories—and, for that matter,
mythology—traverse the demarcation lines that regularly separate
objective from subjective forms of knowledge. Thus, the mythic
story may branch out to allow space for remote, mental or imaginative, domains in which the non-natural (or supernatural) becomes a realistic possibility. Finally, in this respect, myths enable
the crossings of boundaries that are usually considered impass-
able. Thus, myths make it possible for people to relate to the
supernatural as also connect to the unreachable (whether on the
personal level, the distant, belonging to the past, or foreseeable
in the future).

From yet another psychological angle, we may say that myth
sets the facticity of the rationally unknowable. In terms used by
Christopher Bollas, myth is the manifestational organization of
"the unthought known."[3] We may even see, in myth, a representation of a certain reality that creates its own laws of existence.
This reality is imaged in ways that make a desired existence functionally possible. The imaged reality represents a modelled situation. Unlike dreams, however, this reality has been created so
that others may share it. In myth, as in dreams, subjective desires or fears seek full realisation. Behind many a myth, there is
an existential *Sturm* or *Drang* that erupts as a manifestation. This
manifestation crystallises in verbal, pictorial and even musical
representations. Representation, here, means objectification.
Objectification is needed, for it creates a tangible reality to which
rituals, as behavioural factors, can relate. Rituals constitute a mode
of relating to these realities: they create a behavioural dialogue

---

[3] See Christopher Bollas, *The Shadow of the Object: Psychoanalysis of the Unthought
Known*, Free Association Books: London, 1987, particularly pp. 277-283.

with the mythic and constitute behavioural extensions, or enactments, of mythic materials.

As indicated, myth generates ritual. The fact that the mythic "story" connects to a specific ritual or ethos enhances its argumentative potential. It begins as a statement of an imaged reality and moves on to become a behavioural argument. Of course, there are cases, in which the order is reversed, namely, a certain ritual generates a myth or attaches itself to an existing story which, as a result, receives mythic status. In this case, myth must be viewed in somewhat different terms of reference from those described above. Understandably, it is difficult at times to determine the circumstantial sequence of myth and ritual. In any event, the connection of myth to a specific ritual appears to me to be the essential characteristic of myth. This connection also helps us to understand the difference between myth and mythology. Once again, we view myth as a story that exists by virtue of its connection to ritual, whereas in mythology the story exists with no active connection to an existing, active, ritual. Myth can change to mythology, that is to say, it can turn into a story that has no longer an active connection to a ritual. In this case, it functions like any other story: it appears primarily in an aesthetic context, to be looked at and enjoyed.

Myth, then, is a natural form of expression, undeserving of raised eyebrows. Neither is it an exceptional phenomenon. It is a natural expression of the human imagination. Imagination has or shapes a reality of its own. Its first links are not to the fictitious or the untrue, but to the cognitively creative. There is no way of bypassing myth. It *is* an integral part of human consciousness. It is cognitively indispensable. But this does not undermine the human need for, and dependence on other, more rational and critical, forms of judgement. Critical judgement is an indispensable facet of the human mind, as it strives to establish accountability in relation to systemic existences. Myth concerns meta-logical modes of thinking and perception. Myth does not have to account for itself, unless, of course, its being attached to a ritual is viewed as its own way of accounting for itself.

Myth is often described as an allegoric, or symbolic, expression of ideas. From antiquity, this has been the traditional form of rationalising myth. The background of myth is viewed as a spiritual design that is dramatised in the mythic narrative. There are, indeed, instances in which myth functions in this way. However, the approach, presented in this chapter, considers myth as a unique form of cognitive expression. Its essence depends on the unique manner in which it comes into being. Its functionality depends on the kind of links, which it creates between ritual and its role in life. In some cases, myth attempts to provide an interpretation of events. It projects its self-sustained meaning on a specific reality. The unique nature of the interpretative information, that myth supplies, is reflected in the corresponding ritual. Thus, when a myth refers to events connected with specific divine beings or gods, it makes an essential statement in relation to a specific ritual, which these gods allegedly endorse. In the previous chapter we have discussed at length two such examples. When these events have no connection to ritual, or if they have lost that connection, this means that the relevant gods have ceased to prevail or function in the eyes of the people.

The reasons for treating myths with rationalistic suspicion often stem from the strangeness of their narratival setting. Myth, indeed, entails epistemological exceptionality, to say nothing of its interest in the supernatural.[4] As mentioned above, myths cross boundaries of cognitive perception and experiential causality. I am inclined to view myth as an ever-present phenomenon, which embraces the epistemologically exceptional or the supernatural. In fact, myth can endow phenomenological reality with metaphysical qualities. Some readers may be critical of this seemingly loose definition of myth. However, research into religious and cultural studies has shown that myth and, complementarily, mythopoesis are not restricted to the ancient world. Mythic designs are connected to any kind of reality that crystallises in ritual. Rituals are naturally streaming forth from the human mind. Whether they are part of the behaviour of other species or not, is a hotly debated issue in modern anthropology and behavioural psychology. The answer, however, will not significantly bear upon our understanding of rituals. But, if rituals are linked to purposive processes of transformation that are created by a mind set on preserving and safeguarding vital aspects of existence, then their prevalence

---

[4] In the theological debate of the 20th century, the name Rudolph Bultmann needs special mentioning. See Rudolf Karl Bultmann, *New Testament and Mythology and Other Basic Writings*, Philadelphia 1984.

among non-human species is not as self-evident as some scholars believe. Survival is an instinctual drive in humans and animals, alike. The extent to which rituals are motivated by a consciously attentive mind makes their prevalence among animals a matter of diverse speculations. If, however, we view rituals in a context that requires the presence of myths, animals are easily excluded. They cannot verbalise their experience of life. Thus, they have no sense of the cultural setting and function of rituals. In short, then, in as much as rituals assume the existence of a certain myth to sustain them, they cannot be part of the behaviour of animals, even when they reflect a certain repetitive regularity. In the case of myth, consciousness and, for that matter, sub-consciousness, too, play their respective roles. They are the matrix in which myths crystallise. Animal instincts belong to a pre-conscious behavioural stage, and therefore exclude animals from mythical activity. At critical moments of danger to their life and existence animals will, also, engage in repetitive forms of behaviour. But, unlike humans, animals will not repeat these forms of behaviour in situations that do not entail the need to react instinctively. Human rituals are repeatable even in staged ceremonial events. Finally, when myth is linked to rituals, it often provides the world picture, which endows the rituals with their full applicability and function. To the best of our knowledge, animals have no cognitively express-ible world picture.

One conclusion that can be drawn from the above is that, even when the danger is not a real or material one, what matters is that the story that is told in this case is made to sound real by force of its seeking connectedness to a behavioural stance, that is, to ritual. The use of pesticides in coffee plantations seems a rational means of destroying insects and other harmful organisms. However, when priests are called in to recite special blessings, and farmers join in, this is clearly a ritual procedure. In other words, rituals are modes of behaviour and activity that, more often than not, draw on the belief (in our case, the myth) in the efficacy of supernaturally empowered agents. In secular rituals too, (such as extinguishing candles on birthday cakes), one can often discover an irrational element. Thus, all kinds of beliefs (= myths) can find their way into rational forms of behaviour. But matters are much more complex than this and they deserve full scholarly attention, and this leads us to the next point.

III

The uniqueness of the mythic "story" derives from the fact that it creates life patterns that are relevant to ritual and ethos. The linkage between ritual and myth creates special signs that help to shape personal and group identity. Structurally speaking, myth and ritual create identity-marks that, in the eyes of later generations, may appear as codes or coded messages. The "narrative" implied in these codes is the result of the special manner in which a particular myth connects to a particular ritual. Myth can relate to the past, present, or future of the people concerned. The respective rituals, too, may refer to the past, present, or future. Myth may relate to living people, dead people or deities. Rituals endow identity marks with a behavioural configuration, that is to say, people are identified by what they do, and by the manner in which they do it. Divergences in identity, however minute, always emerge in ritual performances, nay, in denominational fractioning.

Since the philosophical way of life, also, aims at establishing fixed patterns of moral and spiritual identity and behaviour, one can argue that philosophy can play the role of myth in shaping human behaviour. Indeed, every ethical code has its own cosmology, which is structured on a worldview, real or imagined, that shapes the end in a manner that justifies the means. It is, therefore, logical for us to say that there is a substantial core, which functions as myth even in a philosophical-rational position such as that taken by Maimonides.[5] Essentially, this is the myth of the eventual unity between the acquired intellect of humans and the active intellect of the divine. In the "Aristotelian" scheme that Maimonides adopts, the divine intellect is an emanated entity, the tenth in line underneath the unrecognisable God. A world structure of this kind must, by definition, sound mythic to an ear attuned to modern rationality. In Maimonides, however, it constitutes the core of his rigidly phrased philosophical-theological programme.

---

[5] Maimonides' stance on this issue—which may be referred to as 'the metaphorisation of the biblical text'—is formulated in these words: "Everything is according to human cognition... and the Torah spoke in the language of humans. Thus, all the names are (to be read as) metaphors. . . everything is a parable and a high flown rhetorical device" (Mishneh Torah, *Yesodei Ha-Torah* 1, 9; 12).

In short, our discussion of myth moves along two complementary lines, which ultimately may converge and constitute a unified statement. The first line defines the principal channels through which myth is directed. In this context, myth is examined along cognitive lines. The second line examines the role that myth plays in shaping ritual, in particular, and religion, in general. Here, criteria deriving from anthropological studies are examined, along with criteria deriving from religious studies. In both cases, the human mind is the common factor that we highlight in our study of both myth and ritual. Myth and ritual complementarily reflect the human mind, which generates a multiplicity of forms of expression, in each case.

I wish to repeat that, in my opinion, myth is not a purely religious factor and it is not unique to this realm. The essence of myth, as we suggest here, is that it supplies the "story" that develops into a ritual, whether religious or not, with all that the latter desires to accomplish. In other words, *the factors that make myth and ritual religious entities are their specific context, not their intrinsic nature.* A guiding point, in this book, is that any fruitful discussion of myth should be carried out from a standpoint that does not include the evaluative stances, which all too often accompany this subject. Myth crosses the boundaries which, in the eyes of many people, differentiate objective and subjective forms of consciousness. The value judgements, which usually accompany any discussion about myth, do not take into consideration those entities evolving in and from this intermediate area between the perceptually objective and the cognitively subjective. These entities have epistemological validity. Since myth unfolds in such intermediate areas, the measure of the epistemological validity that attaches itself to myth considerably decreases in the eyes of people whose measures of cognitive validity are shaped in the symbiosis between rationality and physical objectivity.

The perspective that I am trying to establish, here, follows the approach of the British paediatrician and psychoanalyst, D.W. Winnicott.[6] He writes:

---

[6] See, D.W. Winnicott, *Through Paediatrics to Psycho-Analysis*, New York 1975, mainly pp. 229-242; *idem. The Maturational Processes and the Facilitating Environment: Studies in the Theory of Emotional Development*, International Universities Press: Madison [CT], 1991, pp. 150, 184-85.

In the healthy individual who has a compliant aspect of the self but who exists and who is a creative and spontaneous being, there is at the same time a capacity for the use of symbols. In other words, health here is closely bound up with the capacity of the individual to live in an area that is intermediate between the dream and the reality, that which is called the cultural life.[7]

Another passage makes a similar claim:

It may be necessary... to speak in terms of man's cultural life, which is the adult equivalent of the transitional phenomena of infancy and early childhood, and in which area communication is made without reference to the object's state of being either substantive or objectively perceived. It is my opinion that the psychoanalyst has no other language in which to refer to cultural phenomena.[8]

It is useful to relate Winnicott's words to our discussion. They may be viewed as attaching cognitive value to myth and, consequently, to its epistemological and, hence, scholarly assessment. Indeed, I see, in what Winnicott writes, an element that gives myth (Winnicott refers to symbols) a more positive status and creative value in human culture than is usually the case. Myth can operate as a vital, almost peremptory, factor that maintains the "health" of cultural existence.[9] Winnicott helps us to view myth as a factor that enables dialogue between the world of objective consciousness and its subjective counterpart. Myth exists where and when the commonly maintained borderlines between these two forms of consciousness are either crossed or suspended. This allows for a free flow of the unconscious to this intermediate area where it can bear on the contents of consciously structured forms of cognition and, as a result, on human behaviour. This intermediate area may be viewed as a major factor in facilitating playful imagination to be creatively functional in cultural activity.

In other words, Winnicott may be viewed as offering a creative solution to the problem of myth. I believe that there is no longer any reason to view myth in the context of fictional redundancy or in terms of fantastic unreality. I consider it a point worth arguing that myth lies outside the realm of the merely fictitious. Although myth may have aesthetic values, it functions on a com-

---

[7] *The Maturational Processes*, p. 150.
[8] *Ibid.* p. 184.
[9] Its over-excessive presence may, though, have fatal consequences. The closest example I can think of, in this connection, is Nazi-Germany.

pletely different level of imaginative creativity, that of the intermediate reality between the objective and the subjective. In the
end, it creates, or connects itself to, an existential string that is
concretised in ritual. In other words, it creates cognitively tangible
realities. Myth is the core that sustains culture and human existence. In short, any meaningful study of myth must take into consideration the existence of extraordinary modes of cognition. These
evolve in the space that allows the natural/objective and the su-
pernatural/subjective to interact creatively. I wish to remind the
reader that the full realisation of the mythic takes place in something that is real—in ritual.

IV

Since I believe that myth does not uniquely belong to the realm
of religion, I am seeking a way to present it as a dominant feature in culture. Myth, also, reflects a frame of mind that is engaged in seeking modes of contextualising ritual in a particular
narrative. It constitutes the ethos that sustains ritual. We have
already referred to ethos above, and I wish to add that, in the
modern usage of the term, ethos is a major factor in shaping the
content of the narratival structure that holds together the social,
moral, conceptual (including religious), and even economic, orders. We have seen that the fact that an ethos may constitute pre-
cultural or pre-religious settings. However, this does not detract
from its overall functional centrality.[10] Culture and religion entail social institutions, a structured legal system, and rituals that
are repetitive (rather than spontaneous), communal (rather than
individual), and enacted over extended (rather than sporadic) life
cycles.

My intention, thus far, has been to present the problem of myth
(in relation to ritual) in a broad context. It is true to say that myth
has often been viewed as the rival of intellectual coherence. Judaic modes of religiousness and thinking often led to polemic
positions that tried to minimise the scope and depth of mythic
influence in, and on, the Hebrew Scripture. Judaic monotheism,
it was purported, could only arise in a completely non-mythic

---

[10] For a wider definition of the concept "ethos," see Clifford Geertz, *The Interpretation of Cultures*, Basic Books: New York, pp. 126-141.

environment. Monotheism, as viewed by many, cannot thrive where myth (viewed as epitomising a pagan *Weltanschauung*) is markedly present. This was the position taken vis-à-vis myth by many Jewish, and even non-Jewish, scholars. At times, the scholarly liquidation of the mythic factor in Judaism reached the level of an intellectual crusade. I wish to reiterate in the strongest terms: religion cannot arise in an environment divested of its mythic substance. Any reference to a live—as opposed to a philosophical—God has a mythic essence. Thus, willy-nilly, a scholarly discussion of the concept of a personal god involves the realm of the mythic.

If we follow Winnicott's proposition, myth is a natural factor in the mindset of people, and includes their religious life. Myth is a constructively creative factor sustained by and, at the same time, sustaining human imagination. Thus, whenever human cognition shapes its representations of reality, humans are likely to branch out into the realms of myth. Here, the limitless can be attained, without having to account for breaches of normal human constraints. Epistemologically-speaking, the limitless constitutes a unique reality. That reality unfolds in the transitional realms of which Winnicott spoke. Myth originates in special modes of consciousness, which play a vital role in almost every form of religion or religious expression. In short, religion thrives on mythic forms.

One line of argumentation has often led to curious conclusions, namely that since myths crystallise in the domain of the creative imagination, they can pose a threat to the systemic order set by dogmatic theology. Modern scholarship has often been influenced by this kind of argument. This existential threat may explain the fact that scholars directed their fear against a mythologisation of Scripture. They tried to divest the Hebrew Scripture of any mythic influence, thus activating a normative precedent to their own fears and belief. Myth was essentially "pagan," and believed to cultivate forbidden rituals, *i.e.* idol worship. What could pose a greater threat to their enlightened rationalism than the wild fantasies of the mythic mind as allegedly reified in Scripture? The identification of myth with pagan forms of religion is one of the fallacies introduced into the study of religions and myth by scholars, whose perceptions were based on traditional monotheistic premises. For them, myth signalled chaos, rather than boundless creative imagination.

Whether myths carried, in their movement from culture to culture, elements of indoctrination, which could be described as blasphemy, is an interesting question, but need not be answered here. Scholars have no obligation whatsoever to assess the subjects of their investigation using the measuring scales favoured by theologians. Psychologically speaking, the human imagination can hardly operate with the handcuffs put on it by theological indoctrination. Time and again, a tension breaks out between the predominance of the mythic imagination and the rigid constraints that theological considerations wish impose on the religious mind. The conflict is resolved, though, when common sense is applied. Then, the tension usually subsides with theology losing the game. This may explain, among other things, the failure of the moralising preaching of the prophets of ancient Israel, who persistently tried to ridicule and fight idol worship. They identified it with what may be called today mythic nonsense. Idol worship and mythological materials were commonly thought to go hand in hand. According to the view expressed here, monotheistic religions also have their moments in which the writers of mythic narratives are given a free hand and the whole literary scene. This does not mean that I take sides with the advocates of idol worship. Viewing certain rituals in terms of idol worship reflects a theological bias, not an adequate phenomenological perspective that aims at understanding religions in their own context. My aim here is to explain the dynamics of the human mind: what happens, when it allows the imagination to exhaust its potential for creative freedom? Theologically-minded people may see some danger here, but theological fears are not the subject of the present discourse.

V

As noted, when a myth loses its connectedness to a performed ritual, it becomes part of a mythological inventory. Similar stories can be found in various religions about the origins and lives of gods, the genealogical relationships that connect them, and even their deaths and possible resurrection. Claude Levi Strauss built his anthropological structuralism on the universal occurrence of

similar myths. In his view, they could all be condensed to a critical mass in which structuralism offered unified modes of explanation. However, not adopting a particular myth also makes a
cultural statement, which says, primarily, that this myth has no
ritual connectedness and has been side-tracked to the realm of
mythology. Invalid mythic stories belong to the realm of the aesthetic. However, we cannot tire of repeating that no religion is
free of myth, in the sense that it activates narratives that are ritu-
ally-bound. A ritual is necessary to endow a story with mythic
status.

Notwithstanding these comments, the question remains open:
what is the nature of the mythic, or mythological, materials that
are found in Scripture? These mythic materials (such as the story
of the Garden of Eden and God's combat against archaic monsters) are located in Scripture in a setting that, arguably, calls for
apologetic explanations. The above question demonstrates that,
although we distinguish between myth and mythology, in the
context of the Hebrew Scripture the two may sometimes give rise
to the same question. The question requires more attention than
space allows. I mention it, because I consider it essential to the
understanding of the religion of ancient Israel (and of later times).
One may indeed ask whether the traces of mythic materials in
Scripture are, according to our understanding of the terms, myth
or mythology. It is easy to relegate everything to the domain of
mythology. This amounts to saying that these traces have no ritual
function, that is to say, they can be used for anything that is not
essential to the Law in the religion of ancient Israel. It is interesting to note that such a view brings us close to the rationalistic
presuppositions of monotheistic views, namely, that myths do not
count in the context of a "higher religion". But, different opinions can be expressed on this matter. The question can also be
asked from the following angle: initially, when these materials were
borrowed, did they have a myth-ritual configuration or a mythological setting? The last question, assuredly, has no uniform and
unequivocal answer. In its present form, the mythological configuration of these materials prevails over the mythic one.

A quick look, however, at one example may be eye opening.
When Scripture says that God created the human species ("*the*
Adam") in "[the] *Tselem* of Elohim," the scriptural text hastens
to add that God created "them" (!) male and female (Gen. 1: 27,

5:2). Conceivably, Scripture implies here the bisexual, or the indeterminate sexual, nature of the "*Tselem* Elohim." The Hebrew term *tselem* derives from the Akkadian word *tsalmu*. According to Irene J. Winter, the word means, "consistently and only, image, which then may occur as a statue, or a stele, carved in relief, painted, drawn or engraved."[11] A theologically oriented interpretation of *tselem* emphasises only the spiritual quality.[12] However, if God does not have a physical image how can humans be created in his *tselem*, in the technical sense of the term? Winter's etymological definition repudiates outright the philosophical interpretations of the kind found in Jewish commentaries, to the effect that the term indicates primarily a spiritual representation of a certain being. Professor Simo Parpola has indicated to me that the term may, secondarily, refer to spiritual qualities as well. This does not remove, or displace, the more physical sense suggested by etymology. In the story of Gen. 1, God created humans in his *Tselem,* as man and woman. This cannot but be a signal which, in this particular case, tells us that the word *Tselem* refers to something that is primarily physical.

But can we say that the passage in the Book of Genesis, chapter 1, has a ritual connection, too? That is to say, does it *function* as myth, or is it mythological? I believe the answer to these questions is positive, that is, the passage has a ritual connection and therefore the information it contains operates on a mythic level. The creation of the human species precedes the divine decree concerning human procreation (Gen. 1: 28). The story has a mythic function. It is a myth in the sense described above. It makes procreation an act in the likeness of creation, and the natural result of how things came into being.

Some scholars writing on the creation stories, from Adam to Noah, insist on seeing these materials in an anti-mythological light.[13] Others admit that, in the scriptural texts that recount the

---

[11] See Irene J. Winter, "Art *in* Empire: The Royal Image and the Visual Dimensions of Assyrian Ideology," in: S Parpola and R. M. Whiting, *Assyria 1995*, The Neo-Assyrian Text Corpus Project: Helsinki, 1997, pp. 359-381.

[12] See Yair Lorberbaum, *Imago Dei: Rabbinic Literature, Maimonides, and Nahmanides* [Dissertation (in Hebrew): Hebrew University Jerusalem], 1997. Lorberbaum uses the term "Imago Dei" for the Hebrew *tselem*.

[13] Of interest, in this context, is the way in which M.D. Cassuto relates, in his writings, to this material. In most cases, he refrains from using the word "mythol-

primeval battle between God and certain sea and land monsters, who allegedly attempted to challenge God's absolute hegemony, remnants of mythological materials prevail.[14] They argue that residues of mythological (mostly Ugaritic/Canaanite) materials can be clearly discerned in these texts and that, in their scriptural formatting, these materials functioned in a polemical context. This may well be the case. However, what is of import to us is the question of the relatedness of these materials to ritual, and hence the definition of these materials as either myth or mythology. This consideration does not come up in any of the writings I have in mind. If they functioned in a polemical context, they evidently had no connection to rituals. As such, they were mythology, and therefore they are of limited interest to us here. In contrast, the creation story of the Book of Genesis 1 has ritual functions and it, therefore, is mythic in every possible respect.

It is important to note that the mythological materials in Scripture appear, for the most part, in fragmentary form. They do not reflect any coherent order that tells us what guided their selection and their forms of presentation. However, the various forms in which they appear in Scripture tell a striking story. After all, myth is found in every religious statement that relates to a god or to a divine world. The existence of a divine world, as an entity with personal qualities (anthropomorphism), seeks to create the notion that gods and humans share qualities and attributes. This cannot happen outside the realms of the mythic, or mythological, in the senses discussed here. We can even show greater precision in the discussion of this issue. A personal God requires the doing of rituals. The stories about him, therefore, have a mythic status.

---

ogy." Instead, he talks about "oriental legends" or "early poetic traditions." In contrast, Ezekiel Kaufmann demonstrates how hermeneutic acrobatics can help deal with the subject of "Scripture and mythological idols." He admits that there is an indirect influence of early oriental mythology on certain sections of Scripture. However, he notes that Scripture rejects the mythological idols and is therefore not influenced by these materials in any significant manner.

[14] See, for example, John Day, *God's Conflict with the Dragon and the Sea: Echoes of a Canaanite Myth in the Old Testament*, Cambridge, 1985. This approach is also found Benjamin Uffenheimer's article, discussed below (footnote 20). It should be noted that most scholars do not make a clear distinction between myth and mythology. A noteworthy example is Yehuda Liebes, *Studies in Jewish Myth and Messianism*, SUNY Press: Albany, 1993. Liebes discusses myth and mythopoesis, but he makes no distinction between myth and mythology.

To summarise this part of the chapter, myth activates links between a certain reality and its enactment in structured actions, that is, in rituals. Myth comes to life in a special cognitive space that does not obey the usual constraints of the senses and the material world. As we have seen, the psychology of the mythic condition assumes the existence of an intermediate space in which an attitudinal system is cognitively functional. The existence of this space entirely depends on the imagination. However, this does not affect the way we see myth, namely as an existential reality. Consequently, the boundaries that are usually functional in maintaining a distinction between the internal and external worlds melt away. Finally, it is imperative, in my view, to stress that, in making a distinction between mythology and myth, an essential dilemma presents itself to the reader of the relevant texts. If it is mythology that he finds there, in the sense we attribute to the term here, then why should one bother over the whole issue. If, however, one is inclined to bother, it shows that the materials at hand are mythic, after all.

VI

Since this discussion entails a departure from prevailing modes of discussion, a few more comments are required on the way the subject is handled. Scholars often focus on the historical-archaeological and sociological information that myth, or mythology, purports to convey. Many seek to find, in myth, details that identify the social structure that created it. In principle, there is nothing wrong with this approach. Scholars, with a philosophical orientation, discuss the ontology of myth, regardless of its sociological and anthropological message. From the philosophical perspective, myth is often depicted as representing information regardless of the question of its historical reality or validity. Often, though, in the philosophical approach, the ontological reality of myth and mythology is seriously called into question. However, in the view presented here, the validity of myth does not depend on whether its information is verifiable or not.[15] If we accept a Karl R.

---

[15] The notion of the fictitious, in relation to myth, is highlighted in the title of the book, *Myth and Fictions*, Shlomo Biderman & Ben-Ami Scharfstein (eds.), Leiden 1993. The concept of truth, in the context of myth, is discussed in the various

Popper-like model, we can say that since one cannot prove myth, one cannot deny its truth. As such, myth should be evaluated as a form of meta-scientific thinking. It has cognitive validity, even though it does not organise its information in rational or scientific statements. It is neither pre-scientific nor para-scientific, but it has relevance in the eyes of those who have faith in the myth and do their rituals accordingly.

There is one way of challenging the status-validity of myth: this is when its relevance, that is, its ritual connection is abandoned. A good example of this is the realm of magic. A popular dictum, in the modern study of magic, says: "my miracle is your magic." *Mutatis mutandis*, one may find people say: "your magic becomes a miracle in my hands." Similarly, it is quite common to hear people say: "what they believe in is myth, while what we believe in is true religion." In the Judaic context, the conflict is primarily between different kinds of worship, not between the stories that accompany them. But in the conflict with others, the "other" is the idol-worshipper, the "heretic," or the one who believes in what is called "superstition." His gods are false, not because they teach something that is wrong, but because their respective stories reflect their man-made origins. Hand crafted gods cannot eat, hear or see. Thus, they cannot be recipients of rituals. But, can abstract gods eat, either? Only a mythic god can eat and otherwise act as humans do. Although the God of the Israelites does not eat sacrifices, he can still smell their burnt fragrance. He also hears prayers (or the evil done on earth). In other words, he obeys mythic rules.

The pre-Socratic philosopher, Xenophanes, was the first to hold an anti-mythic approach that, practically speaking, combined religious with philosophical considerations. Xenophanes lived one or two generations before Plato. He waged a fierce polemic against the stories depicted in Homeric literature. According to Xenophanes, the concept that gods are born and die, and even have incestuous relationships, degrades the gods. When Clement of Alexandria joined forces to establish Christian dogma, polemicising against what seemed to be anti-Christian, that is, pagan views, he quoted Xenophanes as a major authority on the subject of myth

studies published in Frank E. Reynolds & David Tracy (eds.), *Myth and Philosophy*, Albany, 1990.

and religious fraud.[16] Views such as those of Xenophanes led many writers to adopt a hermeneutic stance, in which religious myths smoothly translated to become philosophical truths. In Judaic thought, Philo of Alexandria was the first writer who systematically used ways of translating scriptural myth into rationalistic notions. As we know, he applied philosophical allegory to Scripture.[17] We have already noted that an additional change in this opposition to myth came into effect at a later historical stage: this was the theological-rational opposition to mythic (anthropomorphic) language, as voiced by Maimonides. People were persuaded to see, in mythic language, the embodiment of anthropomorphic apostasy.[18]

As stated, I am seeking here to liberate myth from the practice of referring to it in either apologetic or critical terms. I also refrain from placing myth in a position diametrically opposed to what is known as transcendental monotheism. And I refrain from assessing myth in a comparative context involving scientific notions and criteria of comparison. Myth is connected to ritual, and ritual is a behavioural stance that creates transformative events, often in relation to that myth. The breadth and depth of the desired changes and their special character depend on the "cosmos" (or cosmology), which constitutes the frame of reference for the ritual performance. Time and place are among the most important

---

[16] The subject is discussed primarily in the fifth book of the *Stromata*.

[17] Practically, Philo does not polemise against myth: he presents myth as a story that possesses philosophical truthfulness. Philo's approach is facilitated by the allegorical interpretation of Scripture. His hermeneutic method enables him to see, in the scriptural narrative (and particularly in any story in which the gods play a part), a veil behind which an abstract philosophical truth hides. See Ithamar Gruenwald, "Discovering the Veil: The Problem of Deciphering Codes of Religious Language," in: Aleida and Jan Assmann (eds.), *Schleier und Schwelle*, Wilhelm Fink Verlag: Muenchen, 1997, pp. 235-250.

[18] Ezekiel Kaufmann, for instance, outdid himself in establishing that the ancient Near Eastern materials are mythical as opposed to Scripture and its non-mythical exclusiveness. See Benjamin Uffenheimer's discussion of the problem in, Yair Hoffman and Frank Pollak (eds.), *Or Le-Ya'akov: Studies in the Scripture and the Dead Sea Scrolls in Memory of Ya'akov Shalom Licht*, [in Hebrew], Jerusalem, 1997, pp. 17-35. I would like to note that I do not concord with Uffenheimer's view. Uffenheimer believes that, in its presentation of vestiges of ancient concepts from the pagan world, Scripture seeks to fight against them. It seems to me that an opposite interpretation can be made for many of the cases, which Uffenheimer considers support his view. To the best of my understanding, Scripture does not proclaim a philosophical type of monotheism. The issue at stake is monolateria, that is, the worship of one god, not his philosophical mono-existence.

components of this "cosmos." The persistence of this "cosmos"
through time (tradition) may in turn give rise to new phases of
the constitutive myth.[19] Tradition is the framework in which
changes in the ritual practice happen. These create further processes of ritualisation, in which the practice may become stronger
or weaker, as the case may be.

Myths often recount archaic or primordial events. This is especially true of myths which have been created in a religious
context. In this context, they are inseparable from other modes
of recounting history. History is vital for the ongoing processes
of culture. It provides the depth, resonance, foundational background and sequential patterning necessary for culture to function as a coherent and binding structure. It is important to note,
though, that myth is not necessarily an archaic story, as Mircea
Eliade argues (see below). If an event, in the past, constitutes the
narrative behind a particular ritual, then that ritual re-enacts the
relevant event of the past. The past is made present through, and
in, that ritual. The manner in which this happens is by implication, unless an explicit connection is discernable between the event
and the ritual that relates to it.

Emphasising the connection between myth and ritual, however,
does not assume that one event tends more than another to take
on mythic form. Mythopoesis, or myth making, is an immanent
characteristic of stories that wish to inform people about supernatural and charismatic beings. On their surface, these stories do
not point in a specific ritual direction. However, a more penetrat-
ing look will show that there is an element of enactability in these
stories. They bring forth a specific ethos that, in many cases, people
experience on the path leading from calamity to redemption. This,

---

[19] These issues are frequently discussed in the studies of modern anthropologists and have only recently begun to be integrated in the study of the monotheistic religions. For the sake of a general orientation I refer the reader to the study
by Bruce Kapferer, *The Feast of the Sorcerer: Practices of Consciousness and Power*, The
University of Chicago Press: Chicago and London, 1997. See also, Don Handelman,
Models and Mirrors: Towards an Anthropology of Public Events, Cambridge 1990, pp.
191-233 (this chapter in Handelman's book is written in collaboration with Elihu
Katz). See, further, Bruce Kapferer, *A Celebration of Demons: Exorcism and the Aes-
thetics of Healing in Sri Lanka*, Berg Smithsonian Institution Press: Washington, 1991;
Steven M. Friedson, *Dancing Prophets: Musical experience in Tumbuka Healing*, Uni-
versity of Chicago Press: Chicago and London, 1996. See, further, Lawrence E.
Sullivan, *Ichanchu's Drum: An Orientation to Meaning in South American Religions*,
Macmillan Publishing Company: New York, 1988. See also the next footnote.

in my view, is the essence of the stories about the heroic "Judges" in the Book of Judges. These stories were part of an ethos. The processes entailed by it reflected and enacted a pattern of divine intervention in the history of the people. The story told in Jud. 6: 1-10 is telling example of a pattern that shows the predominance of divine vengeance in those cases in which the Israelites did bad things (in Hebrew, *ha-rʿa*). In some cases (e.g., Jud. 3: 7) that evil is identified with idol worshipping. In this respect, a general ethos-like code of values, as discussed in the previous chapter, prevailed regulating the vicissitudes of historical events. We may put this the other way around, namely, that the belief in the existence of divine or charismatic beings calls forth the shaping of stories that function as myths. In such cases, myth is the modus in which lifestyles receive pivotal importance in the shaping, regulating, and preserving the life of the people.

We should be reminded, though, that not every myth is a story about gods. In seeking ways of establishing the case for the omnipresence of myth, even in areas of life that are not necessarily religious, modern anthropology highlights unique aspects of ritual dimensions in human behaviour. Linking myth to ritual, as suggested here, brings the subject of myth closer to anthropological studies—not as an aboriginal curiosity, but as a central factor in human cognition and ways of expression. Since ritual, as we have seen, is not necessarily religious, the myth that is associated with it is also not necessarily religious.[20] These facts open new channels for the discussion of both—myth and ritual.

VII

Mircea Eliade noted several of the major characteristics of myth. He listed, among them: (1) Myth is found in the domain of the "holy" or "holiness;" (2) Myth tells about supernatural beings; (3) Myth is connected mainly with "creation" stories and tells of primordial events; (4) Myth characterises primitive societies; (5)

---

[20] It should be noted, though, that not every ritual is dependent upon myth. More than their secular counterparts, religious rituals tend to seek validation in establishing mythic connections. The resemblance between religious and secular rituals is discussed in Bruce Kapferer, *Legends of People, Myths of State: Violence, Intolerance, and Political Culture in Sri Lanka and Australia*, Smithsonian Institution Press: Washington and London, 1988.

Myth is used as a model story that contributes to the consolidation of certain kinds of behaviour.[21] Other scholars also discuss
myth from this angle, although they use slightly different modes
of characterisation. Myth is, thus, almost universally viewed as a
phenomenon belonging (a) to religion and (b) to the distant past.
Its normative status derives from the manner in which the society
that has been constituted by it handles its messages. It goes almost without saying that I share with Eliade the notion of the
paradigmatic status of myth. However, the connections of myth
with a distant past, a primitive society, and the realm of the holy
seem to me to be individual cases that do not necessarily typify
the cognitively universal nature of myth and its existential presence in human modes of expression, hence, in culture.

   The assumption that myth reflects general, rather than specifically religious, patterns of cognition comes close to the views of
Ernst Cassirer. Cassirer speaks of myth as one of the "symbolic
forms" which characterise human cognition. "Symbolic forms,"
such as language and myth, organise the human experience in
structured—that is, systemically accountable—patterns. These
patterns imaginatively reflect the kaleidoscopic configurations of
the diverse activities of the human mind. Symbolic forms shape
human experience as events and notions that are shared by being communicated. Every symbolic form has its own intrinsic rules
as well as its ideational and practical modes of structuring. But
we should note that Cassirer takes a unique position vis-à-vis ritual.
He views ritual as functional in the creation of myth. In other
words, he points in the opposite direction from the one presented
here.[22] Furthermore, since we view myth as a phenomenon that
is not necessarily connected to the realm of the religious, there is
no need to see it functioning, as Eliade argues, in the context of
the holy. Of course, religion operates through modes of behaviour
that take on specific configurations as rituals. But religion has no
special rights or claims on rituals. The same is true for myth.

   We can give one extreme example. Religious faith is usually
viewed as the cradle in which unquestioning credulity develops.

---

   [21] See Mircea Eliade, *Myth and Reality*, New York 1963, pp. 18-19. The characteristics are enumerated, here, in a different order to that of Eliade.
   [22] For a brief summary of Cassirer's view on ritual and myth, see E. Cassirer,
The Myth of the State, Doubleday: Garden City, 1955.

Initially, faith in God hardly leaves space for what discursive, or logical, thinking can accomplish for the people concerned. However, from an academic standpoint, one can relate to faith in God as to any other type of human faith. It is created where the accepted discernment between the subjective and the objective has disappeared to create a new intermediate realm of cognition. In this realm, cross-fertilisation between the two modes of consciousness cultivates the rich soil upon which the mythopoetic imagination develops. In as much as the imagination bears an influence on human behaviour, its epistemological validity cannot be called into question. The reality of the ritual act projects validity onto modes of cognition that generate rituals. Viewing the imaginative world of myth in these terms represents, to my mind, a crucial stage in assessing the epistemological status of both myth and ritual. Faith helps to shape the subjective in the form of the objective. Rituals are the behavioural platforms upon which this process takes place. Practically-speaking, as also from a psychological point of view, there is no substantial difference between one kind of faith and another, including religious faith. Preferably, in the eyes of the believer who seeks a mode of rationality, faith requires some kind of objective proof or formulation. However, if one follows D.W. Winnicott, the notions of transitional realities and phenomena suggest an intrinsically maintained ontological existence. Hence, they do not require proof, in the ordinary sense of the term.[23]

From our point of view, rituals constitute a self-sustained and self-sustaining system the efficacy of which does not require proof. Rituals create their own experiential edifice, which is efficiently structured to meet targeted aims. An inner coherency connects the situation that gives rise to the ritual practice, the way in which the specific ritual is practised, and the transformed condition that

---

[23] See Winnicott, *Through Paediatrics to Psycho-Analysis*, pp. 229-242. It is worth quoting a few more sentences from Winnicott's discussion of the subject. One of them says: "From birth, therefore, the human being is concerned with the problem of the relationship between what is objectively perceived and what is subjectively conceived of . . . The intermediate area to which I am referring is the area that is allowed... between primary creativity and objective perception based on reality testing" (p. 239). We should note that Winnicott is discussing the process of the children's development. The concepts, presented by him, seem to me applicable to the characterisation of the special transitional stage in which, in my view, myth is shaped.

is shaped by this practice. Since these links are not subject to
rational causality, their existence is assumed. Faith, rather than
empirical testing, applies in their case. To make my point clear,
I shall give one example. It refers to the Laws of Purity, as developed within the Judaic framework.[24]

These laws unfold in the inter-relationship between several
factors: (1) the physical universe in which and through which
impurity and purity come into play; (2) the sanctuary/Temple that
endows the notions at hand with an overall sense of relevance;
(3) the mind/body relationship that is uniquely activated in the
various ritual processes that cause change from a state of impurity to purity. In some respects, the social factor is also involved.
The links between these factors are apodictically assumed in the
texts that prescribe them, but nothing proves their prevalence and
existence. Rituals are effective in, and for, the social structure that
considers them as existentially constitutive factors.

The decrees of the Pentateuch and the *Mishnah* that pronounce
bodily liquid excretions (menstrual blood, semen, saliva) as imparting impurity are a good example. There are other liquids (seven
is their total number) that can also be instrumental in imparting
impurity to edibles. Water is the only liquid that imparts impurity and that is also the main purifying substance and agent. To
understand what purity means, and what its laws are about, one
has to accept certain presuppositions, which concern the ontological
definition of purity. Since the publication of Mary Douglas' work,
the subject of purity has received great attention.[25] Recently, her

---

[24] I am fully aware of the diversity of the materials at hand. Various notions of
purity prevail in Scripture, and this diversity has undergone substantial changes in
rabbinic literature. Thus, any discussion of the subject has to take into account
substantial thematic and temporal nuances. It is significant, in this respect, that
the *Mishnah* Tractate that takes up the subject is *Tahorot* ("Purities"). The plural
form is also preserved in *Miqvaot* ("ritual baths") and in *Ohalot* ("defiling tents").

[25] See especially, Mary Douglas, *Purity and Danger: An analysis of the Concepts of
Pollution and Taboo*, Ark Paperbacks: London and New York, 1966. We need not
summarise the essence of this book here. We can say, though, that Mary Douglas
uses categories that instead of bringing us closer to the understanding of the subject, place us at a point of utter disorientation. I direct my criticism at the manner in which Douglas mixes anthropological categories and notions with religious,
or theological, ones. The reader must by now be aware that the present book
consistently avoids using terms of reference that crystallise in a religious theology.
Furthermore, Douglas brings in notions that were prevalent in the study of regional religion(s) in Africa. Taboo is one of them. The extent to which these notions are directly applicable to the study of the religion in the Book of Leviticus is

work has come under criticism, though from points of view not directly connected to the present discussion.[26] Consequently, she has made a few revisions to her theory, which now focuses on the transmission (which she calls "contagion") of impurity rather than on its functional essence.[27] I agree with Douglas that the discussion of purity/impurity, in the context of ritual and ritual theory, must involve the notion of danger. Whether other categories mentioned in her work—such as uncleanness, defilement, and pollution—are conducive to a correct assessment of the subject is a question of a different order.

Although purity is often connected to notions of defilement, uncleanness, abomination, and contagion, I propose treating it as a category in its own right. In many respects, impurity is caused, not by something that is physically dirty, but by something that is *declared as having the potentials of incurring impurity; that is, impurity entails a serious disturbance in the structural integrity and coherence of the "cosmos" which people hold as sustaining and enhancing vital life processes.* In this sense, the notion of "contagion" as used by Mary Douglas does not create a suggestive analogy to the act of imparting

---

still an open question. I believe that what Mary Douglas writes encourages confusion rather than clarity. See also the reference in the next footnote. Recently Mary Douglas returned to the subject of purity in the book of Leviticus. See Mary Douglas, *Leviticus as Literature*, Oxford University Press: Oxford, 1999. If I read the book correctly, it tries to establish patterns that connect religious notions and religious structures—legal and physical alike. However, the contribution of the book to the understanding of myth (and ritual), as attempted in the present chapter, is rather limited.

[26] See, for instance, John F.A. Sawyer (ed.), *Reading Leviticus: A Conversation with Mary Douglas*, Sheffield Academic Press: Sheffield, 1996. In a paper, "Sacred Contagion," published in this volume (pp.86-106), Douglas courageously admits that she was misled by wrong translations of Hebrew terms in her earlier studies on uncleanness and defilement in ancient Judaism: "I found I was wrong. The scholarly Hebrew translators were exonerated, and I was humbled" (p. 89).

[27] Mary Douglas views impurity in terms of contagion, that is, as a causal notion. However, as we are going to see, impurity cannot be exhaustedly defined as a theory of physical transmission that is usually, but not exclusively, based on the notion of proximity. We shall see that proximity is not the issue. Rather, as Mishnaic sources make clear, the mental factor of intentionality plays a major role in imparting or causing impurity. Sacred contagion directs separation rather than blame. This is not the place to engage in a full-scale discussion of Mary Douglas' new approach. However, I wish to make one further point. While Mary Douglas is concerned with the question of how uncleanness is imparted and what it does to those who impart it, my discussion focuses on the ontological essence of the rituals that impart or remove impurity.

impurity. Contagion is a physical process. Impurity is a matter of ritually categorising causal conditions and substances that incur something that, unlike in the case of contagion, remains to the end physically unnoticed. Impurity happens because of a certain legal or ritual position that states that impurity happens under certain conditions. Without the act of specifically stating the cases at hand in terms of a category-declaration, purity and impurity remain theoretical, or abstract, notions. Impurity is a specific condition. It enacts a specific category, which—*pace* Mary Douglas and others—is not translatable. It is a label that conveys a *sui generis* ontological status. In some cases, when referring in particular to the human body, a location, or a structure made for living in, it may be used as a condition that changes their existential status. This is quite different to physical contagion and pollution, to say nothing of physical danger.

To cut a long story short, I suggest viewing purity/impurity in the framework of category-formation, though in a somewhat different configuration from the one used by Jacob Neusner in the many studies he has published on the subject. Although categories function philosophically in the abstract, "category," as used here, is shaped in the intermediate personal realm discussed above, and what is even more important, it dictates certain modes of behaviour, conceived as rituals. That is to say, in the eyes doing them they are conceived indispensable to maintaining vital life processes. This last aspect is not dealt with in Neusner's work. This realm is as metaphysically real as it is imaginary. The fusion of the metaphysical real with imaginary happens in a mythopoetic world. Both purity and impurity have a strong ontological presence, in spite of the fact that, in most of the cases, everything that happens does so in a world that is fulfilled in its existence as a category. Every category creates its own story, that is, it tells people what they can expect to happen, when certain conditions are fulfilled.

Thus, when a person is defiled by blood, it is not the physically discernible symptom that counts but the attribution of a category related to a changed mode of existence. The fact that immersion in water is believed to remove impurity does not contradict this conclusion. In order for immersion in water to be ritually effective, it has to be effected according to special regulations, which include specifications for the quantity of the water, the manner in which the water is collected there, the type of water allowed, and the specific time when the immersion has taken place. Nothing is visible either before or after the immersion has taken place. Purity comes into effect again, when certain "categories"— that are ritually enacted—create the right conditions. Everything is, then, summarised in a narrative, the narrative in which the ritual unfolds as a decree or a report.

Most of the regulations or specifications, discussed here, refer to the ontological existence of the special cosmos in which impurity happens and rituals of purity become valid factors. This cosmos may be the one that evolves from or emanates out of the Temple. Without the Temple and the qualities of holiness which it diffuses, purity and impurity make no sense. Several of these laws of purity are observed to the present day. They primarily concern the impurity of menstruating women and the ritual baths they take. These laws are tied to the notion of Temple purity. The idea is that some laws of purity (for instance, that which forbids priests from approaching tombs) have to be observed, even without the existence of the Temple, in order to prevent the laws from undergoing a process of ritual oblivion. Mary Douglas is certainly right in demanding that the subject of purity and impurity should be freed from the rationalistic type of criticism levelled against it in intellectual and academic circles, but her reasons for making this demand are different to mine. In my view, the laws of purity and impurity are a living example of the extent to which mythic premises influence daily life.

I also wish to draw attention to the fact that both the creation of the habitable earth and the birth of human beings are linked to "wet substances." Similarly, the disturbance of the cosmic and microcosmic order, even its destruction (by flooding), is conceived as coming into effect in, and through, liquid substances, particularly water. A ritual rebirth, therefore, or the reconstitution of a previously disturbed order or stability (purity), also comes into effect through the purifying agency of water. Entering purifying waters, or a Baptism, falls in the same category. The process cleanses the body from impurity, but it does so at a ritual level that leaves no physically discernible traces and is, above all, unconnected to dirt. In a sense, it enacts the return to the immaculate embryonic-state and to the mimetic enactment of (re)birth.

To return to our initial point, without the acts of purification, the Temple and its wholesomeness remain functionally threatened and even disrupted. The Temple is notionally, and spatially, conceived as the centre of everything. In some sources, it represents the navel of the world.[28] Once this wholesomeness is threatened by something that represents a category of existential disorder, the integrating, constitutive, powers of this centre are critically threatened. All this belongs to a sphere of notions that is predominantly mythic. Finally, it should be noted that the Christian notion of the individualisation of the Temple (every Christian is a temple of God: 1 Cor. 3: 16) carries these notions into completely new realms.

VIII

We have reached a point at which a few detailed examples are pertinent. The ritual performed on Passover night (the "Seder") is the first we shall deal with.[29] In the national ethos, the Exodus from Egypt and everything that is connected with it, serves as the myth behind the Passover ritual. The ritual re-enacts historical memory, though it itself is also a self-sustained ritual that functions on its own performative premises. The "Seder" is one of the most interesting and richest rituals in Judaism. At the core of the Seder is a grand meal. The other parts consist of practices and narratives that recount past events and explaining their relevance to the Passover rituals. Thus, these stories represent mythic materials. The process of recounting them (the technical term in Hebrew is: *Haggadah*,[30] to be distinguished from *Aggadah*, literary Midrash) has a ritual function. According to Halakhic perception, its aim is to instruct the young generation about the great events of biblical times and also to encourage the participants to think of the significance of the Passover events. In other words, the ritual is a multi-layered cultic enactment of historical memory.

I would like to remind the reader that the concept of "myth"

---

[28] See Shemaryahu Talmon, *Literary Studies in the Hebrew Bible: Form and Content*, Jerusalem and Leiden: The Magnes Press and E. J. Brill, 1993, pp. 50-75: "The 'Navel of the Earth' and the Comparative Method."

[29] The reader is referred to the last chapter of this book where the Lord's Supper is discussed in the context of Christian aspects.

[30] The term *Haggadah* also serves as the name of the ritual booklet whose texts are recited on this particular night.

does not mean that the relevant event has no historic reality and, by the same token, it does not say that the event is historically verifiable. The term "myth" indicates that a constitutive narrative has a connection to a particular ritual. The issue of import, here, is the constitutively existential function of rituals and their contribution to life-saving and life-enhancing processes. Remembering the miracles of the past has exactly this function in the life of religious people. Even if a story seems to have ostensibly fictional qualities, the fact that it functions as a myth establishes it as a reality that can neither be eradicated from, nor ignored in, the memory of the people. In short, ritual reflects back on mythic realities as historically valid data.

Memory plays a vital role in establishing the necessary links between myth and ritual. In our instance, the biblical narrator himself initially provided the context that established the binding factor related to the Exodus, with all its ritual overtones. By constructing a ritual event as part of a historical event (the sacrifice of the Passover sheep/lamb in Egypt), and, then, by telling the reader that this event must be re-enacted in the future (initially, not at specific times), the writer determines the mythic function of his narrative. This happens on two complementary levels: the historical event itself and its ritual re-enactment on any future occasion. The reading of the Haggadah, as is done on the Eve of Passover, aims to raise questions. The person in charge—usually the head of the family—recites the Haggadah and thus becomes the leader of a ritual event that commemorates the historical event (in Egypt) of biblical times. The Seder also commemorates the ritual conditions prevailing in the time of the Temple, when this event was ritually enacted in the form of special sacrificial events described in Tractate *Pesachim* of the Mishnah. In the last two chapters of this book, dealing, respectively, with *Leviticus* 16 and the "Lord's Supper," we shall discuss at length the essence of sacrificial acts in the context of ritual theory.

In essence, the principle involved here is one of imitation. The things that are done during the "Seder" night uniquely activate the reality of the rituals that were done in the past. The framework is related to the two commemorative levels discussed above. We shall return to this point later on. Retrospectively viewed, the biblical writer(s) provided Jews, and then Christians, with everything they needed to make the events, connected with Passover, a constitutive factor in their respective religions. The manner in which the Exodus from Egypt is presented in Scripture makes clear—right from the first moment—that it aims at being ritually re-enacted in the future.[31] Thus, for all practical purposes, the initial Passover celebration in Egypt, as narrated in the Book of Exodus, and its following annual commemoration in various ritual forms, were conceptually interwoven from the outset.[32] In this respect, Christianity also constitutes a ritual re-enactment of the myth of the Passover meal, whether the one in Egypt or the one in Jerusalem (the Last Supper).

The annually re-enacted ritual in the form the *Passover Haggadah* emphasises, in its verbal mode, the fact that "The Lord did this for me when I came out of Egypt" and "In every generation every [Jewish] person must see himself as if he himself has come out of Egypt." The commemorative function of these expressions is ritually significant. The reader should understand, by now, what I mean when I say that participating in the Haggadah-ritual signifies entrance into a redemptive cosmos. This is explicitly expressed in the following statements, taken from the Passover Haggadah: "In every generation we are at risk of perishing; but the Holy One, Blessed be He, saves us from their hand;" "Not only did the Holy One, Blessed be He, redeem our Fathers, but even us He redeemed along with them;" and finally, "Blessed art Thou Lord, Our God King of the Universe, who redeemed us and redeemed our Fathers from Egypt, and has brought us to this night to eat unleavened bread and bitter herbs. Thou, Lord our God and God of our Fathers, hast brought us to this Festival and to other Festivals . . . happy in the building of Thy city and rejoicing in Thy work . . . and we shall give thanks to Thee for redeeming us. . ." Every word in these sentences proclaims the

---

[31] Reference to the Exodus is repeated throughout the Pentateuch and, for that matter, in many references to the Sabbath. This becomes clear when the text of the Ten Commandments in the Book of Deuteronomy is compared to that of the Book of Exodus. It is interesting to note that in the Ten Commandments of the Book of Exodus, ch. 20 of all places, the creation motif, rather than the Exodus, is highlighted as the mythic reason for the Sabbath.

[32] A similar connection is created in the text which recounts the receiving of the Law, in the Book of Deuteronomy. The text there is interesting: "Not with our ancestors did the Lord make this covenant, but with us, who are all of us here alive today" (Deut. 5: 3). It is to be noted that the story of the receiving of the Law, in the Book of Exodus, presents a different literary tradition that does not include a reference to the forefathers.

mythic axis leading from the Exodus to Redemption. The ritual re-enactment expresses this concretely in what can be referred to as a trans-subjective reality.

The Passover ritual compresses every aspect of the dimension of time—past, present, and future—into a linearly developing framework. The events of the past and the future are quintessentially entwined within the lives of those participating in the ritual. For the people who take part in it, this compression of time comes to life in the Passover ritual. Myth creates the ambience that facilitates, in a compressed timeframe, a movement that completes itself within the axis of ritual practice. The Seder re-enacts, in a ritualised mode, the fullness of the events to which the respective rituals refer. In this instance, the axis is a transformative one. It enables movement from slavery to redemption, from Egypt to the desert (and then to the Land of Canaan), from destruction to rebuilding, from exile to the ingathering of the people. *Living through* multiple planes of existence, temporal and spatial, can be accomplished only in a framework of a ritual act. In the life of a single person or community, myth and ritual open possibilities of experiencing life that cannot be experienced otherwise. The "there" and "then" can become the "here" and "now." Thus, ritual compresses complex reality (the information about which is told in the myth) into a dynamically liveable experience. It should be noted that, in spite of the fact that the language that is used in the Passover ritual can easily translate into a symbolic one, I—as a matter of principle—view the life processes that are created in and through rituals as real ones.

In this respect, rituals mimetically enact, for those doing them, every mode of reality that people wish to live through. Earlier in this book, I have referred several times to the mimetic dimension of rituals. We have reached a point, though, at which a more detailed explanation is required. Our comments should be viewed against the background of the idea, repeatedly voiced in previous pages, that rituals are not symbolic expressions of ideas and beliefs. What do I mean, then, when saying that rituals are mimetic, and not symbolic, representations? Mimetic representation, here, refers to an event that is condensed into a time span, or space, that achieves complete realisation in the process, not of being repeated, but of being enacted as a ritual. There is no self-explanatory and structural connection between the event, the myth, and, ultimately, the corresponding ritual(s). Thus, everything done in the course of the Passover Seder is made to belong and fit into a compressed form of reality, in which all the components mentioned above—from the Exodus to the future redemption—become a liveable reality. This liveable reality does not refer back to a past event in terms of its symbolic re-presentation. Instead, it operates on a more direct level, that of a re-enactment. We refer to it, here, as a mimetic act. Thus, the Seder enacts—on a ritual plane—the full scope of people's memory of the past and their hopes for the future. *In nuce*, the act of commemoration is consummated in ritually referring to the constitutive myth of the Exodus. Thus, the myth enacts the ritual, and the ritual consolidates the myth. In many respects, myth is the opposite of history. History establishes the "pastness" of an event, while the ritual connection to myth opens ever-recurring possibilities for the event to become a concrete reality in an ongoing present.

As indicated, following the destruction of the Temple, another layer of "memory" was added. It concerned the memory of the altar and the Passover sacrifice in the Temple (there are no records of the Pessach ritual being done in the sanctuary; see 2 Kings 23: 22 = 2 Chron. 35: 18). This layer marks the ever-increasing density of commemorative events that relate to the Egypt-Passover. "A memorial of the Temple [Passover] as done by Hillel. This is what Hillel used to recite, when the Temple was still existing." However, the text of the Haggadah, and particularly the illuminated manuscripts of the Passover Haggadah, reflect memories of events that happened during the middle ages. Those eager to update their relatedness to the Haggadah, use new editions with texts and pictures. Countless publications of the Haggadah, printed even in secular kibbutzim in Israel, have made the Haggadah a ritual centrepiece of Jewish memory.[33] For our purposes, it does not really matter whether Hillel did it this way or the other. The narrative about Hillel is of interest to us, because it constitutes an event that, according to our way of understanding, embodies

---

[33] See, in this connection, Yosef Hayim Yerushalmi, *Zakhor: Jewish History and Jewish Memory*, University of Washington: Seattle and London, 1982. I believe it is fair to say that Yerushalmi underrates the role of myth and ritual in preserving and activating memory. He is more concerned with the role historians, and historiography, have in preserving and shaping memory. We shall return to this issue at the end of the present chapter.

mythic information. It is narrated for ritually constitutive purposes. It purports to enhance a certain layer of the tradition, which crystallises in a certain ritual and its various modes of enactment.

An additional aspect of the myth-ritual relationship needs to be mentioned here. Among other things, the Seder night demonstrates the extent to which ritual status that is accorded to the repetition of the mythic narrative can be stretched to become a live event in its own right.[34] The retelling of the story creates a ritual dynamic that transforms everything that is related to this night. To begin with, the Seder night functions on the level of memorisation. Here, memorisation functions to preserve the actuality of the event as a live memory-factor in the history of the people. Then, the interdependence of ritual and myth creates the dynamics that function mutually effectively for the preservation of both ritual and myth. There is also an additional need, namely, to preserve the up-to-date vitality of the ritual. We have already noted that doing rituals at fixed times reflects a repetitive pattern and prevents their entropy, their cultural extinction. In the type of live ritual tradition that sustains the Seder night, there is never a state of inert relationship to the myth and its ritual. In this respect, a secular approach that purports the irrelevance of the whole event amounts to cultural denial. In fact, it relegates the myth into the domain of mythology. I say this in order to stress what is involved: the axis that makes myth the major active component in sustaining tradition in culture. Since myths and rituals are viewed, in this book, on a larger phenomenological scale than the purely religious one, my comment has no hidden agenda on a theological level.

Those who have reflected on the relationship between myth and history must be aware of the fact that a mythic story does not necessarily replicate an historical verisimilitude. At the same time, myth is not false, deceptive or fraudulent. Its presence in human culture is of relevance to the historian, like any other cultural phenomenon. In as much as people live on myths, historians have to deal with these facts. The ontological question of

---

[34] As we saw, this part of the ritual relates to earlier ritual references, namely, those done in the Temple. One can discern three stages here: the story of the Exodus from Egypt, the ritual of the Temple that relates to it, and finally the Haggadah of the Seder night that relates to the first and the latter. Past, present, and future collapse into a single ritual act.

what is a fact transcends the notion of verisimilitude, or historical verifiability. Just as the alleged dichotomy of "science and
myth" has long lost its conflictual character, so, in my view, has
the alleged dichotomy of "myth and history." In this respect, the
smashing of scholarly arguments as "mythic idols" is either a matter
of self-deception or the peak of cultural iconoclasm. The truth of
myth is its ongoing presence in human cognition, and its actuality is its ritual performance. We have already noted that, when
viewed from the perspective of ritual studies, the occurrence of
the event does not require "proof," nor does it need to come under
the scrutiny of the "historical archaeologist." Historiography, historical realism and rationality, have limited relevance in this area
of human activity.[35] Thus, the dependence of an event on the factor
of the "miraculous"—that is to say, the emphasis given to the supernatural dimension in the story—only tells us that the ritual to
which it is connected is a religious one. It does not add anything
to whether it is truth or untruth. Finally, rituals widen the imaginative spectrum through which mythic dimensions become present.
This explains the predominance of myth in religions. Making the
meta-natural present and realising its presence takes place in modes
of cognition that move between the subjective and objective realms.
Religious myths happen in trans-subjective and trans-objective
realms.

IX

More must be said, at this point, on myth in the context of the
ongoing debate that currently occupies biblical scholars and historians of the biblical period. For a long time, scholars used to
view the beginnings of the religion of ancient Israel as contem-
poraneous with the inception of the monarchy. According to experts on the subject, literacy also emerged in ancient Israel at that
time. Roughly speaking, the early centuries of the last millenni-

---

[35] In recent years, the historical verisimilitude of the scriptural accounts of the
history of ancient Israel until the days of David and Solomon has come under
severe questioning. See, lately, Israel Finkelstein and Neil Asher Silberman, *The
Bible Unearthed: Archaeology's New Vision of Ancient Israel and the Origin of Its Sacred
Texts*, The Free Press; New York, 2001. As indicated, I shall discuss the relationship between myth and history in the last sections of this chapter.

um BCE were viewed by scholars as the beginnings of the insti-tutionalized religion of ancient Israel. More precisely, scholars have told us, this was the time of David and Solomon. Thus, monar-chy, writing, and institutionalised religion were viewed as cultur-ally intertwined. This picture made cultural sense to many scholars. The development of a culture in which literacy was a dominant feature opened the door to the consolidation of a canon of writ-ings that ultimately became Scripture.[36] Scripture, we should re-member, functioned as one of the major factors in fixing the normative status of myths and rituals. The biblical narratives up to the monarchic period—including the constitutive narratives about the Patriarchs, the Exodus, and the conquest of the Land—were viewed, by scholars, as information that could be verified as history, only when scholarly concessions were made.[37] I hope that the present discussion will create the possibility of treating these materials as culturally relevant and having constitutive func-tions, without dealing with the question of their historical truth or untruth.

Indeed, according to the approach adopted here, we can say that, even when historical criticism shakes the verisimilitude of certain biblical narratives, their cultural validity in Jewish tradi-tion is not necessarily shaken. To put it bluntly, culture is shaped

---

[36] On this issue, see the discussion of Nadav Naaman, "The Historiography, Formation of the Collective Memory and the Creation of Historic Consciousness of the People of Israel at the End of the First Temple Period" [in Hebrew], *Zion*, 60 (1995) pp. 449-472.

[37] The radical opinion of those who became known as the "minimalists" (the Copenhagen Group) is well known. They seek to eradicate the historical dimen-sion of the story of David and Solomon. They consider the biblical stories up to, and even after the days of David and Solomon, as a collection of "myths." The first quotation marks indicate that their use of the term myth is completely differ-ent to the one I am trying to establish here. They view myth as a literary collec-tion that does not have the status of historical data. Part of the argument regarding these subjects takes place today in a clandestine manner on the Internet. For the sake of a balanced appraisal of the scholarly situation on this issue, I refer the reader to James S. Strange, "Reading Archaeological and Literary Evidence," in: Jacob Neusner (ed.), *Religion and the Political Order: Politics in Classical and Contempo-rary Christianity, Islam, and Judaism*, Scholars Press: Atlanta, 1996, pp. 49-58. A clarification of the positions on these issues can be found in an extensive article in *Biblical Archaeology Review* 23 (4) (July-August, 1997); 24 (2) (March-April 1998). There is still another dimension to the issue. It concerns the debate over the finds, especially the city gates, at Hazor, Megiddo and Gezer. The question is, whether these gates really represent the architecture of the early kingdom (the period of Solomon) or that of approximately one century later?

by myth more than it is shaped by what historians think is objective judgement. Since this book deals with major factors that shape culture, my position in these matters is self-evident. The Pre-Sinaitic ethos of ancient Israel contains many of the seeds from which the basic forms of religious behaviour of later times grew. As we have seen (in the previous chapter), the marked preference for sheep herding, as the major economic system, is a factor that deserves close attention. This is particularly so, since the nomadic ethos connected with sheep herding highlighted the opposite ethos, the one which led from agriculture to urbanisation, and ultimately to the establishment of the monarchy. One also finds residues of shepherding components in the monarchical ethos (King David began his life as the shepherd of his father's flock and the Christian messiah is designated the Lamb of God). In the sanctuary/ Temple, God persists in his preference for animal sacrifices. God's rejection of the fruit of the earth, which Cain offered, is not concluded at this point. It underwent an interesting metamorphosis. God ordained that tithing the growth of the land is essential to the sustenance of his priestly and Levite servants on earth. The first fruits of the annual growth were brought to the Temple (*Deut.* 26). The unique prayers that were said on those occasions, as the relevant passages indicate, indicated that the fruits of the earth were now sacrificially acceptable.

Another example is the belief in the heavenly origin of the written and the oral Torah. In the eyes of the faithful, this is an undisputed historical fact. However, it represents only a hermeneutic stance. On a literary level, this faith is formulated in a number of ways: "Two kinds of Torah were given to Israel, one in writing and the other in oral mode;" "This is to say that the Torah was given—with all its various kinds of explicatory details— by Moses at Sinai;" "As all the laws of the *Shemitah* year were specified at Sinai, so were the rest of the rulings of the Torah said from Sinai."[38] Many see, in these statements, major theological suppositions with regard to the religion of Israel. From a mythic perspective, the fact that only the parts regarding the written Torah are textually evidenced in Scripture should cause no problem. Scripture itself does not mention any additional code of laws that accompanied the one which received the status of the Written

---

[38] All these quotes come from Midrash *Sifra* (on *Leviticus*), section "*Behar Sinai.*"

Torah and was allegedly given to Moses on Mount Sinai. Constitutive facts have an intrinsic power, whether conceived as myth or as historical reality. Indeed, myth often has a more imposing status than what people consider to be "facts". To people who seek valid relational stances to their existential environment, myths can provide what they seek. Thus, for those whose ability to differentiate between myth and history is impaired, Scripture indeed provides a solid core of information. There is no measuring scale that can absolutely differentiate myth from historical verisimilitude. It is all in the eyes of the beholder. In short, the materials contained in Scripture may function on two complementary levels. For some myth is untruth, for others it is history. For us, here, the distinction has no relevance.

In accordance with the general programme of this book, a new perception suggests itself with regard to the study of Midrashic Aggadah. Aggadic information is usually treated as creative hermeneutics. Yet it often inserts itself in the midst of the scriptural text in a manner that amplifies its mythic resonance. Since Midrash has absolute control over the meaning of Scripture, its mythic dimension, when present, also controls the myth of Scripture. In accepting the Aggadic notion of an Oral Torah that, in many respects, takes over the status of the Written Torah, a mythic fact is created.[39] Those who wish to sustain their belief in the reality of what rituals can accomplish for them will maintain no difference between the Written and the Oral Torah, or between historical reality and mythic reality. For these people, both parts of the Torah have equal status. Determining the authoritative text for the doing of rituals involves a cognitive approach, which is applied to each case. The Qaraites, for instance, consider the Written Torah as the ultimate text for the doing of ritual, while the "rabbis" adhere to the Oral Torah. Each group has its own myth, which ultimately crystallised as theology.

In a line of argumentation that follows Hans Gadamer, facticity is not by necessity dependent on empirical knowledge, that is, on

---

[39] The Oral Law declares itself to be the normative interpretation of the "Written Torah," but it is no more than an interpretative innovation. However, the Oral Law requires the written text. On this matter see, among other studies, David Weiss Halivni, *Midrash, Mishnah and Gemara: The Jewish Predilection for Justified Law*, Harvard University Press: Cambridge (Mass.) & London 1986; *Idem.*, *Derash & Peshat: Plain and Applied Meaning in Rabbinic Exegesis*, New York & Oxford, 1991.

objectively verifiable data. From an epistemological point of view, the ontology of the fact finds its place in the consciousness that relates to it. In this respect, facticity is also independent of any particular text. The text that matters may be that which exists in the mind of the person who imagines its existence. He makes it work for the occasion on which it is used. Since the user is in full command of the hermeneutic situation, he may be the one who adds the mythic dimension to a narrative that he considers worth having a ritual status. Thus, in connection to ritual, even historicity is likely to be modelled in and by myth. To repeat, myth rids us of the need to ask whether this, or that, is historically true.

This line of argumentation should not be taken as establishing the ultimate provenance of myth over history. Myth is a cognitive stance. In many ways, it is one of the most powerful forms of cognition and expression. Since it has no rules to abide by and no limits to observe, it is both omnipotent and omnipresent. Myth can thus be para-scientific and para-philosophical. It creates no conflict with either science or philosophy. It is a way of relating to a reality that exists in its own right. Furthermore, it is a potent tool in making this reality—extraordinary as it may be—existentially present.

X

The link created between myth and ritual is often maintained in an interpretative stance. In this connection, one should mention the name of Paul Ricoeur. He, more than other scholars in this field, contributed to the understanding of the connection between myth and human behaviour. His work, however, takes a hermeneutic path in which symbolism has a major role. In accord with the present discussion, I will refer to this link in terms of a "midrashic condition."[40] A midrashic condition makes the interpretative statement into a fact that shapes the reality of the text to which the interpretation relates. Philosophical interpretation also

---

[40] See Ithamar Gruenwald, "Midrash and the 'Midrashic Condition': Preliminary Considerations," in Michael Fishbane (ed.), *The Midrashic Imagination: Jewish Exegesis, Thought, and History*, SUNY Press: Albany, 1993, pp. 6-22. In this context, it is worthwhile to refer the reader to the various essays published in Eric Hobsbawm & Terence Ranger (eds.), *The Invention of Tradition*, Cambridge 1983, mentioned earlier in this book.

belongs to this domain. However, one of the goals of philosophical interpretation is often thought to be the removal of the basic mythic configuration of a given text. *Prima facie*, it is likely to place the story in a "midrashic condition" that has no connection to a particular ritual. Nonetheless, as we shall immediately see, even a philosophical interpretation can have an important function in establishing a mythic dimension. This happens, when philosophical premises connect the text to a particular ritual.

As noted above, Maimonides continued a line of philosophical interpretation that began with Philo. This line of interpretation argued that there are latent philosophical agenda in the biblical story, which require special deciphering and assessment. When does such an interpretation acquire, as argued above, a mythic status? It does so, when it attaches a non-negotiable element of truth to the philosophical interpretation of Scripture. In *The Guide for the Perplexed*, Maimonides advocates the view that the ultimate purpose of all philosophical activity is political. This view is succinctly maintained at the very end of the book (Third Part, Ch. 54),[41] where Maimonides writes that this philosophical activity reaches its peak in the maintenance of "steadfast love, justice and righteousness in the Land (Jer. 9: 23)." The models for this form of behaviour can be found in every part of Scripture. According to Maimonides, this political aim constitutes the essence of the philosophical discourse, which is latent in Scripture. Exegetically speaking, it is revealed with the sophisticated tools of interpretation that philosophy offers. In principle, it does not necessarily extract the mythic substructure from the biblical materials. It should be noted that I use the word "myth" here, in a different sense to that which Maimonides would have used. Maimonides takes a philosophical approach to myth: He argues that scriptural stories that do not fit his (= any) philosophical views can be accounted for only when explained as using a type of language that is suited to philosophically uneducated people, mostly, as he puts it, to women and children. However, one point needs to be mentioned here. When a philosophical interpretation is con-

---

[41] Various opinions have been expressed of late concerning the status of Chapter 54 in the philosophy of Maimonides. For our purposes, there is no need to inquire into this issue. See Shlomo Pines, "The Philosophical Purport of Maimonides' Works and the Purport of *The Guide for the Perplexed*", in: *Studies in the History of Jewish Thought*, The Magnes Press: Jerusalem, 1997, pp. 463-476.

nected to a ritual, it creates the same kind of linkage that constitutes the subject of this chapter. In other words, a tendentious philosophical interpretation, like that of Maimonides, that is connected to a ritual is likely to take on a mythic configuration. In this respect, any interpretation that is annexed to the ritual act is likely to function like any mythic story that is positioned in relation to the same or any other ritual. Thus, to claim that a certain interpretation is the "absolute truth" does not, in principle, change its ultimate function as the myth that goes before the ritual. There is no functional difference between a philosophical and a mythic interpretation. In both cases, the explanatory truth has the same function; the difference lies not in the explanatory essence but in the contents and the way it is expressed.

We have described above the notion of the "midrashic condition." In many respects, any specific myth may be viewed as the midrashic condition of a particular ritual. Establishing a "midrashic condition" means that, an interpretation desires to achieve a status of binding relevance. Relevance is understood as fixing the institutionalised mode of ideas and rituals. Once a myth becomes relevant to a particular ritual, it is exempted from the need to prove its bearing on historical verisimilitude. Thus, when we refer, for instance, to the story of the reception of the Torah on Mount Sinai as a myth, we mean that the story is a functional factor in the ritual history of ancient Israel. It says nothing about the "archaeological," or material, truth of the story. On the other hand, though, it does not say that we have any information that can disqualify its historical verisimilitude.

The space that is created for the mythic dimension to evolve and remain is supposed to do the same for the rituals in question. This space does not necessarily emerge directly out of a specific text; it can also emerge out of a hermeneutic stance or an ideational presupposition.[42] Furthermore, if a particular text

---

[42] Naturally, there are interpretative dimensions within Scripture itself. The most extensive discussion of this issue is found in Michael Fishbane, *Biblical Interpretation in Ancient Israel*, Clarendon Press: Oxford 1985. Recently, Professor Fishbane has studied the subject of Mythopoesis in Midrashic literature. If I understand the essence of Fishbane's discussions correctly, his primary preoccupation is with the way that mythic foundations are created in Midrash and how mythopoesis operates in serving the midrashic interpretation of Scripture. Fishbane's approach differs from that taken here. See Michael Fishbane, "'The Holy One Sits and Roars':

is not originally conceived in a ritual context, it may be viewed as such later on. Scripture says, "You shall eat your fill and bless the Lord your God for the good land that he has given you."[43] These words wish to institutionalise natural expressions of gratefulness. Nothing is said how this should be done. With time, though, the verse was retrospectively viewed as the basis of a decree of ritually binding status, which later covered all the ritual blessings prescribed in Tractate *Berakhot* (= "Blessings") in the Mishnah, and elsewhere.

It may be argued that carrying out the commandments in the mode of the "Oral Law" is a ritual enactment of the principle of the "midrashic condition."[44] One may even say that doing the ritual according to the "rabbinic mode" retrospectively determines the interpretative reality into which Scripture is forced to enter. This reality bears an essential similarity to myth. Its aim is to account for the doing of all rituals. In a very general sense, its assumptions epitomise the structure and status of the rabbinic programme. In this case, the myth is forged in the interpretative reality that develops from the all inclusive order to follow the legal advice of "the Levitical priests and the judge who is in office in those days" (Deut. 17: 9). Thus, myth and ritual create together an exclusive interpretative reality, which emerges out of the unique relationship that binds them together.

I have suggested, above, that there is a mythic construct in the legal reality created by the doctrine of the dual Torah. For orthodox observant Jews, this is a commonplace assumption, but, in scholarly eyes, the cognitive structure of this belief is of great interest. The historicity of the giving of the Torah at Sinai is believed to arise from Scripture itself. However, this fact was not known, in the cognitive sense of knowing, by those who had another version of the history of ancient Israel. There were indeed people who were, either unfamiliar with the story or, for one reason or another, consciously passed it over as if non-existent. Thus, for example, one can find Psalms that tell of the won-

---

Mythopoesis and the Midrashic Imagination," *Journal of Jewish Thought & Philosophy*, Vol. 1 (1991), pp. 1-21.

[43] See Deut. 8: 10. Deut. 11: 15, however, omits the "blessing."

[44] See Ithamar Gruenwald, "The Midrashic Condition: From the Derashot of the Sages to the Derashot of the Qabbalists" [in Hebrew], *Jerusalem Studies in Jewish Thought*, Vol. 8 (1989), pp. 255-298.

drous acts of God when liberating Israel from Egypt, without even
mentioning the Sinai revelation. This cannot be attributed to
oversight or accidence. It is repeated in at least three instances:
(1) "A *Maskil* of Asaph" (Psalm 78) declares: "I will open my mouth
in a parable; I will utter dark sayings from of old, things that we
have heard and known, that our ancestors have told us." In what
follows, one finds many familiar details, but the giving of the Torah
is not included in the poetic account. (2) The Psalmist (Psalm 105)
asks: "Remember the wondrous works He has done, His miracles,
and the judgements of His mouth." The ensuing poetic narrative
mentions the history of the Israelites in detail. It is instructive on
two counts—what it includes and what it excludes. To our great
surprise, the giving of the Torah is, once again, omitted from the
story. (3) The famous litany (chapter 136): " . . . for his steadfast
grace endures forever") is another remarkable example of the literary omission of the reception of the Torah. Thus, at least three
psalms, and perhaps another one (Psalm 68), refer to the Exodus
history with no explicit reference to the giving of the Torah on
Mount Sinai.

If the giving of the Torah was as foundational an event in the
history of ancient Israel as it is almost universally assumed to be,
it is striking to find that it is omitted in these Psalms. The omission of the event in the poetic narrative surely has a reason. I would
therefore suggest a somewhat paradoxical explanation. The omission in one set of texts creates an essential distinction between
those events that are mentioned and the one event that is not.
There is no official history that has to be told by everybody and
at all times. History was what people thought and told it was. In
the eyes of certain people, then, the Sinai theophany was a unique,
sui generis, event, not to be mentioned with other ones. Singling
out the Sinai event in its exclusion from certain historical accounts
strikes interesting notes, and one may assess it from two opposite
points of view. Either it was beyond history, in a sense it was a
mega-myth, or, else, it was not mythic enough to be part of the
material history. In any event, its historic validity was not a relevant issue in the ordinary sense that defines, in our case, relevance; at least, it was not in the eyes of some of the psalmists. I
would argue, therefore, that the manner it was handled showed
our point here: religious history is not different from any other
kind of history. One may present it according to needs and wishes.

Its validity emerges from mythic considerations, in the sense we discussed them above.

One must, however, leave the door open to yet another explanation, namely, that in not referring to the revelation on Mount Sinai the Psalmists in question maintained a polemical attitude towards the event. This seems unlikely, but it still constitutes an (alternative) explanation.[45] The polemic may follow the same line as that taken by the angels who argued with God over his willingness to give the Torah to the Israelites. This subject is frequently discussed in modern scholarship.[46] Various interpretations have been given, and the antinomian one should not be dismissed off hand. Antinomianism, we should not forget, is tantamount to a dismissal of myth. Where there is no "law" there is no myth.

It seems to me that Maimonides would have agreed with this assertion: without the philosophic interpretation of Scripture (to which we have here given the status of myth), many biblical utterances would have remained in the domain of falsehood (in Hebrew, *kazav*), in the epistemological sense of the term. Many

---

[45] It would be interesting to examine Maimonides' opinion on this problem. In *Mishneh Torah*, Maimonides elaborates on the subject of the Torah from Heaven, in and of itself, as a subject that is "a clear and explicit thing in Torah, that it (=Torah) endures forever and ever" (*Hilkhot Yesodei Ha-Torah* 9, 1). However, Maimonides does not say here that the Torah is from Heaven. On the other hand, the subject of the Torah from Heaven, apparently without a metaphoric interpretation of any kind, surfaces in *Mishneh Torah* in the context of the prophecy of Moses: "And what did they believe in? In the giving of the Torah, that our eyes saw and not a stranger's and our ears heard and not another's... thus Moses, our teacher, all Israel are witnesses to him after the giving of the Torah. And he does not need to perform a [miraculous] sign for them... " (*Yesodei Ha-Torah* 8, 1-2). In the ensuing discussion Maimonides writes concerning Moses: "There is no parable but the matter is seen straightforwardly, without any riddle and without parable... he does not prophecy in a riddle but rather in [direct] vision for he sees the thing clearly..." (*Yesodei Ha-Torah* 7, 6). It seems to me, that an in-depth examination of Maimonides' views in *Mishneh Torah* will show the ambiguity of his views on the subject. Maimonides expresses himself in formulations that can be interpreted as mutually contradictory. There is no need to go into the details of what Maimonides writes on this issue in *Guide for the Perplexed*. His opinion there is decisive and consistent and does not stray from his pedantic metaphoric formulations. We note one last example: "But they said 'and Moses went up to God' (Ex. 19: 3)—not that the Lord, may he be exalted, has a place that one ascends to it or descends from it. God is above and above any of the fantasies of fools" (*The Guide* I, 10). In other words, Maimonides highlights the mythic function of the biblical story and does so to justify the need for the philosophical interpretation of Scripture.

[46] See the references and discussion in Ithamar Gruenwald, *Apocalyptic and Merkavah Mysticism*, E.J. Brill: Leiden/Koeln, 1980, p. 60, fn. 115.

biblical stories require hermeneutic adaptation (*alias*, a myth), that
is, before they can be incorporated in a coherent theological framework. Establishing the truth of the details contained in a particular story is determined, therefore, by the type of interpretation
that is given to the story. In other words, it is all a matter of hermeneutics, which according to our way of looking at it is tantamount
to myth. At times, this hermeneutic stance entails an unequivocal digression from the simple, straightforward, sense of the scriptural text. According to Maimonides, this form of interpretation
is essential in order to maintain reasonable coherence between
the word of Scripture and the philosophy that Maimonides believed was Aristotelian. In his eyes, as long as this coherence can
be maintained, the status of the decrees is safeguarded.

The type of analysis, suggested in this chapter, has demonstrated
the relevance of myth to ritual performance, *i.e.* Law and
Halakhah. It has also demonstrated that myth is a much broader
concept than is usually assumed and should be separated from
the prejudices that view it as fraud and deception. It is a mode
of cognition, in which even philosophical notions can find an
interesting venue for their own contextualization in a myth-sta-
tus.

CHAPTER FOUR

IN QUEST OF NEW PERSPECTIVES IN RELIGIOUS STUDIES: HALAKHAH AND THE STUDY OF RITUALS

I

This chapter takes us to the heart of the discussion of how religious rituals are done. More specifically, it discusses the relevant subjects in the framework of a wide range of issues and methodological considerations, all of which have a common denominator, namely, an in-depth assessment of the various scholarly issues that address rituals in their *doing*-modes. It should be noted that, in referring to Halakhah, I intentionally use the term 'doing' rather than the more common one 'practising', because there are a number of macro-forms in which Halakhah is practised (Orthodox, Conservative, Liberal, etc.), and these have a more theological connotation. Questions that relate to the manner in which people view Halakhah in theological terms are not the subject of my concern, here. As indicated earlier, theology becomes part of the scholarly discussion of rituals, when a theological notion comes to bear directly on *how* a ritual is done.

In short, the present chapter focuses on a specific aspect of the subject matter—the doing-modes of Judaic Halakhah.[1] Since people use the term Halakhah in various ways, I need to state the manner in which I use it. I distinguish between two different

---

[1] The Hebrew term *Halakhah* is interpreted in very different ways, in scholarly writings. It has a linguistic kinship with the word that indicates walking, *Halikhah*. Thus, walking in the ways of God means obeying his decrees (see, for instance, 1 Kings 3: 14). This has become a paradigmatic notion in the world of the Halakhah. However, another meaning of the verb הלך, in Hebrew, is "to study." Studying the Law and observing its decrees are considered in rabbinic practice two sides of the same coin. See Wilhelm Bacher, *Die Exegetische Terminologie der Judischen Traditions Literatur*, Reprint: Wissenschaftliche Buchgesellschaft: Darmstadt, 1965, pp. I. 42-43; II, 53-56.

notions of Halakhah. The first concerns the prescription of a specific Halakhah. The phrase "this is the Halakhah" means "this is the final decision taken with regard to a particular issue in the legal matter concerned." In its literary and conceptual genres, Halakhah takes the form of jurisprudence. Thus, one may generically justify its description in legal terms. The second sense, in which the term is used and to which we shall not refer in the present chapter, concerns the process of formulating and codifying Halakhah.

Halakhah is a generic term. It concerns the branch of knowledge that covers religious rituals. For reasons that will become clear, I shall use the term Halakhah primarily in its sense referring to doing, as described above. One should note that the prescriptive aspect of Halakhah often uses a descriptive language, that is to say, it describes what people do in order to fulfil their religious duties in a ritual narrative. There is a legal narrative that characterises Halakhah in its documented phases, and one has to learn how to read the information at hand in order to make it relevant to scholarly work.

In as much as Halakhic writings refer to specific issues, they still speak a shorthand language. What appears to be a detailed description is in fact a series of succinct headings, behind which one always finds a chain of details that require specification. These details undergo, in turn, another process of specification, which presents itself in the form of comments and commentaries on the previous stages. There is, thus, a constant process of adding explicatory materials to previous statements and decisions. In the case of Halakhah, explication often receives the status of a ruling. The entire process is known as the 'Oral Torah,' which complements the 'Written Torah' (= the Pentateuch). The Oral Torah, already discussed at some length in the previous chapter, aims at explicating the Written Torah. In a sense, the Oral Torah translates the written words of the Pentateuch into do-able actions. But since the Oral Torah was also put in written form, one can speak of a continuum and even conclude that the various forms of practising Halakhah follow fixed patterns of development. They shape and bring into effect practicable manuals (such as the *Shulchan 'Arukh*, "The Set Table") which, in turn, become normative texts. These are also followed by explicatory stances that introduce new approaches and contribute to the shaping of these manuals into legal codices with a scriptural status. All these texts specify in detail what to do, when, and how. When these manuals undergo the critical scrutiny of later authorities, new layers of views and recommended changes are added to former ones. In practice, therefore, a bulk of commentaries and exegetical studies always accompanies the printed editions of the texts of the Oral Torah, and they become another "Written Torah" for the next generation(s). This makes Halakhah an ever-growing corpus of rulings. It is a dynamic process that creates a diversified ritual tradition.

Briefly stated, the Oral Torah discusses Halakhic issues and decisions. Since, as we have noted, the common way of presenting these issues is a legal one, jurisprudence is the major status-context of the Halakhah, that is, the ritual process in Judaism. Jurisprudence is the preferred form of stating ritual obligation in the rabbinic circles represented in *Mishnah* and the subsequent Halakhic literature. As noted in the previous chapter, the cognitive presuppositions of Halakhah are set in the myth of the dual Torah. The hermeneutic framework suggested is the exegetical venue in which the Oral Torah unfolds. These hermeneutic stances are believed to have been normatively established from the days of the revelation on Mount Sinai. This is also the trademark and cornerstone of rabbinic Judaism. Thousands of learned books incorporate Halakhic lore covering almost twenty centuries. One has to view Halakhah, therefore, in its endless forms of expansion and diversification. Halakhah reflects different motivations, considerations, and personal inclinations. Indeed, the Halakhic corpus is so diverse, and its modes of presentation so diffuse, that submitting it to a generic discussion does not do it justice. We shall therefore concentrate on one aspect of the subject. In line with the programme of the present book, we shall refer to the term Halakhah in a manner that is not often used in scholarly discussion—as the Judaic form of ritual, whose natural place of discussion is the phenomenology of ritual and issues of ritual theory.

The major question that we shall ask here is composed of two parts: in what sense can the study of rituals contribute to our understanding of Halakhah, and in what sense can the study of Halakhah enrich our understanding of the doing of rituals and the relevant ritual theory? Since the major point that this book wishes to establish is that rituals are the key factor in religious systems, the natural conclusion follows that Halakhah has a sim-

ilar status in Judaism.[2] This is not a theological statement, although I am aware that it has a strong theological ring, the implications of which cannot be ignored. People usually express
themselves first in deeds, then in thoughts, ideas, and feelings.
Since rituals belong to the behavioural side of human expression,
the study of rituals will gain from areas of knowledge and study
that focus on behaviour within systemic structures of actions, such
as Halakhah. This makes anthropological studies a relevant area
of research in the scholarly discussion of Halakhah.[3] Religious
studies, too, are a relevant area of research. Religion provides the
context in which rituals are done. In this context, I include two
major factors, theology and myth. Myth was the subject of the
previous chapter. In the present chapter, more concentrated attention will be given to the role that theology plays, or does not
play, in the study of rituals.

One should, in fact, remember that the terms of reference that
I apply here exclude theological stances from the study of rituals. However, I view theology as a major factor that gives rituals
a context and an added sense of direction and meaning. In addition, theology contextualises rituals into a coherent system.[4] This
system highlights possible reasons and motivations, although the
latter do not explain the actual manifestation of rituals in their
doing-modes. In as much as reasons and motivations play a role

---

[2] It is crucial, in my view, not to confuse "Law" and "Ritual." The two terms
represent two distinct notions. The confusion is found primarily in scholarly writings written with a Christian agenda. Since the days of Paul, prominently established circles in the Christian world have shown opposition to the Judaic concept
of Law. This opposition to the Law inadvertently spread over to include rituals
and, as we shall see, it often extended to the scholarly study of rituals. It should be
noted that the theological notion of "the Law" (*nomos*), as discussed in the Letters
of Paul, is basically directed against the Pentateuchal [or Priestly/Deuteronic]
Law, not against rituals, in principle. There are, in fact, quite a number of ritual
practices in Christianity. Paul, himself, introduced the Eucharist [see, below, Chapter
6]. In general, the notion of ritual suffered from prejudiced underrating in scholarly circles. This came about as a result of Christian opposition to the "Law."
Symptomatically, Christian Bible scholarship does not discuss the "Old Testament"
notion of ritual but the nature of the "Old Testament Law"! See, for instance, J.
Alberto Soggin, *Introduction to the Old Testament*, Westminster/John Knox Press:
Louisville, Kentucky 1989, pp.164-175. We shall discuss this issue at some length
further on.

[3] Although there are some studies, in this area, the subject does not receive the
methodological and epistemological attention it deserves.

[4] We shall return to this subject, in the last chapter of this book, which focuses
on ritual as it crystallised in early Christianity.

in the doing of rituals,[5] theology becomes part of the study of rituals.

Theology emphasises the primacy of the believing spirit in the doing of rituals. From a theological point of view, rituals play a subservient role in religion. They are instrumental in processing factors relevant to faith and belief. However, if one accepts the behavioural approach presented in this study, rituals should be viewed as an autonomous expression of the human mind. The mind, we argued in Chapter 1, generates rituals in an almost automatic manner. Thus, in principle, rituals function *beyond* and *apart from* theology and other ideational components and, at times, in spite of them. One may see in the foregoing comments an absolute affirmation of rituals, irrespective of theological considerations. Once again, this does not mean that theology has no place in religion or that it is completely irrelevant to the study of rituals. It means that the basic explanation of religious rituals is not grounded in theology, but in an indigenous form of expression of the human mind. This means that rituals are autonomous extensions of the human mind, regardless, at this moment, of the question, in which areas of human activity they evolve.

Since this book is based on the assumption that, in order to formulate a specific theory of rituals, one must examine, in each case, the rituals to which the specific theory is supposed to relate, the question that needs to be asked is: how should scholars proceed in handling the reconstruction of the theoretical dynamics embedded in rituals that came into being a long time ago? Scholars work with written documents that prescribe the rituals, but these documents tell us, in an explicit manner, very little that is usable for scholarly purposes.[6] The texts which incorporate prescriptions or descriptions of rituals speak of processual actions. But the ritual narrative becomes somewhat frozen as a result of the textual configuration which dictates a certain degree of stasis.

---

[5] Mystical trends in Judaism highlight the factor of intention (*Kavanah*) in the doing of rituals. Indeed, there are special rituals intended to enhance and intensify the factor of *Kavanah* in the doing of rituals. Extensive attention will be given to this subject later on.

[6] Interestingly, religious people constantly refer to texts, that is, to an authoritative voice to direct them in their actions. They try to do the rituals in their true sense, which means by tracing the true meaning of Scripture. Sophisticated tools of hermeneutics are applied in order to show that the accumulated tradition derived from Scripture. Scholars are apt to show more care with regard to, and respect, criteria of historical differentiation.

Thus, the reconstruction of rituals from texts benefits from terms of reference accumulating in the process of studying as many forms of purposive and specifically targeted human actions as possible. As indicated, rituals are a special mode of human action and behaviour. Thus their discussion requires the application of behaviour-oriented parameters that reflect a wide spectrum of considerations. I include, among these: intentionality,[7] timing,[8] choosing a special place,[9] unique modes of sequencing the details,[10] specifying the exact measures and quantities required,[11] and establishing the correct order (when the ritual process at hand consists of a number of sequential rituals).[12] All these factors create the special "cosmology" that sustains the ritual process and they create the inner logic that makes rituals function in the way they should.

In comparison to the transformation factor, which is an essential component in making rituals what they are, the above factors are primarily instrumental in function. They play a subservient part in the process of achieving the major goal, which *is* transformation. To remind the reader, transformation means that signif-

---

[7] This factor will be discussed at some length later on.

[8] An oft-quoted example is found in the opening sections of Mishnah Tractate *Berakhot*, where time spans are specified for the recitation of the *shem'a* prayers in the evening and morning. Correct timing of rituals is often discussed in Scripture and in Halakhah. An oft-repeated expression says: "if its day has been exceeded, its sacrificial status is annulled" (*Bavli Berakhot* 26/a; the subject here is prayer). In magic, which can be viewed as the epitome of ritual, timing (sunset, midnight, sunrise, etc.) is not only crucial for an effective performance, it is also believed to provide protection against the evil spirits that may interfere with the magical deed. Untimely actions call forth unwarranted processes.

[9] The Temple, and then the synagogue, was considered such a place. In magic, once again, the circle drawn around the magician not only defines the magical space, it is also believed to provide protection against outside powers that may harm, or interfere with, the performing magician. Various other places are also often chosen as the places for magical performances. Magic shows a predilection for river banks, lakes and uninhabited regions.

[10] See, for instance, Mishnah Tractate *Yoma* 5, 7: "The entire rite of the Day of Atonement stated in accord with its proper sequence — if he [the high priest] did one part of the rite before the next in order, he has done nothing whatsoever."

[11] There are a number of examples of such cases. A famous one is Mishnah Tractate *Middot* [=Measures], which discusses the dimensions of the Temple, its furniture and vessels. There are also other kinds of "sacred" measures, which indicate quantities, time spans and weights.

[12] One can mention, here, the famous Halakhic principle: "the one that is more commonly done always precedes the one that is less frequently done" (Talmud Bavli, *Berakhot* 51/b).

icant changes take place, whether in the person doing the ritual, in the "cosmos" in which the person lives, or in the principles that regulate this "cosmos." In a religious framework, all this is linked to a divine decree. Rituals aim at bringing about substantial—I have referred to them as metaphysical—changes in existence. These changes are planned and programmed and concern basic forms of existence.[13]

There are, of course, numerous studies of various aspects of Halakhic practice but, to the best of my knowledge, no extant study exists that comprehensively and systematically explores Halakhah as ritual, in the anthropological sense of the term. The interest of scholars in this particular subject is often limited to such subjects as religious holidays, laws of marriage and divorce, ownership of property, damages, and, last but not least, laws of purity. This is not a comprehensive list; nonetheless, it is a fair reflection of the interest shown by scholars in the domain of ritual. What is missing in studies of these subjects is a detailed examination of the ritual process itself and how it brings about what it claims to do.[14] Baptismal laws in Judaism obviously catch the scholarly eye, because of their link to baptismal rites in Christianity. But Christian scholars rarely pay attention to the ritual process as a subject in its own right.

Since Halakhah is the Judaic equivalent of rituals and cult,[15]

---

[13] In this respect, the definition of sacrifice as suggested in Henri Hubert and Marcel Mauss, *Sacrifice: Its Nature and Functions*, University of Chicago Press: Midway Reprint, 1981, p. 13, deserves a comment. This definition comes close to the one I would adopt for the discussion of sacrifices in the present book (see next chapter). Hubert and Mauss write: "Sacrifice is a religious act which, through the consecration of a victim, modifies the condition of the moral person who accomplishes it or that of certain objects with which he is concerned." The important words, in this definition, are "modifying the condition of." I should point out, though, that such modification happens not only, as Hubert and Mauss argue, in the case of a "moral person" but on a much wider scale.

[14] A notable exception is the voluminous scholarly output of Professor Jacob Neusner. In numerous communications with Professor Neusner, I discussed the difference in our respective approaches at length. In spite of the differences between our respective approaches and the conclusions we have reached, I believe that Neusner's work, in the study of the religion and law of rabbinic Judaism during its formative period (the first centuries of the Christian era), is the most relevant one to the present study. See further, footnote 66.

[15] A few words of clarification are due as to how I use a few key terms in the present chapter. Scholars often use the terms "cults" and "rituals" interchangeably. However, I would prefer to consider "cult" as a term that designates a clus-

the attempt to understand Halakhic rituals, in their intrinsically performative essence, means that the self-formulated agenda of Halakhah will receive scholarly priority. It also means that if one wishes to prevent the study of Halakhic rituals from becoming a disguised form of involvement in theological issues, then it is important to avoid enabling the latter from setting the agenda of the scholarly discussion. Thus, the type of sweeping generalisations produced by the theological approach to rituals and cult (and, hence, Halakhah) will not satisfy our purposes. My goal is to explore new paths, which can help us to understand the praxis of Judaic forms of Halakhah as rituals. In as much as the materials at hand allow me to do this, I shall use Halakhah as a model of the practice of rituals in general.

II

We have already seen that the study of the performative aspects of rituals requires the application of anthropological considerations or criteria.[16] For various reasons, some of which go back to the nineteenth century, anthropological studies gained the upper hand in the study of the practised aspects of rituals. The societies, which were studied by anthropologists, were primarily illiterate societ-

---

ter of ritual acts consisting in the worship of a certain deity or deities. In many cases, the term is used in connection with heathen deities. I would also suggest using the term "rite" in a similar sense, that is to say, as a series of ritual acts that are connected to a particular event, for example, a festival or the consecration of a temple. It should be noted in this connection, that "ceremony" sometimes indicates a rather loose and minimally structured type of ritual that accompanies a particular public event. These ceremonies are not essential to creating the kind of transformation that is discussed here as constituting the essence of rituals. Ceremonies, as discussed here, are usually structured *ad hoc*, as festive events with colourful displays of various kinds. In any event, usually no transformative purposes are connected to them. See, however, the discussion at the beginning of the next section.

[16] In modern scholarship, anthropology is usually connected with studies and fieldwork that focus on the behavioural aspects of individuals and groups. This is also the sense in which the term is used in the present study. However, there are important aspects of anthropology that are connected with philosophy and existential psychology (and also, in this respect, with theology). See, Wolfahrt Pannenberg, *Anthropologie in theologischer Perspective*, Vandenhoeck & Ruprecht in Goettingen, 1983. Pannenberg writes that the purpose of his book is to study "... die religioese Dimensionen der menschlichen Lebenswirklichkeit in ihrer strukturellen Eigenart und in ihren Wichtigsten Erscheinungsformen" (p. 7).

ies. The major source of material for the anthropological studies was the daily lives of the people among whom the anthropologists lived and whose customs they observed and learned. Their lives were defined by a series of events in which basic social processes were channelled through ceremonial enactments. A ceremonial enactment here means *a single ritual event that usually does not systemically connect to other events and rituals*. From the point of view of ritual theory, then, ceremonial enactments may turn daily into festive events; nevertheless, they always fall short of events that make a grid of constitutive factors in the life of a people. Unlike rituals, ceremonies have a playful element. Like rituals, ceremonial events are functional even when no theology is involved. In short, the power of ceremonies is less conspicuous than that of rituals.

Scholars who were trained in religious studies found, in the reports published by anthropologists, interesting materials that testified, in their view, to elementary forms of religion. The anthropological material seemed to shed light on the simple forms and nature of religion, and comparative religion found in them a popular subject that in some ways showed the universal, rather than the particular, in religion. There was an element of an enlightened criticism entailed in this procedure. But scholarly fascination with the subject should favour the scrupulous analysis of differences rather than the assessment of accidental similarities. A value judgement prevailed in these studies: "primitive" was often the characteristic qualifier attached to the societies and cultures studied by these anthropologists. "Primitive" was a label that marked the space in which a sense of distance produced assertions whose validity always had an ascertainable appearnce.

Arguably, the philosophical stance, that reached its peak in the work of Kant, constituted the intellectual compass of these studies. The mention of Kant cannot go without tracing the Kantian tradition back to the Orphic-Platonic notion of the body being the prison of the soul. One finds this tradition, with a slight variation, in the Pauline writings.[17] Since rituals cannot be done without

---

[17] This may seem to be a somewhat oversimplified and stereotypical view of the state of affairs in Christianity. See, Kallistos Ware, "'My Helper and My Enemy': the Body in Greek Christianity" in: Sarah Coakley (ed.), *Religion and the Body*, Cambridge University Press: Cambridge, 1997, pp. 90-110. Other essays in this excellent collection analyse the alleged omnipresence of the Orphic-Platonic *topos* in Christian religion and culture.

using one's body, the prison house of the soul so-called, they were a priori degraded to satisfy only the needs of the material world. For us today, the Orphic-Platonic tradition appears as a philosophical idiosyncrasy that puts chains on phenomenological research.[18] In the intellectual tradition of the West, the inferior status of the body and, consequently of, rituals was a cultural constant.[19] In a number of cases, though, the Christian West bypassed this difficulty by paradoxically conceiving the spirituality of the body. In any event, Kant, more than anyone else, contributed to intensifying, from a philosophical point of view, the position that Paul forged in relation to the Law, *alias* the Pentateuchal ritual, done "in the flesh."[20] Indeed, Kant echoed the voice Luther raised against Catholic forms of "Liturgy",[21] or cult. Kant presented Christianity, and especially its Protestant version, as the prototype of a "high religion." A "high religion" epitomises conformity with spiritual ideals, particularly ethics, that bring with it eternal bliss.[22] A breach with anything that material or terrestrial bonds signify or represent is a *sine qua non* in the Kantian vision. A major point, in this line of argumentation, was that, since rituals are confined to material expressions, they can separate people from their sense of humanity, as characterised by the ultimate good and perfection. Kant's view was quickly accepted as the trademark of cultural enlightenment. Furthermore, it became affiliated with the enlightened face that Protestantism showed vis-

---

[18] It is often argued that, in these matters, Paul was influenced by the flesh-spirit duality as followed by the Qumran community.

[19] The various aspects that this dichotomy took, in Western culture, are discussed in Peter Brown, *The Body and Society: Men, Women, and Sexual Renunciation in Early Christianity*, Columbia University Press: New York, 1988.

[20] In this respect, the author of the *Letter of Barnabas* took a more radical approach than Paul. He diligently collected all the utterances in the Hebrew Scripture that voiced criticism of offering sacrifices with defiled hands and an evil heart. This protracted list of antisacrifice statements fought Judaism on its own grounds. In a Jewish medieval setting, Maimonides argued that sacrifices were granted to the people as a concession. God knew that the custom of the day was to bring sacrifices. Maimonides could quote the relevant verses in Scripture to support his philosophical views with regard to sacrifices. However, as has been noted often, the philosophical attitude in the *Guide for the Perplexed*, Part III, is not corroborated by the positions taken in *Mishneh Torah* and other Halakhic writings of Maimonides.

[21] I use the term "Liturgy" in the technical sense it has in Catholicism, meaning the entire way of life as it unfolds in cultic-relevant modes.

[22] Kant's indebtedness to Spinoza should be mentioned, at this point, though it will not be discussed.

à-vis Catholicism. Protestant Christianity, for that matter, saw it-self as the natural upholder of cultural enlightenment in gener-al.[23]

One should note that Paul preached the rejection of the "flesh."[24] The notion of "flesh," in Paul and in the writings of the Qumran, is a theological notion. It is used in connection with what people should do and how, in line with a specific under-standing of the scriptural law. Needless to say, it is a notion that has ritual implications. With time, this notion was given an eth-ical interpretation, and came to advocate a total rejection of the carnal body and materialism in general.[25] Ultimately, rituals were philosophically—and theologically—degraded in the scholarly discussion, too.

It is easy to say, as I have done, that religious studies should avail themselves of the research methods and tools of anthropol-ogy. In practice, however, the casual adoption of anthropologi-cal notions by religious studies is liable to cause confusion, and even to miss the mark. Indeed, researchers in religious studies often argued that field anthropology caused such a disciplinary confu-sion. What I believe is needed, at this point, is a word of clarifi-cation. By adopting certain modes of perception current in an-thropological studies, such as assessing the behaviour of the body and the various forms of organisation of the individual human mind, scholars can still maintain religious studies within familiar

---

[23] Interestingly, Kant refers to Lev. 19: 1—"You should be holy, for I am holy" —as the proof text for the Christian, though philosophically phrased, idea of per-fection. See, Immanuel Kant, *Die Religion innerhalb der Grenzen der blossen Vernunft*, II, 3. However, as noted in the previous chapter, the etymology of the Hebrew term *qadosh* does not refer, as all too often in Christian interpretations, to the notion of holiness, but rather to the notion of separation. The Greek term *hagios*, which usually renders the Hebrew *Qadosh* in the sense of "holy," is rather vague. Liddell & Scott quote negative senses for the term. In any event, the verse in the Book of Leviticus begins a series of ritual acts that are required from those who wish to be holy. Kant uses the term in a completely different sense, one which, among other things, ultimately led to Rudolf Otto, *The Idea of the Holy* (a rather strange trans-lation of the German, *Das Heilige*, The Holy).

[24] In this respect, Paul followed the line of thinking advocated by the Qumran community. See David Flusser, *Judaism and the Origins of Christianity*, Jerusalem: The Magnes Press, 1988, pp. 23-74: "The Dead Sea Sect and Pre-Pauline Chris-tianity."

[25] Daniel Boyarin, *Carnal Israel: Reading Sex in Talmudic Culture*, University of California Press: Berkeley, 1993, over-emphasises, in some respects, the opposite pole to that which is advocated in Talmudic Judaism. The book, nonetheless, contains discussions of interesting texts and ideas, which clearly amplify, in their own man-ner, the discussion of Paul's anti-carnal attitude.

limits. Field anthropology, as distinct from its philosophical and religious counterparts, makes available to researchers the technical vocabulary that religious studies need in order to include behavioural and cultural factors in their area of consideration. As argued, in previous pages, rituals are not confined to religion. They are a much more common and widely spread form of experiential expression and behaviour than one that is limited to the religious domain. Ignoring this fact encourages the approach, which holds that religions can be studied only in the framework of the belief in the supernatural, whatever this may represent to critical students of religion.

But how far should religious studies go in adopting the anthropological discourse? Religious studies have been slow in accepting the terminological approach of anthropology, although the real issue is not terminological but epistemological. Anthropology has created its own epistemology, according to which the human mind, rather than divine will, is the generator of ritual behaviour. Through rituals, the mind seeks a way to express itself at the behavioural level, in structured actions related to changing modules of the "cosmos." While religious studies tend to emphasise the theocentric view of rituals, anthropology does the opposite— it puts the emphasis on the anthropocentric essence of rituals. Thus, from the epistemological point of view practically the same "texts" are seen as completely different entities in the two areas of study. In anthropology, the "text" is observed in a detached manner. The anthropologist reports and assesses what he has observed and his observations have no status in the community, which is the object of his research. In religious studies, the "text" is connected to a canon; the major concern in this respect is the ideas that sustain the whole structure, even the rituals.

Canonical texts tell people what *to do*, and disobedience is not an option. It is a punishable sin. In anthropology, as we have seen, sin has no (theological) meaning, and whether it is punished or not, and how, remains a question that is answered confined to a phenomenological discussion. Religious studies demonstrate little interest in relating to the question of how rituals work. Instead researchers in religious studies examine messages contained in written and other forms of documentation. No specific attention is given to the manner in which people do rituals. If they show some interest in how people do rituals, it is in the framework of the following questions: What is the history of the things people are told to do? What is the idea behind these acts (theology)? Are they in line with what their canonical books prescribe and, if not, are they an expression of denominational fragmentation, of a heretical stance, or of sectarian fractioning? This interest develops into questions that focus on the nature of the texts being studied. The ideas contained in the relevant documents, their textual development in history and in different societies are also of major concern to scholars in religious studies. It is time, though, for scholars of religious studies to allow themselves more freedom in their way of reading the documented configuration of rituals and take into consideration experienced rituals. The reading of written texts that describe or prescribe rituals should be informed by the way in which their prescriptions are carried out. All this depends on how we understand human actions.

The present chapter is, thus, an attempt to explore the possibilities of the interdisciplinary integration suggested above, with the domain of Halakhah at the centre of the investigation. A systematic linkage between anthropological and religious studies can produce fruitful results for the study of rituals in general, and for the study of the practised aspects of Halakhah in particular. Indeed, religious forms of behaviour can gain considerably from being assessed in a non-religious framework.[26] A few examples of non-religious rituals that may play a part in assessing religious rituals are bureaucratic organisations, industrial projects, maintenance manuals, and protocols of etiquette. All these involve ritualised, although not necessarily religious, forms of actions and behaviour. A common feature in all these is that any conceivable deviation from what they prescribe is liable to bring about "disaster" for the people concerned.

Anthropological studies tell us something valuable about the various ways in which humans respond to their surrounding environments, social and mental. The presence of the mind-factor

---

[26] It has variously been suggested that the sacrificial parts of Greek drama constitute the original context in which the technical sense of the concept of ritual first appears. See Hugh Lloyd-Jones, "Ritual and Tragedy", in: Fritz Graf (ed.), *Ansichten Griechischer Rituale: GeburtstagsSymposium für Walter Burkert*, B. G. Teubner: Stuttgart und Leipzig, 1998, pp. 271-295. Modern views of drama and theatre often take their departure from a similar perception, though religion is not necessarily a factor in these views.

shows that structured behavioural reactions are more than just mechanical acts. They are an extension of the human spirit. I use the word spirit with great caution. I see no more than an inferential connection between spiritual activity and ritual behaviour. This does not take me to the other extreme, namely, that there *is* a biological basis to rituals, a view that several modern scholars highlight. The main point I wish to make is that rituals are not mere "materialistic" manifestations of something that is divorced from the spiritual. There is a subtle element to ritual behaviour, which transcends instincts and automatic practices. Human rituals can be repeated at pre-planned times, when instinct stimulating conditions do not prevail. To repeat, this does not mean that rituals figuratively translate mental positions into physical gestures. They support a form of expression that, ontologically speaking, is *sui generis*. Furthermore, rituals are often ceremonialised, that is, all kinds of aesthetic embellishments are added to make them look and function more conspicuously.

Anthropological studies, thus, help to present rituals as indigenous forms of human—often socially oriented—behavioural expression. More specific even, in the approach outlined in the present book an attempt is made to distinguish between the automatic and instinctual, on the one hand, and the structured response, on the other. There is also a distinction between the behavioural and the ideational, including, for that matter, the symbolic. However, I would resist simplistic interpretations of these distinctions. I believe that the reader by now realises that the body is *positively* involved in making the mind achieve things that only the rituals can do. What the mind generates has meaning, although the manner in which we approach and assess the nature of this meaning is through, and in, behavioural gestures. The meaning of rituals is what the mind generates as a structured form of action. Structure, here, is tantamount to purposively oriented entities. It is a behaviourally intrinsic type of meaning.

Language serves as a good example of what I have in mind. Linguistic expression is explained by means that apply to language, not to the special signs, for instance, that are used in choreography. The same is true the other way around. Similarly, what rituals say or may mean is contained in the rituals themselves. Which interpretation does a better service—one that derives from outside the ritual or one that attempts to decipher the meaning of rituals from their own performative essence—is an open question. I feel more inclined to favour the hypothetical answer based on internal suggestions rather than the allegedly more certain answer that is based on an external theory. The unique merit of the present approach to rituals is that it annuls the negative attitude that prevails in moralistic evaluations of bodily actions. When the body does things that have structure and purpose (as in dancing, playing a musical instrument, painting or sculpting), it reflects features to which I would refer as "the aesthetics of patterned action."[27] The same applies to the bodily gestures that prepare and accompany states of possession. The notion of aesthetics indicates that something is done which stimulates the mind to perceive and respond in an aesthetic manner.[28] The comparison with artistic expression indicates that rituals involve modes of corporeal subtlety which are not present in other forms of action.[29]

When viewed as vital factors in shaping life and maintaining its orderly functioning, rituals significantly contribute to upgrad-

---

[27] A good example, in this respect, is carpet weaving. The patterns of each carpet draw, almost subconsciously, from an inventory of notions of artistic perfection that are rarely understood by the weavers. However, each detail, and the Gestalt of the whole, define the carpet artistically and its commercial value. Mistakes in the execution of the patterns decrease the value of the carpet. We have referred to the fact that minor differences in ritual performance can create denominational differences. Major differences create sectarian schisms and often justify notions of heresy and idol worship. A major difference between Persian and Turkish carpets is in the knotting technique and both nations take great pride in their respective techniques. Other examples are gardening (especially knot-gardening) and flower arranging (*i.e.* the Japanese Ikebana with its strict rules of arrangement).

[28] See Elaine Scarry, *On Beauty and Being Just*, Princeton University Press: Princeton, 1999. The opening words of Scarry's book are quite enlightening on this subject. She writes (p. 3): "What is the felt experience of cognition at the moment one stands in the presence of a beautiful boy or flower or bird? It seems to incite, even to require, the act of replication. Wittgenstein says that when the eye sees something beautiful, the hand wants to draw it." The relevance of Scarry's aesthetic and ethical observations is of great interest to the discussion of art and ritual. Limitations of space prevent us from elaborating further on this theme.

[29] It should be noted that sports have a close affinity to rituals, not so much in their ceremonial features (flags, processions, uniforms, strict rules, etc.), as in the structured training process (the preparation) and the competition (the ritual) itself. Games, also, have their ritual features. Breaking the rules of the game, means breaking the "cosmos" in which the game is played. In Hebrew, there is a metaphorical expression used mainly by children, saying "the vessels have been broken." It means that the game is interrupted and broken off. The subject requires a theoretical assessment from the point of view of ritual theory, but this is not the place to do it.

ing bodily gestures and other forms of expression. This statement should not be underrated. Taking a ritual bath, building a Suk- kah, slaughtering an animal for sacrificial purposes, lighting the Sabbath candles and many other ritual actions involve doing things with the body. Ritual goals are not, as a rule, accomplished in a "Quietist" manner, simply by thinking about them. Each ritual mentioned, here, deserves detailed analysis. Without the details, the whole does not function.

In respect of human behaviour, one is reminded of the obser- vation made by several scholars, Catherine Bell among them, to the effect that the departure from the perennial dichotomy be- tween body and spirit opened new possibilities for the scholarly study of rituals.[30] For religious studies to accomplish a complete change in its approach to rituals, a complementary change has to occur in the manner in which religious studies view the ontology of bodily behavioural expressions. It is not a matter of formally treating the body in ameliorative terms in the discourse on its ontology—it is a matter of attributing vitally positive significance to what the body does and accomplishes in rituals. This is direct- ly connected to what the body, or (to use a more Pauline expres- sion) the "flesh,"[31] succeeds in accomplishing in the way of trans- formative events. We should not forget that transformation, apart from being a cultic issue, is a mental process.

It is common to describe the power of the mind in terms of its intellectual, emotional and creative capacities. People seldom think of the human mind in connection with structuring human behav- iour in a manner that brings about changes which are vital for maintaining human existence. What is unique, in ritual behav- iour, is that human action is not logically and pragmatically con- nected to what it is expected to do. The connections between the means (rituals) and the expected results become effective in a special "cosmos," already extensively discussed above. This "cos- mos" brings together the mind that is behind the ritual act and

---

[30] See Catherine Bell, *Ritual Theory, Ritual Practice*, New York and Oxford: Oxford University Press, 1992. The extent to which this change is carried through, in modern scholarship, is discussed by Dennis E. Owen, "Ritual Studies as Ritual Practice: Catherine Bell's Challenge to Students of Ritual," *Religious Studies Review*, Vol. 24/1, January 1998, pp. 2330.

[31] I am fully aware of the fact that, in Paul, "flesh" may have an evocative sense. It may signify a distorted view of man's relationship with God.

the situation or condition addressed by the ritual. I suggest refer-ring to this cosmos as a mythic reality, in the sense discussed in the previous chapter. I have also referred to it as a metaphysical reality. This mythic reality has an ontology that one cannot but define as paradigmatic in a metaphysical sense. To envision this reality metaphysically is not self-evident. The appellation meta-physical indicates that this reality has a status in its own right and that, in this case, it cannot come into being other than by myth-ic-ritual means.

An additional attempt to clarify this part of the discussion fol-lows in the next section. What is clear is that one cannot con-ceive of the realm, or reality, in which the mind is functional, in a ritual setting, in terms that refer to normal conditions. Rituals presuppose the existence of a different kind of reality to that which prevails when normal modes of perception and behaviour oper-ate. In short, the human mind dynamically activates behavioural actions to accomplish certain desired aims in a *sui generis* condi-tion. In a sense, this line of argumentation creates a closed cir-cle: the mind and the ritual action are intrinsically interconnect-ed. They shape the "cosmos" to which they relate and in relation to which they become constitutively functional. The mind also shapes the intrinsic logic that structures the sequential coherence of the details of the ritual action in a manner that creates a func-tional totality or a working Gestalt.

III

We can also refer to this "cosmic order" as a mode of imaging the world. The people concerned create modes of configuring reality in which rituals are enabled as major life-enhancing fac-tors. Without this process of configuring reality, rituals are like words written on ice. Conditions have to prevail, or be created, for rituals to exercise their purposive functionality. This "cosmic order" is not necessarily a pre-existing entity into which people are born. On the contrary, it is they who create it. Cognitively-speaking, this makes living one's life an ongoing process of im-aging the world in conditions that require responses that entail a ritual reaction. Generally, human consciousness develops in con-stantly creating models of imaging the world. This is an experi-entially diversifying process that marks life, or constantly changing growth, from infancy onward. Patterns of ritual behaviour are forced on humans almost from the very moment of their birth. The infant learns that physical safety and mental stability are acquired by watching people in its live environment (*i.e.* the mother) do things in a repeatable manner. Action (including breast feeding, changing diapers, singing, and talking to the child) is the essence of life, in this respect.

Rituals add, to this process of imaging the world, the factor of creating the repetitive rules by which this imaged world exists and, at the same time, the means of maintaining these rules in working condition. Expressed in different terms, rituals help the human mind to engage in essential life processes. They can be said to enhance the relational attitudes towards the realities in which people live. The ability to relate to reality in a ritual mode is a unique quality of the human mind. I believe that rituals come into effect once the need arises either to keep intact or repair the life-enhancing conditions of a specific cosmos. Its specificity is its being dependent on rituals for moment-to-moment existence. A cognitive process that accompanies the ritual process means that ideological and theological factors have entered the scene.

Many people feel that a certain ideational stance accompanies their ritual activity. One should note that the mental processes that are complementarily active together with ritual activity induce the conceptual framework that creates the metaphysics of the "cosmic order," discussed above. The mental or conceptual layout that often accompanies rituals (though it is not an intrinsic part) has to do with the mind and the various ways in which it functions. Thus, while ideational stances are often intertwined with ritual behaviour, they are not necessarily two sides of the same coin.

As already noted, religion imparts normative status to rituals. This means that something is added to a behavioural activity that is not necessarily an integral part of its essence. At the beginning of his treatise "On the Creation of the World," Philo wrote that when God created the world, he looked at the "Law" (the Greek word, *nomos*, indicates the Hebrew word Torah, the Pentateuchal Law) in the way an architect looks at plans of the "palace he is building." In this manner, Philo created a metaphysical bridge between the cosmic laws and the laws of the Torah.[32] This idea,

---

[32] See E. E. Urbach, *The Sages: Their Concepts and Beliefs*, Harvard University Press: Cambridge (Mass.) and London, 1987, pp. 184-213.

often repeated in Jewish lore, expresses something that anticipates, in theological terms, the ideas presented here: rituals are essential to maintaining existence and order. Indeed, rituals control the universe (the "cosmos"). In this connection, the notion of a cosmic order no longer requires inverted commas. In this connection too, those who break the law of the Torah are considered among those who, literally, "destroy the world." Idolatry is a striking example of what people are likely to turn to in such cases.[33] When rituals state or create differences,[34] dogmatic schisms quickly set in to mark theological borderlines that should not be crossed. Rituals enact, or bring into effect, borderlines. Any attempt at encroaching these borderlines means warfare. Waging war against those who worship other gods (heathen people) was always, and continues to be, the ritual justification of warfare.[35]

An important aspect of religious rituals is their meta-rational setting, although the meta-rational is not necessarily religious. In a religious context, the meta-rational qualities of rituals make them functional in organising reality in modes that link human actions to the will of the gods. In this respect, even human social relations easily become a religious issue. The "Golden Rule" is a good example of this. In ritual terms, the love shown to a friend and that shown to God have the same status.[36] Indeed, the social order finds ways of integrating with the divine. It does this, using

---

[33] Idolatry still requires an exhaustive study at the level of ritual and ritual theory. This aspect is completely missing from Moshe Halbertal and Avishai Margalit, *Idolatry*, Harvard University Press: Cambridge (Mass.) and London, 1992. As is customary, the authors discuss concepts of idolatry rather than ritual configurations.

[34] Jonathan Z. Smith, *To Take Place: Towards Theory in Ritual*, The University of Chicago Press: Chicago and London, 1987, p. 109, succinctly writes: "Ritual, above all, is an assertion of difference." However, I find it difficult to follow the line of argumentation presented by Smith. Its characterisation of rituals is too inclusive: it includes the notion that rituals translate ideational, emotional, and symbolic stances.

[35] In discussing the ritual/sacrificial aspects of war, Bruce Lincoln, *Death, War and Sacrifice: Studies in Ideology and Practice*, The University of Chicago Press: Chicago & London, 1991, p. 138, writes: "For our purposes, war may be defined as organized and coherent violence conducted between established and internally cohesive rival groups... Being a complex phenomenon, war has multiple dimensions that are deeply interrelated, chief among them being economic, ideological, and social factors."

[36] See the comparative study of the subject in Jeffrey Wattles, *The Golden Rule*, Oxford University Press: Oxford..., 1996.

terms of reference that present the social order as abiding by divine norms. The notion of *Imitatio Dei*, in its various shades of meaning, is a telling example, in this respect.[37] God sets the scale by which people relate to each other in forms of ritual that express His will. In other words, unlike forms of ritual behaviour that are not specifically religious, religious rituals have a metahuman configuration that forges their special setting. The language of revelation, theology, and religious experience demonstrates the extent to which the supernatural is involved in each case.

The academic study of religion is not attuned to assessing mental experiences that are considered supernatural. This suggests another reason for the preference of scholars to study religion in the framework of its human accountable experience: history, texts, philosophical-theology, and language. Experiential aspects of religion, in which I include rituals, remain outside the range of scholarly discussion. In rituals, there is the assumption that something happens that is not fully accountable in rational and (non-Marxian) material notions. Conventional areas of research—the "traditional" artefacts of the academic study of religion—exempt scholars from the need to refer to these supernatural components. The study we have undertaken, here, follows a completely different path. Our discussion does not even include the realm of symbolic expression.[38] But I can affirm that I take no shortcuts in the discussion of the very essence of rituals. The essence of rituals is their purposive doing, not their contextualising theology, history or textual configuration, even not its symbolic features.

The discussion of rituals in their non-performative aspects is problematic from yet another angle. When Halakhah is discussed in dry legalistic language—that is, in mostly theoretical rather than experiential or practice-related terms of reference—this often leads

---

[37] In rabbinic writings the notion often occurs, namely, that walking in the ways of God means acquiring the moral standards that he sets in his omniscience: compassion, piety, and holiness, etc.

[38] This trend is mainly represented, in modern scholarship, in the writings of Victor Turner. Symptomatic of his approach is, *The Forest of symbols: Aspects of Ndembu Ritual*, Cornell University Press: Ithaca and London, 1967. Another striking example of the same approach is Raymond Firth, *Symbols: Public and Private*, Cornell University Press: Ithaca, 1973. As noted in the title, the book is a study of symbols. However, its main subject matter is the various forms in which symbols are expressed in ritual. The thesis of the book could thus read as "the symbolic components of rituals."

the discussion into formal deliberations where hermeneutic interests—that is to say, a philosophical-exegetical stance—play a major
role. Other aspects that are prominent in the discussion of Halakhah are the various schools or methods of Halakhic study, as well
as their respective historical settings and development. Finally, but
of importance in this respect, come the Halakhic considerations
themselves: when and under what conditions a specific Halakhic
issue applies or does not apply. At times, the theological reasons
and purposes of a particular Halakhah (the Hebrew term is: *ta'amei
ha-mitsvot*) are also discussed. The study of Halakhah requires an
enormous amount of knowledge and technical expertise and such
knowledge and expertise are rarely accessible to scholars of religious studies, not to mention anthropologists. Thus, with a few
exceptions, Halakhah is rarely included in the academic study of
religions.[39] Even in those cases where the study of Judaism is part
of the curriculum of religious studies, the parameters of the scholarly discussion do not include the theoretical foundations of the
practised aspects of the religion or its experiential modes. The
inevitable conclusion can hardly be avoided: the type of assessment proposed, here, is a priority.

There are several questions that can be asked at this point. The
first one, "what do Halakhic rituals do?" has a simple answer:
"they just do what they are expected to do in their own specific
manner and context." This is a very general answer, and applies
to any ritual done whether in a religious or other context. It means
that there is nothing that rituals wish to accomplish beyond their
purposive end(s). They do not, for instance, establish a certain
meaning that is not specifically included in the very act of doing.
If we ask, "what, then, is their unique nature or their intrinsic
essence?" the answer is: "they are unique expressions of the human mind set on addressing specific issues which individuals and
communities consider vital to maintaining a liveable cosmos." If
we furthermore ask: "is it not true to say that the overall characterisation of rituals, as presented in the present book, seems rather

---

[39] There are a few exceptions to this rule. One of the first attempts to study
Judaism from the point of view of religious studies is Jonathan Z. Smith, *Imagining
Religion: From Babylon to Jonestown*, The University of Chicago Press: Chicago and
London, 1982. Smith developed suggestions that had been previously made by
Jacob Neusner. But the direction taken by Smith is completely different to the one
taken here.

mechanical and leaves no room for ideational or cognitive components?" the answer is: "yes, the characterisation is intentionally mechanical, in that it stresses behavioural aspects. The reason
is self evident—any kind of ideology that is alleged to exist in
relation to a particular ritual is almost never reflected in the ritual actions as they are done."

If I am asked, "why do you insist on such a narrow characterisation of rituals?" the answer gets more complex and consists of
several parts: (1) Rituals are performative entities, in the sense that
people do rituals rather than think about them. Even prayers should
be viewed in this perspective of doing. Thus, the study of rituals
should begin with what is done and how it is done, rather than
with what people think or feel. (2) Focussing on the doing-aspects
of rituals enables us to study them as uniquely shaped behavioural
extensions of the human mind. Nothing intervenes between them
and the human mind. It is my view that all the other factors come
into play at a later stage, if at all. This means that the extensions
of the human mind into the realms of the behavioural and the
ideational do not necessarily go together. They are, in essence,
ontologically apart. In addition, as can be seen in many societies
that have rich inventories of ritual practices, they rarely have an
explanation that amounts to a full-fledged theological explanation. (3) We have seen that the aim and purpose of rituals are
defined by and within their performative context.

In attempting to define rituals in a context that is broader than
the performative one, the choice is normally between two kinds
of discourse, theological and scholarly. The difference between
the two is obvious: while the theological discourse highlights religious motivations, as they are defined in their faith-engender-
ing parameters, the scholarly discourse is free (even obliged) to
find channels of reference that are disengaged from theological
considerations and motivations. One should be aware that seeking the context of rituals in theological deliberations reflects an
attempt to adopt a discourse that is usually not articulated in the
doing of rituals and in the manner in which they are prescribed.[40]

---

[40] The first of the Ten Commandments (in the Books of Exodus and Deuteronomy, respectively) can be read as a theological statement. It declares the "God-
ness" of the God of Israel and is clearly a statement of religious particularism
rather than philosophical universalism. It says: "I am *your* God..." What follows is
immediately linked to the commandment which forbids idolatry. In other words,

Scholars should be able to use a discourse that does not require commitment to issues of religious faith and belief. However, even in the case of the scholarly discourse two options prevail: one speaks for fetching the explanatory materials from external, comparative, sources; the other—and this is the scholarly practice adopted here—tries to find the explanation in the phenomenon, rituals, itself. Since the human mind generates and regulates rituals as a structured (that is, planned) activity, a somewhat mechanical approach to the subject becomes inevitable. Rituals, we have seen, emerge from a mind that reacts to certain circumstances that threaten to interfere with a particular "cosmos" which ideally consists of a coherent system of factors. Preserving this coherency is the ultimate goal of rituals.

Finally, there is one more angle to this question. Although it is commonly agreed that academic work should not propagate religious belief, I believe that the study of religion cannot be carried out in an intellectual vacuum, or in a framework that is hostile to religion.[41] In the past, the study of rituals suffered from the prejudices discussed above. Then, it was a victim of philosophical positions that presented themselves under the guise of secular enlightenment. We have noted that the secular enlightenment followed in the footsteps of the Protestant criticism of Catholic indulgence in the Christian cult. Questions of belief and disbelief thus entered the scholarly domain from the back door. Cults and rituals were not studied for their own sake but for the support they gave to the sides taking part in the disputes about what the prophets of ancient Israel thought with regard to the Law. Here, the views of the early Church, and the ones reiterated in Lutheranism, played a major role. Thus, the negative assessment of most sacrificial rituals was ultimately due to theological considerations. One result was that a selective approach, in the Protestant Church, preferred to identify with the teaching of the proph-

---

God introduces himself, but immediately demands ritual actions. He tells his people what they should and should not do. The ritual connection is, therefore, clear. Only in later Jewish thought, for instance in medieval Jewish philosophy, does the introductory clause of the Ten Commandments receive full theological attention. Before that, it was mostly read as a call for monolateria, that is, the worshiping of the one God of the Israelites.

[41] See Ithamar Gruenwald, "The Study of Religion and the Religion of Study," in: Lukas Bornmann et al. (eds.), Religious Propaganda and Missionary Competition in the New Testament World, E. J. Brill: Leiden..., 1994, pp.3-21.

ets of ancient Israel rather than with the priestly Levitical code in
the Hebrew Scripture. Thus, dismissing rituals became the *bon ton*
in circles that believed it their duty to control the discussion of
what constitutes a "true religion."[42] However, as Catherine Bell
has pointed out, a new attitude towards the body in modern culture brought about not only a revival of the scholarly interest in
rituals but also a new approach to their study.

IV

We have already mentioned the fact that rituals delimit boundaries.[43] In every possible respect, rituals communicate what is
included and what is excluded, in terms of social structure, place,
and specified time limits. Rituals demarcate ethnic and cultural
zones. Rituals are functional in creating, maintaining, and preserving denominational and regional diversity. In some respects,
they can be compared to dialects. Indeed, one can argue that
rituals, like language, are modes of communication in predefined
operational codes. Every detail (special clothes, colours, sequence
of performed acts, bodily gestures, etc.) represents an important
part of a given whole, and contributes significantly to the completion of the process. The details create and maintain the appa-
ratus of signs, which enable a community to develop its specific
identity.[44] Furthermore, rituals create the context in which the

---

[42] Symptomatically, one finds that a modern scholar has written a much-ac-
claimed book on religion without taking up the subject of ritual. See Leszek
Kolakowski, *Religion*, Oxford University Press: New York, 1982. For a long time
the modern study of religion was concerned principally with theorising about religion. See, for instance, Ninian Smart, *The Science of Religion & the Sociology of Knowledge:
Some Methodological Questions*, Princeton University Press: Princeton, 1973. It would
seem that "The Science of Religion" does not deal with rituals; at least, this is the
picture that emerges from Smart's book. Numerous books can be quoted to the
same effect. The general trend, in these books, appears to be the need to justify
religion to an audience that defines itself as secular, modern, rationalistic and sceptical.
In this sense, they all share an underlying apologetic agenda.

[43] This fact has been recognised and discussed in various works. To give one
example out of many, see E. Thomas Lawson and Robert N. McCauley, *Rethinking Religion: Connecting Cognition and Culture*, Cambridge University Press: Cambridge,
1990, pp. 45-59: "Ritual as Language." The discussion is rather formal and concerns such issues as communication and meaning. The new perspective, which I
propose, deals with the performed aspects of rituals (note the plural), that is, how
actions create messages and what are the messages they create.

[44] A telling example, in this respect, is the kilt worn by Scotsmen, particularly

specific traits of the 'clan' are empowered to exercise their identity-enhancing functions. It is only in the framework of this identity-"cosmos" that rituals acquire their unique functionality. Practically speaking, being allowed to share in a ritual, or being excluded from it, is the decisive factor that defines rituals in terms of social boundaries. Factors of this kind mark the demarcation lines between "innness" and "outness." The question of who can participate in a ritual and the reason why is also essential to the manner in which rituals are practised as a cultural totality. Thus, an uncircumcised person is not permitted to share in the Passover sacrifice (*Ex.* 12: 48) nor are impure Israelites (*Num.* 9: 6-11).[45] The fact of excluding people from participation in certain rituals makes rituals speak an intensely separatist language. In this way, rituals create notions of belonging and non-belonging. These notions are also relevant to the discussion of rituals from the point of view of the sociology of religion.[46]

Viewed in the context of the sociology of religion, a new approach emerges regarding the phenomenology of rituals. One should consider rituals not only in their almost inexhaustible diversity but also in their changeable dynamics, for rituals are subject to endless changes. In this respect, rituals engender, reflect, and preserve sociological changes. Paradoxically, the notion of the changeability of rituals is a constant in their development. In Judaism, development and change create tradition(s).[47] Tradition is another factor that sustains and preserves the specific traits of social structures. In many respects, Halakhah is the major vehicle of tradition in Judaism. Rabbinic Judaism, as a social structure, owes its existence and extension in time and place to the Halakhic activity that it generates. It is a process that constantly renews itself while being viewed, at the same time, as an unchanging continuum. It is said in the Mishnah (Tractate *Avot* 1: 1), as

---

when they gather to celebrate their national identity. See Hugh Trevor-Roper, "The Invention of Tradition: The Highland Tradition of Scotland," in: Eric Hobsbawm and Terence Ranger (eds.), *The Invention of Tradition*, Cambridge University Press: Cambridge, 1983, pp. 15-41.

[45] These issues will be taken up in the last two chapters of this book.

[46] One should keep in mind that, in the area of the sociology of religion, ideological stances play a major role. In this respect, rituals are part of the sociological structure, though not all of it.

[47] This factor has been mentioned above, with regard to the tradition in which Halakhah evolves.

also in many other passages in rabbinic literature, that the Torah was handed down from generation to generation. In rabbinic Judaism, this process entitles and obliges every generation to interact actively with the materials and customs that have been handed down. Although orthodox circles argue that they do not change but only refine ancient interpretations, tradition, even for them, is the fulcrum that generates a process that makes life change. In other words, in each phase of the development of Halakhah, people introduce their own changes and adjustments and so redefine themselves from a sociological point of view. These changes reflect and address the specific concerns of each generation regarding the changes that life enforces on it. Each generation leaves not only its learned imprint on the Torah-phase it has received but also its indelible mark on the shaping of its social structures. This may be a destabilising factor but it is, at the same time, a clear testimony that the process of creation and re-creation is constantly active.

Hermeneutic considerations play an instrumental role in these changes and adaptations. It is a fact that when Halakhah is left to its rather accidental—though repetitive—modes of performance, it is less given to change than when, in light of changing circumstances, its rulings are studied and subjected to hermeneutic scrutiny. The study of Halakhah, particularly when engaged in as a religious duty, is seen as a ritual act that has its own dynamics and status. Thus, practically-speaking, the process of studying Halakhah is a ritual in its own right. Study, in this case, resolves the polarity that normally exists between self-conserving stagnation and reformative evolution.[48] Interesting as is the subject of sociology and rituals and the dynamic of change, we are obliged to leave it at this point.

Changes are sometimes intentional, sometimes un-intentional. The subject of intention, however, is an important aspect in the doing of rituals and requires special attention. In discussing the mental factors that accompany the doing of rituals, Judaic sources often refer to the notion of *kavanah*, intention. For reasons that will become clear immediately, our discussion makes a distinction between intention and intentionality. Numerous debates, both in rabbinic sources and in scholarly research, discuss the

---

[48] I do not use these terms in any modern denominational sense.

question of how essential *kavanah*, intention, is to the doing of religious law. *Kavanah* is a theological notion and its application in the religious life of Jewish people has a number of ramifications. Briefly, the debate centres on the question of whether the *Mitsvot*, the Hebrew term for ritual acts, should be done with or without *Kavanah*.[49] More specifically, *kavanah* indicates an "oriented action" and refers to the targeted will of the person doing the ritual, whose mind is set on fulfilling a specific religious obligation.

Intentionality is a more complex notion. To clarify this point, I shall give one example. Other examples will be discussed further on. Mishnah Tractate *Makhshirin* ("instrumental causes") states that edibles can become impure when a dead insect falls on or touches them. However, they must be wet in order to contract impurity. If they have become wet without the knowledge of the owner, or if he disapproves of their having become wet, the fact that they have become wet does not count as a valid instrumental cause making them susceptible to contracting impurity. Wetness, in this case, must be something that the owner is aware of and consciously approves. Intentionality refers to any mental process that is considered critically instrumental in the *shaping of conditions* that result in a ritually valid action or status. Intentionality thus constitutes the state of mind required for positing the right conditions without which a ritual event is void. In many cases, some of which will be examined below, the factor of intentionality is activated even without any conscious intention by the party concerned to create a ritual event. In these cases, intentionality is the mental factor that activates instrumentally valid conditions to also become ritually valid. Intentionality is needed to make certain ritual events possible. Understandably, shaping the conditions for an event to connect to a ritually relevant situation does not automatically come under the rubric of *kavanah*. Intentionality also means instrumentally preparing the inclusion of a certain situation in a ritually relevant category (*i. e.*, impurity). Intention-

---

[49] Most of the scholarly discussions of the term, known to me, deal with the notion of *kavanah* in philosophical, theological, and Talmudic frames of reference. An attempt to bring the discussion closer to religious and anthropological studies can be found in Howard Eilberg-Schwartz, *The Human Will in Judaism: The Mishnah's Philosophy of Intention*, Scholars Press: Atlanta, 1986. The extent to which my approach differs from that of Eilberg-Schwartz will be explained when our discussion focuses on intentionality. A classic *locus* that discusses the notion of *kavanah* is Bavli *Berakhot* 13/a.

ality defines (a) the key factor that causes this inclusion to happen, and (b) the circumstances in which this factor crystallises.

The *kavanah* type of orientation usually indicates two other factors. The first is that, in doing a ritual act (for instance, reciting a prayer), the person concerned is mentally orienting himself towards fulfilling a specific religious obligation. The right timeframe, place, and specific mode of doing the ritual are basic conditions. In order to do what they are expected to do, rituals cannot be done casually or in an offhand manner. In the absence of *kavanah*, the Halakhic question arises of whether the ritual act fulfilled a religious obligation or not. There are different opinions regarding this question, but they need not concern us here. The second factor involves issues that entail an accidental change in a person's intention. Mishnah Tractate *Sanhedrin* 9: 2 addresses the issue of a person who intends to do one thing and by mistake does another:

> If he intended to kill a beast and killed a man, a gentile and killed an Israelite, an untimely birth and killed an offspring that was viable, he is exempt.
> If he intended to hit him on his loins with a blow that was not sufficient to kill him when it struck his loins, but it hit his heart, and there was sufficient force in that blow to kill him when it struck his heart, and he died, he is exempt.
> If he intended to hit him on his heart, and there was in that blow sufficient force to kill when it struck his heart, and it hit him on his loins, and there was not sufficient force in that blow to kill him when it struck his loins, but he died, he is exempt.
> If he intended to hit a large person, and there was not sufficient force in that blow to kill a large person, but it hit a small person, and there was sufficient force in that blow to kill a small person, and he died, he is exempt...
> Rabbi Shim'on says: "Even if he intended to kill this party, and he actually killed some other party, he is exempt.[50]

The cases discussed by Tractate *Sanhedrin* are rare. They raise unpleasant issues but the principle is clear. Intention, *kavanah*, makes a great deal of difference in such cases. Indeed it constitutes the entire difference, for a person's conscious attitude when carrying out a specific act decides whether the person is liable or not. The

---

[50] A similar case is discussed in Tosefta Tractate *Sanhedrin* 12: 4: "... If a person intended to kill an animal but killed a human being... he is not liable".

above cases demonstrate, once again, how the mind factor operates in rituals. Another example will clarify what is at stake:

> He who was going along behind a synagogue, or whose house was near a synagogue, and who heard the sound of the *shofar* (a ram's horn blown on the high holidays)… if he paid attention [thereby intending to carry out his obligation], he has fulfilled his obligation. But if not, he has not fulfilled his obligation. [That is the rule] even if this one heard and that one heard, [for this one] paid attention, and that one did not pay attention [to what he heard] (Mishnah Tractate *Rosh Ha-Shanah* 3: 7).

In theological terms, the notion of "orienting one's heart" (Mishnah Tractate *Berakhot* 4: 5) implies that a mental turn of direction towards the Holy One or the Holy of Holies has taken place. This mental turn of direction indicates the element of spiritual geography (the "place" factor) in prayers. Initially, "the Israelites would set their eyes upward to heaven and submit to their Father in heaven" (Mishnah Tractate *Rosh Ha-Shanah* 3: 8). Later, when the Temple became a point of ritual orientation, the prayers were recited, with the face of the praying person turning in the direction of the Templeplace, or Jerusalem (1 Kings 8: 30). When turning one's face is technically impossible, turning one's heart assumes the same function. The conditions which prevailed in the Diaspora dictated other means of orientation. The *Mizrach* ("East") was fixed as the "North Pole" of the cultic compass. Facing the East, while praying, implied a spiritual connectedness to the site of the Temple or to Jerusalem. Thus, rituals must be done with a certain mind-set, and, often, in a specific place. One is even told that, if one is unable to turn physically in the direction of the Temple or Jerusalem, one can do so mentally (Mishnah Tractate *Berakhot* 4: 5).[51]

V

We have already referred to the factor of intentionality and to the manner in which it shapes ritual conditions. Intentionality

---

[51] Although a few striking examples have been given, the subject of *kavanah* is not exhausted here. Two famous schools—that of Hillel and that of Shammai argued over whether to include *kavanah* or exclude it from ritual performance. See Yitzhak D. Gilat, *Studies in the Development of the Halakhah* [in Hebrew], Bar Ilan University Press: Jerusalem, 1992, pp. 72-83. It should be noted that Gilat, and others who have dealt with the same subject, confuse issues of *kavanah* with those of intentionality.

crystallises in the subjective attitude of the person to whom, or to whose property, the ritual conditions apply. Evidently, intentionality plays a crucial role in shaping the ritual act and in making it happen. In its religious configuration, intentionality implies a state of mind that sets the right conditions for the ritual event to become effective, with the aim of fulfilling God's will, or making his law effective. Intentionality defines the state of mental participation that is needed to create conditions that are ritually valid. Intentionality is present in almost every area of Halakhic ruling.[52] It can be said that intentionality sometimes minimal, if at all, activates intentional participation. In one of the examples discussed below, the person involved is pleased with the fact that the fruits have become wet. He may be completely unaware of the fact that being pleased is a decisive factor in creating the conditions that make his edibles susceptible to contracting impurity.[53]

The presence of intentionality in the domain of purity and impurity, as noted above, is an important one. To begin with, it makes the issue of purity/impurity less arbitrary than it seems. It is not superfluous to point out that this factor is not discussed in any of Mary Douglas' treatments of the subject.[54] As we have noted in the previous chapter, Douglas focuses on *existing* categories of hygiene and, particularly, pollution and danger. Most recently she has connected these notions with the Pentateuchal urge to overcome heathen beliefs. Mishnaic sources, in contrast, emphasise the process of *creating* categories. Rituals create categories that are effective in shaping the religious "cosmos." Category formation is one of the chief issues discussed in Jacob Neusner's more recent studies.[55] What matters, here, is how the human mind uses rituals to create lived-through realities. Living through a ritually relevant reality creates conditions that are essential to defining a

---

[52] See Jacob Neusner, "Intentionality and Life Processes in the Law of Judaism: *Hallah* and *Makhsirin*," *The Review of Rabbinic Judaism* IV/1 (2001), pp. 59-77.

[53] Mishnah Tractate *Makhsirin*, chapter 1. See Jacob Neusner, *A History of the Mishnaic Law of Purities*, Brill: Leiden, 1977 [Classics in Judaic Studies Series, Vol. XVII], *Makhshirin*. (Reprint: Global Publications: Binghamton, 2002).

[54] This also holds true of Mary Douglas's most recent book, *Leviticus as Literature*, Oxford University Press, Oxford, 1999.

[55] See, for instance, Jacob Neusner, *The Hermeneutics of the Rabbinic Category-Formations: An Introduction.*, University Press of America: Lanham, 2000.

ritual category. This category is the label that is now applied to that reality.

Several additional examples will illustrate what I have in mind. I shall focus again on the laws of purity and impurity which, in many respects, most strikingly exemplify the notion of intentionality. In this connection, I shall refer, once again, to Tractate *Makhshirin*. This Tractate discusses the instrumental factors (in Hebrew: *makhshirim* [*makhshirin* is the Aramaic form]) that cause impurity.[56]

Makhshirin 1: 1 says regarding liquids that may render edibles impure, when a dead creature or insect touches them:

> Every liquid that from the outset is agreeable [to the owner of the edibles], even though at the end it is no longer agreeable, or which at the end is agreeable, even though it was not so from the outset...

Thus, the owner's thoughts regarding the liquid, even without making them known explicitly, makes all the ritual difference. If a person takes a bath and the water drips from his body onto edibles, nothing will occur that is liable to have ritual consequences. However, if a person uses his garment to wring out his hair and the water drips onto edibles, this is instrumental in rendering the edibles susceptible to impurity (1: 5). If a person floats his fruits in the rushing stream of a river, the fruits do not become susceptible to impurity (1: 6). The watershed in all these cases is the wishful wetting of the edibles. If it is a wishful act or event, it is liable make the waters (liquids) active agents in incurring impurity. If it is not, there is nothing that changes the status of the waters (liquids) to be such active agents. If the person concerned did not want to wet the fruits but only to float them from one place to the other, the fact that the fruits were wet did not make them, in this case, susceptible to contracting impurity. Similarly, the drops of sweat that accidentally drop onto edibles do not create the required conditions for becoming susceptible to impurity. But sweat that is caused after entering hot water makes edibles susceptible to impurity (2: 1), since one obviously enters a sauna in order to make the body sweat. Finally, consider this case:

---

[56] The translations are primarily those of Jacob Neusner, *The Mishnah: A New Translation*, Yale University Press: New Haven and London, 1988. I have made a few modifications, because I believe they serve my purposes better than the translations offered by Neusner.

> The ass drivers who were crossing the river and their sacks fell into the water—if they [the ass drivers] were happy [with the wetting of the sacks and what they contained], the load of foods is susceptible to impurity (3: 7).

There are many more examples of this kind, all of which tell the same story, namely, that the human mind does not only generate ritual actions but also specifies the conditions necessary to impart ritual relevance.

In the cases quoted above, the element of intentionality is prominent. Jacob Neusner writes about intentionality as manifested in the case of *Makhshirin*: "There [in *Makhshirin*], what is deliberately wet down is subject to uncleanness, but what is accidentally wet down is not".[57] In contrast, I believe that these examples demonstrate that the factor of intentionality does not depend on whether or not the act was done deliberately. In the case of the rituals discussed, deliberateness and intentionality are not always, or necessarily, interconnected. What matters is the factor of mental compliance towards one of the segments of the "event." Thus, liquids that wet edibles in a manner that does not show any explicit sign of being a deliberate act may still create the potential conditions for impurity. It is the implicit expression of compliance with the fact that the edibles are wet that makes them susceptible to taking on the impurity imparted by dead insects.

One encounters the same principle in another case—the tithing of a portion of bread dough, *Hallah*. Here, too, the factor of intentionality is dominant. We have observed, several times, that the logic of the ritual is expressed in the order and correct sequencing of its various parts. In the first chapter, we noted that when this order changes, the ritual status vanishes.[58] Mishnah Tractate *Hallah*, Chapter 3, contains a number of examples that illustrate the importance of the orderly sequencing of details in each case, particularly regarding intention and intentionality.[59] Any

---

[57] See Jacob Neusner, "Intentionality etc.", p. 67.

[58] Neusner uses the notion of a conflict between life and death with regard to the ritual tithing of the *Hallah*-portion (p. 67). I will do the same further on, in my discussion of sacrifice. But I strictly avoid notions of "sanctification" and uncleanness, because I consider that these terms give an unnecessary theological twist to the entire issue.

[59] Neusner writes: "... intentionality plays no role in the liability of the dough to dough-offering" (p. 67). My analysis demonstrates the opposite.

change from the correct order (the "protocol") exempts a baker from the duty of tithing his dough. In other words, one can by-pass the tithing by changing certain details of the standard order. In such cases, intentionality negatively interferes with the prescribed order. What I have tried to show, is the centrality, even power, that mental processes have in shaping an act into a ritual or a ritual into an ordinary act. The chief mental factor on which we focus here is intentionality.

Another set of examples comes from Mishnah Tractate *Zebahim* ["burnt offerings"]. But before I quote them, I would like to refer the reader to a dictum that says it all very clearly:

> Thought causes all utensils to enter (lit., "descend into") a state of impurity, but they cannot ascend (be purged) from their state of impurity save by a change effected by an act. For an act can cancel both an [or: another] act of usage and a thought, but a thought cannot cancel an act of usage or a thought. (Mishnah Tractate *Kelim* 25: 9).

In other words, the mental process of intentionality creates the conditions that make a certain utensil susceptible to impurity. But a full-fledged ritual act is necessary in order to revert to, or restore, the original condition. This is the quintessence of an important branch of rituals and its ritual theory. A ritual act reconstitutes a reality that has been disturbed, damaged, or gravely unbalanced, even by the tiniest thought.

Mishnah Tractate *Zebahim* (1: 1) begins with this statement:

> All animal offerings which were slaughtered for any other but their designated purpose [lit., "name"] are ritually approved of [so that their blood is tossed and their entrails burned as a sacrifice]. However, they are not accredited to the owner in fulfilment of the [originally] designated obligation.

The deviation from the designated purpose of the sacrifice takes place in a mental process. This demonstrates the powerful role, which the factors of the mind and intentionality play. In the discussion of the various details for bringing a sacrificial offering to the altar of the Temple, Tractate *Zebahim* (1: 4) lays great emphasis on the manner in which the blood is "received, conveyed, and tossed." What is of great importance, apart from the slaughtering and burning of parts of the sacrificial-animal on the altar, is the manner in which the blood is handled. Handling blood is a ritual procedure in its own right: although it is part of the sacrificial

event as a whole, it has its own individually defined functionality. For this reason, anything that is improperly done in the course
of the blood-ritual can render the *entire* sacrificial event invalid.
   Tractate *Zebahim* (1: 4) says:

> ... in the situation in which he *has* to convey [the blood], [wrong] thought
> can generate sacrificial invalidation. [If he does so] in a situation in
> which he does not have to convey [the blood], [wrong] thought can-
> not generate sacrificial invalidation.

Thus, in general, a [wrong] thought or intention can generate
sacrificial invalidation, provided the thought comes from some-
body whose sacrificial act is, in the first place, ritually acceptable
(*Zebahim* 2: 2; 3: 1). The question, of course, is what constitutes a
wrong thought. Mishnah defines wrong thought *ad hoc*. Tractate
Zebahim clearly shows that different categories of "wrong thought"
prevail in different sacrificial circumstances. In any event, these
examples clearly demonstrate the important role that thought, not
necessarily ideas, has in rituals. As indicated above, the mind does
not only generate ritual acts, it is functional in keeping them intact. Any "change of mind" regarding what should be done and
the correct order of the performance will have an annulling effect on the ritual act. The mind generates rituals and the mind
can also alter their efficacy.

VI

The above examples illustrate, from a new perspective, the manner in which I perceive the study of rituals in their embedded
performative modes. Evidently, it makes a great difference whether
ritual is studied as a generic notion or as an individually crafted
construct with a dynamic of its own. This difference can best be
seen in the diverse modes of relating to rituals. One can say that
a priest stands up and blesses the community; or the prayer book
will indicate "Here, the priest blesses the community." One may
even give a detailed description of how the priest says the blessing, the very words he uses, and the bodily gestures he makes while
saying the blessing. Specifically, attention should be given to the
intentionality of the performing priest and the community present,
which is needed in order to make the ritual process effective. This

is precisely what Midrash *Sifri* on *Be-midbar*, parag. 39-40, says on the priestly blessing, mentioned in Num. 6: 22-27.

Knowledgeable observation that focuses upon participation in the rituals is certainly the best recommendation that can be given, at this point, to those wishing to study rituals in the manner suggested above. This is the approach favoured by anthropologists, although the latter often lack the knowledge needed in order to classify the materials observed in a context that is specifically relevant to rituals studied, and to religious studies. In contrast, the study of rituals from texts, which is the approach of religious studies, places students at a considerable distance from rituals as they are/were done. There are pictorial "texts," which may contain depictions of rituals, such as those found on ancient wall paintings and vases. The process of deciphering pictorial depictions, however, is no easier task than that of interpreting verbal texts. There are, in addition, prescriptive and descriptive texts. Obviously, the different texts contain different perspectives and approaches to the presentation of the information they contain. This is true even in cases where both the prescriptive and the descriptive texts converge regarding the details of the same ritual.[60] The study of rituals thus involves several methodological difficulties that have to be clarified before additional research can be done. This is particularly true of any attempt to assess the cognitive aspects of rituals. Since rituals are viewed here as direct expressions of the human mind, they entail a mode of cognition that is expressed primarily in behavioural modes. After consulting experts on the physiology of the brain, I learnt that current knowledge of the various phases of brain activity that may relate to ritual behaviour is limited. Thus, a more sophisticated analysis of the subject matter than that which I have undertaken here must wait for the acquisition of more knowledge on the function of the brain in ritual activity. As noted before, I am not convinced by the recent trend to explain ritual behaviour in humans

---

[60] In some cases, such as the Feast of Booths, even Scripture contains versions that vary on the prescriptive level. One should compare Lev. 23: 33-34 with Num. 29: 12-38, Deut. 16: 13-16, Neh. 8: 14-18, and Zech. 14: 16-19 to see that different versions of the same feast prevailed in ancient Israel. Then, following a further comparison of the scriptural materials with Mishnah and the Tosefta, additional layers of stratification become evident. This can be seen on both the prescriptive and descriptive levels.

through biological data and biological terms of reference. Some
rituals may indeed reflect biological needs, but the repetition of
rituals at particular times and circumstances, when these biological needs do not exist, removes the study of rituals from the
exclusive realm of biological explanation.[61]

One major question arises here: how are rituals empowered to
do what they are expected to do? The notion of empowering rituals indicates that rituals are not performed in a careless, accidental, mechanical, or matter-of-fact manner. It also indicates that
the mere doing of a certain act does not necessarily endow it with
the fully enacted properties of a ritual event. To give a ritual act
status and power, it has to be configured in a special manner; it
has to possess a special inner logic that works towards achieving
specific ends.[62] In short, there are certain factors that endow rituals with their power to do what they are expected to do. Admittedly, this power is an assumed component, which comes into being
when a number of factors interact (for instance, time, place and
intention). Achieving this structural interplay means that the specific ritual has been performed correctly, at the right time and place.
The small pieces that make up the ritual performance are fitted
together—by the mind, of course—to create a coherent action.
The proper conditions are created for the action to accomplish
what it is supposed to bring about. The complexity of each Halakhic prescription is a striking example of the complex nature of
rituals, in general.

VII

I would like to wind up this part of the discussion by reminding
the reader of two notions that have been discussed at length in
the first chapter. They provide the reader with a sense of fixing

---

[61] Sexual behaviour may be a good example, in this respect. Sexual relations
are a biological need. But they are ritualised in order to sustain courtship, marriage and encourage childbirth, and are subdued in monastic life and in the Catholic
priesthood. Freudians even speak of processes of sublimation (a mental process) of
sexual drives in humans.

[62] A striking example of an empowering prayer is the *ana beko'ah*, "I adjure You
with great might..." It originated in medieval Qabbalistic circles. Regarding the
notion of theurgy, empowering the performance of the divine decrees, see Moshe
Idel, *Kabbalah: New Perspectives*, Yale University Press: New Haven and London,
1988.

the point of departure of any discussion of ritual. The first is "attitudinal space." Every ritual process creates a certain "ritual space" or "cosmos," and since each process consists in a behavioural attitude that is mentally generated, I have referred to these "spaces" in terms of "attitudinal spaces." An attitudinal space relates to a specific event as an existentially vital environment. In these spaces, rituals are endowed with their special features and functions, and these are specifically fixed in order to realise specific results. The actual manner in which the desired goals are achieved is still a riddle. Most of the relevant research deals with the psychology of cognition and memory rather than with rituals or ritual behaviour and their origins in the physiology of the brain. I have mentioned the notion of "attitudinal spaces" here in order to provide a framework for future discussion of the subject.

The second notion I have used is "transformation." Everything that happens in the "attitudinal space" is conducive to creating a transformative event or transformative results. Transformation is the change that a ritual performance brings about, whether in the performing person, in his physical or social environment or status, or—in a religious context—in a particular deity to whom the ritual has been addressed.[63] This process involves specific psychological stances. The discussion, on this level, is on safer ground than at the level of brain functioning and biological explanations. I indicated a few guidelines that took us in the direction of the work of Donald Winnicott. More needs to be done, in this area, than I am competent to do. Needless to say, when rituals are performed in a community, the transformation is likely to affect the whole community and, in this respect, group psychology and sociology are vital areas for the study of rituals. The important question then is: how are rituals structured to bring about the expected *social* transformation? From the point of view of ritual theory, the best answer that I can give is that the special structure and inner logic of rituals is essential to empowering them for their designated goals, individual and social alike. They configure a type of reality that is primarily shaped by the interplay of subjective and objective materials. These materials stimulate the mind

---

[63] Almost every religious act does this. The passage from a state of impurity to one of purity, from profanity to sanctity, from sinfulness to righteousness—all entail transformative processes.

to generate actions and modes of behaviour that, when desired, take on ritual form.

As noted above, from the point of view of theoretical structuralism, rituals are a language.[64] They have their own vocabulary, grammar, and syntax. They create an argument, a sequential process of making something to happen. One may even go a step further and argue that rituals create meanings. But, in the line of thinking developed here, meaning *in* rituals is exhausted in the very doing of the rituals. Clearly, this is a performative language: I am attempting to translate the behavioural phase into a verbal argument. When theology and ideology enter the arena, the situation changes completely. At this point, rituals may serve a specific theological stance or idea. Thus, rituals may use linguistic and vocal forms of expression in a purely behavioural context or in the service of ideas and symbols. What matters are the structured forms of the actions that are viewed here as "statements" or "arguments" in their own right. Rituals are, thus, processual events: they create "arguments" that spread out in time and space as long as they have not completed what they are supposed to accomplish. It is clear that rituals speak to us on the performative level. Ritual statements also have another kind of communicative function: they make people relate to one another in terms of the shared ritual experience. This point will receive more attention in the last chapter of this book. Finally, rituals, particularly those of a religious nature, function in establishing a relationship of (conditional) mutuality and reciprocity with divine beings.

This chapter, together with Chapter 5, examine the manner in which the practice of scriptural law and Halakhah respectively function as Judaic forms of ritual. I believe that a full-scale and paradigmatic study of Halakhah as ritual is a desideratum. In this chapter, we have just laid the foundations of such a study. Halakhah is one of the most complex forms of ritual known to us. It creates models for scholarly work that have paradigmatic importance for the study of rituals, in general. It is possible to speak of

---

[64] The language of rituals is not identical to the language in which rituals are either prescribed or described. In most cases, the performance of rituals entails an act of translation, from text to praxis. How this is done is a question that has to be discussed separately. However, we may say that the Oral Torah contains the principles of this translation for the religion of the Israelites.

the Halakhah-stage in Judaic religiousness, in a similar way as one speaks of the Church-Fathers stage in Christianity and the Hadith stage in Islam. In terms of historical length, this is the longest period in the Israelite religion. Judaism was often criticised for what was viewed as its over-indulgence in the performance of Halakhah. In rabbinic Judaism, Halakhah has become the one and only factor that obliges the Judaic believer to lead a religious way of life. His entire existence is shaped by the precepts that are meticulously formulated in one of the richest legal libraries known to us. There is hardly any aspect of Judaic life that is not governed by Halakhah. The following is a striking example:

> Even when a person is sleeping so as to intentionally give rest to his mind, and also allow his body to rest so that he will not be sick and consequently prevented from worshipping God, one cannot but conclude that this kind of sleep has the status of divine worship.[65]

Maimonides' advice combines issues of Halakhah and philosophical ideology.

As noted, it is impossible, here, to discuss all the issues relating to the study the nature of Halakhah. We have, however, suggested a new scholarly approach to its study and understanding. We have already mentioned several prejudiced stances against ritual. One that has not yet been mentioned in the present context relates modern Jewish secularism. This sector proffers the argument that Halakhah is typical of *Galut* (exile) Judaism and therefore declares Halakhah obsolete and redundant in modern Jewish life. Halakhah is viewed in terms that swing from irrelevance to absolute negation. It must be clear by now that this is not a position we can accept here for scholarly purposes. Rituals can never be obsolete and redundant, unless they are moved to the domain of mythology. Any scholarly discussion of Halakhah and ritual must first disengage itself from such pejorative notions. Indeed, Halakhah can no longer be excluded from the study of rituals, and, by the same token, ritual studies have to pay full attention to the kind of behavioural attitudes that mark religious law. As noted, Halakhah is usually studied in various scholarly connections and under various categories of discussion. However, they rarely include ritual. Furthermore, we have noted that Halakhah is usually found under headings like jurisprudence and

---

[65] See Maimonides, Mishneh Torah, *Hilkhot De^cot* 3:3.

religious law, hermeneutics, history and sociology. The study of Halakhah seldom includes anything that is of substantial relevance to religious studies.[66] This means that the parameters of religious studies are rarely taken into consideration in the study of Halakhah.[67] True, scholars of religious studies have their own agenda and are mostly oriented towards the study of Christianity, the religions of East Asia, Islam, and the native religions of the Americas, Africa and the Pacific. Unless Halakhah is connected to the world of Hebrew Scripture and Midrash (its theology, history, archaeology, and literature), it is usually not included in the academic programmes of religious studies. More generally, though, in American scholarship, one finds Judaism frequently included in Near Eastern Studies. In Europe, it comes under biblical and theological studies. The relevant conclusions with regard to the study of Halakhah must be obvious by now.

The present chapter has discussed a few aspects of the study of Halakhah that give an indication of what a full-scale discussion would entail. Scholars studying the Judaic background of Christianity often found in Halakhah a source of understanding for some of the stories told about Jesus in the New Testament.[68] Nonethe-

---

[66] With all the differences in their views, the two names that stand out, in modern scholarship, as exceptions to this rule are: Professors Jacob Neusner and E. P. Sanders. Neusner subjected the corpus of rabbinic writings in Talmudic times to various scholarly disciplines (religious, political, economic and social), which are not Talmudic in the narrow sense of the term. His work is particularly relevant to a discussion of rabbinic law from the point of view of religious studies. Although, in many respects, Neusner's voluminous work can be considered a point of departure for the present study, it is essentially different. Neusner clarifies the corpus of rabbinic writings and its major themes, categories, and forms of narrative in relation to a wide spectrum of theological considerations. But, *grosso modo*, he does not open the discussion to the question of ritual and ritual theory. His scholarly ontology is emphatically theological.

[67] This holds true in spite of the fact that a number of scholars who write about Halakhah are affiliated to departments of religious studies.

[68] It should be noted that very little Tannaitic Halakhah can historically be ascertained to be relevant to the study of the New Testament. As Neusner demonstrated in his writings, there is no guarantee that what is presented in rabbinic writings as the Halakhah of the Tannaim can be truly accredited to them. What we know about the Tannaim is paradigmatically correct but not historically ascertainable. Jesus lived almost one hundred years before the apex of the Tannaitic period. In this respect, New Testament materials can help scholars to understand the Tannaim rather than the other way around. The Halakhah of Qumran is more relevant to the study of New Testament Christianity more than the study of the Tannaim.

less, in terms of ritual studies, Halakhah continued to remain an ignored area of study. It is to be hoped that the comments made here, and further on in the present book, will stimulate a new kind of discussion with regard to Halakhah.

CHAPTER FIVE

SACRIFICES IN BIBLICAL LITERATURE AND RITUAL THEORY

I

Since I consider that sacrifices constitute the heart of rituals, everything that has been said so far is inherently connected to this chapter and to Chapter 6. These two chapters represent the core, and essential test case, of the preceding discussions and their methodological deliberations. Sacrifices, in the Israelite religion, are usually discussed in the framework of biblical studies, which, initially, is their natural context. However, in order to discuss their embedded ritual theory, it is necessary to use different terms of reference to those generally used in biblical studies. Discussing biblical texts from their exegetical, text critical, hermeneutic, historical, or theological perspectives is of limited use to our goal. Biblical texts that either prescribe or describe sacrifices use highly coded forms of expression and provide almost no information that contributes to a scholarly assessment of what is actually done and how.[1] Furthermore, they do not make it clear to those who are interested in ritual theory, rather than in theology, what the sacrifices bring into effect, beyond the theological assumptions that tend to accompany their doing. It is generally believed that sacrifices atone for grave sins or express gratitude to gods; but belief

---

[1] I wish to repeat that the phrase "to do a ritual" is a common expression in modern anthropology. Accordingly, throughout this book, I have chosen to use the expression "doing" rituals rather than "performing" rituals. Let me also repeat the reason for doing so. The word "perform" is associated with artistic and theatrical settings. "Doing" (in Hebrew: *la-ʿasot*) rituals and sacrifices was a common form of expression in ancient Greece, as also in Judaism. In Scripture, one finds "to do a sacrifice" (Num. 28-29); "to do Shabbat" (Ex. 31: 16); "to do the laws [of the Torah]" (Deut. 6: 24); etc. For other, particularly Greek, parallels, see Walter Burkert, *Homo Necans: The Anthropology of Ancient Greek Sacrificial Ritual and Myth*, The University of California Press: Berkeley... 1983, p. 3.

is not an issue that can substantiate scholarly assessments. Thus, a different language to that which is presently accessible to biblical scholars needs to be applied in the study of sacrificial rituals.

It follows that scholars, wishing to study sacrifices in terms of reference that relate to anthropological issues, first need to decipher encoded textual messages and make them available to a behavioural assessment. No wonder, then, that only few scholars have given systematic attention to the subject matter and to its proper assessment in the framework of ritual studies. The most systematic studies, in this respect, are by Henri Hubert and Marcel Mauss, *Sacrifice: Its Nature and Function*, and *The Gift* by Marcel Mauss.[2] These seminal works attracted a lot of scholarly attention and exercised considerable influence on this field of study. In many ways, they represent a continental divide in this area of study, for they mark a transition from accidental observation to systematic study.[3]

Mauss and Hubert present their case in a comparative framework that highlights the relevant Hindu sacrificial materials with their counterparts as presented in the religion of ancient Israel. However, when it comes to the study of detailed cases, their studies make general observations rather than specific ones.[4] The books lack a segment-by-segment reading and analysis of sacrifices, which is what I propose in this chapter and in chapter 6. Their books offer primarily an external reading of the subject matter rather than an internal one. Judging from my knowledge and understand-

---

[2] What Hubert and Mauss write on the sacrificial system in the Pentateuch requires comment. I assume that the Judaic materials mentioned in their study, *Sacrifice: Its Nature and Function*, are mostly contributed by Mauss. Astonishingly, little is said in the main text of the book on the Judaic materials that can be compared to Hindu sacrificial texts and rites. The Judaic materials are mentioned primarily in the endnotes and their discussion is hardly satisfactory. As I read it, the book presents a discussion of Hindu sacrificial rites with comments on Judaic parallels, rather than a well-balanced discussion of parallel materials. See footnote 4, below.

[3] For a recent and comprehensive evaluation of Mauss's contribution to the study of the nature of gifts and sacrifices, see Maurice Godelier, *The Enigma of the Gift*, The University of Chicago Press: Great Britain, 1999, pp. 10-107: "The Legacy of Mauss."

[4] It is interesting to note, in the present connection, that several scholars have pointed out that Mauss's studies were informed and influenced by his Jewish origins. See, for instance, W.S.F. Pickering, "Mauss's Jewish Background: A Biographical Essay," in: Wendy James and N.J. Allen (eds.), *Marcel Mauss: A Centenary Tribute*, Berghahn Books: New York and Oxford, 1998, pp. 43-60.

ing of the Judaic materials, I can say that there is a disturbing degree
of misinformation, and it would make a detailed study in its own
right to examine case by case each of the examples the writers
give.

It should be pointed out, that in any discussion of sacrifices
cross-religious observations, such as those made by Hubert and
Mauss, should be handled with caution. Every religion has its own
systemic structures, its endemic context. Consequently, the amount
of materials that make sense in a detailed comparison between,
for instance, Greek forms of sacrifice and their Israelite counterparts, is quite limited. Thus, when Hubert and Mauss attempt to
show that Israelite and Hindu forms of sacrifice share the same
comparative umbrella, one must read their comments with critical caution. To give one example, out of many, Israelite forms
of sacrifice are very sparing in their descriptions of what is actually said during the sacrifices. Israel Knohl has even argued that
total silence prevailed in the Israelite sanctuary.[5] Hardly any form
of speech is reported in connection with sacrificial services and
there is clearly an attempt, in relevant biblical materials, to avoid
almost any reference to verbal expressions that may have accompanied the ritual acts.[6] This is a dominant feature in the Temple
worship, and symptomatically it is not mentioned in Mauss' studies. Most sacrificial rites, known to us from outside the realms of
the religion of ancient Israel, contain references to the verbal
expressions (lyrics, prayers, conjurations) that used to accompany
sacrifices offered in Temples. To take another example: in ancient Greece, the dates chosen for various sacrificial cycles were
often connected to specific events in the lives of the people
(whether in villages or in towns) and the various gods while, in
ancient Israel, sacrifices were commonly associated with "mythic"

---

[5] This is one of the major points made in Israel Knohl, *The Sanctuary of Silence:
The Priestly Torah and the Holiness School*, Fortress Press: Minneapolis, 1995.

[6] There are two notable exceptions to this rule. They are mentioned in Deut.
26, and refer to the *Bikkurim* and *Ma'aser* [*Sheni*] (the first yielding of the fruits of
the earth and the second year tithing, respectively), when brought to the Temple.
In both cases, the scriptural text mentions specific prayers (in later sources they
are referred to as "confessions") that must be said on these occasions. The reason
is that originally God rejected the sacrifices of the land offered by Cain (see Gen.
Chapter 2). The Deuteronomist presents a completely different attitude to vegetarian offerings and the unique ritual act, the "confession" endorses this change
of attitude.

events in the nation's past and with the agricultural cycle.[7] Previously, we referred to the fact that once the "religion"-stage had been established (as opposed to the ethos stage), all sacrificial events took place in the "chosen place," *i.e.*, the Temple. This notion is particularly associated with the position taken by the Deuteronomist. However, in many other religions cultic places are dispersed. Local temples and sanctuaries are one of the major targets of the prophets' criticism of the forms of idol worshipping that used to prevail in ancient Israel. I should note that, in pointing to these differences, I am not making a value judgement, or reflecting an intellectual preference. Cultural and religious differences are context-dependent and, in this respect, they are essential factors to any study of sacrifices carried out at a cross-cultural level. The extent to which such comparisons are essential to general statements on the subject matter is a question that need not be resolved here.

In Mauss, and a few other studies, one quickly realises that the Israelite sacrificial materials are relevant to shaping concepts of sacrifice, in general. However, these studies omit from the discussion a number of aspects that are essential if one wishes to draw a full picture and formulate a ritual theory. One such aspect is the study of the logic, which, from the point of view of ritual theory, constitutes the inner structure of rituals. This remains a lacuna in many studies of ritual. Paying attention to these issues will also help us to reach new conclusions regarding sacrifices and their special configuration in ancient Israel.

Two basic notions serve as guidelines in many studies on sacrifice: they are "gift" and "substitute." But, as we shall see, something essential is missing from this picture, when one focuses only on these notions. The demonstration of what is missing constitutes one of the major tasks of the present chapter. Every sacrifice is a ritual process and is composed of various details, the sum total of which brings into effect the sacrificial goals. It is, therefore, essential to concentrate on what is done in every part of the sacrificial process and how it is done, then draw conclusions regarding the overall ritual theory implied in the sacrificial act. Only then, can we move onto the next stage, which is to examine how all the factors involved shape the manner in which the sacrifice

---

[7] See Chapter 3.

functions in a specific social order. Following this procedure will allow us to reach valid conclusions on the manner in which sacrifices, as the epitome of rituals, should be studied. The study of sacrifice can neither limit itself to the volitional aspects of the act (the "gift" element) nor only stress the ideational aspects (the "substitute" element).

Recent anthropological work on sacrifices suggests a new approach to the study of the subject. I believe that these studies introduce a new direction to the discussion: they concentrate on the sacrificial act itself and all that it entails from a ritual point of view, rather than stressing what ideational components the act gives expression to.[8] In this approach, sacrifices are separated from any theological context, and are presented as a universal factor in human behaviour. This is the approach adopted here, for I believe that what makes a sacrifice a ritual event is not its specifically religious context, but its behavioural essence.

Jacob Milgrom's recent study of the *Leviticus*-materials is unusually richly informed.[9] It highlights almost every aspect of sacrifices, presented in the Book of Leviticus and, to my mind, no study of sacrifice in biblical literature compares with this wealth of information. The book marks a landmark in the study of the priestly traditions of ancient Israel, supplying the reader with a wide panorama of comparative materials, particularly, from the ancient Near East. The book takes an interest in historical, literary, cultic, as well as exegetical, issues and subjects. What it lacks is also missing from many other studies of sacrificial rituals in the religion of ancient Israel and in other religions, namely, the examination of the materials at hand in the framework of a comprehensive theory of ritual. The present chapter points in the direction that I believe should be followed in this respect.

In order to accomplish the goals of this chapter and Chapter

---

[8] Writing, in the *Anchor Bible Dictionary* (1997), *s. v.* "Sacrifice," Gary A. Anderson notes: "The reader should know that much work still remains to be done here by the biblical scholar... By and large, biblical scholarship has not kept up with the theoretical work of recent anthropology." I fully agree with this assessment of the situation, and I hope that this book fulfils the type of work suggested in Anderson's comment.

[9] J. Milgrom, *Leviticus 1-16: A New Translation with Introduction and Commentary*, [The Anchor Bible], Doubleday: New York..., 1991. Two additional volumes complete this extraordinary undertaking, but the main thrust of Milgrom's argument in relation to sacrifices in contained in the first volume.

6, I pursue a rather complex line of argumentation and a brief outline of the contents of the two chapters is therefore in place. This outline serves, in each case, as a general introduction: it offers a few theoretical guidelines and delineates clear points of orientation. The two chapters focus on sacrificial practices in ancient Israel and in early Christianity, respectively. As in the case of rituals, it is assumed that sacrifices sustain life at crucial points of existence. Because of their dramatic modes of performance, sacrifices are able to do what other forms of ritual cannot. Sacrifices do what they are expected to do, only when special modes of consciousness exist in which the basic life processes that are addressed by the sacrifices are viewed as real and vitally present. A basic assumption that runs through the present study is that humans do not only interpret reality to make it what they believe it to be (= cognitive hermeneutics), but that special modes of consciousness can create unique realities that operate in accordance with, or as a result of, these modes of consciousness. Rituals, and especially sacrifices, are major examples of unique forms of existence, whose presence is intensely liveable and existentially relatable to and by human beings. I previously examined the psychological, intra-subjective, domains in which these realities exist.

It will be argued, here, that, as in the case of ritual in general, a major factor in the shaping of sacrifices is the intimation that a certain reality, or existence, is either under threat or actually undergoing disintegration. The sacrificial ritual is done to prevent this from happening or to repair the damage that has already been done. In the first place, the sacrificial act enacts or repeats an act of breaking:[10] it mimetically repeats the essence of a disastrous event. It is often said that healing begins with an intensification of pathological symptoms. The act of breaking—henceforth referred to as violence—repeats, at the ritual level, a destructive process mimetically similar to the one which reality has under-

---

[10] A typical example is the rite of the heifer, whose neck is broken, "when any one is found slain, lying in the open country, and it is not known who killed him"—Deut. 21: 1-9. This is an exceptionally brutal act. Slaughtering an animal, however, is also an act of breaking, even when what appears to be a more merciful way of killing is applied. Comparatively speaking, any ceremonial killing of an animal, which is viewed as part of a religious or social system (ceremonial hunting, the stabbing of a bull [generally white) in Mithraism, the killing of humans, bulls and other animals in the Roman forum) represents such an act of breaking and often has—or is given—sacrificial functions.

gone. It can be safely said that sacrificial rituals enact the reality
in which they are done and to which they relate. What the rest
of the sacrificial acts does and how it does it, can be likened to
the process of healing or resolving conflictual situations. The main
example, discussed in this chapter, *Leviticus* 16, clearly demonstrates that the two poles of the sacrificial act are often marked
by polarised extremes such as life and death, continuation and
discontinuation, existence and non-existence.[11]

In terms of methodology, the main question, here, that requires
full and careful attention is: How do the special perspectives of
sacrificial practice inform ritual studies and improve our understanding of their relationship to religious studies? In attempting
to formulate guidelines for the study of ritual theory, we began
with the rituals themselves. In approaching the subject of rituals
in the manner suggested here, we had to define first some methodological principles. I hope that it is clear to the reader, by now,
that the present study is not another study, in a long series that
assesses the study of religion in historical and theological terms
of reference. As indicated earlier, almost all the studies, I know
of, take off from historical, textual, literary, and hermeneutic platforms. Even when not explicitly declared as engaging in theological discussions, these studies are often tainted with theological
or ideological concerns. Inevitably, this entails certain value judgements, which cannot be swept under a carpet of assumed neu-
trality, even if presented against a wide range of comparative materials and interests.

It is particularly important to note that, when ritual theory is
placed at the centre of scholarly discussion, the subject of sacrifices should be given full prominence. It is in the interest of the
scholarly undertaking to maintain a clear separation between a
discussion of sacrificial practices in terms of reference of ritual
theory, and the theological presuppositions that mentally sustain

---

[11] See Victor Turner, *Schism and Continuity in an African Society: A Study of Ndembu
Village Life*, Manchester University Press: Manchester, 1957, p. 303. He writes, "A
society continually threatened with disintegration is continually performing rein-
tegrative rituals." It is argued here that sacrifices are, in a sense, such reintegra-
tive rituals. Turner adds an interesting aspect: "Ritual among the Ndembu does
not express the kinship and political structure as in firmly organized society; rather
it compensates for their deficiencies in a labile society." Turner dialectically argues that rituals replace political power and authority. It should be noted, however, that "power" (kingship, state and authority) inspires its own ritual practices.

sacrifices in their own religious framework. In my view, it is immaterial whether a theological position exists behind the sacrificial practice or whether that position emerges out of the sacrificial act. What matters is the assessment of the sacrificial act in its own terms of reference, which are emphatically performative. In other words, sacrifices should be studied in a manner that facilitates bringing to light their own, self-maintained, ritual theory. Such a theory is primarily linked to what is done and how. Proceeding, in this manner, is essential to studying the efficacious nature of sacrifices as rituals.

It is often argued that sacrifices create a multi-faceted form of dialogue with gods. When gods are connected to the discussion of sacrifice, nothing but religious or theological considerations is given visibility. When one says that a particular sacrifice aims at drawing the attention of the gods, this does not tell us anything about what is done or how it is done. Nor does it relate to the inner logic of the ritual process. The label that describes a medication and what it is expected to do, does not tell us how the medication actually works. This information is reserved to those trained in pharmaceutics. If this comparison makes sense, then the study of rituals is the study of the chemistry, or the physics, of structured forms of behaviour. Highlighting the manner in which sacrifices are structured, in either their prescribed or described modes, has little to do with the alleged receiver of the sacrificial donation. The notion of gods, who expect to receive sacrifices, can at best serve as a canopy under which theological arguments unfold. Such arguments, though, *do not explain* the nature of the sacrificial act; nor do they have anything significant to say on how it is structured to function in a purposive manner.

A ticket that specifies destination has no connection with knowledge of how trains work or how the railway system operates. Theology—and, for that matter, morality—are viewed, here, as playing a confined role. Theology creates the ideological framework in which rituals are embedded but its relevance, or contribution, to the structuring of rituals is not decisive.[12] Those who

---

[12] A word is due here on the rather strange position taken by Hyam Maccoby on the relationship between ritual and morality. He writes: "The proliferation of ritual rules in Judaism, especially in the area of ritual purity, tends to obscure the fact that ritual in Judaism is ultimately subordinate to morality, or more accurately, exists as the self-identifying code of a dedicated group whose main purpose

do rituals clearly want to know why, or for what purpose, they *do* whatever they are told to do. However, the theological response that is given in each case has little to say about what is done, how, and how it becomes ritually potent and effective. From the point of view of ritual theory, one has to demonstrate that theology plays an important role in explaining the structuring of rituals, before it can become part of the discussion. Sociological considerations, on the other hand, in as much as they provide an insight into the social structures that sustain rituals, are relevant to understanding who does the ritual, the type of social structure favoured by the doer, and the social statement made by the ritual.

Some readers may find this approach somewhat artificial, if not altogether unacceptable. If, as we argue here, theology is not important enough to play a significant role in the study of religious rituals, then what is important in this respect? Admittedly, theology is so much a part of religion that it is hard to configure a situation in which a central element, such as sacrifices, is discussed completely apart from theology. In our case, instead of making theological notions the basic motivation of ritual behaviour, we speak of behavioural or mental *transformation*. It should no longer be necessary to justify the advantage of using a theologically neutral term as the main axis around which various aspects of ritual behaviour rotate.[13]

As we have seen, transformation highlights the *behavioural* aspects of rituals. The reference to behaviour indicates the activity of a purposively-oriented mind. Acts become agents through which the mind relates to, and even shapes, specific modes of existence.[14] If this existence is impaired or threatened with non-existence, the mind generates acts that aim to reverse the fatal process. Behavioural notions do not cancel out the operation of the human mind, as such. On the contrary, behavioural acts constitute a language of their own, and language is an expression of the mind.[15] This

---

is ethical." See, Hyam Maccoby, *Ritual and Morality: The Ritual Purity System and its Place in Judaism*, Cambridge University Press: Cambridge, 1999, p. viii.

[13] See also Walter Burkert, *Homo Necans*, p. 40: "Sacrifice transforms us. By going through the irreversible "act," we reach a new plane. Whenever a new step is taken consciously and, irrevocably, it is inevitably connected with sacrifice."

[14] I am aware of the fact that, in saying this, we come very close to the way the mind operates in magic.

[15] For a slightly different presentation of ritual as a form of communication, as language, see Walter Burkert, *Homo Necans*, p. 29.

special kind of language utilises structured acts as its specific mode of expression. One could say that the human mind models acts to make them constitutively functional in life processes that support and maintain existence. Every act, and, particularly, every ritual act has its own grammar. Thus, acts speak for themselves and serve as communicative transmitters. Understanding what they "say" depends on our ability to discover the nature of the language used, in each case. This is a goal that can be achieved either, by sharing in a ritual, or by exploring in depth the mechanism that operates in each ritual act. Clearly, the ultimate goal of the researcher is to uncover the ritual theory that is functional in activating each ritual.

In many respects, sacrifices constitute the core of religion. Since they involve issues of life and death, they touch upon the deepest aspects of religion. Sacrifices, even more than do rituals in general, operate on a thin thread that marks the delicate divide between existence and non-existence. In, paradoxically, linking destruction to the revitalisation of life processes, sacrifices restore existence and prevent it from collapsing into non-existence. The reader may note that the language I use here highlights religious issues in a scholarly or academic framework. That is to say, every effort is made *not* to disguise, as is often the case, theological considerations as phenomenological observations.

For scholars doing research in religious studies to bypass theology they have to disengage themselves from criteria that promote theological interests and goals. Naturally, special efforts must be made, first, to define these criteria and show how they function. This, too, requires a scholarly approach. The main advantage of this procedure is that it avoids prejudices and the disguised, or latent, desire to promote propaganda. Scholarly work, from Victorian times, has often been affected by such propagandistic undercurrents, whether positively or negatively oriented to religion. The results of fieldwork carried out in those days and in many parts of the world, mostly by Christian scholars, were coloured by a scale of values, which placed monotheism (particularly in its Christian phases) at the top and everything else at the bottom. The notion of a high religion was polarised against religions that, in the mind of the scholars, appeared to be primitive and superstitious. Everything that did not fit European ideas and standards of religion was depicted as "aboriginal," "superstitious,"

"primitive," "magical" or "mythic." In those days, and even today, these categories used to define cultural inferiority and phenomenological marginality.[16]

This does not mean to say that religion can be divested of its
most treasured assets, namely, the belief in the omnipresence,
omniscience and omnipotence of divine beings. These are all issues
that require theological assessment. However, in order to understand the distinctly performative, that is, behavioural, language
used to prescribe or describe religious rituals one has to apply a
more inclusive discourse than the theological one. Theology and
ritual behaviour are complementary entities in religion, however
they need not necessarily be discussed in conjunction with each
other, nor should they be confused with each other. In order to
understand the one, we do not necessarily have to consider the
other. On the contrary, at the behavioural level, rituals are much
better understood when viewed in their own contextual framework, as performances.[17] As indicated earlier, theology defines
motivation, but does not necessarily explain the behavioural
mechanism of rituals.

Being aware of this does not mean the opposite—namely, that
religion has to be de-sacralised before it becomes the object of
scholarly examination. There is no need to cause a contextual
displacement of the religious element. However, even when addressing religious issues and language at a scholarly level, one
should always be aware that a certain degree of conceptual and
contextual translation is being applied. Being aware of this fact
means that scholars should beware of applying scholarly over-
translation, that is to say, arbitrarily de-contextualise the issue at
hand.

In other words, the academic study of religion often highlights
aspects of religion in ways that differ completely from the way

---

[16] In this respect, it is interesting to note that one of the major studies of magic
in Judaism discusses *Jewish Magic and Superstition: A Study of Folk Religion*. The author, Joshua Trachtenberg, does not hide his aversion from the subject matter and
his criticism of its non-rational aspects. Another issue, which cannot be discussed
here, is the tendency to relegate matters that do not reflect critical knowledge and
understanding to the realm of folklore, thus making folklore the stepchild of a high
culture, so to say.
[17] Here, I use a term that Victor Turner used in relation to rituals. See Victor
Turner, *The Anthropology of Performance*, PAJ Publications: New York, 1987. But, for
reasons mentioned above, I favour the terms "doing" and "practice" in this study.

they are formulated in the texts themselves. The epistemology of religion covers a domain that stretches between ascertainable knowledge and maintained belief. So what is the special methodological ontology that should be used by the researcher? Once he enters the domain of belief, the researcher should be conscious of the need to explore reliable ways of terminological contextualisation, rather than apply a direct translation. What is at stake here is risking distortion and a mistranslation from one mental mode to another. No doubt, the language of religious belief and behaviour must be re-cast before it can be included in the scholarly discourse. Since the academic study of religion should not indulge in, or promote, theological considerations (including the theological justification for the practice of rituals), it should be conducted in a way that completely neutralises theological associations and implications.

Admittedly, the "belief"-component forces into the scholarly discourse issues, which require a process of *mental* translation. This translation presupposes, above all, a de-theologisation of the materials at hand. Thus, the scholarly study of the phenomenology of sacrifices requires cognitive presuppositions, which view the mind as generating realities that are not explicitly addressed in scholarly research. In these realities, phenomena related to magic, mysticism, exorcism, witchcraft, demons and angels play an important role. In other words, modes of alternate states of consciousness, (or better, substantial extensions or expansions of consciousness) have to be moved into the centre of the scholarly discussion. This is a task, which has not yet met with a wide approval and scholarly sophistication in academic circles. In the past, theologians inclined to treat these realities, or issues, as aberrations of the human mind, matters that defy institutionalised forms of religion. This was a fallacy that scholars should be able to discard in the scholarly discourse. The same applies to the modes of consciousness that are connected to divination (including "Shamanism"). In short, a new cognitive approach has to prevail in the study of phenomena that ordinarily appear to be of less import in the general esteem of the academic community.

II

One of the major arguments of the present study is that the texts
that prove to be relevant to the discussion should not be used to
illustrate "external" ritual theories. Instead, we should enable these
texts to display their embedded ritual theory. This means that we
must examine the specific manner in which each ritual creates its
own narrative and assess its inner logic, or functional structure.
Each ritual has its own mode of practice, and different rituals rarely
follow the same line of practice. The difference between one ritual and another is not only in what is done and how, but, also in
the way in which each ritual is narrated, whether on a descriptive or prescriptive level. These differences constitute the key that
is used here to discover the hidden aspects of rituals, *i.e.* their
embedded ritual theory. In the final resort, however, similarities
create a common discourse.

   We have repeatedly noted the need to bring about a radical
change in the manner in which rituals are studied and assessed.
If we keep in focus the issue of ritual theory, as viewed here, it
becomes evident that it is also essential to modify the manner in
which sacrifices are studied. Since the above perspective presupposes that many forms of life, or ways of living, include ritualised and sacrificial modes of behaviour, the study of sacrifices is
not specifically limited to the religious domain. One should add,
however, that the religious context of sacrifices adds interesting
components and dimensions to the subject matter. Sacrificial acts
are part of what constitutes humanity in general, and social life
in particular. But, to repeat, in their religious context, sacrifices
have special dimensions that project on sacrificial modes of behaviour in general.

   We assume that people are not always aware of the extent to
which ritual forms of behaviour regulate their everyday lives.
There are phases, in the culture of people, when the stage direction "enter" or "exit" is missing from the script to indicate to the
reader, when a religious stage is entered or exited. Life is neither
profane nor sacred, although there may be times when people
feel the need to relate to the divine more intensely than at other
times. In respect of ritual modes of behaviour, the religious and
the profane do not have the kind of mutually exclusive animos-
ity that is found among theologians who are constrained to pro-

fess the borderlines that mark the "in" and "out" of the ultimate truth of their position.

Rituals are not studied, in this book, because of their alleged connectedness to the realm of the sacred: the sacred is a relevant factor in as much as it informs us about a specific aspect of ritual theory that cannot be assessed otherwise. This may happen, for instance, when religious tradition influences rituals and the way they are done. However, in view of the fact that we give close attention to every single ritual in our study of rituals, the individual context plays a greater role in their study than tradition. An epistemological approach to rituals, nonetheless, requires some generalisations to be made, particularly with regard to the manner in which rituals are contextualised in the lives of human beings. Context, in the case of rituals, means a lot, if not everything. However, the epistemological context is not identical to the context in which each ritual operates. In any event, in both cases, context means more than simply a circumstantial framework, though each form of context has to be assessed individually.

More specifically, in sacrificial rituals, context means that altars and temples play a pivotal role in the existence of the individual and the community. They are the "centre" that holds the "cosmos" together. What makes them bring this task into effect is the sacrificial rite. If rituals are meant to reconstitute a frail or disturbed form of existence, sacrifices address this issue in a more intensified manner. Sacrifices go with the conviction that omitting the sacrificial ritual can cause something fatal to happen— an existing life cycle may collapse, a state of paralysing frailty may set in, or a sense of total failure may take over. In short, rituals, and particularly sacrifices, exist in order to avert existential entropy.

Before progressing further, we have to bring up once again the question as to how scholars inform themselves about, and, then, present, the materials on which they base their knowledge of sacrificial ritual(s). The question was already discussed above. It is not unique to the study of sacrificial rituals, but it deserves special attention, in this particular context. In many cases, the sacrificial materials studied (a) become removed from their original *in-templo*-setting, and (b) are viewed at a mental distance from the cultural context of the people who did the rituals. Conceivably, the people who initiated the rituals had more information than that contained in the texts from which the scholar of today draws his information. It is true to say that, by dint of his metaphysical presuppositions, the scholar of today is to some degree, if not totally, alienated from the form of consciousness that shaped the rituals he is studying. Scholars of religious studies are expected to maintain a mental distance from the object of their research and beware of falling into the trap of sharing in the religious experiences, which they are studying. Following this advice, in a strict manner, can deprive the scholar of important information and the absence of the 'sharing' perspective is likely to render his research deficient, in essential aspects.

If accompanied by a critical approach, the insider's view can prevent scholarly work from stopping at the periphery of facts. Indeed, the insider's view helps the scholar to discover the inner core of the materials at hand. Since the scholar has full control of the materials, he is not only in charge of their selection but also of their modes of explication and assessment. Scholarly knowledge, in this respect, reflects the scholar's ability to perceive and critically process the selections that he has made. We should be aware, however, that these selections, whether made arbitrarily or not, constitute the scholar's own idiosyncratic "theology," that is to say, the scholar's special relationship to the rituals he is studying is contextualised in his own research ontology.

Clearly, in resolving these problems, we open new ones. The scholar, who is usually told to keep himself at a mentally safe distance from the materials he is exploring, must now place himself, once again mentally, at a viewing point from which he may discern the relevant details and complexities that reflect the consciousness of the people who created the rituals he is studying. This is a requirement that is often discussed under the subject of the "participating observer." When the observer participates in a ritual, even at a mental level, he is expected not to do this without, in most cases, aiming to bring about the type of transformational event, which the people doing the ritual wish to generate.[18]

---

[18] One finds, in recent scholarship, an interesting shift in the ontology of research. Scholars make their own experiences available to the reader as the starting point of the research report. See, for instance, Steven M. Friedson, *Dancing Prophets: Musical Experience in Tumbuka Healing*, The University of Chicago Press: Chicago and London, 1996. The first chapter of this book gives a detailed description of the writer's dance experience. The chapter begins with a statement: "At

This is a reasonable position taken in the academic world. However, the argument, which I put forward in this book, entails a rather more demanding spectrum of mental attitudes than is usual in such cases. At times, it may entail entering states of mind that are diametrically opposed to what is normally assumed as a *sine qua non* in scholarly work, namely, controlled critical rationalism and holding back. In some cases, even alternate, or extended, states of consciousness must be accepted. What is the scholar to do, in such cases? I believe that scholars have to take into account that such states of mind are real, at least, in the eyes of the people whose rituals they study. It is my view that we need to adapt ourselves to the fact that the realities of other people cannot be dismissed as irrelevant simply because they differ from or are irrelevant to our own realities. If a scholar believes the reality he wishes to study is not true, he would do better to abandon the matter altogether. This said, I would go further and argue that the study of lies and fictional fantasies has a place in the study of culture, although I would never consider treating any subject connected with the various phenomenologies of religion as opium distributed to cheat the masses. Lies have their own, epistemological and psychological, truth. They constitute a reality that cannot be dismissed as non-reality, as perversion, in the first place. These phenomenologies deserve to be treated with scholarly tools. In certain cases, the adequate tools still need to be developed, or considerably refined, but the scholar still has a duty to refer to these special states of mind, or cognitive realities, in a manner that shows scholarly interest, curiosity, and responsibility. This excludes the possibility of referring to the sacrificial rituals connected with exorcism, possession and magic as experiences that belong to the domain of the superstitious. They are as true to the believer as are all other kinds of sacrifice. Their untruth—fraud and deception—belongs into the realm of theology and the prejudices it sometimes fosters. In brief, value judgements that go with

---

my last research site, the compound of a woman named Lusemba, I danced *vimbuza* for the first time" (p. 9). See also Michael B. Bakan, *Music of Death and New Creation: Experiences in the World of Balinese Gamelan Beleganjur*, The University of Chicago Press: Chicago and London, 1999, p.13: "The 'science' of ethnomusicology inevitably begins and ends in understandings and perceptions that stem from the researcher's personal experiences, especially during the fieldwork process." The section, which begins with this sentence, is characteristically called: "How Music Lives: Toward an Alternative Epistemology."

"traditional" modes of rationalism should not interfere with the scholarly work done on realms that include such extraordinary experiences.

In short, the realms of the extraordinary should be part of the scholarly work. They entail what can be one of the most interesting and challenging parts of the scholars' activity. Studying these materials does not mean that a scholar who is assessing them necessarily leaves the track of critically oriented rationality. If he does not abandon himself in the ontological premises that make such experiences possible, his status as a scholar is preserved. At every point, he should feel himself able to return to the point of departure where scholarly parameters set his methodological agenda. In fact, there is nothing in the experiences of the kind mentioned above forcing a scholar to abandon for good his academic principles. In my opinion, the time has come for scholars to disengage themselves from the constraints dictated by fashionable consensus. They should risk excursions that take them to experiential realms in which something altogether other than the ordinary and the usual rules prevails. They can do this and still preserve their scholarly integrity.

Clearly, these aspects of the study are missing from the discussion of sacrifices as carried out by Henri Hubert and Marcel Mauss. These scholars contributed significantly to the academic study of sacrifice, but their omission of central issues in the religious experience is not the only problem I find with their book. As indicated above, they adduce materials from Judaic sources, but the picture, which they draw, is seriously impaired by partial, or even deficient, information.[19] They read the relevant materials, in a highly selective manner, choosing evidence, which primarily reflects what is of interest to them. The missing points from their studies constitute a non-negligible lacuna, which turns what seems to be a systematic case study into a somewhat incidental chain of observations. Their book does not contain even a single ritual that is studied from beginning to end, in all its detailed complexities, and in the context of its ritual theory.

An even more serious problem stems from the way the authors

---

[19] I would add that the remarks made by Hubert and Mauss on the sacrificial system in the Pentateuch raise serious concerns regarding other materials that are used or referred to, in their celebrated book, *Sacrifice: Its Nature and Function.*

use the source materials. They apply a selective mode of collecting materials that serve illustrative purposes, making them fit *their* theory rather than allowing the materials to express their embedded ritual theory. In doing this, their attempt to go beyond what is considered important by the scholarly consensus is not topped with significant success. For instance, a more careful handling of the textual evidence would have refined their scholarly observations.[20] Finally, the materials they study are often subjected to modes of interpretation that do not necessarily reflect the ritual reality of the materials. This will become evident, when one compares the analysis of Lev. 16, as presented below, with what these authors write. The kind of hermeneutics used by Hubert and Mauss does not provide protection against criticism of arbitrary selectivity and inaccuracies. In the study of practised rituals, the formulation of each hermeneutic stance is a delicate matter. It requires the ability on the part of the scholar to differentiate between exegesis and a systematic analysis of rituals in their practised modes. I believe that the body of materials used by Hubert and Mauss should be studied not as texts that prove certain existing theories, but as sources that inform scholars about what is relevant, in these materials, to the study of ritual theory.[21]

III

To direct the reader to a better understanding of the way I approach the sacrificial rituals in Lev. 16, I wish to mention the names of W. Robertson Smith and Frits Staal. Indeed, in many respects,

---

[20] When I discuss the text of *Leviticus* 16 further on, I shall show the role of language in establishing notions of ritual theory.

[21] The reconstruction of ancient rituals is indeed a major issue in their study and analysis. Walter Burkert says: "Thanks to the descriptions in Homer and tragedy, we can reconstruct the course of an ordinary Greek sacrifice to the Olympian gods almost in entirety..." (see, *Homo Necans*, p. 3). However, he does not specify what constitutes the principles of reconstruction, as he sees them. As I see it, Burkert only offers a hypothetical synthesis and not a real reconstruction of any given sacrifice. It is based on a number of sources that may not have the same value and the kind of accurate information that others have. The connection between ritual and theatre is a much-discussed topic. See, for instance, Victor Turner, *From Ritual to Theatre: The Human Seriousness of Play*, PAJ Publications: New York, 1982; and more recently, Fritz Graf, *Ansichten griechischer Rituale: Geburtstag-Symposium fuer Walter Burkert*, B.G. Teubner: Stuttgart und Leipzig, 1998. Several of the papers in this Symposium deal with the subject of ritual and theatre.

the present study is influenced by the scholarly tradition that began with Robertson Smith. His position was that, ritual and myth are the two major components in religion, and that, in many cases, rituals precede myth.[22] Staal's major position is that rituals should be foregrounded in the study of religions, and that (particularly in the case of mantras) they have no meaning at all.[23] Indeed, the meaninglessness of ritual (and of myth) has become the trademark of the Staal School of ritual and ritual studies. Staal's position can be viewed as extreme, particularly because it is maintained with regard to an area of human attitudes that usually fulfils itself in mental realms, that is, in purposive actions.[24]

As noted above, I believe that rituals are best viewed in a context where their meaning is established through the process of doing.[25] In principle, this position comes close to that of Frits Staal, although there is one essential difference. I use the word *meaning* in connection with rituals, and avoid the kind of reductionism characteristic of Staal. As I have repeatedly argued, I believe that rituals create, or establish, their own meaning in the very act of doing and in the logic that constitutes the processual manner in which they are done. Meaning is also shaped through the manner in which rituals operate and through their effect on those who do them. Evidently, this is a different kind of meaning to the meaning, which emerges in an ideational context. Meaning is created

---

[22] See W. Robertson Smith, *The Religion of the Semites*, Meridian Books: New York, 1956, pp. 15-16. Because of the seminal importance of this book, it is worth quoting Robertson Smith's view, here: "... However, the antique religions had for the most part no creed; they consisted entirely of institutions and practices. No doubt, men will not habitually follow certain practices without attaching a meaning to them; but as a rule, we find that while the practice was rigorously fixed, the meaning attached to it was extremely vague... The rite, in short, was connected not with a dogma but with a myth" (pp. 16-17). The extent to which these views are followed or adopted in the present study must be clear by now.

[23] See, in particular, Frits Staal, *Rules Without Meaning: Rituals, Mantras and the Human Sciences*, Peter Lang: New York... 1989. See, for instance: "The meaninglessness of the ritual and the myth... are two tips of the iceberg of human nature" (p.453). Staal considers that meaning is created only in language.

[24] Here I fully concur with Walter Burkert, *Structure and History in Greek Mythology and Ritual*, University of California Press: Berkeley... 1979, p. 39: "In this way, we need not start from any reconstructed 'ideas'; we need not assume that there was, first, a conscious or even verbalized idea and then, secondly, some ritual action."

[25] See Frits Staal, *Op. Cit.*, p. 453: "... what counts in rituals is what the ritualist *does*."

in relation to, and as a result of, *transformation*. Since the subject of this chapter is sacrificial ritual, we shall explore the different modes in which transformation is attained in this type of ritual. Let me repeat that, to say that there is meaning in rituals is not tantamount—as many scholars believe—to saying that they are symbolic expressions of ideas. The meaning is contained in the performed essence of the rituals. As noted, rituals are performed acts, which work to bring about an essential factor to existence (of individuals and groups) and, which cannot be brought about by other means or in a different manner.

One of the tasks, which the present study wishes to accomplish, is to explore the degree to which a non-ideational approach to rituals and sacrifices makes sense, and to evaluate what kind of sense it makes. In this sense, we should be aware of the fact that human acts derive from a background that often carries meaning or wishes to establish significance. Kissing is a physical act. Its performative physicality is clearly expressive of certain emotions that give the gesture significance. However, the question is an open one, whether the people giving or receiving kisses are aware of what kisses are in relation to the emotions that accompany them. In this respect, the act is done almost regardless of an articulate feeling or idea that may explain the kiss. Similarly, jogging is a routinely performed act that is justified by a multitude of ideas: it is supposed, for instance, to relax muscles and enhance cardio-vascular endurance. However, jogging does this not because there is an idea behind it, but through the very act itself. Physiological explanations cannot do what the act achieves in the doing. Finally, in this respect, the idea behind prayer, or even sacrifice, is to please the gods and thus ensure a safer or better life for the person reciting the prayer. In many cases, though, sacrifices make the gods present (see, for instance, Lev. 9: 6, 23; 1 Kings 8: 5-11). Thus, sacrifices are expressive of the relative power that humans have over divine beings. In this sense, we may say that every sacrificial act has an idea that sustains it or that it sustains. No idea accounts for what is done and how. Thus, when I say that the meaning of rituals is in their very doing, I use meaning in a non-ideational sense. Meaning is established in the very structuring of the ritual act. This is meaning which crystallises in a performative setting, in the doing of the ritual. However, since every ritual consists of a certain sequence of acts, something must hold the various parts together. One could say that this something is similar to the harmonic structure of a musical phrase. Harmony, in music, has its own rules and its logic is defined through its own terms of reference. Harmony is responsible for building a coherent musical statement or, sentence, in a manner that finds aesthetic resonance in the listener. Harmony, though, is not the musical phrase itself, nor can it build a statement or argument that is verbally expressed. In other words, harmony crystallises in a way that is musically defined. It is the fountainhead, from which the aesthetics of music wells out.

One can still ask: if the present study argues that religious rituals should be studied in their own performative context—largely divorced from any kind of doctrine or theology—how is it that rituals enjoy the status they usually have in religion? The answer to this question is not difficult. Theology creates ideational paradigms that have a wide range of implications. But, as we have argued above, theological considerations are no essential part of the very doing of rituals. These paradigms require knowledge and understanding, and many people find it difficult to relate to them. Rituals are done on what appears to be a mechanical basis, so it is easier for people to relate to them. One may even say that rituals are more user-friendly than the philosophical deliberations connected with theological truths. Furthermore, rituals promise to achieve something concrete for those doing them. If one believes in the efficacy of rituals, they function like medicine. Their effects are "physically" real. Theology, in contrast, speaks a language that is hardly translatable into a language of material cause and effect or the attainment of something practically beneficial. Theology cannot easily demonstrate its transformative achievements and, even when it does, this mostly happens in spiritual domains. It is much more common to find theological explications of rituals than theological deliberations translated into ritual behaviour.

Theology can sustain people's motivation to do rituals, but is seldom directly convertible *into* acts. The difference may appear insignificant but, in my view, it is a decisive factor. The relevance of theology to the study of rituals is that it formulates the concept-labels that stimulate ritual activity. Notions such as repentance, purity, commemorating past constitutive events, and one form or another of communion with God—all these involve transformative events that have a theological label. In the religious context, giving the transformative event a theological justification is an essential procedure. Without some kind of theological motivation to do them, rituals can lose their attraction, in the eyes of the people concerned. The question, however, remains: what does theology contribute to the understanding of rituals from the point of view of ritual theory? The answer is the same: theology is relevant to setting the context of religious rituals but not to structuring them in terms of performative essence.

The fact that the sacrificial materials discussed below derive from canonical writings, *i.e.* from a documentary milieu densely packed with theological agenda and issues, is another issue that is likely to render our position somewhat difficult to accept. Theology, almost by definition, is the contextual framework for everything that carries the stamp of Scripture. One is therefore justified in asking: how can rituals be severed, or extracted, from their immediate theological milieu? Alternatively, if theology cannot be altogether dispensed with, can it still be used to inform ritual theory? We have touched on these matters above, and more will be said about them in the ensuing discussion.

In summary, we have argued that rituals are acts that are done for a special reason and purpose, and the manner in which they are done has no connection to the ideology that claims to sustain their behavioural setting or even wishes to control their provenance. Let me give an example. Belief in God is the cornerstone of prayer and a certain theology always stands behind the content of prayers. However, the issue of how prayers are said, at what times, on what occasions, which bodily gestures should accompany the prayers and how one should dress have nothing to do with the theology that maintains this belief in God. Thus, people doing these rituals are not necessarily conscious of a particular chapter in their theology books. They do their rituals because they believe, or are told, that rituals will accomplish, for them, something that cannot be accomplished in any other way. We have furthermore seen that rituals are vital for the continuation of basic life processes, which are the essence of existence. It is for this very reason that no theological statement or formal declaration of belief can substitute for a ritual act. Something comes into play here that, by its very doing, resembles what, in another context, comes under the heading of magical efficacy.

IV

The principle example we use of a ritual text, which is studied to uncover its underlying ritual theory is Lev. 16.[26] Ancient and modern writers, alike, all too often associate this chapter with the ritual of the Day of Atonement. It should be noted, though, that the introductory verses do not mention the Day of Atonement at all, but the death of Aaron's two sons. I wish, therefore, to argue that their death in the sanctuary is the immediate context of the sacrificial ritual described in this chapter. In fact, death or its proximity is the ultimate context of sacrificial rituals. Admittedly, the Day of Atonement is mentioned in this chapter, although only towards the end.[27] According to our understanding, this chapter describes the ritual done by the High Priest when he entered the innermost part of the sanctuary (or Temple)—a ritual that, in post-biblical times, was adopted as the major ritual of the Day of Atonement.[28] The reason for choosing this ritual for detailed discussion

---

[26] The extent to which the analysis, offered here, is used for either exegetical or interpretative purposes is in the hands of the reader. This is a study in ritual theory, and the interpretative application is completely in the hands of the reader. Later developments of this particular ritual, as known from Second Temple literature and from rabbinic writings, are not included in the present discussion.

[27] See Israel Knohl, *The Sanctuary of Silence: The Priestly Torah and the Holiness School*, Fortress Press: Minneapolis: 1995, p. 27 ff. Knohl emphasises the distinction that Lev. 16 maintains between the ceremony for the purification of the sanctuary and the laws of the Day of Atonement. The latter are discussed in Lev. 23: 26-32 (see, also, Ex. 30: 10). For reasons that are not specified in Lev. 16, the Day of Atonement and, particularly, the self-affliction and sabbatical rest, are attached to the ceremony of entering the Holy of Holies. While Knohl considers Lev. 16 as describing a ritual that deals with the purification of the sanctuary, Milgrom speaks of Lev. 16 in terms of the Day of Purgation. Purgation is the central issue in Milgrom's discussion. It should be noted, though, that, if vss. 2 and 3 shape the contents of the whole chapter, which I believe they do, then Lev. 16 deals with the ritual that the High Priest has to do in order to enter the innermost section(s) of the sanctuary without causing damage to himself or, even risking his life. This may happen irrespectively of a specific day or date in the ritual calendar. The reason for his entry is not stated, though it could be said that purging the sanctuary/temple is the main issue (Ex. 30: 10), since the venue of the sacrificial rites is the existential axis-mundi. From the point of view of ritual history, it is also interesting to compare Lev. 16 and the ritual of the Day of Atonement, as described in Mishnah Tractate *Yoma*, and all the rabbinic sources that are dependent on it. The differences are quite remarkable not only in terms of ritual development, but also in terms of the ritual theory that is involved. One interesting point that Mishnah makes is the importance of the right order and sequence for each part of the ritual.

[28] As noted (see previous footnote), Milgrom also uses the heading "The Day of Purgation" for Lev. 16: 1-34. The Day of Atonement is on the tenth of the

is that it contains interesting materials regarding the nature of the ritual theory of sacrifices.

As already noted, what should direct the reader in his reading of Lev. 16 is its self-proclaimed point of departure—the death of Aaron's two sons.[29] The details of their death, enigmatic as they are, were given earlier in Lev. 10: 1-7. Whatever the stated circumstances, ("they offered before the Lord unauthorised coals" ['esh zarah], Lev. 10: 1)[30] their death created an interesting circumstantial, even causal, link to Aaron's entry into the sanctuary:

> The Lord[31] spoke to Moses after the death of the two sons of Aaron, when they drew near before the Lord and died. The Lord said to Moses: Tell your brother Aaron not to come just at any time into the *holy section*[32] inside the curtain before the *kapporet* that is upon the ark, or he will die; for I appear in the cloud upon the *kapporet* (16: 1-2).[33]

Elsewhere (Lev. 10: 8-10), entering the sanctuary is strictly forbidden to priests who have drunk wine or ale.[34] The link between the death of Aaron's sons and the sacrificial rites is made clear in vs. 3: "*Doing these [rites]*, Aaron *may* come into the holy place". In other words, the sacrificial rites are aimed at removing the hazard of death from Aaron's entry into the sanctuary. In a broader sense, the connection made, in the biblical text, between the death event and entering into the sanctuary, makes a clear point in terms of the ritual theory that is implied.

---

seventh month (Tishri), while the death of Aaron's two sons must have been in Nissan, during the days allocated to the inauguration of the sanctuary.

[29] In a wider context, Lev. 16 comes after long sections that discuss personal and domestic categories of impurity. The ways of regaining purity are also discussed at length. Thus, it is not surprising that Temple purity/impurity comes next in the line of discussion.

[30] The translation is from Milgrom's *Leviticus 1-16*, p. 595.

[31] "Lord" here stands for the Tetragrammaton.

[32] The Hebrew text here reads *ha-qodesh*, whereas on other occasions the *kapporet* is located in the *qodesh ha-qodashim*, that is, the holy of the holies. Milgrom (p. 1013) remarks: "This terminological anomaly is one of the many reasons for regarding vv 2-28 as comprising a discrete literary unit that was not originally composed by the author or redactor of P."

[33] Note that the chapter highlights three morphologically-linked terms: *parokhet* (=curtain), *kaporet* (ark covering), and *kaparah* (covering for sins). When not otherwise stated (and marked by italics), the English translation is that of the New Revised Standard Version. Following this procedure will give the reader an idea of the various problems that I see in the English translation. In important instances, the reason for departing from the NRSV will be given.

[34] Milgrom, p. 613, lists other instructions by which the priests must abide before they can enter the sanctuary.

In the first place, death dramatically highlights what kind of signals sacrifices give. Sacrifices place, in the foreground, a completely different factor to the gift factor usually associated with them. I shall discuss, later on, the extent to which the factor of substitution can be maintained with regard to sacrifices. In any event, the text in *Leviticus* creates a strong link between the killing of animal victims and the death of Aaron's two sons. It builds an axis of mortality that activates the link between the event and the ritual. In terms of ritual theory, what can be more telling than this connection between death and sacrifice? As we shall see below, approaching a sacred place or touching a sacred object, involves risking one's life, a sacrificial act is required to protect those whose life can be endangered. Thus, the words "lest he dies" dramatically convey the main point of the whole story. If, as we are going to see below, sacrifices entail the rectification of a disturbed order, one may interpret what is said in Lev. 16 as giving directions on how to approach the sacred cosmos.[35] It cannot be approached without a sacrifice that functions as an act of rectification. Sacrifices are often described as acts that are intended to appease the gods. Using these terms engages a theological language. Ritual theory requires different terms of reference. Sacrifices, such as those described at the beginning of Lev.16, are done to enact a programmed, and thus controllable—hence, also mimetic)—moment of disturbance that anticipates the major disturbance that is likely to come into effect, if sacrifices are ignored. In short, sacrifices avert danger. When the sacrificial rite is omitted from the protocol, danger may take over and prevail.

If the foregoing line of argumentation is accepted, it shows that theology, in the usual sense of the term, is not necessarily part of the ritual procedure. It does not play the type of role it is usually accorded in the regular discourse of religious studies. Theology does not cause death, unless humans incur death for reasons that are stipulated in the theological system. We cannot avoid expressing this in paradoxical terms: death caused by either looking at (Num. 4: 20) or touching (2Sam. 6: 7) sacred objects, and, in a completely different context, the death penalty incurred for trans-

---

[35] In developing this line of thinking, here, and in the following paragraphs, I have benefited from the detailed comments made by Professor Don Handelman who read an earlier version of this chapter.

gressing a religious law, ultimately have constitutive functions. They guarantee—through an act of cathartic purgation—the wholeness and totality of the cosmos that was previously affected by incorrect behaviour, sin or moral corruption.[36] This is easy to understand with regard to religious law and the manner in which the community is made to depend on observing law and order. Indeed, the community is responsible for maintaining the integrity of its cosmos as a live, or life preserving, factor.[37] Thus, the community is obliged to deal with any transgression of the law in a manner that shows that it is well aware of the need to do away with evil (Num. 25: 5; Jos. 7). Evil carries with it the seeds of destruction and social disintegration. If nothing is done to correct the disturbance, the entire community is liable to suffer, for it is implicated and its very existence is endangered (Num. 8: 19). Furthermore, the "land" does not tolerate people who transgress: it vomits them out (Lev. 18: 28; 20: 22).

Sacrificial rites are thus one of the major instruments used to prevent a potential disturbance from gaining control over a situation. In a deeper sense, sacrifices represent acts of breaking and destruction: they enact a processual "ceremony of destruction" that mimetically enacts the actual disturbance, or destruction. In some cases, they signal that destruction has already set in. In other words, they protectively enact a destructive event and indicate that no further corrective acts need be done. At the community level, the members participate in a sequential process of destruction, which has a specific ritual configuration, and functions as an act of prevention or rectification on behalf of all, even if only a few members take an active part in the ritual. A sacrifice, therefore, can preserve the wholeness of a community before it is overcome by calamity. The community and, in many cases, the sanctuary/temple

---

[36] See, Hyam Maccoby, *Ritual and Morality*, p.193: "In every case where there is a conflict between ritual and morality, ritual gives way to morality." I must confess that I do not understand what Maccoby means. He does make, though, a clear distinction between Scripture and the Rabbis. The latter, he argues, emphasize the morality factor over ritual. Sweeping generalisations of this kind should be taken with caution.

[37] In this respect, the notions of *'edah* and *'adat B'nei Yisrael* are of particular importance. The entire congregation was called to stone, first, "him who cursed" (Lev. 24: 14, 16) and, on another occasion, the man who was found gathering sticks on the Sabbath (Num. 15: 33, 35). See also Num. 19:20, where a negative relationship is maintained between a sinning person, the congregation (*qahal*), and the Temple. The subject will come up again in our discussion of Lev. 16.

as well, has to preserve its wholeness. This wholeness is expressed in ritual terms.[38] By its very nature, the eating (even by the gods) of the various parts of a sacrifice gives a functional indication of reverting to, or restoring, a life-enhancing process. The next chapter will take up this point and discuss its various implications.

The sacrificial rite in Leviticus begins with the words, "with a young bull for a sin offering and a ram for a burnt offering." This act involves the shedding of blood. As we shall see, the blood of the slaughtered animals plays an important role in the sacrificial procedure. This is explained by the fact that Scripture conceives animal offerings in the context of doing certain things (which will be discussed below) with the blood that is shed. This is what Scripture says about blood: "for the life *essence*[39] of the flesh is in the blood..." The enactment of shedding blood brings about "atonement":[40] "... and I have given it for you upon the altar *to cover for your own life essence*, for the blood [of the slaughtered animal] covers by reason of its [containing] the life essence" (Lev. 17: 11). We should note that this verse appears to give, what may be referred to as, a "theological" explanation. However, the level at which the explanation presents itself is more technical than theological. In a sense, it introduces a notion of substitution, which is not necessarily theological but mimetically practical.

I have introduced the factor of substitution not in the sense of replacement but in conjunction with the Aristotelian notion of mimesis. For our purposes, I would translate mimesis as programmed imitation, not in the sense of a theatrical display but as a ritual enactment "of the same." In both cases, it involves catharsis. If this is accepted, we can view sacrifice as an enactment on a parallel—or even binary—plane-of-existence of events that involves a crisis. Shedding the blood of a sacrificial victim con-

---

[38] It is interesting to note, in this connection, what the Israelites are told: "And if you make me an altar of stone, you shall not build it of hewn stones; for if you draw your sword upon her (stone in Hebrew is feminine) you profane her" (Ex. 20: 25). The altar must be built "of whole stones (*avanim shelemot*)"—Deut. 27: 6.

[39] The Hebrew text, here, reads *nefesh*, which is often translated as soul. However, it seems to me that the sense in which the word is used here indicates "life essence."

[40] The RSV, on which my translation is based, is clearly inaccurate. The Hebrew text uses the word *yekhapper*, which is commonly understood as implying the notion of "achieving atonement." However, it is used, here, in the sense of covering. The blood of the sacrificial animal is shed to cover for the need to shed the blood of a sinning person. We shall return to this point later on.

stitutes a moment of crisis, which resolves a potential crisis on another level. There is, however, one essential difference between the lived event and its mimetic enactment as a sacrificial rite: while the lived event marks a crisis that ran out of control, the ritual enactment mimetically signals a crisis that is kept carefully under control. Mimesis is a planned, controlled event. It has structure, in every conceivable respect. Mimesis plays out something that is related to a previously lived reality. On the artistic level, it involves mental or emotional catharsis. Sacrificial mimesis, on the other hand, is purposively structured and, thus, it can aim at rectifying an event to which it analogically relates. This is where the notion of replacement enters the scene as conterminous with mimesis. Instead of creating catharsis in mental, or aesthetic, realms, as mimesis does in art, ritual mimesis is believed to create it in a real life-factor, and its process of rectification relates to a disturbed *reality*. Sacrificial rituals also aim at reconstituting damaged conditions. In short, what sacrificial rituals bring about is the restoration and rectification of life processes. In all these cases, a mimetic process is involved at the enactment level, which cannot always be rationally explained.

Let us take a closer look at theatrical mimesis. Although it concerns and affects human behaviour, it relates to staged conditions and situations. It differs from sacrificial mimesis in several ways. Theatre may have ritual functions and theatrical performances may be part of ritual cycles, as was clearly the case in ancient Greece. However, ritual acts that are performed on the stage never completely lose their role as part of a theatrical event. In ancient Greece, theatrical events were often part of the ritual life of the polis. Some ceremonies still have a ritual function as local public events in modern Greece today. However, they do not have that function when performed in a non-Greek locality. In other words, rituals take place as place-bound events. Furthermore, in modern theatre, actors are not the priests of ancient times, or people acting on their behalf. Finally, the modern audience watching the theatrical performance participates in a story (drama, in Greek), no matter how meaningful it is, from a religious point of view, not in a staged event that has ritual functions. Participation in an artistic event is limited to an emotional—an aesthetically mimetic—experience. In real rituals acts, aesthetic borderlines are crossed and the event becomes a purposively targeted act. These acts focus on participation that is best characterised as real (not mental) sharing. The end- result is a transformative experience, in the full sense of the term. I believe, though, that more has to be said on the similarities and differences between catharsis, in its Aristotelean sense, and transformation, as used here. As the next chapter will demonstrate, the factor of sharing is an essential feature of rituals. It does not have this status in art. In fact, no act of ritual sharing is required on the part of those who go to the theatre. Although they pay for admission, an act that has a few similarities with the subject matter discussed above, this is not a sacrificial act in the full sense of the term.

Let us return to the scriptural text. What do the terms *le-hattat* and *le-'olah* imply? Sacrifices done in the sanctuary/temple have labels and names. They are listed according to certain ritual categories and clearly have special functions, although these are not always specified. Spontaneous sacrifices, such as those described in the Book of Genesis, have no special designation and the manner in which they are done receives little attention. However, the cultic environment of the sanctuary leaves nothing to chance or to non-systemic performance. Indeed, it activates a more sophisticated systematization of rituals, in which clearly specified names and functions play a major role (e.g., Num. 28-29). Careful instructions as to how to do the sacrifices, including handling of blood and remains, are part of this system. Milgrom (p. 256) comments: "By daubing the altar with the *hatta't* blood or by bringing it inside the sanctuary... the priest purges the most sacred objects and areas of the sanctuary..." If this is the case, and I think it is,[41] then the *hatta't* offering prepares the way for the other offerings that are brought to the sanctuary/temple on the same occasion. In our case, the *'olah*-offering follows the *hatta't*. Bulls usually come first in the sacrificial rites of the sanctuary. Even when their purpose is not explicitly stated,[42] the fact that they are being sacrificed establishes an essential and sequential act of purgation, which, in this case, is the essence of the *hatta't* sacrifice. In other words,

---

[41] In saying this I raise an objection to what Hyam Maccoby says by way of disagreeing with Milgrom's "Proposition 3," namely that "the purpose of the 'purification offering' is to cleanse the Temple, not to atone for the sin of the offerer." See *Ritual and Morality*, p. 175.

[42] The sacrifices mentioned in Num. 28-29 contain many examples to this effect.

an initial act of cleansing the sanctuary/temple is required before the other sacrifices can be offered.

On some occasions, several acts of cleansing and purgation are repeated in the course of a single sacrificial rite. The overall sacrificial program is split into several sections, acts and scenes. Sacrifice, in fact, is a generic term, that covers a sequence of segmented parts in which several animals, and other edibles (such as salt, fine flour, oil, and wine), are offered.[43] The complexity of the sacrificial act most probably reflects the complex nature of the situation to which it relates. Sacrificial rites that consist in the slaughtering of several animals are a probable indication of either the complexity of the issues addressed, the importance of the event, or the gravity of the situation to which the sacrificial rite relates. It must be clear by now that sacrificial events speak a language of their own and this language requires an act of deciphering. This is how the relevant aspects of ritual theory are brought to the surface. Sacrifice is a word that designates a ritual process and entails the act of making an animal a ritual victim. The victim mimetically enacts another reality in which victimisation has already set in or is likely to happen. In this respect, sacrifices image a reality in which averting danger is an existential necessity.

In discussing sacrificial rituals in the context of ritual theory, one should pay attention to every detail that is involved. The information contained in the relevant texts is so scanty that, indeed, every word should be made to count. A key question is, what is implied by the various specifications such as what is done before and after the slaughter of the victim and how is the victim's blood to be handled? However, we shall first address another issue, that of the garments worn by the priest.

> He shall put on the *sacral*[44] linen tunic, and shall have the linen undergarments next to his body[45]; and he should fasten *a* linen sash, and *tie around [his head]* the linen turban; *all* these are sacral vestments. He shall bathe his body in water, and then put them on.

---

[43] It is worth repeating that sacrificial foods are not only meals offered to the gods. On a larger scale, they also epitomise the notion of life sustaining processes in which sacrificial rites play a major role.

[44] We have already referred to the fact that the Hebrew word *qodesh* is all too often translated (as also in this case by the NRSV) as "holy." In a ritual context, Milgrom's suggestion, as adopted here, makes more sense.

[45] Literally, the sentence says "on his flesh."

One could say that special garments and their specific colours are conspicuous indications of office and rank, and symbolic expressions of authority and power. This may well be the case. However, we view garments, and particularly the ritual acts involved in changing them, as indicating something different. In many cases, changing clothes in the course of a ritual indicates a transition from one stage of the ritual to another. Garments also speak a language of ritual empowerment (as distinct from marking status). Since garments empower those who wear them, they are effective in empowering rituals to reach efficacy. Changing garments constantly reconfigures the status and condition of the person who does the ritual. The very act of changing garments incarnates the essentials of the ritual process as a transformative event. Ritual transformation is not achieved instantaneously. It crystallises in a process, whose main feature comprises in a multi-level aggregate of ritual acts that move from one stage to another. Changing garments is of cardinal importance, in this process. The garments indicate the kind of stage that has been reached in the ritual process. People visiting India who watch rituals done over several (often seven) days, will notice that the persons who do the rituals are dressed differently for every day's ritual. The colours of the flowers are changed, too. Interestingly, people, who are expected to know, were unable to inform the writer about the meaning of the colours chosen for every stage (day) of the ritual. Wearing garments with special colours and decorations clearly depicts those who can do the ritual and mark them off from those who are not allowed or cannot do it. Understandably, the fabric or material from which the garments are made is another important factor in the mechanism that activates rituals. As indicated, decorations, too, may add, in various ways, to the factor of empowering the person to do the rituals, as do woven patterns. All these elements speak a coded language, which implies, among other things, nuances of conscious differentiation and structured changes.[46] In part,

---

[46] Earlier, in this study, we referred to the stories that kilts worn by Scotsmen are supposed to tell. The colours and the patterns of these kilts reflect factors of identity related to clan and family kinship. An outsider may wonder why males wear skirts (and special hats), being ignorant of the fact that what matters is not only the form but also the colours and patterns that establish identity factors. In other words, these kilts represent a coding system. See Hugh Trevor-Roper, "The Invention of Tradition: The Highland Tradition of Scotland," in: Eric Hobsbawm and Terence Ranger, *The Invention of Tradition*, Cambridge University Press: Cam

they also reflect cultural identity and the presence of a certain tradition. In short, garments and vestments tell a multi-layered and multi-functional story about the creation of change, difference, and diversification in rituals.[47]

V

Returning to the text in *Leviticus*, the next two verses raise an interesting question. If logical sequence means anything, then vs. 6 should come before vs. 5. Verse 6 continues vs. 4, while vs. 5 seems to be inserted in the wrong place. Moreover, vs. 11 is a repetition of vs. 6. Thus, one cannot but reach the conclusion that the editorial process of this text does not meet modern standards.[48] Verses 5 and 6 read:

> He shall take from the congregation of the people of Israel two male goats for a sin offering [*hatta't*], and one ram for a burnt offering [*'olah*]. Aaron shall offer the bull as a sin offering for himself, and shall *bring into effect ritual covering* for himself and for his house.

We may append to this vs. 11:

> Aaron shall present the bull as a sin offering for himself, and shall *bring into effect ritual covering* for himself and for his house; he shall slaughter the bull as a sin offering for himself.

It should be noted that the passage makes an interesting distinction between presenting the bull and slaughtering it. This observa-

---

bridge, 1983, pp. 15-41. See, also, Ithamar Gruenwald, "Discovering the Veil: The Problem of Deciphering Codes of Religious Language," in: Aleida Assmann and Jan Assmann (eds.), *Schleier und Schwelle: Geheimnis und Öffentlichkeit*, Wilhelm Fink Verlag: Muenchen, 1997, pp. 235-250.

[47] Jonathan Z. Smith, *To Take Place: Toward Theory in Ritual*, The University of Chicago Press: Chicago and London, 1987, p. 109, writes: "Ritual is, above all, an assertion of difference". In paraphrasing this notion, we may say that the changes that occur in the doing of a certain ritual declare that more advanced phases of the ritual have been reached or sectarian differences have been established. Although rituals look as repetitive, one must open one's eyes and ears to notice the nuances of change that occur within the sequential process. We have noted, that the use of different colours or signs in a ritual that stretches over a certain time span (hours or even days) indicates the different stages of the ritual. Reading rituals accurately means that full attention is given to the various changes that happen in the course of the rituals. The development of a certain ritual in the course of history (the factor of tradition) is an issue that requires special attention.

[48] Milgrom seems not to be worried by this fact. In fact, his respective translations of vss. 6 and 11 give the impression that he wants to lay flat the difficulties in the respective texts.

tion is more important than it seems. The Hebrew word for sacrifice is *qorban*. It links to *we-hiqriv* (in vss. 6 and 11), "he shall
present." Thus, the factor that lends rituals their generic term is
the act of presenting the victim before God, *not* the implied meaning of the term in the sense of slaughtering the victim.[49] Thus,
the ritual process begins with the presentation of the victim animal before God. It culminates[50] in the slaughtering of the animal, the ritual handling of its blood, and finally in the burning
of certain parts of the animal on the altar.

A linguistic point needs to be made here. The words "he shall
cover," which translate the Hebrew *we-khipper*, are problematic.
The Hebrew KPR is normally taken to belong to the semantic
field of "atonement." Thus, *Yom Kippurim* is translated as "the Day
of Atonement." In my view, the notion of *Kapparah* as the remorse-
ful removal of sinful behaviour is rather problematic. Milgrom
introduces the semantic field of purging.[51] I believe that it also
semantically indicates the idea of "covering." Gen. 6: 14—"and
cover it (*we-khipparta*) inside and out with pitch (*ba-kofer*)"—is instructive, in this connection. I would therefore suggest that KPR,
initially, involved the semantic field of "covering." Another example in which KPR is used in relation to blood seems to strength-
en this point. Num. 35: 33 reads:

> You shall not thus pollute the land in which you live; for blood pol-
> lutes the land, and no covering can come into effect (*we-l'o yekhuppar*)
> for the land, for the blood that is shed in it, except by the blood of
> him who shed it.

Blood that is lawlessly spilled covers the land. The blood of the
killer has to cover for the blood of the person who has been killed.
This may sound somewhat strange to a modern mind; but it seems
to express the ancient notion of *lex talionis*, measure for measure.
Thus, any good deed, or sacrificial act, can cover for an evil deed,
including a breach of the law.[52]

---

[49] There are a number of hermeneutic attempts to explain the meaning of the
term *qorban*, sacrifice. However, there is no need to discuss them here.

[50] A few of the things that are done prior to the slaughtering of the animal
are: checking the physical wholeness of the animal; the laying on of hands on the
animal's head; a confession of the sin that is said; etc

[51] Milgrom writes: "...it is determined that the verb *kipper* literally means 'purge'"
(p. 1033).

[52] One should note that the ancient Babylonian New Year rite (performed in

The RSV, for its part, endows the Hebrew *yekhapper* with the notion of expiation. Interestingly, Onkelos and the "Targum Yerushalmi" both use the same verb, *mitkepper*, which indicates to me that they found the Hebrew term difficult to translate. If my interpretation is correct, then the drama of the sacrificial act turns around the interplay between the blood, that epitomises real destruction, and the life-blood that deserves deconstruction unless the sacrificial blood reconstructs its right to existence.[53] As we saw, in the case of the killing of a human being no substitute-sacrifice is accepted—the killer must be killed. He is legally made into a sacrifice of his own self. Similar principles prevail in the entire sacrificial spectrum.

At this point, the ritual takes a most dramatic turn. Referring to the two goats mentioned in vs. 6, the texts continues:

> He shall take the two goats and set them before the Lord at the entrance of the tent of meeting; and Aaron shall cast lots on the two goats, one lot for the Lord and the other lot for 'Azazel. Aaron shall present the goat on which the lot fell for the Lord, and offer it as a sin offering; but the goat on which the lot fell for 'Azazel shall be presented alive before the Lord to *bring into effect ritual covering* over it, that it may be sent away into the wilderness to 'Azazel.

By all standards, this is an extraordinary passage.[54] It describes a

---

the month of Nissan) is called "Kuppuru-ritual for the temple." See, James P. Pritchard (ed.), *Ancient Near Eastern Texts Relating to the Old Testament* [Third Edition], Princeton: Princeton University Press, 1969, p. 333. In contrast to the ritual, as described in Scripture, the Babylonian text contains extensive praying sessions and acts of exorcism. Notwithstanding the differences, the most striking parallel to Lev. 16 is: "He [the king] shall call a slaughterer to decapitate a ram, the body of which the mashmashu-priest shall use in performing the *kuppuru*-ritual for the temple. He shall recite the incantations for exorcising the temple. He should purify the whole sanctuary, including its environs... The mashmashu-priest shall lift up the body of the aforementioned ram and proceed to the river. Facing west, he shall throw the body of the ram into the river. He shall then go out into the open country... The mashmashu-priest and the slaughterer shall go out into the open country" (p. 333, col. 2). One should also note that these acts of purification are done not only to safeguard the functioning structure of the temple, but as a New Year rite that involves the king, the city and the state. The gods are thus called to do their cosmo-political functions on behalf of the empire.

[53] This brief discussion by no means exhausts the scriptural attitude to blood. Under certain circumstances, blood pollutes (the blood of dead people, menstrual blood); under other conditions, (slaughtering animals for human consumption) blood must be spilled on the earth "like water" (Deut. 12:16, 24; 15:23). In Ex. 12:7, 13, blood serves apotropaic functions.

[54] Hyam Maccoby, *Ritual and Morality*, p. 85 writes: "Redolent of primitive thought

unique and unparalleled ritual. I think that the two goats epitomise two aspects of destruction: one goat is slaughtered while the
other is sent away to *erets gezeirah*, (Milgrom, p. 1046: "a cut-off
land"). Although in later Jewish tradition (see Mishnah Tractate
Yoma 6: 6) the 'Azazel goat is—brutally—killed, the scriptural
regulation regarding this goat only speaks of sending it away.[55] It
is frequently argued that the goat was just sent, and not killed,
because it was intended to satisfy the appetite of a weird being,
ghostly or demonic, called 'Azazel.[56] Allegedly, the idea was to
ward off 'Azazel and prevent him from entering the Israelite camp
(in the desert) or the temple mount (in Jerusalem). The fact that
the goat is escorted by a special person (*ish 'ithi*; in Mishnah Tractate *Yoma* the task is allotted to the "celebrities of Jerusalem") to
its designated destination shows that it was not just sent away to
roam aimlessly the wilderness. Since it was supposed to carry the
sins of the Israelites to the wilderness, there was an cleansing ritual involved.[57] The goat was expected not to return to the camp/
city.

For the High Priest to enter the sanctuary safely he, and the
community that he represents, have to be cleansed of all sins. He
has to be—and represent—an unblemished cosmos. As we noted
above, sins affect the wholeness of the social cosmos. Consequently,
the physical cosmos of the people is affected, too. The notions of
destruction and exile are a direct expression of this state of affairs. Lev. 15: 31 makes clear that ritual uncleanness is likely to
defile the sanctuary/temple.[58] That other forms of moral misbe-

---

and practice is the rite of the Scapegoat. Here we have a rite that is openly revealed as stemming from pagan belief in demons..." Fortunately, Maccoby's ensuing discussion of the scapegoat does not fall into the dismissive trap reflected in
this statement.

[55] That this is not accidental is attested by Flavius Josephus (*Antiquities*, III.240).
Josephus, who lived in Temple times, had fresh memories of how matters were
done in the Temple. To all likelihood, the Temple practice preserved the scriptural protocol. However, the rabbis, in Tractate *Yoma*, reflect a line of development that puts together a new set of principles and elements.

[56] See, for instance, Hyam Maccoby, *Ritual and Morality*, pp. 90-91. Maccoby
writes (p. 90): "That the Scapegoat is sent into the domain of a demon or minor
deity called Azazel, carrying the sins of the community, is too much of a scandal
to be admitted into monotheistic consciousness." I believe that my readers have
outgrown this kind of rationalistic superciliousness.

[57] See the discussion of this subject of carrying sins away by Baruch Ya'acov
Schwartz in *Tarbiz*, Vol. LXIII (1994-5), pp. 149 ff, in Hebrew.

[58] See, in this connection, Jonathan Klawans, *Impurity and Sin in Ancient Juda-*

haviour could do the same thing becomes clear from Lev. 16: 16 and the opening chapter of *Isaiah*. In contrast to views that confine themselves to laws of purity/impurity, I suggest considering a wide range of implications for notions of "uncleanness" and "pollution" that crystallise in other than just the realms of purity/impurity. In fact, I suggest viewing sins, in general, in such a context.

As noted, the sanctuary/temple was likely to be polluted by the moral misbehaviour of the people.[59] Sins connected with idol worship are constantly referred to, in the Pentateuch, as *to'evah* and *tum'ah*—terms that designate ritual abomination. Thus, as long as the sin has not been removed, people risk being endangered by all kinds of existential hazards. Nothing should be done that is likely to endanger the life of the person officiating on behalf of the community. He represents the social structure, and whatever happens to him is likely to affect the whole community. Indeed, too much is at stake, when the priest takes it upon himself to purge the community of its sins. Kings, in particular, and High Priests in a priestly governed society, are the *axis mundi*, in this respect. The entire social structure rests upon them. Conditions have to be created for them to be free of all cares. As Mishnah Tractate *Yoma* (5: 1; 7: 3) vividly describes, incurring danger on behalf of the community constitutes a dramatic moment for the community, for it depends on the flawless performance of the messenger ritually acting on its behalf. Sacrifices involve particularly risky moments. As many descriptions of rituals in Scripture and rabbinic literature show, many things can go wrong and disturb the ritual efficacy of the sacrifice. Only the most clean and expert can do the sacrifice and set aright the damaged cosmos. We have seen that the killing of the animal victim(s) epitomises in a concentrate manner mimetic destruction. Indeed, as the first two verses of the *Leviticus* 16 indicate, the entire ritual is intended to prevent unnecessary destruction from setting in during one of the most essential rituals in the rite. The presence of the High Priest in the Holy of Holies is often viewed as the ultimate purpose of this ritual. In principle, I agree with this view. However, the real is-

---

ism, Oxford University Press: Oxford, 2000. Although the notion of "ritual" plays an important role in Klawans' study, his approach is mostly conceptual. In this respect, he leans heavily on the work of Mary Douglas.

[59] As we have seen above, Maccoby rejects this idea.

sue is not entering the innermost section of the temple but emerging from it safely. According to an ancient belief, variously documented, the High Priest took great risks while sojourning in the
Holy of Holies. It was a major ordeal, in which—all kinds of things
could happen to him. In this sense, it was a transitional event
constituting liminal qualities (Mishnah Tractate *Yoma* 7: 3). Although it potentially entailed moments of danger, in most of the
cases known to us the kind of transformation that the High Priest
underwent were physically and spiritually beneficial. Some sources
even tell of prophetic visions that a High Priest could experience
there.[60] The various sacrificial elements, that *Leviticus* 16 introduces,
are exactly intended to subvert this danger and make it possible
for the High Priest to officiate undisturbed.

VI

This brings us to the main issue of our discussion. Recently, the
factor of violence has received prominence in the scholarly discussion of ritual and sacrifice.[61] The slaughtering of the sacrificial victim can hardly be interpreted in a context other than the
notion of violence. More generally, sacrificial rituals often relate
to events that are likely to have, or already had, fatal consequences.
Violence, one way or the other, plays a crucial role in these events.
We have noted that sacrifices mimetically assume the victim-sta-
tus of a guilty person or a group. They ritually shift the focus from
the potential human victim to the animal, which is made to carry
the sin to a place of total destruction (the slaughtering house). The
fact that sins can be moved from humans to sacrificial objects (this
is the meaning of the Hebrew notion of לשאת) shows that sins have
a material reality. We have just seen that the sins of the people
are loaded onto the 'Azazel goat and it is made to carry them
into the wilderness. In the case of a sacrificial animal, the sin that
it carries is also destroyed. One can speak of the ontological reality of sin and, in this context, of the metaphysical "realness" of

---

[60] See footnote 79, below.
[61] The notion of violence in connection with ritual is particularly associated
with the work of René Girard: *Violence and the Sacred*, The John Hopkins University
Press: Baltimore, 1977; *Things Hidden Since the Foundation of the World*, Stanford
University Press: Stanford, 1978; *The Scapegoat*, The John Hopkins University Press:
Baltimore, 1986. See, more recently, *City of Sacrifice: The Aztec Empire and the Role
of Violence in Civilization*, Beacon Press: Boston, 1999.

evil. I wish to emphasise that, as I see it, what we have in Lev. 16 are *not* symbolic gestures. Ritual destruction, or deconstruction, is a real event that relates to something that is indeed real. Before it is slaughtered, the sacrificial animal takes upon itself everything—*i.e.* the sins—that could have ruined the lives of the people who offer the sacrifice. Once the animal victim is destroyed, the evil that it carries is destroyed too.

In brief, sacrificial rituals redirect the consequences of acts that incur destruction, from humans to sacrificial victims. The sacrificial act generates a ritual dynamic that re-locates the act of destruction (= the factor of violence) from those who should have undergone victimisation (= punishment) to the sacrificial animal. It re-locates destruction and places it in a realm that does not cause any damage to the human, or social, cosmos. Sacrificial relocation protects the social order from loss and destruction. The reader may have noticed that I avoid the obvious term in this context, substitution. Indeed, I consider it important that the notion of substitution is abandoned for the sake of "relocation" or "transplacing." Substitution entails a factor of agreement on the part of the one who substitutes, while relocation is a more technical and, for our purposes, a more adequate term. Substitution also means that the "real thing" is no longer there or that it is not at hand.

The element of cutting and parting (= violence) characterises almost every stage of the sacrificial act and involves a more complex procedure than one would think. It begins when the victim-animal is slaughtered. One part of the blood is collected in a special vessel, while the rest drains (in the Temple) through special pipes into the earth. Then, the body of the animal is cut into pieces: some are placed to burn on the altar, while others are distributed among the priests, even the ex-owner of the animal. Thus, sequences of cutting and parting make up the sacrificial act. We may add that the sacrificial gesture, in itself, means parting from something that is given to another (a god or other "sacred entity").[62] Finally, it is significant to note that the *'Azazel* goat is sent to "a cut off land" (*erets gezeirah*).[63]

---

[62] Mishnah Tractate *Hullin* 2: 8, mentions mountains, hills, seas (lakes), rivers, and deserts. The Bab. Talmud 40/a adds the sun, the moon, the stars, the constellations, Michael the Great Prince, and a small worm.

[63] The term *gezeirah* may also mean "forced decree" or "fatal decision" (also

In another context, the process of handing out food or wine to people who share a meal entails essential components in the acts of breaking, *i. e.*, cutting the bread or meat, and sharing the wine.[64] On the ritual level, meals and sacrifices comprise two opposites: deconstitution and reconstitution. The act of handing out food represents an act of [sacrificial] deconstitution, the aim of which is to create the opposite, a momentum of social reconstitution. As noted above, when the element of sacrifice is introduced into the scene, one can assume that something has been done that initiated a process that could end in the disintegration of a specific cosmos. The group, or person, was exposed to a threat of defragmentation. However, the instinctive urge to survive catastrophes and escape dangers prevails among people. As a rule, people do things that they feel will guarantee their survival. At a deep level, sacrifices are one of the most radical ways of achieving this goal.[65] Sacrifices do this by enacting opposite, though complementary, processes. In the first place, there is the slaughtering of the animal. This brings about the deconstituting act of sin that the animal is meant to accomplish. Then, there is the mending process in which the parts of the sacrifice are distributed and eaten, either by gods or by human beings. Partaking in a meal naturally signals that a life enhancing process has begun again. Paradoxically, then, the community regains its life and wholeness through a sacrificial act. This act creates a ritual bridge between a process of deconstruction and reconstruction-by-deconstruction.[66] Sacrifices thus become a major factor in regaining and preserving the existential unity of the community, indeed, its very existence.[67]

---

magically applied). Although the principal semantic field of the verb *gazar* is that of "cutting," it is often used in a legal context.

[64] See the discussion of this issue in chapter 6.

[65] I would include here thanksgiving sacrifices, which give expression to the joy of being rescued from something evil or dangerous.

[66] One can argue that the Hebrew term for blessing—ברך—etymologically carries also a sense of breaking, since the act of blessing entails parting with a "good" thing and sharing it with another being. If this suggestion is correct, then ברוך is not Benedictus (= the one who is said to be blessed) but—parallel to קדוש—the one who is (viewed in his being) selected, separate, or exalted in his divine singularity.

[67] See René Girard, *Violence and the Sacred*—(mentioned above), p. 93: "...the sacrificial rite—which protects the community from the same violence and allows culture to flourish." In other words, the danger that threatens a community is subverted by making the sacrificial victim the surrogate for the endangered society. The extent to which we can fully subscribe to the theory of sacrificial substi-

Finally, if we keep in mind that temples are often considered the centre of the universe, then sacrifices sustain not only society, but also the whole world.[68]

As noted above, the scholarly discussion of the goat that is sent to 'Azazel often leads to the conclusion that this part of the rite aims at eliminating the demonic. Milgrom writes (p. 1072): "Elimination rites are... employed to drive the demons from human habitations and back to the wilderness, which is another way of saying that the demons are driven back to their point of origin, the underworld..."[69] However, one may argue, in line with the above, that the 'Azazel goat is a sacrifice *to the demons inhabiting the wilderness*.[70] A similar interpretation is suggested by the Tannaitic Sages, in their interpretation of the "calf of the herd" that Aaron was told to bring as a purification offering on the eighth day of the consecration of the sanctuary (Lev. 9: 2). Curiously, the Sages comment in *Siphra* [*Torat Kohanim*]: "You must give [it, the calf] into the mouth of Satan. Send a gift [*doron*, a Greek loan word] ahead, before you enter the Temple, lest he hates you upon your entering the Temple..." The demonic was always a source of serious concern. *Siphra* even assumes its presence in the Temple. Doctrinal statements and decrees often proved inadequate in erasing the satanic from people's minds: it had to be fought on another level, with other means and tools—that is, with rituals.

We return here to the axis that links myth and ritual, as discussed in an earlier chapter. From the point of view of its consequences on ritual behaviour, the creation of demonic entities is a subject that requires separate study. These entities make human fears concrete and therefore manageable. In terms used in the present study, these entities are mythic configurations that are

---

tution is an issue that I touched on briefly, above. I prefer to avoid further discussion of this issue at this point. As we saw, there is an element of substitution—or relocation—in almost every sacrifice. However, I believe that there is evidence to the fact that sacrifices do not substitute but mimetically duplicate the sacrificing person or community and their fate.

[68] For comparative discussions of this and similar ideas, see the various studies collected in Michael V. Fox (ed.), *Temple in Society*, Eisenbrauns: Winona Lake, 1988.

[69] The demonic element of 'Azazel is also emphasised in rabbinic writings.

[70] One may even go a step further and argue that the sins that the 'Azazel goat carries into the wilderness were generated by the wilderness ghosts that succeeded in infiltrating the city and created sinful opportunities.

handled at the level of rituals. It is common for people to place
their fears onto external entities or beings; they separate the destructive forces from within themselves and turn them into demonic
beings. Since demonic beings have separate, external, forms of
existence, they are fought as such and can be physically annihi-
lated. The principle of "if you cannot win them over, destroy them"
is very applicable in the case of demons. Of course, one may try
to appease them by supplying them with food but, ultimately, their
destruction is intended. It is interesting to see how the rabbinic
Sages handled this issue and how it fits our understanding of the
rite of the 'Azazel goat. One cannot leave it to theology to fight
the demonic. Proving the un-truth, even the non-existence, of the
demonic, or declaring it idolatrous, has had little effect—demons
continue to thrive in, and celebrate, theology's futile endeavour
to annul them. Whether we like it or not, what has become the
central ritual in the Jewish calendar—the Day of Atonement—
engages in a ritual that takes for granted the realness of the demonic. It addresses the demons of the wasteland.[71]

In existential terms, evil is often present as sin. In this respect,
sacrificial rituals handle only certain manifestational aspects of evil,
not its metaphysical essence. In its metaphysical configuration, evil
creates a duality. In the phenomenal world, the drama in which
this duality unfolds is reflected in the battle between the forces
of light and darkness. In the metaphysical realm, the conflict
between these dual opposites cannot be annulled.[72] On the phenomenal level, however, people may control evil or sublimate its
effects. Its total annihilation, though, is the subject of apocalyptic
dreams. In any event, rituals are believed to be one of the more
effective ways of, first, controlling evil, then of destroying it. The
rite of the 'Azazel goat entails just this: the ritual tells the story of
how an innocent goat is chosen to become instrumental in the
fight against the demonic. In the process, it becomes almost iden-

---

[71] We do not need to enter into a full-scale discussion of all the "rituals" done
in response to the presence of the demonic. Qabbalah enriched the ritual life of
the Jews, in this respect. Those interested in the subject can start with the blowing
of the ram's horn on New Year Day (*Rosh ha-Shanah*). Its aim, as suggested by the
Talmudic Sages, was to "confuse Satan," (Bav. *Rosh Ha-Shanah* 16(b).

[72] In Jewish and Christian eschatology, though, one finds lengthy speculations
and mythic descriptions on the subject of the nullification of evil. The speculations
reflect an attempt to force utopia on facts. However, a discussion of these issues
will take us off the main track.

tical with the demonic—it carries the entire load of Israel's sins.

I consider it significant that the sacrificial rite in Lev. 16 includes a section that is not carried out as an act of slaughter. The sending away of the goat to the wilderness entails an act of parting but not a direct execution. According to Scripture, the scapegoat can roam the wilderness until it meets a natural or unnatural death. From the point of view of ritual theory, one can argue that the rite of the *'Azazel*-goat entails a sacrificial act without the direct infliction of sacrificial victimisation.[73] The change from the usual sacrificial procedure is indicative of the change in function: it does not constitute a sacrificial gesture vis-à-vis God, but in relation to *'Azazel*. Furthermore, the story changes in Mishnah tractate Yoma, where the procedure leaves no room for doubt: here, the *'Azazel*-goat is brutally victimised. Violence is enacted in the full sense of the term. There is no sacrificial sublimation of violence.

The notion of the *'Azazel*-goat being sent away to satisfy the appetite of wild beings living in the areas "outside the camp" still holds priority in the common interpretative imagination.[74] It is not difficult to imagine that, in mythic terms, these beings would be identified as demonic. However, they are sometimes associated with nomads who have to be warded off from everything that the non-nomadic stability of the temple-city, or the organised camp, represents.[75] Thus, the aim of the scapegoat is to prevent the camp/city from being invaded and its political and economic system exposed to chaotic fragmentation. Paradigmatically expressed, this is the primordial conflict between the city and the desert.[76] The city (the camp) can survive only if the desert, like the sea, is kept within its natural limits. The wilderness, and the fact that it can spread into civilised areas, represents the end of

---

[73] The notion of the "Scapegoat" was first highlighted as an issue, deserving special attention in the study of comparative religion, in James George Frazer, *The Golden Bough*, Chapter LVII: "Public Scapegoats", and Chapter LVIII: "Human Scapegoats in Classical Antiquity." See also Milgrom, *Op. cit.* pp. 1020-1021. The logic of this idea is that, if a human being is given the chance of running away to the wilderness instead of being killed by the sword, he will very likely opt to run away. With all the risks that escaping into the wilderness entails, he has a chance if he is lucky to save his life.

[74] See Milgrom, pp. 1020-1021.

[75] See the discussion of this issue in Chapter 2.

[76] See, above, Chapter 2.

civilisation, of existence. The "city" makes a statement vis-à-vis the steppe: it marks the boundaries of uninhabited areas.

In short, this part of the ritual has a wider range of implications than is usually assumed. It re-enacts the primordial principle of creation by separation, which is also present in the creation story in Gen. 1. In Lev. 16, the separation establishes civilisation over wilderness, with all that this separation implies. The ritual of sending the goat into the wilderness makes it clear who is in charge of the situation and who, in the final resort, will benefit from the expulsion. In any event, the sending away of the goat, bearing the sins of the Israelites, indicates that the people inhabiting the city (or the camp, as the case might be) have restored wholeness and are therefore worthy of continuing their existence and do not deserve destruction. An uncontrollable expansion of *erets gezeirah* into the camp/city is no longer conceivable.

Before proceeding further, another aspect of this part of the ritual deserves our attention. Vs. 10 reads:

> But the goat on which the lot fell for *'Azazel* shall be presented alive before the Lord, to bring into effect ritual covering *over it*, that it may be sent away into the wilderness to *'Azazel*.

Here, the italicised words, over it, translate the Hebrew, עליו. Milgrom assumes that עליו reflexsively refers to the goat. But this word can also be translated as "over him," referring back to God, who is mentioned just before the word עליו. Thus, the act of וכפר עליו refers to God! Why does God need *kapparah*, a ritual covering? Probably, because he has taken the lives of the two sons of Aaron, the event that suggests the context for this ritual. Or is it because the sanctuary is under a rigid process of *kapparah* and God, too, has to undergo a similar process? One should mention, in this connection, that, in the ancient world, the gods were washed and their "bodies" venerably treated (Mishnah Tractate *Sanhedrin* 6: 7). If God is the object of *we-khipper 'alav*, then this explains the sending away of the goat into the wilderness. The only logical conclusion that one can draw in this case is that the object of the *kapparah*, God, cannot receive a sacrifice that does the *kapparah* for him. To the best of my knowledge, this is the only case in which an act of "covering for" or ransoming is applied to God.

VII

We now come to the part of the ritual in which the incense offering comes into focus.[77] Once again, the "natural" narratival sequence is interrupted and is continued in verse 14. What we see here is one of the most controversial rituals in Jewish history. The fact that two groups, the Pharisees and the Sadducees, reportedly (see Mishnah Tractate *Yoma* 1: 5; 5: 1) split over the manner in which the incense-ritual should be done is a clear indication of its centrality. According to the Sadducees, the incense should be burning already when the High Priest enters the Holy of Holies. The Pharisees, on the other hand, maintained that the fire should be applied *in* the Holy of Holies. The plain text of Scripture supports the position taken by the Sadducees, and it is not clear what made the Pharisees hold a different view. Scripture says:

> He shall take a censer full of coals of fire from *atop* the altar before the LORD, and two handfuls of crushed [*and*] *scented* incense, and he shall bring it[78] inside the curtain and put the incense on the fire before the LORD, [so] that the cloud of the incense may cover the *kapporet* that is upon the covenant, or he will die.

It is striking that death is mentioned, once again, in connection with a possible deviation from the correct protocol of the ritual. Considering the evidence given by several rabbinic sources, death is likely to occur in the presence of a divine appearance in a cloud over the *kapporet*.[79]

What does the incense do?[80] In Scripture, incense is mentioned as an important ingredient in the protocol of the daily Temple-service. Its purpose, in all likelihood, was first to perfume the air that was filled with the smell of burnt meat. It is also plausible to

---

[77] The incense offerings are one of the most difficult subjects in the history of ritual in Temple, and post-Temple times. Interesting aspects of this history are discussed by Paul Heger, *The Development of Incense Cult in Israel*, Walter de Gruyter: Berlin and New York, 1997.

[78] The word "it" is added in the translation. The Hebrew says: "and he shall bring inside..."

[79] See J.Z. Lauterbach, "A Significant Controversy between the Sadducees and the Pharisees", *Hebrew Union College Annual*, Vol. IV (1927), pp. 173 ff.; Ithamar Gruenwald, "The Impact of Priestly Traditions on the Creation of Merkabah Mysticism and Shi'ur Komah" (in Hebrew), *Jerusalem Studies in Jewish Thought*, Vol. VI/1-2 (1987), pp. 65-120.—Milgrom, p. 1014, points to the untranslatability of the word *kapporet*.

[80] See Milgrom's detailed discussion of this question, pp. 1024-1030.

assume that, when used inside the Temple, the smell of the incense was intended to ward off evil spirits that could interfere with a specific ritual.[81] Clearly, the smell of the incense transformed the air, and created a more pleasant condition for Temple worship. When, later on, in the Second Temple period, the preparation of the incense was claimed to be a secret known to a select group of people, the power of this sacrificial component was dramatically enhanced.[82] Since Tosefta *Kippurim* 1: 8 mentions the fact that the High Priest must add a smoke-increasing ingredient to the incense, it is very likely that the smoke created many figurative shapes. With his (perfume intoxicated) imagination, the High Priest could imagine seeing a divine being emerging out of the dense smoke.[83] It should be noted, too, that once the ark was removed from the Temple, a stone "out of which the world has been woven" replaced the ark.[84] This adds a new dimension to the danger motif entailed in the ritual described here. Unless the protocol of the ritual is carried out "punctiliously," the whole cosmos is in danger.[85]

In this connection, another aspect of the fragrance which incense spreads should be discussed. When its fragrance becomes part of the ritual, it enhances, with olfactory means, the atmosphere in which the ritual is expected to work.[86] Furthermore, aroma creates a perfumed area—a specifically configured cosmos into which no other smells are allowed to penetrate. The presence of scent demarcates, in a somewhat aggressive manner, the boundaries of the cosmos in which the ritual act operates.[87] The

---

[81] See Milgrom's reference (p. 1025) to ancient Egyptian and Canaanite practices of offering portable censers.

[82] See the Mishnah, *Yoma* 3:11.

[83] Mishnah, *Yoma* 5:2, mentions the fact that the whole "house" was full of smoke.—Although I came to this conclusion independently, I should point out that Milgrom's discussion ends with a similar conclusion. However, another interpretation is possible: the dense smoke screened all kinds of apparitions that the High Priest was likely to encounter in the Holy of Holies.

[84] See the Mishnah, *Yoma* 5:2.

[85] See Milgrom, p. 1030, who makes this point about punctiliousness.

[86] See, for instance, Tosefta, *Miqva'ot* 6: 16, where myrrh, one of the ingredients used in the preparation of incense, is said to create a "firewall" against ritual uncleanliness.

[87] This point is variously made in Constance Classen, David Howes and Anthony Synnott: *Aroma: The Cultural History of Smell*, Routledge: London and New York, 1994.

fragrance makes a clear distinction between the scented and the non-scented areas. Only the scented area provides the venue in which the ritual can work. A bad smell is likely to attract evil or hostile beings that might adversely interfere with the ritual act. Bad smells could become the substance on which these evil beings draw their sustenance. Odours define the "class," that is, the beneficial purposes of the ritual.[88] Finally, very strong smells have intoxicating potentials. When alternate states of consciousness were desired, the various ingredients used in the preparation of the incense could render a valuable service. The strong fragrance was also a signal to people that the olfactory environment provided them with shelter.[89] In short, the High Priest was right to expect that he would meet no harm in the scented environment.

In addition to these *ad hoc* considerations, one must pay attention to the sequence of events, as described in Scripture. The burning of the incense is inserted between the slaughtering of the bull and the various ways in which the blood of the animal is administered. This highlights the axial role that the incense plays in the whole procedure. The scriptural text is not very clear with regard to the details, but the sequence may be more revealing about the ritual theory implied. The burning of the incense purifies the interior of the adytum before the major event takes place, namely, the carrying of the blood into the Temple and the ritual of sprinkling it there. It is significant to note that an act of burning, *i.e.* destruction, is performed here. This fits the ritual pattern that we have noted above, namely, that the reconstitutive parts of the ritual can come into effect only after an enactment of destruction has been carried out on the ritual level.

Next comes the sprinkling of the blood:

> He shall take some of the blood of the bull, and sprinkle it with his finger on the *kapporet on the east side*,[90] and before the *kapporet* he shall sprinkle the blood with his finger seven times."

---

[88] Scent and social class is another subject discussed in *Aroma*. I use the notion "class" in a different sense from that used in *Aroma*.

[89] See Ps. 45:9; Prov. 7:17; Songs 4: 12-14.

[90] Here, I follow Milgrom's translation, p. 1010. The NRSV makes no sense. It says: "in front of the mercy seat." This misses the point on two counts: the *Kapporet* is not the mercy seat, and the Hebrew *qedmah* does not mean "in front" but "east side" or "eastward".

Milgrom (p. 1032) notes: "The purpose of the blood sprinkling is to purge the adytum of its impurities." He also notes: "The text is silent concerning the manipulating technique." A further comment is worth quoting: "it [the blood] should be brought into the adytum where it becomes consecrated and is thereby empowered to sanctify the altar" (p. 1033). Milgrom is aware of the transformative functions of this part of the ritual but does not fully investigate the consequences of its terms of reference.

I would like to add, though, that the various acts done with the blood tell us that the blood is spread out before God. The drained blood is collected and brought into the adytum, where it is sprinkled and then put on the four corners of the altar. The blood is thus displayed and is visible everywhere. Its omnipresence makes it a key factor in the ritual and its expected consequence are made present. The presence of the blood clearly demonstrates that basic life processes, or existence as such, are at stake. Blood that is accepted by God removes the evil that caused it to be sacrificially spilled.[91]

We understand, from this ritual, that blood cannot be dispensed with. In sprinkling the blood or in putting "it upon the horns of the altar all around" (vs. 18),[92] the blood is made to function in a sacrificial context of its own. It is not burned. Its unused parts are poured into the earth "at the base of the altar of burnt offering" (Lev. 4:7).[93] Clearly, blood is the sacrificial quintessence of the entire sacrificial act. It is handled in a way that tells us that

---

[91] The notion of – ("[to] the will of God") is often mentioned in the scriptural account of sacrificial rites. God is expected to accept the sacrifice, otherwise it is a vain offering.

[92] Milgrom (p. 234) comments: "The altar's horns are right-angle tetrahedra projecting from the four corners... In the Ancient Near East, the horns are emblems of the gods..." Milgrom associates these horns with strength and force. It is unlikely, though, that an essential part of the altar would be an emblem of power. I therefore suggest that the four horns are indicative of the four directions, *i.e.* the cosmos. In other words, sacrifices sustain the world.

[93] Rabbinic literature tells us that there were שיתין, special pits through which the blood reached subterranean domains. According to Rabbi Yohannan, these pits existed since the six days of the creation (Bav. *Sukkah* 49/a). Another tradition recounts (*loc. cit.*) that, when King David (i. e., Solomon) built the Temple, he dug out the holes of these pits. He reached the depth of the waters of the Abyss (*tehom*), which threatened to burst through and destroy the world. The blood of the sacrifices that is poured through these pits would quench the destructive forces of the abyss. In its special way, this mythic tradition highlights what is at stake in these sacrificial practices.

the sacrificial act functions on a number of levels. Blood is like a meridian that endows the entire sacrificial act with its points of ritual co-ordination.

Let us turn, next, to the blood of the goat that is slaughtered.

> He shall slaughter the goat of the sin offering that is for the people and bring its blood inside the curtain, and do with its blood as he did with the blood of the bull, sprinkling it upon the *kapporet* and before the *kapporet*.

The text adds:

> Thus he shall *cover* for the sanctuary, because of the uncleannesses of the people of Israel, and *from* their transgressions,[94] *related to* all their sins; and so he shall do for the tent of meeting which *is present* with them in the midst of their uncleanness.

The point that deserves attention, here, is the fact that the sanctuary has to be cleansed of the wrong doings (Milgrom: "malfeasances") of the community for it is assumed that the Temple has been physically affected by what the people did. To prepare the Temple to do what it is expected to do, it first has to be cleansed of all the sins that have stained it. In mythic terms, one can say that the sacrificial rites prescribed in Lev. 16 aim at covering (*i.e.*, "atone for") the sins that adhere to the Temple. An annual event of purging the temple or cleansing it from evil beings or doings is also recorded in Mesopotamian documents and extensively discussed by Milgrom. As is indicated, further on, in Lev. 16, the ritual ultimately helps to remove the malfeasances of the people. The incantations and exorcisms in the ancient Babylonian ritual indicate that evil spirits found their way into the temple: their presence was a real threat to the temple and, consequently, to the entire social order. We have already seen what is implied when evil takes on mythic aspects and experientially shapes the life of the people. It is common for religious systems to view the fight against evil as a struggle against its personified configurations. One may go a step further and state that religion (or better: rituals) systematises the fight against evil.

It is interesting to note the role played by human beings in this process. Human beings are the ones who are most affected by any

---

[94] The type of disorderly behaviour referred to here is not clear. The Hebrew mentions *tume'ot*, *pesha'im*, and *hata'ot*. Milgrom translates these as "pollution... transgressions... sins".

kind of disorder and they, therefore, play a crucial role in correcting disturbed conditions through rituals. In the particular context discussed above, the High Priest takes the entire responsibility upon himself. This is not only a status-symbol; it is the result of his special status.

> No one shall be in the tent of meeting from the time he enters *to bring into effect the covering of sins* in the sanctuary until he comes out and has *accomplished this covering* for himself and for his house and for all the assembly of Israel.

This decree indicates the exclusive role played by the High Priest in bringing about the transformation that is the ultimate purpose of the ritual. It is unlikely that the decree that he should be alone in the sanctuary/temple is part of a priestly power game. It may point instead to the fact that, since so much is at stake at these moments, the danger of a mishap should involve only the person who must be there in order to do the job.[95]

> Then he shall go out to the altar that is before the Lord and *bring into effect the covering of sins* on its behalf, and shall take some of the blood of the bull and of the blood of the goat, and put it on each of the horns of the altar. He shall sprinkle some of the blood on it with his finger seven times, and *purge it and consecrate it*[96] from the uncleannesses of the people of Israel. When he has finished *the act of covering the sins* for the holy place and the tent of meeting and the altar, he shall present the live goat. Then Aaron shall lay both his hands on the head of the live goat, and confess over it all the iniquities of the people of Israel, and all their transgressions, all their sins, putting them on the head of the goat, and sending it away into the wilderness by means of someone designated for the task. The goat shall bear on itself all their iniquities to a barren region; and the goat shall be set free in the wilderness.

The confession of sins is noteworthy in this passage. It clearly indicates that something is said, although what this is remains a question. It is hard to believe that the confession would have been said *ex tempore*. Since it concerned the High Priest, an element of secrecy or essential privacy could have been attached to it. We

---

[95] Milgrom writes that when the process of purging the Temple begins, "the shrine is just too dangerous a place for anyone but the High Priest" (p. 1036).

[96] In this case, I follow Milgrom's translation. He also discusses, at length, the differences between purging and consecrating in the various stages of this ritual. Evidently, these two aspects of the ritual are complementary. Purging ends in consecration, and a higher degree of consecration affects the power of the purging.

can assume that the confession quintessentially expressed the entire burden of the ritual and may have functioned as its major incantation.

What follows next is an essential part of every ritual. It concerns the special garments that are used in all rituals. As noted above, the change of garments is an important part of the ritual process. The special garments, or vestments, that are worn on every occasion, represent specific details in the ritual process. The changing of garments—often made of different materials and different colours—indicates a phase of completion and a consequent change in the narrative. The ritual ablutions or washing of hands and legs are yet another way of indicating transition from one part of the ritual to another.

> Then Aaron shall enter the tent of meeting, and shall take off the linen vestments that he put on when he went into the holy place, and shall leave them there. He shall bathe his body in water in a holy place, and put on his vestments; then he shall come out and offer his burnt offering and the burnt offering of the people, *thus bringing into effect the covering of sins* for himself and for the people.

An essential question in every sacrifice is what is indicated by the parts that are burned on the altar and those that are shared by the priests (and, eventually, by the community). I confess that I do not have a clear answer to these questions. It is reasonable to assume, though, that the inner parts of the animal are used as burned offerings to the gods, for the inner parts represent the life-generating and life-preserving parts of the animal. However, in some cases they are also the parts that humans are less likely to eat.

The main part of the ritual ends when the *'Azazel* goat is sent away to the wilderness. It is not clear to me what exactly dictates the order or sequence of the events, however, this part of the ritual is delayed to a point that makes it almost the climax of the entire rite. The same can be said of the order implied in Mishnah Tractate *Yoma*. In both texts, the description of the end of the rite seems a little confused and the disjunction may indicate some textual confusion.

> The one who sets the goat free for *'Azazel* shall wash his clothes and bathe his body in water, and afterward may come into the camp.

This indicates the completion of this part of the ritual, as does this:

> The bull of the sin offering and the goat of the sin offering, whose blood was brought in *to bring into effect covering of sins* in the holy place, shall be taken outside the camp; their skin and their flesh and their dung shall be consumed in fire.

Interestingly, there are some other parts of the sacrificial rite that belong, too, to the wilderness. The ritual ends thus:

> The one who burns them shall wash his clothes and bathe his body in water, and afterward may come into the camp.

The rest of the chapter is devoted to the subject of the Day of Atonement. This part does not concern us here. There are, however, two verses that summarise the chapter and the ritual process it describes:

> He shall make atonement[97] for the sanctuary, and he shall make atonement for the tent of meeting and for the altar, and he shall make atonement for the priests and for all the people of the assembly. This shall be an everlasting statute for you, to make atonement for the people of Israel once in the year for all their sins. And Moses did as the Lord had commanded him.

These concluding verses summarise one of the most interesting rituals in ancient Israel. Our approach to the subject has provided an example of how to study rituals and their embedded ritual theory without engaging in theological discourse. The attempt to make a systematic analysis of sacrificial acts in terms of their own ritual theory is, I believe, central to changing the conventional perspective of religious studies in general, and Judaic studies in particular. The first part of this chapter discussed the subject of ritual theory, which we consider vital for the understanding of sacrificial rites, while the second part investigated at length one specific ritual event.

---

[97] Here, I consider the word "atonement" to indicate the later developments of the ritual.

CHAPTER SIX

THE "LORD'S SUPPER" AND RITUAL THEORY

I

We can now wind up our discussion and examine how the preceding discussions on ritual and ritual theory are reflected in Paul's position regarding ritual, in general and sacrifices, in particular. The present chapter takes issue with a number of scholarly presuppositions that are based, to some degree, on theological and scholarly stereotypes. Jesus is depicted, in the Gospels, as arguing with the rabbinic "leaders" of his time over issues of religious laws. As is known, Paul's utterances with regard to the Mosaic Law are controversial. Since, in the days that followed the destruction of the Temple, Judaism developed along lines that put increasing emphasis on the doing of rituals—indeed, it regulated life within Halakhic parameters (see above Chapter 3)—it is understandable that those who wished to bring about a parting of ways with the mother religion had to formulate antithetical agenda and positions. Allegedly, the early Christians felt that they had to present their new creed in entirely different terms of reference. In some cases, this resulted in Christianity being associated with anti ritualistic views. These processes had an accumulative effect both on the manner in which the new religion developed and, subsequently, on the manner in which Christianity was and still is discussed in theological and—hence, also in—scholarly circles. As noted, earlier in the book, a rather reserved attitude towards rituals, in general, developed, which negatively affected its study.

In the eyes of many, Paul is seen as putting great emphasis on the negation of "doing" and "works"—the ultimate expressions of the "flesh"—while positively emphasising "belief" and "righteousness"—the ultimate expressions of the "spirit." These are well known facts. However, in dealing with these notions in the present

context, I hope that a new perspective will be reached in the discussion of both Paul and ritual theory. For the sake of a general
orientation, I will begin the discussion by highlighting a few aspects of this perspective and compare Paul's position with that
taken in the *Letter of James*. There are a number of differences
between James and Paul, a sample of which will clearly illustrate
the Christian dilemmas of the time.

Paul says, (Rom. 4: 1-5), "What then shall we say about Abraham... For if Abraham was justified by works, he has something
to boast about, but not before God... his faith is reckoned as righteousness." James, in contrast, says (2: 21, 24): "Was not Abraham our father justified by works, when he offered his son Isaac
upon the altar... You see that a man is justified by works, and
not by faith alone." These statements say it all and create an inner Christian confrontation. It is, nonetheless, premature to conclude that, for Paul, ritual played no role whatsoever. The truth
is quite the opposite. The manner in which Paul utilised rituals—
often dramatically changing the Jewish practice of rituals—makes
him an interesting case for the study of rituals and ritual theory,
in general. In discussing the position taken by Paul on the "Law,"
the following statement was quoted to justify an antinomian interpretation of Paul: "Let me ask you only this: Did you receive
the Spirit by works of the law, or by hearing with faith?" (Gal. 2:
2). Thus, the following quote is likely to create a cognitive dissonance for any Christian who expects to find homogeneity in the
ancient Church: "For as the body apart from the spirit is dead,
so faith apart from works is dead" (James 2: 26). In saying this,
James clearly confronts Paul who says in Rom. 4: 13-14: "The
promise to Abraham and his descendants... did not come through
the law but through the righteousness of faith. If it is the adher-
ents of the law who are to be heirs, faith is null and the promise
is void." Finally, when James speaks of the "law of liberty" (1:
25; 2:12), he must have been reacting to Paul's words: "For the
law brings wrath, but where there is no law there is no transgression" (Rom. 4: 15). These references provide a striking example
of the degree to which Paul created tension and antagonism among
the early Christian communities that preserved their Judaic connections. In Gal. 2: 16, he says: "A man is not justified by works
of the law but through faith in Jesus Christ. Even we have believed in Christ Jesus in order to be justified by faith in Christ,

and not by works of the law. For, no one is justified by works of the law." This is to be viewed as one voice in the early Church but not the one that was from the start unanimously accepted.

No further discussion is necessary in order to show that Paul's theological argumentation differs from that of James. One point is worth mentioning, though, in connection with the theological triad of sin, ritual, and atonement. In stating that sin is hereditary and that it affects humans from the time of their birth (Rom. 5: 12), Paul proposes a new ontology of sin. In the terms described in this book, this means that the cosmos in which humankind exists is disturbed from time immemorial. Thus, not every new-born human being is directly responsible for the disorder that prevails and the subsequent cessation of life processes. Paul seems to wish to remove the cause of all sin, which he locates in the archetypal event in the Garden of Eden and in the Pentateuchal Law. Sin, in his view, is an existential essence, which appears as an "original" event in the life of every human being. Adam was its cause (Rom. 5: 15) and Jesus, allegedly, was able to remove it. Until the days of Jesus, the right way to righteousness led through the Pentateuchal Law. Jesus changed the rules of the game, and made his death the ultimate rectification of all evil. Consequently, the main Christian objective, as Paul saw it, was to place the death event of Jesus at the centre of the new creed. It is not altogether insignificant that, in spite the great emphasis placed by Paul on the spirit, "works done in the flesh"—*i.e.* rituals—*are given* a prominent role in his theological system. Admittedly, Paul would claim that everything a Christian does is defined as an experience of, or in the framework of, belief (*pistis*). Although belief is a mental predisposition, rituals, in the ordinary sense of the term, still play a role for Paul. As we shall see, the Lord's Supper is a striking example of this position.

What, then, does Paul reflect, in terms of inner Judaic developments, during the generation(s) preceding the destruction of the Temple? He rightly identified the preoccupation, in the mother religion, with issues of ritual behaviour in which sacrificial rites played a major role. However, his views on these issues gradually shaped as those typical of Jews living in the Hellenistic Diaspora. That is to say, he saw himself as a person who had disengaged himself from the cultic life connected with the Jerusalem Temple. Thus, Paul brought into effect the inevitable break with the

Temple oriented Judaism, with the cult and the Pentateuchal law. To many, this may sound that Paul abolished ritual. However, as we are going to see, this was not exactly the case. The issues of ritual praxis and the Judaic concept of the Law are not identical. Law (*nomos*) was an essential part of this break, but not ritual. Contrary to what is often said on this matter, Paul understood that, in splitting from the mother religion, the issue of ritual could not be dumped altogether. He placed certain events, in the life Jesus, in a paradigmatic model that shaped not only the new Christian cult—and its ritual aspects—but also the very narrative that sustained it. Earlier, in Chapter 3, we saw that this kind of narrative has the status of myth. Since the sacrificial factor, in these narratives, constituted a central position, the new cult possessed everything needed to place the Jesus-event as a substitute for Temple worship. If this is the case, we can reach the conclusion that we do not find an absolute annulment of ritual in Paul, but rather a transformed form of cult. Indeed, one may view Paul's attitude to the issue of rituals as a reification of rituals in new models and forms.

As noted above, there are different approaches in the New Testament to the question of abiding by the Pentateuchal law. Jesus himself directed his criticism at a few prevailing legal issues, including, for that matter, the Temple. However, looking at that criticism in retrospect—that is, from the point of view of the crucifixion—people were made to believe that everything Jesus had said was expressive of a most outspoken rejection of the Jewish authorities and ways of life. However, a case for case study of these disputes can show that the disputes Jesus had with people over legal issues did not come from a point of rejection but from a deep concern with regard to the manner in which people viewed and treated the axis Law-God. Thus, from the point of view of establishing ritual paradigms, it is not accidental that the crucifixion in its self-sacrificial mode was placed at the centre of the ritual life of Christianity. From a Judaic point of view, though, the theological thrust of the Letters of Paul poses a more targeted threat than the polemical utterances of Jesus, for they take issue with the entire legal structure of Judaism. Nonetheless, the sacrificial issue remained a crucial one for Paul as well, although it surfaced in a transformed mode. In short, Paul did not altogether abandon the concept of ritual.

If one accepts the previous line of argumentation, a similar question to the one posed in the previous chapter can be asked. In what way can the subject of the "Lord's Supper," as formulated in 2 Cor. 10 and 11, gain from being examined in the context of the study of rituals; and in what way can the methodology of the study of rituals be enhanced by a new examination of the "Lord's Supper"? In other words, I wish to examine Paul's handling of the "Lord's Supper" and shed light on it from the viewpoint of ritual theory. I also wish to explore the ways in which ritual theory can gain from a close examination of this specific "Pauline" case. I would add that this is not another study of the "Lord's Supper," informed by the long tradition of New Testament scholarship, with its specifically historical, textual, and theological interests. Rather, it is a case study in ritual theory and aims at foregrounding a new angle in the study of religion, in general, and in the study of the New Testament, in particular.

I think that in the context of Paul's ways of thinking, a reminder to the reader is needed. This study views rituals as the major component in religion, even before ideas, theology and belief come into play. We shall examine this assumption and see its implications for understanding the case at hand. We shall also examine how this new approach generates additional modes of understanding in the study of the "Lord's Supper." The "Lord's Supper" will be treated here as a case study that brings into focus and summarises some of the central points of ritual theory, which were discussed in previous chapters. It is in the case of the New Testament in particular that rituals are rarely studied for their own sake. Moreover, their study is seldom emancipated from theological concerns and interests. It is, therefore, apt to remind the reader that the theological context is not fully suited to the study and assessment of the rituals, which it sustains. The assumption that directs this chapter is that the study of how Paul transforms a communal meal into the "Lord's Supper" requires the kind of scholarly attention that ritual studies specifically facilitate.

We have assigned theology a contextualising role rather than made it the essence of the ritual event. In more advanced phases of religion, theology is functional in setting specific goals and targets for religious acts. Thus, when Paul speaks of the "Lord's Supper," he has in mind a meal to which he has first to assign ritual functions and, only then, theological meaning. It is a ritual with con-

stitutive functions in the religious life of the people. Its configuration, though, brings together ritual function and theological
meaning. The ritual is intended to create a community with a
specific structure, a Christian one. Hence, the question that needs
to be asked is: what is there, in the ritual under consideration,
which renders it functional in attaining this specific goal? There
must be something in the various stages of the doing-process that
makes the ritual useable for this specific end. Evidently, there is
a belief in the efficaciousness of the action. The factor of intentionality, to which we referred previously, has an important role
to play, too. However, nothing can replace the doing of the ritual, as prescribed in a given setting.

II

The question of the status of rituals in the New Testament is
generally discussed under the aegis of theology. This is certainly
a safe harbour to anchor the discussion of religious texts. Theology is connected to historical, textual and hermeneutic inquiry
and is quite often presented in a comparative setting. However,
one cannot avoid asking: can the academic study of theological
issues avoid the pitfall of becoming theology in disguise? In view
of the history of New Testament scholarship, this pitfall is, to use
an understatement, not easily avoided. Scholarly discussions of
Paul's position with regard to ritual deal with the theological
concerns of the texts themselves.[1] Discussing, as we do, rituals in
the framework of anthropology will help to reduce the theological overload that is often present in scholarly discussions.[2] There
is no need to repeat, at this point, the essentials of our approach

---

[1] See, for instance, the use of the term in connection with the "Lord's Supper,"
in Bruce Chilton, "Ideological Diets in a Feast of Meanings," in: Bruce Chilton
and Craig A. Evans, *Jesus in Context: Temple, Purity, and Restoration*, Brill: Leiden...
1997, pp.59-89. The title of Chilton's paper speaks for itself.

[2] The references will be given in due course. However, it should be noted that
the term "anthropology" is used, in the present book, in a non-theological and
non-philosophical connection. In theology and philosophy, the word designates a
particular concept or evaluation of human nature. A good example, in this respect is, Rudolf Bultmann, *Theology of the New Testament*, Charles Scribner's Sons:
New York, 1951-55, Part II, pp. 191ff. "The Anthropological Concepts." The sense
in which I use the term derives from theories of human behaviour and the function
of the mind in that behaviour, as developed in modern social anthropology.

to the study of rituals and ritual theory. However, we shall see that the Pauline materials contribute, in a significant manner, to highlighting interesting aspects of ritual theory in a way that other materials do not.

The sense, in which the term ritual has been used in this book, draws upon scholarly resources and notions that are usually bypassed in the study of early Christianity. I use the term "ritual," in the context of Paul in a manner that is closely related to Arnold van Gennep's notion of "Rites of Passage."[3] Christianity, from New Testament times, is replete with rites of passage, that is, with rituals that facilitate different modes of religious change and conversion.[4] The New Testament reports of and establishes various forms of transition from the old religion to the new one. Baptism is just a first stage in the process of initiation into the new framework. The Eucharist, the historical precursors of which will be discussed in the present chapter, is another example. Curiously, though, *Christian* notions of conversion, new birth, and spiritual regeneration (or transformation) are only sporadically referred to in van Gennep's work. Indeed, van Gennep refrained from applying his theory and terminology to religious experiences in Christianity. Christianity remained outside the direct range of his interests and scholarly oeuvre. To give another example, more relevant to the present chapter, van Gennep refers to "eating and drinking together" as an example of what he calls "rites of incorporation".[5] However, the obvious Christian example of this case, the Eucharist, is barely discussed by him. Typically, too, most of the examples that van Gennep discusses are taken from

---

[3] See Arnold van Gennep, *The Rites of Passage*, Eng. Trans., The University of Chicago Press: Chicago, 1960.

[4] A. D. Nock, *Conversion: The Old and the New in Religion from Alexander the Great to Augustine of Hippo*, Oxford University Press: Oxford, 1961, discusses a wide range of conversions and rites of conversion. Nock's book is written from the viewing point of the history of religion, reflecting a strong inclination to discuss theological issues. Nock places rites of initiation at the centre of his understanding of conversion. I present a different notion of conversion. Accordingly, I will show that conversion can include a wider range of religious transformations that is usually allotted to it. The two chapters on Conversion in William James, *The Varieties of Religious Experience*, treat a wider spectrum of experiences than is found in Nock, although James also speaks of conversion in terms that derive from a basically religious inventory. He speaks of notions such as receiving grace and being "unified and consciously right, superior, and happy" (p. 157).

[5] See van Gennep, *Op. Cit.*, p. 29.

non-European cultures and societies. In other words, van Gennep leaves ample space to the present discussion.

In fact, it did not occur to van Gennep that a more inclusive range of references could enhance the applicability of the term—rites of passage—that became his trademark, and indeed changed the agenda on the scholarly scene.[6] Van Gennep's mistake, however, seems to be that he wanted to leave the so-called "high religions" out of the range of his scholarly vision. He may have thought that his thesis would receive a better hearing if the subject matter was a distant, rather than a close, neighbour. Van Gennep also drew essential demarcation lines between the religious and the profane, which prevented him from considering essential life processes that crystallise in non-religious areas, but still entail ritual processes of passage. Furthermore, the range of van Gennep's study covers the whole life cycle of humans, from birth to death. However, once again, *the* religion that enacts it all in a sequential ritual process, Christianity, was left out of consideration. In short, Christianity, which was viewed as a "high" religion, was lost in his work.[7] In a domain of what was generally conceived as a religion that evolved in the spirit (πνενμα), ritual was out of reach. In other words, van Gennep set boundaries to his research that prevented him from making the type of contribution, which has been enabled by modern anthropological studies.

The person who deserves the credit for re-introducing van Gennep's work into contemporary scholarship is Victor Turner.[8] However, we shall omit a full discussion of his work, here, because Turner made symbols function as the prism through which he viewed rituals. If rituals are at all derivative, one must foreground their setting in myth, not in symbols and ideas. In Chapter 3, I have tried to give the reasons for this view.[9] Myths, we

---

[6] Van Gennep admits, though, his indebtedness to Robertson Smith's study, *The Religion of the Semites*.

[7] See Ivan G. Marcus, *Rituals of Childhood: Jewish Acculturation in Mediaeval Europe*, Yale University Press: New Haven and London, 1996. Marcus refers to interesting materials of which van Gennep was not aware.

[8] Nuances in the respective views of Van Gennep and Turner are discussed in Don Handelman, *Models and Mirrors: Towards an Anthropology of Public Events*, Cambridge University press: Cambridge... 1990, pp.65-66.

[9] As we have seen, the subject of myth and ritual is one of the most contested areas of modern scholarship. For a general point of orientation relevant to our

saw, are neither symbols nor narratival configurations of ideas, but stories that are linked to rituals.[10] Furthermore, despite their awareness of the need to take advantage of new scholarly notions, several books that were recently published on the subject of rituals (as specified earlier in this book, I prefer the plural notion) have to be left out of the present treatment of the subject. The reason is that, in my view, they contribute very little that constitutes a departure from common notions on rituals. Thus, for instance, Catherine Bell concentrates on generalities rather than on detailed analysis of specific rituals. When she refers to specific rituals, she does so for illustrative purposes, shifting quickly from one example to the other.[11] If she refers at all to Christianity, it is only in sporadic references. Generally speaking, in most of the works known to me ritual practice in Christianity is hardly ever studied systematically, from the point of view of ritual theory. Scholars have often overlooked aspects of rituals that would help to bring about a real change in the study of rituals.

In the past, terms such as "worship" and "liturgy" were the preferred terms, in the study of the Christian way of life, as opposed to terms such as "ritual." If we examine Paul's attitude towards what we would today call ritual, we cannot avoid feeling the loud theological ring of the terms of reference applied. However, we should not fall into the trap of discussing *rituals*, in general, in light of Paul's critical views of the νόμος, the Mosaic Law. In the eyes of many, Paul was often viewed as taking an antinomian position.[12] However, if we take 1 Cor. 9: 20-21—"To the Jews I became as a Jew, in order to win the Jews; to those under the law I became as one under the law, that I might win those under the law. To those outside the law I became as one outside the law, *not being without law toward God but under the law of Christ*, that I might win those outside the law"—then the common view with regard to the subject if "Paul and the Law" has to change

---

discussion, see Walter Burkert, *Greek Religion*, Harvard University Press: Cambridge (Mass.), 1985, pp. 54-118.

[10] As I suggested earlier, stories about divine beings that have lost their connection to rituals come under the rubric of mythologies.

[11] See Catherine Bell, *Ritual Theory, Ritual Practice*, Oxford University Press: New York and Oxford, 1992; *Ritual: Perspectives and Dimensions*, Oxford University Press: New York and Oxford, 1997.

[12] See, for instance, Alan F. Segal, *Paul the Convert*, Yale University Press: New Haven and London, 1990, p.144.

radically. These verses, and particularly the italicised words, show that Paul did not reject the "Law" as a matter of principle. If Paul still maintains a "law toward God," he cannot be considered antinomian. Nor can he be identified with views that underestimate the place and role that rituals have in religion.[13] Paul *is* under the law, but as one who considers the Christ-event as binding. Very generally expressed, this is the new law of the Christ (Gal. 6: 2). The meaning of this cannot be discussed at length here, but one thing is clear: Paul's position in relation to the Law, in the sense of ritual, is not epitomised by its total negation and rejection. It has a direct bearing on the manner in which Christianity should be enacted as a religion. Paul does not express strong opposition to the rich presence of rituals (and sacramental views), nor is his critique of the Law based on a total aversion to rituals, *per se*. On the contrary, Paul's Letters show how conscious he was of the need to practice Christianity in a variety of rituals.

On the other hand, Paul makes no effort to either hide or disguise the anti-nomos vocabulary, which he uses in his Letters. Scholars are often at pains to explain this kind of discrepancy in Paul's theological exposé. In face of a striking lack of consistency in the Pauline way of expression, I can only give one explanation: Paul voices a sharp criticism of the Pentateuchal (Priestly and Temple-oriented) Law, for which he finds support in the writings of the Prophets of ancient Israel and their criticism of sacrificial rites. At the same time, he voices an inevitable affirmation of rituals, in which he reflects his intuition concerning the ritual essence of religion. Indeed, New Testament Christianity—and the corpus of the Apostolic Fathers—demonstrates criticism of the Law, which for them epitomises "the old" Judaism. However, these writings, reflecting the "new and true Israel", are replete with sections about what the believers should do or avoid doing. In

---

[13] Some scholars still fall into the trap of identifying the Law and rituals. See, for instance, David Flusser, *Jesus*, The Magnes Press: Jerusalem, 1998, pp. 56: "... Western culture contributed to Christianity's de-emphasis on ritual or ceremonial prescriptions concerning 'food and drink and various ablutions' (Heb. 9: 10)... Had Christianity spread first to the eastern Asiatic regions, it would have developed specific ritual and ceremonial practices based on the Jewish law in order to become a genuine religion in that part of the world." One need not add italics to impressionistic observations of this kind. Obviously, this is based on a stereotypical reading of Paul's notions of the Law and its sweeping interpretation of the "concept of freedom from the law" (p. 53).

other words, these writings do not hold back their explicit sayings about rituals. For them, rituals cannot be considered a negligent factor. As an institutionalised religion, Christianity clearly
shows a dependence on order, that is, on law and ritual. The
inevitable conclusion from all this is that Christianity is indeed
an interesting case for the study of a religion *with* rituals. In light
of this conclusion, it is surprising to see how little attention was
given in the relevant scholarship to this aspect of study. It cannot
be said emphatically enough: the presence of ritual themes in no
other writings than Paul's demonstrates how essential rituals are
in structuring religious behaviour and institutions. In short, the
subject of Paul and the Law justifiably figures as the apex of our
discussion of rituals and ritual theory.[14]

III

We have just seen that Paul's views of the Pentateuchal Law easily epitomise the Christian attitude toward the Judaism of the
time,[15] but do not summarise his views with regard to the subject
of rituals. It should be noted, though, that, when we speak of the
Judaism of the time, Mishnah and rabbinism are not the natural
candidates for a comparative discussion. Mishnah was finalised
circa 200 CE, that is, at least two generations *after* the completion
of the last book included in the New Testament. The time difference between the major writings incorporated in the New Testament and the finalisation of Mishnah limits the evidentiary value
of Mishnah for the study of the New Testament, its historical setting
and interpretation. This point has been made by several scholars
in the past, most emphatically by Jacob Neusner. I reiterate it here,
only as a reminder. In many respects, the New Testament informs

---

[14] See James D. G. Dunn's detailed discussion in *The Theology of Paul the Apostle*,
T & T Clark: Edinburgh, 1998 pp. 599-623. Dunn has interesting insights on the
nature of the Eucharistic meal in 1 Cor. However, he characteristically uses "theology" as the framework of his discussion.

[15] See James D. G. Dunn, *The Parting of the Ways: Between Christianity and Judaism and their Significance for the Character of Christianity*, SCM Press: London, 1991.
Here, the context is even wider than in Dunn's work, referred to in the previous
footnote. Dunn's book may serve as a good introduction to the problem raised, in
the present chapter, though the notion of rituals in its various aspects, in the context of religious studies, is missing. See further, James D. G. Dunn (ed.), *Jews and
Christians: The Parting of the Ways A. D. 70 to 135*, J.C.B. Mohr: Tuebingen, 1992.

us about Judaic Law and ritual in pre-Mishnaic times, rather than
the other way round. Thus, what Judaism was really like at the
time of Jesus can be surmised from the New Testament itself, along
with the information found in the writings of the Dead Sea Scrolls
and of Flavius Josephus, rather than from Mishnah and its contemporary Midrashic compilations. Philo, also, comes closer to
the centre, in this respect,[16] although his writings inform us more
specifically about Judaism in the Diaspora than about the Jews
living in their own Land. Since Paul travelled in the Diaspora and
addressed his letters to communities there, Philo may be more
relevant than is sometimes conceded to the study of Paul. However, we should keep in mind that Paul spent his formative years
in Jerusalem before he travelled to Asia Minor, Greece and Rome.
In this respect, Paul may have had better information of Judaic
life in Jerusalem than Philo, who visited Jerusalem once or twice.

However, before we turn to a verse for verse examination of
the relevant Pauline texts, I want to refer the reader to the definition of ritual as given by Stanley J. Tambiah in his 1979 Radcliffe-Brown Lecture, *A Performative Approach to Ritual*. Tambiah says:

> Ritual is a culturally constructed system of symbolic communication.
> It is constituted of patterned ordered sequences of words and acts, often
> expressed in multiple media, whose content and arrangement are char-
> acterized in varying degree by formality (conventionality), stereotype
> (rigidity), condensation (fusion), and redundancy (repetition). Ritual
> action in its constitutive features is performative in these three senses:
> in the Austinian sense of performative wherein saying something is also
> doing something as a conventional act; in the quite different sense of
> a staged performance that uses multiple media by which the partici-
> pants experience the event intensively; and in the third sense of in-
> dexical values—I derive this concept from Peirce—being attached to
> and inferred by actors during the performance.[17]

Tambiah's definition makes a lot of sense in the context of many
discussions of rituals in modern scholarship. It should be noted
that Tambiah does not use religious language, which makes it clear
that he views ritual forms of behaviour as not necessarily religious.
Here, I am in complete agreement with Tambiah. Unlike van

---

[16] Interestingly, no extant study systematically examines the subject of Philo
and Halakhah. The issue is discussed in many scholarly writings, but an in-depth
monograph on the subject is still a desideratum.

[17] From the Stanley J. Tambiah, *A Performative Approach to Ritual*, Proceedings
of the British Academy, London, Volume LXV (1979), Oxford University Press,
p. 119.

Gennep, Tambiah argues that "... in a discussion of the enactments which are quintessentially rituals... the traditional distinction between religious and secular is of little relevance..." (p.121). Tambiah's understanding of rituals is informed by general concepts, such as the formation, structuring, and organisation of human behaviour. Religion, in this sense, constitutes an important aspect of human behaviour, but does not exhaust the field of ritual behaviour in humans.

I should make clear, though, at what point I part ways with Tambiah and favour a different approach. Tambiah offers what I consider is a static definition of ritual. There is nothing in that definition that reflects an awareness of the essentiality of the processual features of rituals. Throughout this book, I have made it clear that I view rituals as dynamic processes. They come into effect through the systemic streaming of the various parts that constitute their self-structured essence. I need no longer to repeat what I have said in the previous chapters. I consider it vital, for the understanding of rituals, to consider the manner in which their dynamic aspects first come into being, then into effect and, finally, how they bring about the type of transformative event that happens in each case. The various components that comprise the ritual event generate a process. This process is vital for the ritual event to move from inert stasis in the mind to a purposive end in external reality. In other words, what matters is the energising of the various segments that set the ritual process into motion and make it a factor that energises effectiveness.

It is therefore necessary to highlight the special ways in which each ritual is made to create the process that brings about the expected transformative event. We have described the major formative aspects of rituals, and shown how they are fulfilling functions that enhance life or existence.[18] The reversal of the generative process means the extinction of central life processes. The function of rituals is to control and, hence, prevent, change the

---

[18] Lev. 16 gives a very powerful example of this notion. See the discussion, in the previous chapter. For a general reference, in the context of the present study, see the various studies included in Maurice Bloch and Jonathan Parry (eds.), *Death and the Regeneration of Life*, Cambridge University Press: Cambridge, 1999. It should be noted that, in that collection of papers, the subject is not death caused by violence (as in the case of the two sons of Aaron and, in a different context, Jesus), but the ritual handling of death and funerary ceremonies.

course of, or redress the consequences of adverse events. Thus, since the notions of change and transformation are essential to the definition of rituals, this definition has to include a language that foregrounds the processual dynamics of change. In my view, then, one of the major characteristics of rituals is missing from Tambiah's definition.

We have already mentioned the fact that arguments advocating the need to use a behavioural discourse, in the study of rituals, may give the impression that rituals are mechanical acts dependent on biological instincts. Indeed, many people consider that behaviourism is a domain of human activity that does not involve a consciously operating mind. Behaviour and cognition are often viewed as two opposites. There can be nothing more misleading than such a view. Rituals, even in their behavioural setting, cannot be viewed in the same way as instinctual acts. Rituals are the channels through which the mind transmits and activates structured messages, which can be transmitted only in this manner and which aim to achieve a self-defined target. In this respect, rituals function as language, but do so in other means of expression. These forms of expression are indispensable to the continuation, or prolongation, of essential life-enhancing processes. In a deep sense, they cannot be randomly configured or accidental forms of expression. As previously noted, the factor of intentionality should receive full attention, in this connection. Intentionality represents the participation of the human mind in creating conditions for minimal volition to be a decisive factor in defining the validity of the process as a ritual event.[19]

Finally, we have seen that rituals presuppose a cultural context that meaningfully sustains their constitutive and communicative power. We have viewed this cultural context as paradigmatically structured by four types of attitudinal or orientational spaces. These are: (1) the initial predisposition—social and individual—that generates the multifaceted forms of the rituals and their pro-

---

[19] To avoid any misunderstanding, I would like to repeat that rituals are neither biologically instinctive nor automatic acts, such as found in animal life and behaviour. Acts that are repetitive and shared by a herd have the appearance of or resemble forms of ritual behaviour. See Walter Burkert, *Creation of the Sacred: Tracks of Biology in Early Religions*, Harvard University Press: Cambridge (Mass.), 1996. However, rituals, among humans, are the expression of a structure-oriented mind. As pointed out above, Burkert's interest in the systematic assessment of rituals is somewhat limited.

cessual unfolding; (2) the specific circumstances that trigger the need to do the rituals; (3) the manner in which rituals are done; (4) the ultimate results or goals that come into effect through the doing of the rituals. These paradigmatic spaces are conditional settings for bringing together various ritual functions into existentially coherent entities. They activate, and then energise, the ritual processes, which ultimately do what they are expected to do. In many cases, rituals contain a corrective process. This is particularly true of sacrificial or penitential acts. It is generally believed that disrespecting the ritual process, failure to do it properly, or missing the appropriate time and place for doing it is liable to adversely affect the integrating powers of the ritual process. We have shown that this characterisation of rituals covers the phenomenon in a more systematic manner than found elsewhere: it moves away from Tambiah's definition by focussing on aspects of the dynamics implied in ritual processes rather than highlighting their static characteristics.

Yet another component in Tambiah's definition calls for comment. Tambiah's definition begins with the statement: "Ritual is a culturally constructed system of symbolic communication." This is important, though in my view, requires some explication. It is, admittedly, very common to find a unique ritual defined as a symbolic performance. Evidently, in the example discussed below, one cannot eat the body of Christ nor drink his blood. However, the ritual that marks these events does not, as is often thought, replicate them symbolically. Rituals operate on a different, and in this sense non-symbolic, plane. However, when suggesting a different view on this issue, the subject of ritual and symbolism has to be clarified.

What exactly is implied by Tambiah's "symbolic communication"? The thrust of Tambiah's definition is based on his perception of rituals as signs or as socially contextualised signifiers. That is to say, linguistic components play an important role here. In giving expression to this idea, Tambiah uses a highly technical language adapted to his own purposes from various authorities. He argues that, due to their communicative functions, rituals operate as language. This is not new to us, and we, too, have followed similar lines of argumentation, although we approached them from a different angle. In this respect, we have argued that the primary function of rituals is communicative, but the specifics of communication in this case are transformative. How this transformation functions on a communicative level will be explored later on, when we discuss the details of the "Lord's Supper". The analogy of rituals to language will therefore be viewed somewhat differently to Tambiah's approach. Language is a world creating entity or factor. This is the notion explicated in the *Genesis* story, in the concept of the Logos, and, in a highly sophisticated manner, in *Sefer Yetsirah* ("The Book of Creation"). Every ritual creates its own cosmos, or dynamically relates to an existing one. To carry the analogy a little further, every specific utterance conveys an expressive cosmos, that is, a self-sustained unit of speech that can easily be likened to a cosmos. Every ritual makes its own statement and its communicative elements should be established with regard to what it specifically does or does not do. Since rituals are viewed here as conveying meaning only in or through what they bring into effect, their analogy to the communicative nature of language has to be defined in a special way.[20] Magic will show this point clearly. In magic, rituals empower words to do their transformative function even on the material-physical world. Prayers are another example to the same effect. Without the ritual mechanism, words cannot acquire the status of prayer.

The manner in which Tambiah expresses himself may give rise to an understanding of rituals in which they are highlighted as vehicles expressing symbols. As noted, Victor Turner stressed this approach in several of his studies. It is indeed a common fallacy of modern scholarship to treat rituals in this manner. Scholars tend to believe that, if rituals have anything worthy of scholarly attention, they are the ideas or concepts that nourish or sustain rituals rather than their doing. If ideas are behind them, it could be argued that a latent agendum is being served in the doing of rituals. This may amount to the unmasking of the "real" content of the rituals. Although my understanding of rituals involves the mind that acts in, or through, them, this happens without necessarily involving an ideational component.[21]

---

[20] For the theoretical discussion that helped the present writer reach his own conclusions, the reader is referred to William F. Hanks, *Referential Practice: Language and Lived Space among the Maya*, The University of Chicago Press: Chicago and London, 1990; *idem. Language and Communicative Practices*, Westview Press: Boulder, Colorado, 1996.

[21] In this respect, I share Roy Rappaport's view on rituals. See, Roy A. Rappaport,

I attach great importance to this way of presenting rituals, since it moves the study of rituals from the ideational sphere, which is more often than not formulated by no other than the critical onlooker, to the sphere of the person who does the rituals. Among other things, my approach allows the factor of empowering intentionality to play its full role in the scholarly assessment of rituals. Intentionality, in my view, is *not* an idea-forming component. It is a mental or volitional predisposition that instrumentally functions in making the ritual process an effective factor in the lives of people. When ideational and theological considerations are left out, the space is given over to the real factor, namely, intentionality, in the sense described above. Intentionality is not connected to any ideational component: it is simply a subtle moment of volitional consciousness.

One should note that very few people, even those performing a specific ritual, are able to account for the ideas that allegedly sustain rituals. People *do* rituals, because a mental space is opened for ritual behaviour to come into effect, or because they are told to do them. Explanations usually follow at a later stage, when resourceful sophistication is a *sine qua non*. However, the inner logic that sustains the special sequence creates the ritual event as a Gestalt, without necessarily demanding a detailed explanation.[22] In fact, the doing of rituals creates its own modes of behavioural expression. The success or failure that believers attach to the ritual act has very little to do with whether they understand the technicalities and nature of the ritual act.

With regard to the Pauline materials that we intend to discuss here, the question will arise: what makes the difference between

---

Ritual and Religion in the Making of Humanity, Cambridge University Press: Cambridge, 1999, p. 24, where ritual is defined: "... the performance of more or less invariant sequences of formal acts and utterances not entirely encoded by the performers." This is a rather narrow definition of ritual, but it is significant. As Rappaport himself says (p.26): "Certain features often associated with ritual are notably absent from our definition. First, the term "symbol" docs not appear... That ritual is not entirely symbolic is one of its most interesting and important characteristics..." One element that is disturbingly absent from Rappaport's definition is the mind-factor, repeatedly highlighted above.

[22] To illustrate my position, I believe that Stanley Tambiah would have used something like "are structurally constituted," instead of the words "are done." The difference is between the approach, which focuses more on the generative process rather than, as I do, on the parts that create the functional process, and, hence, meaning.

a ritual act that is repudiated and a very similar one that is approved? Paul criticises sacrifices that are offered to pagan Gods, but he does not shun meals that are taken with sacrificial agenda, such as the "Lord's Supper." To suggest a vantage point, in rabbinic Judaism both are treated as idol worship. Paul does not oppose sacrifices *per se*, only those that are wrongly directed to idols. In this sense, one can argue that, the targeted context, or theology, creates the measuring scale that defines correctness or the wrongness of the ritual act. Context and theology, however, are external factors that do not intrinsically connect to the very doing of rituals. Regarding external factors, a myth that is told in connection with a certain ritual often *is* the most relevant explanation of that ritual, but it is rarely part of the doing process itself. Myth is a communal narrative that directly sustains the ritual act. The question whether it has theological status or not is a secondary one. People doing the ritual share the relevant myth; but, like theology, myth does not directly bear upon the manner in which the ritual is done and on how it becomes an efficacious process.

V

We now come to the main topic of this chapter—the "Lord's Supper,"[23] the ritual as described in Paul, and its practice. Along with Baptism, the Eucharist is a central ritual event—more specifically, a sacrament—in the Pauline writings. Both cases involve what recent scholarship views as essential to rituals, namely, transformative events. These events are usually regenerative and reconstitutive, often involving a preliminary stage or event of a deconstitutive nature.[24] Baptism is the first transformative event in the life of a Christian and is often conceived as a purifying, that is a regenerative, event. Allegedly, it purges Christian believers from their dependence on a birth-event that connects them to the Original Sin of Adam and Eve. However, from the point of view of ritual studies as presented here any immersion in water entails a return to pre-existence or non-existence. This can be likened

---

[23] The Greek term is mentioned in 1 Cor. 11: 20—κυριακὸν δεῖπνον.

[24] What these deconstructing elements or factors are will be discussed in the example that follows, namely, the "Lord's Supper."

to a return to the maternal womb. One may even say that it constitutes intentional deconstruction, drowning in total abandonment. Thus, before there can be a new birth that has a regenerative function and status, there has to be a mimetic return to the quasi-uterine state of pre-existence.

The "Lord's Supper" is also a central event in Christian life. Its centrality underwent a series of changes before it has become part of the Catholic Mass in church. It should be noted that Protestant criticism of Catholic indulgence in the cult focused on the centrality of the "Lord's Supper" in the life of the Catholic Church. Whatever is involved in the "Lord's Supper," and we shall examine the Pauline evidence only, involves a process that is intended to bring about a ritual transformation of a group of individuals into a community of believers. As we shall see, the Lord's Supper also involves a preliminary stage of annihilation (the breaking of the bread), before re-generation becomes possible (creating the totality of the community that shares in the bread and is consequently reunited by and through the ritually reassembled pieces of the bread).

We shall now try to apply this characterisation of rituals to New Testament materials that deal with the "Lord's Supper." As noted, rituals are structured to be processual. This means that they generally have to be meticulously prescribed and learned before they can be done and shared at a community level. Structure, here, means that the people concerned carry out rituals in a fixed sequence, at given times and, in many cases, in specifically chosen places. Changes, in this sphere, can either invalidate the rituals or create denominational splits. Observing the correct patterning of these conditions guarantees that not only the form is duly preserved but also that the performed ritual is empowered in such a manner that guarantees the accomplishment of its ends.

This becomes evident in the manner in which the "Lord's Supper" is prescribed in 1 Cor. 10-11. One may distinguish between the descriptive—"historical"—formulations in the Gospels, where the "Last Supper" is described as it allegedly took place[25] and the prescriptive formulations as stated in 1 Cor. 10 and 11. The one that will be discussed first is found in 1 Cor. 10: 16-

---

[25] Of course, one can argue that traces of the Pauline texts are clearly visible, even here, but this is not a point we want to discuss in the present study.

18.[26] The other formulation, which is significantly different, is found in 1 Cor. 11: 23-26. The first is mentioned in connection with the avoidance of sacrifices that are offered to idols. The second is mentioned in connection with the establishment of the Christian community in unity and the complementary wish to avoid communal fragmentation. Significantly, in both cases, meals, rather than the service in the Church, are the context. An important difference between the two formulations is that, in the first formulation, the wine comes before the bread, while in the second, the order is reversed and the bread comes before the wine. As will be shown below, both formulations can be accounted for, in Judaic practice.[27]

Paul creates a strong link between the formalities of the performance and the final goal, which is the sacrificial act essential to establishing a Christian community. Viewed from a ritual point of view, creating the community cannot be accomplished by a simple verbal declaration or formal pledge of allegiance, authoritative as each of these may be. It has to come about by a ritual act! This act does not replace a verbal declaration, but creates the desired goal in its own way and in its own terms of reference.

An interesting question is how one should read the words of Jesus on the wine and the bread (Matt. 26: 17-30; Mk. 14: 12-25; Luk. 22: 7-23,).[28] Arguably, they reflect the same source material that Paul uses. Even the change in the order of their occurrence—bread followed by wine and wine followed by bread—is reflected in the Gospels. While Mark and Matthew have the bread first followed by the cup of wine, Luke describes the

---

[26] Usually, these verses do not receive priority in the various discussions of the "Lord's Supper". For instance, they are not included in the synoptic texts presented in Kurt Aland, (ed.), *Synopsis of the Four Gospels* [Greek-English Edition], German Bible Society: Stuttgart, 1984, p. 284.

[27] This depends on whether a regular meal is described or the meal of Passover Eve. In a regular meal, the bread usually comes first, and the wine that comes with the meal generally does not require a special blessing. However, on Passover night, and in Sabbath and festival meals, the wine comes first, and a special sanctification prayer is said before it is drunk. The bread is covered to indicate that the regular order is reversed. This is because the major blessing said over the meal mentions the "bread growing out of the earth," and, for ritual purposes, this includes everything consumed during the meal. Thus, the wine indicates the "day" not the meal. We shall immediately see what Paul makes of the blessing over wine.

[28] The words, added by Luke (22: 19), "Do that in my memory" reflect acquaintance with 1 Cor. 11: 24 - 25.

Passover event in the reverse order. In any event, one can see, in the different accounts given in the Gospels, the myth behind the ritual as formulated by Paul. This does not tell us anything regarding the true historical order of the descriptive (Gospels) and prescriptive (Paul) materials, but it establishes the myth-ritual linkage of the materials. Initially, one may read the words of Jesus, in the context of the Passover event, which he celebrated with his disciples, with no real Christological intentions or meaning. The Last Supper (as distinct from the Lord's Supper and the Eucharist) is set as a Passover event. Paul takes the event out of its Passover context and turns it into the "Lord's Supper," that is, into a communal meal that can take place in any circumstance. This is a unique feature of rituals: although they can be done at any time, place, and by any person, it is usually mandatory that the factors of time, place, and officiating person should be strictly fixed. Despite the fact that, technically speaking, all the essential ingredients are still there, the "Lord's Supper" becomes a new ritual no longer connected to the original setting of the Passover night. In its new formatting, it has transformative goals that are completely different to those of the Jewish Passover ritual. The new ritual is no longer set in the framework of enacting the memory of the Exodus, but in the framework of the Passover Supper that Jesus and his disciples celebrated, with its new redemptive functions.

As in the case of every ritual, the "Lord's Supper" has repetitive characteristics that can be shared by any community. Moreover, as we shall see, it addresses important sacrificial issues through which the community is constituted. As noted above, these issues have a covenantal status. The universal aspects of this status are enhanced by the fact that neither a specific place nor time is mentioned, only the circumstances, *i.e.* whenever the community sits down to take a communal meal.[29] Thus, the "Lord's Supper" is given the ritual modes of a ceremony that has specifically stated functions. Initially, it involved the community at Corinth. Subsequently it helped to establish Christian consciousness everywhere and at all times.

A closer examination of the text will reveal Paul's understand-

---

[29] This made it possible for the Protestant Church to maintain its own concepts concerning the practice and frequency of the "Lord's Supper."

ing of the function of ritual. We should remember that, in 1 Cor.,
Paul refers twice to the "Lord's Supper." In the first instance, he
says:

> The cup of blessing which we bless, is it not a participation in the blood
> of Christ? The bread which we break, is it not a participation in the
> body of Christ? Because there is one bread, we who are many are one
> body, for we all partake of the one bread. Consider the people of Is-
> rael; are not those who eat the sacrifices partners in the altar?" (1 Cor.10:
> 16-18).

It is important to note that food is the core of the ritual. Food
sustains life. Its life-enhancing qualities are intensified by the sacrificial dimensions that are added here to it. Sacrifices sustain life
in a more intense sense than food eaten by an individual person
or by a community. In spite of the interrogative mode of this text,
it contains everything a student of ritual needs, or can wish to find.
It is deeply informative about its embedded ritual theory. It sets
constitutive regulations, describing how this specific ritual works
in order to accomplish what it is supposed to do. Further issues
emerge later (in chapter 11), and they will be given full attention
when we come to that point.

What else do we find in the text that is of interest to the student of rituals? In the first place, Paul's words contain a distinct
element of intentionality, implied in the blessing that is said over
the cup of wine. Intentionality, as we have seen, points to the mind
working through and in ritual. The blessing actively defines the
intentionality that is embedded in the sharing in the cup of wine.
Although the actual words of the blessing are not mentioned here,
the "missing" words must have ritual potency.[30] *Mutatis Mutandis*,
a ritual setting can endow words with the potency to carry out a
special transformative "mission." In our case, the blessing creates
a ritual connection between the cup, the blood of Christ and the
community.[31] Thus, sharing the wine creates a communal act of

---

[30] This raises the subject of magic and theurgy, which requires a special handling in the context of rituals and ritual theory. Briefly, magic shows how vital,
even indispensable, rituals are for a "deed" to be empowered to do its designated
action.

[31] It is significant that Paul, here, does not identify the blood with the wine, as
Mark and Matthew, unlike Luke, do in the Passion story. More specifically, Jesus,
in the Gospel of Matthew, conveys the notion: "*Drink of it*, all of you, for this is my
blood..." (26: 28).

participation with broad implications. It is not acted out symbolically: rather, as Paul himself says, it is done in/through a blessing that is said, a verbal empowerment. In short, the words of the blessing, although unvoiced here, create a reality that generates a constitutive process, which shapes the community that receives the ritual status of being allowed to participate in the blood of Christ. Since rituals do not happen symbolically or automatically, the ritual at hand must possess certain empowering specifics that make it work in the way it does. In the case of the blessing of the cup, sharing in the act of blessing creates the momentum, or reality, that facilitates the sharing in the wine.[32] The wine is wine, not blood. However, the mimetic act makes the wine act as blood. The theological notion of transubstantiation is still not present. However, intentionality is at work at this early stage.

Initially, Paul assumes that blessing the cup creates the necessary predisposition for people to participate "in the blood of Christ," *alias* the wine. At first, it is not even stated what this participation entails, or how it comes into effect. The same is true of the "participation in the body of Christ" which, initially, comes into effect by breaking the bread. If we take Paul at his word, both acts of "participation" entail neither drinking from the cup nor eating from the bread. Blessing and breaking are mentioned here as *the* crucial acts. This, in my view, cannot but be intentional. It focuses all the initial attention on the issue of doing, something that is *not* directly connected to the act of consuming. It should also be noted that drinking from the cup is not mentioned at all in this passage. Eating, however, is directly referred to in the second part of this passage. Once it is mentioned, the eating itself—not its symbolic enactment—creates *the* momentum for the act of participation. The question, then, is, what are the parameters that one should use to define this act of participation. In line with the previous discussions, I prefer to avoid theological parameters. Instead, I view this participation as a socially constitutive act that aims at bringing into effect a specific reality, a unitive event enacted at the communal level. A ritual correspondence exists between the act of breaking the bread and eating it. The correspon-

---

[32] It should be added that the manner in which Paul refers to the "Lord's Supper" demonstrates that he has in mind an already existing custom. This becomes particularly evident, when this passage is compared with 11: 27-29.

dence crystallises into a sacrificial event. Wine, (like oil and salt), also has a special status in the sacrificial acts of the Temple. However, unlike Dionysian cults, in the sacrificial protocol of the Jewish people, wine only accompanies sacrifices and has no sacrificial status in its own right. It is poured on, or simply brought to, the altar along with many sacrificial victims. This, however, is not the case with the lamb slaughtered for Passover ritual, which, in the Christian view, prefigures Jesus. On a practical level, we may assume that the acid components of wine have cleansing capabilities that help to remove the smell of burnt flesh. We know from many sacrificial rites, in the ancient Near East, that fermented liquids (such as beer) were part of meals that had sacrificial status.

The interrogative mode with which Paul introduces the passage, furthermore, emphasises the fact that no symbolic gesture is intended. The cup cannot qualify as "a cup of blessing" unless a ritual blessing *is said*. In our case, it also intentionally enables the process of participation.[33] Focussing the mind on a ritual object—the cup—can do a lot, but it cannot make the participation possible before the words of blessing are said. The words enable the *ritual* enactment of intentionality, not just as a formal affirmation of a theological truth. The words literally "do it." The blessing that is involved, in this case, receives a new transformative function, which it does not normally have in Judaic practice. In the Judaic practice, the blessing formally precedes the drinking. In fact, Mishnah Tractate *Berakhot* ("Blessing") stipulates that blessings have to be said before—and after—eating and drinking. In my view, this indicates the ritual act of transferring to humans something that initially belongs to God. Thus, before a blessing is said, no one is expected to relish from the food that God supplies. It should be noted, though, that technically speaking the term "cup of blessing" (*kos shel berakhah*) ritually declares that the meal is over, as is the case in Chapter 11 (where the words

---

[33] From the point of view of the ritual act, I believe that it is important to avoid the theological language of transubstantiation so characteristic of John 6: 51-58 and Paul himself in 1 Cor. 11: 23-25! We shall elaborate on this issue later on. In any event, Paul may be understood to say that the wine is the blood of Jesus, but he does not say, here, that the wine *is* turned into blood. I intentionally engage in this kind of interpretative acrobatics in order to avoid unnecessary theological language and speculation.

"of blessing" are missing).[34] In chapter 10, however, Paul mentions the "cup of blessing" to define commencement of the meal, rather than its conclusion. The cup is made into the ritual "foundation" that creates the community (of Christians) and makes it ready to participate in the blood of Christ.[35] What matters, here, is the communal, rather than the individual, participation. This is a point that is stressed by Paul further on, in chapter 11.

The next stage is the act of breaking (not cutting) the bread. This is yet another significant segment, which is expressive of the structural sequence that constitutes the inner processual logic of the ritual. We shall soon see its significance in a sacrificial framework. The blessing over the wine is the preliminary act that has to be accomplished before the act of sharing in the bread becomes possible.[36] The next act, breaking the bread, can come into ritual effect, only after reciting the blessing over the cup. Then the

---

[34] The term "cup of blessing" technically means the cup that is held in the hands of the person who says, in a group, the grace *after* the meal. If the expression "cup of blessing" has the technical meaning that it has in *TB Berakhot* 52a, it is strange that, in the present context, the bread comes *after* the wine! The meal should by now, be over. For this reason, the text of the "Lord's Supper" in 1 Cor. 11, which reverses the order, is more in line with the above-mentioned Halakhic procedure. In any even, we cannot avoid noting that Paul speaks, here, of the "cup of blessing" and "the blessing" rather than the drinking of the wine. This may be a formal difference with no real consequences, but if words count, then this has to be mentioned.

[35] In Scripture, prophets and priests say the blessings over sacrificial meals: 1 Sam. 9: 13. See also the [Qumran] *Rule of the Community*, VI, lines 4-5. Before the blessings are said, no one is allowed to eat. Obviously, this keeps the community together, if it does not actually create it. In the Mishnah Tractate *Berakhot* 6: 6, the same rule is made to apply, although the priestly predominance is no longer preserved. In none of these cases is it specifically indicated what the words of the blessings are. However, Mishnah *Berakhot* Chapter 6, begins with a list of benedictions that must be said on eating various fruits and dishes. Although Mishnah *Pesachim* mentions the *Chavurah* or *Chavurot* several times, when it comes to the description of the evening meal (as distinct from the slaughtering of the Passover lamb), only the housemaster is mentioned, and this in the singular! Can this be taken to mean that the last chapter of Mishnah *Pesachim* was composed with an anti-Christian focus? For a translation of relevant texts relating to communal meals and their protocol, see Jacob Neusner, Tamara Sonn, and Jonathan E. Brockopp, *Judaism and Islam in Practice*, Routledge: London and New York, 1999, pp. 23-27.

[36] Paul also stresses the negative side, that is, what is likely to happen if the meal is not conducted properly. In 1 Cor. 11: 18 ff. Paul addresses the issue of the disagreements that split the assembling community (εκκλησία; the regular English translation, Church, is an over-translation! The Hebrew equivalent would be *Knesset*, or better even in this case, *Chavurah*). Paul argues that participating according to the etiquette of the "Lord's Supper" will make it clear who belongs in

community becomes one ("for we all partake of the one bread"—
10: 17).[37] The full communion of the people partaking in the
bread (re-)creates the oneness, the totality, of the broken (and, in
the case of Passover, unleavened) bread.[38] This totality works
backward and creates the integrating factor that is needed to make
the ritual segments into a working Gestalt.

Interestingly, the participation in the body of Christ becomes
possible by a seemingly paradoxical, if not antithetical, act: First,
the bread is broken; then, the members of community, which has
been constituted by the meal (initially, by "the cup of blessing"),
eat the parts of the bread that have been broken off.[39] In eating
the bread together, the broken pieces of bread are ritually reassembled and become one again, a united totality.[40] The bond that

---

the community and who does not. This is one of the constitutive aspects of the
meal. See Hans Dieter Betz, *Paulinische Studien* (= *Gesammelte Aufsaetze III*), J.C.B.
Mohr (Paul Siebeck), Tuebingen, 1994, pp. 240-271: "Transferring a Ritual: Paul's
Interpretation of Baptism in Romans 6." Betz discusses interesting comparative
materials on the practice of rituals in the Hellenistic world. However, he keeps to
the level of describing the circumstances that made rituals possible in that world,
and does not offer a detailed discussion of the manner in which the very ritual
act—in this case, Baptism—is phenomenologically made to work in the Christian
Church. See also Betz's discussion of ἐκκλησία, *ibid.* p. 244. Relevant to our discussion of Paul's words on the "Last Supper" is Betz's observation to the effect
that "One of the most common ways of introducing new cults into a city was by
founding a cult association" (p. 243). Paul does exactly that, when, with the aim
of creating a community constituted in the sharing of the ritual aspects of the
meal, he gives instructions to the "Corinthians" as to how to participate in their
"Last Supper".

[37] This *is* the sequence and functional purpose of the ritual, as enacted in the
Sabbath and festivals evening meals. However, the cup of wine that consecrates
the Sabbath and other religious festivals is the "cup of the *Qiddush*," "the cup of
separation". Its transformative function is to make a separation between the regular working day and the Sabbath. It must be noted that the one who says the
blessing over the wine also drinks of it. In many families, the cup is handed out to
those present. According to another custom, each person has his own cup of wine,
while the master of the house recites aloud the blessing(s) over the wine. In the
case of the bread, it is cut or broken, then a slice or piece is handed out to all
those gathered for the meal.

[38] See the exposition of this idea in 1 Cor. 12: 12 ff.

[39] It is tempting, in this connection, to bring up the subject of cannibalism,
particularly the eating of dead bodies in certain societies. See, for instance, Andrew Strathern, "Witchcraft, Greed, Cannibalism, and Death: Some Related Themes
from the New Guinea Highlands," in: Maurice Bloch and Jonathan Parry (eds.),
Death and the Regeneration of Life, above fn. 22, pp. 111-133.

[40] This is a somewhat different interpretation to that suggested by Henri Hubert
and Marcel Mauss, *Sacrifice: Its Nature and functions*, Midway Reprint (The Univer-

is ritually created among those sharing the meal causes the pieces of bread to regain their initial wholeness. "Because there is one bread, we who are many are one body, for we all partake of the one bread" (10: 17).[41] The paradox—it is almost a *mysterion*—can be resolved if we keep in mind the fact that, in participating in the previous act of blessing the cup, the individual members of the community have already reached a stage of unity-creating intentionality.[42] As a community, they can now enact the next stage, which is the main one in the ritual process: the deconstitution of the bread, and, complementarily, its reconstitution. The reconstitution of the bread reconstitutes for them the body of the Christ. This raises the degree of reconstitution that is accomplished. First, the bread is restored to its wholeness; then, the members of the group sharing the meal enhance their communal existence.

We should not forget, though, that first the assembled members have to break up as a group. They do it at a ritual level, when they break the bread. In the final resort, they regain existence as a community—and as individuals, too—through the sacrificial participation in the bread, which for them mimetically functions as the body of Christ. In terms deriving from the history of religions, this amounts to an act of initiation. Something that concerns the group happens in a marked-off territory—the ritual act. The ritual act then reflects back onto the community and then onto every individual who is part of the community.

The blessing over the cup creates a community that is prepared to share, and ritually enact, the bread-event. The "broken" pieces

---

sity of Chicago Press): Chicago, 1981, p. 40: "By eating a portion of it [= the victim], he [= the sacrificer] assimilated to himself the characteristic of the whole."

[41] It is essential, in my view, to note the socially creative factor of this meal. It ritually builds the early community of believers who sacrificially share in the body of Jesus. The notion of *pistis*, belief, that is so essential to Paul, provides the redeeming meaning and function of life "in the Christ." It constitutes Christian life in the theological—and, if we follow Albert Schweitzer's understanding of it, also mystical—dimension. It is, however, significant to note that the factor of *pistis* is not included in Paul's discussion of the "Lord's Supper." Ritual and theology are strictly held apart in this case!

[42] The Christian notion of a community, or even "Church," is an interesting extension of the ancient notion of kinship. In making this observation, I follow Frank Moore Cross, *From Epic to Canon: History and Literature in Ancient Israel*, The John Hopkins University Press: Baltimore and London, 1998, pp. 3-21: "Kinship and Covenant in Ancient Israel." Cross does not carry his arguments over to the religious realms of Christianity.

of bread are re-assembled to become whole bread again. This process happens in and through a community that has assembled for a ritual act that creates communal dependence and relatedness. In 1 Cor. 11, the bread of the "Lord's Supper" is identified with the body of the Christ.[43] In this sense, the unity that is constituted by the community brings into effect the wholeness of the crucified Christ. As we shall see, this gives the cup (in chapter 11, the words "of blessing" are significantly omitted) a new status.

VI

We shall now examine the text of the "Lord's Supper," as formulated in chapter 11. This will help us give special attention to the sacrificial structure of the breaking of the bread, and its function, from the initial de-constitution to the final reconstitution.

> For I received from the Lord what I also delivered to you, that the Lord Jesus on the night when he was betrayed took bread, and when he had given thanks, he broke it and said, "This is my body which is for you. Do this in remembrance of me." In the same way also the cup, after supper, saying, "This cup is the new covenant in my blood. Do this, as often as you drink it, in remembrance of me." For as often as you eat this bread and drink the cup, you proclaim the Lord's death until he comes (1 Cor. 11: 23-26).

This passage repeats several elements, mentioned in the previous passage, but it also contains some significant changes. As already pointed out above, the context in which it is said is different from that of the first passage, and it reverses the order of the bread and the wine. It also reports that Jesus said a blessing over the bread and that the cup marked the end of the meal. In addition, it mentions the new covenant. All these elements add up to

---

[43] The formulation in John 6: 51 - 58 is, in this respect, the most radical of all. Jesus is quoted as having said: "I am the living bread that came down from heaven; if any one eats of this bread, he shall live for ever; and the bread which I shall give for the life of the world is my flesh... Truly, truly, I say to you, unless you eat the flesh of the Son of Man and drink of his blood, you have no life in you." The bread from heaven constitutes a new image-category. This is not the "unleavened" bread of the Passover meal, but the manna, which in Judaic (midrashic) tradition imparts eternal life. B.J. Malina, *The Palestinian Manna Tradition*. Brill: Leiden, 1968; Peder Borgen, *Bread from Heaven: An Exegetical Study of the Concept of Manna in the Gospel of John and the Writings of Philo*, Brill: Leiden, 1981.

emphasising the sacrificial character of the ritual.[44] The ritual character of the event is enhanced by the fact that it is presented as repeatable ("For as often as you eat this bread and drink the cup..." 1 Cor. 11: 26). However, no specific details are given with regard to when and in which circumstances this is to happen. Finally, the factor of "remembrance" (ἀνάμνησις) is emphasised in both parts of the passage. We need not enter, here, into a full-scale discussion of the semantic field created by this term. Nonetheless, its ritual implications cannot be overlooked, although Paul makes clear that the ritual act creates a memory-event and not the other way around, namely that memory is the creative factor in ritual.[45]

This passage identifies the bread and the wine with the body of Jesus (1 Cor. 11: 27; 12: 27). It enhances the sacrificial nature of the ritual. Although many reasons can be given for interpreting this ritual, particularly the remembrance part, in symbolic terms I consider it essential to keep the actual sacrificial act in focus. In this, I find the work of René Girard, to which we have already referred above, of great interest and relevance.[46] In referring to Girard's work, I use a selective approach, highlighting from it only those elements that I consider relevant to the present discussion. Girard rightly concentrates on the act rather than on its symbolic meaning or significance. Generally, I am in full agreement with those who argue that the efficacy of the sacrificial act is taken away, if it is viewed as a symbolic act. If one wishes to be protected against, or to ward off, events that cause anxiety and a sense of existing danger, more than mere symbolism has to come into play.

---

[44] The notion of meals or sacrifices, in covenantal acts, is an ancient and well-attested theme. For two famous examples, the reader is referred to Gen. 15 and to Ex. 24. Cutting and destruction as elements of "sacrificial violence" are discussed in the previous chapter.

[45] Yosef Hayim Yerushalmi, *Zakhor: Jewish History and Jewish Memory*, University of Washington Press: Seattle and London, 1982. Yerushalmi deals with different modes of cultural memory, as reflected in Jewish historiography. It should be noted that memory plays a major role in Jewish Halakhah (e.g., the memory of the creation of the world or that of the Exodus from Egypt). However, the ritual functions or dimensions of memory have not been explored, in this connection.

[46] Girard's work has been mentioned earlier in this book. I refer again to Rene Girard, *Violence and the Sacred*, John Hopkins University Press: Baltimore, 1977, pp. 1-38, where "Sacrifice" is the subject of the discourse. See further the discussion of the relevance of Girard's views to the understanding of the "Lord's Supper" in Bruce Chilton, *The Temple of Jesus* (mentioned above), pp. 14-28.

Rituals do what they are expected to do in actual practice and reality. Girard says that sacrifices deflect mischief from the people who are threatened by it onto a sacrificial victim. In this respect, sacrifices are more than just appeasing acts of substitution.[47] When discussing sacrifices, Girard mentions, among other things, the notion of the "scapegoat." In doing so, he appears, though, to retain the notion of substitution.[48] There are, of course, good reasons for maintaining the "scapegoat" (as we saw, in Lev. 16 it is sent out into the wilderness) in the domain of sacrificial substitution.[49] However, what is of great importance, for our purposes, is the emphasis Girard places on the notion of *participation*.[50] As must be clear by now, I consider this element to be of major concern to Paul and his notion of ritual theory. Full, almost mystical, participation is required of those concerned if the ritual act is to fulfil its function as a life-enhancing factor. In the case of the "Lord's Supper," life refers to the community and all that it stands for.

The factor of substitution may be viewed as central to *the theme* of sacrifice, but its bearing on the understanding of *the essence* of the ritual act itself is limited. I consider the notion of the scapegoat to be more essential to the understanding of the sacrificial

---

[47] For a recent emphasis on this view of sacrifice see Walter Burkert, *Creation of the Sacred: Tracks of Biology in Early Religions*, Harvard University Press: Cambridge (Mass.) and London, 1996, pp. 34 ff. Although seemingly unaware of Burkert's work, Roy A. Rappaport, *Ritual and Religion in the Making of Humanity*, Cambridge University Press: Cambridge, 1999, develops some of the lines of thinking discussed in Burkert's study.

[48] This is what Girard writes: "The general direction of the present hypothesis should now be abundantly clear; any community that has fallen prey to violence or has been stricken by some overwhelming catastrophe hurls itself blindly into the search for a scapegoat" (p. 79). However, the next sentence makes clear that the notions of "scapegoat" and "substitution" can easily be confused: "Its members instinctively seek an immediate and violent cure for the onslaught of unbearable violence and strive desperately to convince themselves that all their ills are the fault of a lone individual who can be easily disposed of" (pp. 79-80). See the discussion of the subject of the scapegoat in the previous chapter.

[49] Girard writes "In destroying the surrogate victim, men believe that they are ridding themselves of some present ill" (p. 82).

[50] Girard writes, "If the community is to be freed of all responsibility for its unhappy condition and the sacrificial crisis converted into a physical disorder, a plague, the crisis must first be stripped of its violence. Or rather, this violence must be deflected to some individual—in this case, Oedipus. *In the course of the tragic debate all the characters do their utmost to assist in this process*" (pp. 77-78). The italics were added to highlight the factor of communal participation.

act than the notion of substitution. The scapegoat inherently assumes an initial status of participation. As the description in Lev. 16 makes clear, the scapegoat acts on behalf of the group (in Lev. 16 this is defined by the term *'edah*, "the covenantal community") of which it used to be a part. As we saw, substitution introduces the notion of an existing gap between the sacrificer and the sacrificed. This is not what the scapegoat stands for. In the previous chapter, I explained the reason for preferring, in this context, the notion of replacement. The act of breaking the bread and the eating of it by the members of the community demonstrates how real, in this particular case, the sacrificial ritual is and how vital is the act of [mimetic] participation, on the one hand, and the factor of replacement (the bread for the body of the Christ), on the other. Only participation safeguards the community against its own fragmentation (1 Cor. 11: 18-34; cf. 12: 12-27).

In the terms used by René Girard, breaking is an act of violence, and there is no sacrifice without an initial act of violence. An interesting question that need not be answered here is, are all acts of violence essentially sacrificial? Violence is essential to Girard's understanding of many human acts, not only of sacrifices. Briefly stated, Girard's contribution to our discussion is that the theological notion of sacredness is not the decisive factor in establishing the nature of a sacrifice. If I understand Girard's arguments correctly, the notions that are essential for understanding sacrificial acts transcend the realms of the specifically religious.[51] Something that is more telling of human nature, cognitively and behaviourally, is involved. If we refer to violence as a central element in the sacrificial act, it is implying the enactment of deconstruction at the every conceivable level. The fact that the scapegoat (the bread and the body of the Christ, too) is part of,

---

[51] Some of the people who read previous versions of this chapter asked me why I had chosen Girard to highlight aspects of the sacrificial act. Girard seems to be stretching the phenomenological blanket beyond what is indeed necessary for covering the subject of sacrifice. This seems particularly correct, when Girard maintains the existence of connecting links between the subject of sacrificial violence and patricide and incest. My answer is that Girard, more clearly than many other scholars in the field, views sacrifices in their own ritual reality, without attaching to them much that is, in my view, extrinsic to their very nature and understanding. Furthermore, when Girard refers to violence, I think that he comes close to what is maintained, here, with regard to the crucifixion and to its ritual enactment in the "Lord's Supper".

or incorporated into, the community for which it is supposed to act, is an intrinsic element in the notion of re-placing the community on the scapegoat.[52] The scapegoat is not a substitution (=*pars pro toto*, a part *for* the whole), but a part *of* the whole. Once it takes upon itself the burden (in the physical sense) of the guilt, the community is freed to resume life, once again.

What is at stake is the potential prolongation of conditions in which the community's life processes are likely to be critically suspended. It is essential for the existence of the group that *part of it* is given away so that the whole can regain the vitality of its life processes, that existence can be reconstituted. At a ritual level, regeneration becomes possible only after its opposite, degeneration, has been separated from the main body, as radically as possible. Sacrifice does just that. The sacrificial animal, which belongs to the community (or the individual, as the case might be) enacts for the community the aspect of destruction from which the *'edah* has to separate. The animal enacts the role of instrumental agency rather than of substitution. In Pauline language, this is "the old man in us." In the context of the "Lord's Supper," community fragmentation and the erroneous practice of (pagan) sacrifices are the two issues that are dispensed with through, and in the course of, the new sacrificial meal.

VII

Having reached the conclusion of this book, I would like to introduce some comparative material, by way of a general summary. Let us look at the way sacrifices are assessed in a completely different cultural setting to the one described above. I refer to certain sacrificial rituals in Sri Lanka, as presented and analysed by Bruce Kapferer.[53] Kapferer studied these sacrificial rituals and

---

[52] For instance, this is done by the laying of hands on the scapegoat, as described in Lev. 16. We have already referred to the fact that the scapegoat is sent into the wilderness, accompanied by a person chosen for that purpose (Lev. 16: 21). In Mishnah Tractate *Yoma* 6: 4 the "celebrities of Jerusalem" do the job. Although one may argue that this is necessary to show the goat its way, it seems to me that part of the community, for which the scapegoat enacts atonement, is assigned the task of constituting the scapegoat-group.

[53] See Bruce Kapferer, *The Feast of the Sorcerer: Practices of Consciousness and Power*, The University of Chicago Press: Chicago and London, 1997, particularly pp. 185-

advanced this argument: what is at stake, in a situation that requires a sacrificial act, is the reintegration of the community that
previously went through an act of decomposition or is in need of
social composition. The group has to do something that will regain, or reconstitute, its existence, not before it does a ritual act
that unites its members into a community. What is unique about
a community—as opposed to a group—is the notion of recipro-
cal responsibility. There is something in the existence of a community that is more binding than its getting together, its shared
location, or its formal identity. It is very likely that this is exactly
what Paul had in mind, when he addressed the issue of the constitutive powers (in the terms used here) of the meals taken in the
framework of the community. Everything that is done receives a
special status from the fact that it is configured as a community-
event. Thus, the eating of the broken bread plays a central role
in the re-composition of the group into a whole.

The act of breaking the bread deconstructs, in Kapferer's terms,
the very same society that is later on reunited by sharing the pieces
of the same broken bread. I have already referred to the fact, that
the re-composition of the bread through the act of sharing its
broken pieces is an act that has almost mystical dimensions. It
demonstrates the power of the mind to transform social and essential realities and transcends normal notions of causality.[54] It is
not a symbolic act because the people who share the bread eat
it, but also because they consider the bread, in our terms, as
enacting a re-placing of the body of the Christ. *Mutatis mutandis*,
the existence of the communal unity is the ultimate condition for
the reconstruction of the wholeness of the bread, that is, the re-
placing entity of the body of the Christ. No wonder, then, that
people came to believe that this would virtually restore Jesus to
life. To begin with, the restoration comes into effect through a
communal event. It equals the reconstruction of the society whose
cosmos requires re-integration through participation in the fatal
event of the crucifixion.[55] Thus, the bread that is broken and then

---

220, and elsewhere. We shall immediately discuss Kapferer's characterisation of
sacrifice.

[54] See the discussion in Don Handelman, *Models and Mirrors*, p. 29.

[55] The notions of "cosmos" and "cosmology" are variously used in modern
anthropology. Generally, they relate to any kind of systemic structure in which
people organise their lives or certain aspects of their lives. The terms rank high in

distributed among the various members of the community, in order to accomplish its unity again, constitutes the processual event that Paul refers to as "participation in the body of Christ."

As we have seen, modern scholarship emphasises the element of violence that is involved in the sacrificial act. The sacrificial animal has to be dismembered,[56] before it can be used in the act of being shared by the priests and the people who share in the sacrificial act.[57] In Christian terms, Jesus *had* to die to become efficacious in the redeeming function of his resurrection—that is, in a dialectic series of transformative acts.

Examining Paul's utterances with regard to the ritual act of the "Lord's Supper," one cannot fail noticing the strong polemical tones with which he argues against pagan, and even Judaic, practices of sacrifice. Paul even criticises certain acts of assembly for prayers and other purposes,[58] including casual meals.[59] In other words, Paul argues that, without a correctly oriented sacrificial aim, every meal causes separation instead of communal unity. The "Lord's Supper" clearly points in a new direction. What Paul is saying is that pagans and Jews alike do not possess the key that can open, for them, the door to the correct realisation of their own sacrificial acts, unless they accept the new line he advocates.

One can see that there is a vast literature on the subject of sacrifice. However, when the subject of the "Lord's Supper" is discussed, its sacrificial aspects are generally discussed in a theological framework and the theological discussion focuses primarily on the symbolic nature of ritual. Most discussions of the "Lord's Supper" do not examine the ritual aspects of this event in their own anthropologically-centred setting. What I have tried to accomplish, in this book, and in my assessment of the nature

---

the study of Don Handelman mentioned above and in Jadran Mimica, *Intimations of Infinity: The Cultural Meanings of the Iqwaye Counting and Numbers System*, Berg: Oxford... 1988.

[56] See, for example, Gen. 15: 10 and Lev. 1: 6, 12.

[57] See the comments made by Bruce Chilton, "The Hungry Knife: Towards a Sense of Sacrifice," in: Bruce Chilton and Craig A. Evans, *Jesus in Context: Temple, Purity and Restoration*, Brill: Leiden... 1997, particularly pp. 97-101.

[58] 1 Cor. 11: 17-18: "... because when you come together (συνέρχεσθε) it is not for the better but for the worse. For in the first place, when you assemble in a gathering place (the Hebrew was probably *Knesset* or *Chavurah*, the Greek word used here is: εκκλησία), I hear that there are divisions among you, etc."

[59] See 1 Cor. 11: 21 - 22.

of the "Lord's Supper," is to examine rituals in the framework of ritual theory.

Returning to Kapferer, I find his characterisation of sacrifices extremely informative. Although he refers to exorcist sacrifices in Sri Lanka, Kapferer writes in a manner that recapitulates much of what has been said, in the present chapter, and in the rest of this book:

> The Suniyama is a sacrifice that restores social agency to the victim. The victim becomes a world maker who simultaneously engages in acts of self-recreation and is endowed with the capacity to constitute and reshape relationships in the world as these affect the victim's life chances... The regeneration of human beings in this sense is at the heart of... sacrifice —the reconstitution of human beings as being capable of manifesting a sociality that is immanent in existence... This relates to the strong sense in which I use the word sociality—that is, the capacity to form and participate in the process of world construction and even against the forces that are integral to such processes but may blast apart both the construction of the world and the human beings within it... Therefore, at some risk, I regard sacrifice as a total act of (re)origination by which human beings radically reconstitute, remake, or maintain their life and its circumstances. It is in my view *the* total act which condenses or has immanent within it qua act the generative processes constitutive of human beings and their life worlds... (p. 185-187).

I believe that almost no comment is necessary here. Every part of Kapferer's characterisation neatly summarises our understanding of the nature the "Lord's Supper," as described in 1 Corinthians. The sacrificial death of Jesus, "the victim," is re-enacted ritually by every one in the Christian community, thus contextualising the breaking of the bread in the framework of the subject of the "sacrificed-sacrificer."[60] Kapferer's assessment of the mind of the individual in relation to the group is also of interest to us. This relation is established in the sacrificial act. It represents an important element that has not yet received the scholarly attention

---

[60] We should note, though, with René Girard, *The Scapegoat*, John Hopkins University Press: Baltimore, 1989, that the ritual act of violence, i. e., the sacrifice, can fulfil its role only if it re-enacts the factor of violence that, in this case, was incurred upon Jesus. In other words, though Girard himself does not exactly say so, we may surmise from his line of argumentation that the scapegoat fulfils its sacrificial function, that is, it can be a scapegoat, only if it relates to an act of violence that can be removed in a sacrificial manner. In being sacrificed, that is, in becoming a victim of an act of violence, the scapegoat or the sacrificial animal, is made to fulfil its sacrificial function.

it deserves. It has the advantage of speaking in a language that is of primary interest to us, here. It is a language, which is not loaded with theological notions.

I wish to reiterate that Christianity, in particular, cannot fully function without theological notions. A theological understanding of the "Lord's Supper" is an essential part of the understanding and correct assessment of Christianity, in general, and of the place that the "Lord's Supper" is accorded in Christianity, in particular. However, when one chooses to discuss a particular ritual, *per se*, and understand it in its own terms of reference, it is essential to establish and observe clearly marked boundaries. The discussion of the ritual itself, what it consists of, and how it is done, are subjects that need to be examined first. Only then comes the turn of the issues relating to its theology, history, and inner development.

BIBLIOGRAPHY

Affricate, W.E., et al. (eds.), *Urbanism in Antiquity: From Mesopotamia to Crete*, Academic Press, Sheffield, UK, 1996.

Aland, Kurt, (ed.), *Synopsis of the Four Gospels* [Greek-English Edition], German Bible Society, Stuttgart, 1984.

Assmann, Aleida, and Jan Assmann (eds.), *Schleier und Schwelle: Geheimnis und Öffentlichkeit*, Wilhelm Fink Verlag, München, 1997.

Assmann, Jan, *Moses the Egyptian: The Memory of Egypt in Western Monotheism*, Harvard University Press, Cambridge, MA, and London, UK, 1997.

Bacher, Wilhelm, *Die Exegetische Terminologie der Jüdischen Traditionsliteratur*, Reprint: Wissenschaftliche Buchgesellschaft, Darmstadt, 1965.

Bakan, Michael B., *Music of Death and New Creation: Experiences in the World of Balinese Gamelan Beleganjur*, The University of Chicago Press, Chicago, IL, and London, UK, 1999.

Baudy, Gerhard, "Ackerbau und Initiation: Der Kult der Artemis Triklaria und des Dionysos Aisymnetes in Patrai", in Fritz Graf (ed.), *Ansichten griechischer Rituale: Geburtstags-Symposium für Walter Burkert*, B.G. Teubner: Stuttgart und Leipzig, 1998.

Baumgarten, A.I., "Urbanization and Sectarianism in Hasmonaean Jerusalem," in M. Poorthuis & Ch. Safrai (eds.), *The Centrality of Jerusalem: Historical Perspectives*, Kok Pharos, Kampen, 1996.

Bell, Catherine, *Ritual Theory, Ritual Practice*, Oxford University Press, New York, NY, and Oxford, UK, 1992.

——, *Ritual: Perspectives and Dimensions*, Oxford University Press, New York, NY, and Oxford, UK, 1997.

Betz, Hans Dieter, "Transferring a Ritual: Paul's Interpretation of Baptism in Romans 6" in: *Paulinische Studien* (= *Gesammelte Aufsaetze III*), Mohr & Siebeck, Tübingen, 1994.

——, "Jesus and the Purity of the Temple (Mark 11:15-18): A Comparative Religion Approach", in: *Antike und Christentum: Gesammelte Aufsätze IV*, Mohr Siebeck, Tübingen, 1998.

Biderman, Shlomo & Ben-Ami Scharfstein (eds.), *Myth and Fictions*, Leiden 1993.

Bloch, Maurice, and Jonathan Parry (eds.), *Death and the Regeneration of Life*. Cambridge University Press, Cambridge, UK, 1989.

Bodson, L., *Hiera Zoia: Contribution à l'étude de la place de l'animal dans la religion grecque ancienne*, Academie Royale de Belgique, Brussels, 1975.

Bollas, Christopher, *The Shadow of the Object: Psychoanalysis of the Unthought Known*, Free Association Books, London, UK, 1987.

Borgen, Peder, *Bread from Heaven: An Exegetical Study of the Concept of Manna in the Gospel of John and the Writings of Philo*, Brill, Leiden, 1981.

Bornmann, Lukas, *et al.* (eds.), *Religious Propaganda and Missionary Competition in the New Testament World*, Brill, Leiden and Boston, MA, 1994.

Bourdieu, Pierre, *Outline of a Theory of Practice*, Cambridge University Press, Cambridge, UK, 1977.

Boyarin, Daniel, *Carnal Israel: Reading Sex in Talmudic Culture*, University of California Press, Berkeley, CA, 1993.

Brown, Peter, *The Body and Society*, Columbia University Press, New York, NY, 1985.

Bultmann, Rudolf Karl, *Theology of the New Testament, Part II*. Charles Scribner's Sons, New York, NY, 1955.

——, *New Testament and Mythology and Other Basic Writings*, Philadelphia, PA, 1984.

Burkert, Walter, *Structure and History in Greek Mythology and Ritual*, University of California Press, Berkeley, CA, 1979.

——, *Homo Necans: The Anthropology of Ancient Greek Sacrificial Ritual and Myth*, The University of California Press, Berkeley, CA, 1983.

——, *Greek Religion*, Harvard University Press, Cambridge, MA, 1985.

——, *Creation of the Sacred: Tracks of Biology in Early Religions*, Harvard University Press, Cambridge, MA, and London, UK, 1996.

Burton-Christie, D. *The Word in the Desert: Scripture and the Quest for Holiness in Early Christian Monasticism*, Oxford University Press, New York, NY, and Oxford, UK, 1993.

Cassirer, E., *The Myth of the State*, Doubleday, Garden City, KS, 1955.

Chilton, Bruce, and Craig A. Evans, *Jesus in Context: Temple, Purity and Restoration*, Brill, Leiden, 1997.

Classen, Constance, David Howes and Anthony Synnott: *Aroma: The Cultural History of Smell*, Routledge, London, UK, and New York, NY, 1994.

Coakley, Sarah, (ed.), *Religion and the Body*, Cambridge University Press, Cambridge, UK, 1997

Day, John, *God's Conflict with the Dragon and the Sea: Echoes of a Canaanite Myth in the Old Testament*, Cambridge, MA, 1985.

Dodds, E.R. *Pagans and Christians in an Age of Anxiety*, Cambridge University Press, Cambridge, UK, 1968.

Doniger O'Flaherty, Wendy, *Other Peoples' Myths*, Macmillan Publishing Company, New York, NY, 1988.

Douglas, Mary, *Purity and Danger: An analysis of the Concepts of Pollution and Taboo*, Ark Paperbacks, London and New York, 1966.

——, *Leviticus as Literature*, Oxford University Press, Oxford, UK, 1999.

Dunn, James D.G., *The Theology of Paul the Apostle*, T & T Clark, Edinburgh, UK, 1998.

——, *The Parting of the Ways: Between Christianity and Judaism and their Significance for the Character of Christianity*, SCM Press, London, UK, 1991.

——, (ed.), *Jews and Christians: The Parting of the Ways A. D. 70 to 135*, J.C.B. Mohr, Tübingen, 1992.

Eilberg Schwartz, Howard, *The Human Will in Judaism: The Mishnah's Philosophy of Intention*, Scholars Press, Atlanta, GA, 1986.

Eliade, Mircea, *The Sacred and the Profane: The Nature of Religion*, Harcourt Brace: San Diego, CA, 1959.

——, *Myth and Reality*, New York, NY, 1963.

Finkelstein, Israel, and Neil Asher Silberman, *The Bible Unearthed: Archaeology's New Vision of Ancient Israel and the Origin of Its Sacred Texts*, The Free Press, New York, NY, 2001.

Firth, Raymond, *Symbols: Public and Private*, Cornell University Press, Ithaca, NY, 1973.

Fishbane, Michael, *Biblical Interpretation in Ancient Israel*, Clarendon Press, Oxford, UK, 1985.

——, "'The Holy One Sits and Roars': Mythopoesis and the Midrashic Imagination," in *Journal of Jewish Thought & Philosophy, Vol. 1*, 1991.

Flusser, David, *Judaism and the Origins of Christianity*, The Magnes Press, Jerusalem, 1988.

——, *Jesus*, The Magnes Press, Jerusalem, 1998.

Fox, Michael V., (ed.), *Temple in Society*, Eisenbrauns, Winona Lake, IN, 1988.

Frankfurt, H., *The Birth of Civilization in the Near East*, Doubleday Anchor Books, Garden City, NY, 1956.

Frazer, James George, *The Golden Bough*, Chapter LVII: "Public Scapegoats", and Chapter LVIII, "Human Scapegoats in Classical Antiquity." MacMillan, New York, NY, 1922. Reprinted by Bartleby.com, New York, NY, 2000

Friedson, Steven M., *Dancing Prophets: Musical Experience in Tumbuka Healing*, University of Chicago Press, Chicago, IL, and London, UK, 1996.

Geertz, Clifford, *The Interpretation Of Cultures*, Basic Books: New York, 1973.

Gennep, Arnold van, *The Rites of Passage*, The University of Chicago Press: Chicago, 1960.

Gilat, Yitzhak D., *Studies in the Development of the Halakhah* [in Hebrew], Bar Ilan University Press, Jerusalem, 1992.

Girard, René, *Violence and the Sacred*, John Hopkins University Press, Baltimore, MD, 1977.

——, *Things Hidden Since the Foundation of the World*, Stanford University Press, Stanford, 1978

——, *The Scapegoat*, John Hopkins University Press, Baltimore, 1989.

——, *City of Sacrifice: The Aztec Empire and the Role of Violence in Civilization*, Beacon Press, Boston, MA, 1999.

——, *I See Satan Fall Like Lightning*, Orbis Books, Maryknoll, NY, 2001.

Godelier, Maurice, *The Enigma of the Gift*, The University of Chicago Press, Chicago, IL, 1999.

Graf, Fritz, *Ansichten griechischer Rituale: Geburtstag-Symposium für Walter Burkert*, B.G. Teubner, Stuttgart und Leipzig, 1998.

Gruenwald, Ithamar, *Apocalyptic and Merkavah Mysticism*, Brill: Leiden and Köln, 1980.

——, "The Impact of Priestly Traditions on the Creation of Merkabah Mysticism and Shi`ur Komah" (in Hebrew), *Jerusalem Studies in Jewish Thought, Vol. VI.1-2*, 1987.

——, "The Midrashic Condition: From the Midrash of the Talmudic Sages to that of the Qabbalists" [in Hebrew], *Jerusalem Studies in Jewish Thought, Vol. 8*, 1989.

——, "Midrash and the 'Midrashic Condition': Preliminary Considerations," in Michael Fishbane (ed.), *The Midrashic Imagination: Jewish Exegesis, Thought, and History*, SUNY Press, Albany, NY, 1993.

——, "The Study of Religion and the Religion of Study," in Lukas Bornmann *et al.* (eds.), *Religious Propaganda and Missionary Competition in the New Testament World*, Brill, Leiden and Boston, MA, 1994.

——, "How Much Qabbalah in Ancient Assyria? Methodological Reflections on the Study of a Cross-Cultural Phenomenon," in: Simo Parpola and Robert Whiting (eds.), *Assyria 1995*, The Neo-Assyrian Text Corpus Project, Helsinki, 1997.

——, "Discovering the Veil: The Problem of Deciphering Codes of Religious Language," in Aleida Assmann and Jan Assmann (eds.), *Schleier und Schwelle: Geheimnis und Öffentlichkeit*, Wilhelm Fink Verlag, München, 1997.

Halbertal, Moshe, and Avishai Margalit, *Idolatry*, Harvard University Press, Cambridge, MA, and London, UK, 1992.

Handelman, Don, *Models and Mirrors: Towards an Anthropology of Public Events*, Cambridge University Press, Cambridge, UK, 1990.

Hanks, William F., *Referential Practice: Language and Lived Space among the Maya*, The University of Chicago Press, Chicago, IL, and London, UK, 1990.

——, *Language and Communicative Practices*, Westview Press, Boulder, Colorado, 1996.

Heger, Paul, *The Development of Incense Cult in Israel*, Walter de Gruyter, Berlin and New York, NY, 1997.

Hobsbawm, Eric, *On History*, The New Press, New York, 1997.

——, and Terence Ranger, *The Invention of Tradition*, Cambridge University Press, Cambridge, UK, 1983.

Hoffman, Yair and Frank Pollak (eds.), *Or Le-Ya'akov: Studies in the Scripture and the Dead Sea Scrolls in Memory of Ya'akov Shalom Licht*, [in Hebrew], Jerusalem, 1997.

Hubert, Henri, and Marcel Mauss, *Sacrifice: Its Nature and functions*, Midway Reprint, The University of Chicago Press, Chicago, IL, 1981.

Hubert, Jane, "Sacred Beliefs and Beliefs of Sacredness," in: David L. Charmichael, Jane Hubert, Brian Reeves and Audhild Schanche, *Sacred Sites, Sacred Places*, Routledge, London, UK, and New York, NY, 1994.

Humphrey, Caroline, and James Laidlaw, *The Archetypal Actions of Rituals: A Theory of Ritual Illustrated by the Jain Rite of Worship*, Clarendon Press, Oxford, 1994.

Idel, Moshe, *Kabbalah: New Perspectives*, Yale University Press, New Haven, CT, and London, UK, 1988.

Jacobsen, Thorkild, *The Treasures of Darkness: A History of Mesopotamian Religion*, Yale University Press, New Haven, CT, and London, UK, 1976.

James, Wendy, and N.J. Allen (eds.), *Marcel Mauss: A Centenary Tribute*, Berghahn Books, New York, NY, and Oxford, UK, 1998.

James, William, *The Varieties of Religious Experience*. 1903. Reprinted by Routledge, London, UK, and New York, NY, 2002.

Kant, Immanuel, *Die Religion innerhalb der Grenzen der blossen Vernunft*, II, 3. Königsberg, 1793.

Kapferer, Bruce, *Legends of People, Myths of State: Violence, Intolerance, and Political Culture in Sri Lanka and Australia*, Smithsonian Institution Press, Washington, DC, and London, UK, 1988.

——, *A Celebration of Demons: Exorcism and the Aesthetics of Healing in Sri Lanka*, Berg Smithsonian Institution Press, Washington, DC, 1991.

——, *The Feast of the Sorcerer: Practices of Consciousness and Power*, The University of Chicago Press, Chicago, IL, and London, UK, 1997.

Kedar, Benjamin Z., and R. J. Zwi Werblowsky (eds.), *Sacred Space: Shrine, City, Land*, Macmillan and The Israel Academy of Sciences and Humanities, Houndmills, London, UK, and Jerusalem, 1998.

Klawans, Jonathan, *Impurity and Sin in Ancient Judaism*, Oxford University Press, Oxford, UK, 2000.

Knohl, Israel, *The Sanctuary of Silence: The Priestly Torah and the Holiness School*, Fortress Press, Minneapolis, MN, 1995.

Kolakowski, Leszek, *Religion*, Oxford University Press, New York, NY, 1982.

Lane Fox, Robin, *Pagans and Christians*, Alfred A. Knopf, New York, NY, 1987.

Lauterbach, J.Z., "A Significant Controversy between the Sadducees and the Pharisees", *Hebrew Union College Annual*, Vol. IV, 1927.

Lawson, E. Thomas, and Robert N. McCauley, *Rethinking Religion: Connecting Cognition and Culture*, Cambridge University Press, Cambridge, UK, and New York, NY, 1990.

Liebes, Yehuda, *Studies in Jewish Myth and Messianism*, SUNY Press, Albany, NY, 1993.

Lincoln, Bruce, *Death, War, and Sacrifice: Studies in Ideology and Practice*, The University of Chicago Press, Chicago, IL, and London, UK, 1991.

Lloyd-Jones, Hugh, "Ritual and Tragedy", in Fritz Graf (ed.), *Ansichten Griechischer Rituale: Geburtstags Symposium für Walter Burkert*, B. G. Teubner, Stuttgart und Leipzig, 1998.

Lorberbaum, Yair, *Imago Dei: Rabbinic Literature, Maimonides, and Nahmanides* [Dissertation (in Hebrew)], Hebrew University, Jerusalem, 1997

Maccoby, Hyam, *Ritual and Morality: The Ritual Purity System and its Place in Judaism*, Cambridge University Press, Cambridge, UK, 1999.

Malina, B.J., *The Palestinian Manna Tradition*. Brill, Leiden, 1968

Malinowski, Bronislaw, *Argonauts of the Western Pacific*, reissued by Waveland Press, Prospects Heights, IL, 1984.

——, *Magic, Science and Religion and Other Essays*, reissued by Waveland Press, Prospect Heights, IL, 1992.

Marcus, Ivan G., *Rituals of Childhood: Jewish Acculturation in Mediaeval Europe*, Yale University Press, New Haven, CT, and London, UK, 1996.

Mauss, Marcel, *The Gift: The Form and Reason for Exchange in Archaic Societies* (English Translation by W.D. Halls), W.W. Norton, New York, NY, and London, UK, 1990.

Mieroop, Marc Van de, *The Ancient Mesopotamian City*, Clarendon Press, Oxford, UK, 1997.

Milgrom, J., *Leviticus 1 - 16: A New Translation with Introduction and Commentary*, The Anchor Bible, Doubleday, New York, NY, 1991.

Mimica, Jadran, *Intimations of Infinity: The Cultural Meanings of the Iqwaye Counting and Numbers System*, Berg, Oxford, UK, 1988.

Moore Cross, Frank, *From Epic to Canon: History and Literature in Ancient Israel*, The John Hopkins University Press, Baltimore, MD, and London, UK, 1998.

Naaman, Nadav, "The Historiography, Formation of the Collective Memory and the Creation of Historic Consciousness of the People of Israel at the End of the First Temple Period" (in Hebrew), *Zion* 60, 1995.

Neusner, Jacob, *The Presence of the Past, and the Past of the Presence: History, Time, and Paradigm in Rabbinic Judaism*, CDL Press, Bethesda, MD, 1966.

——, *A History of the Mishnaic Law of Purities*, Classics in Judaic Studies Series, Vol. XVII, *Makhshirin*. Brill, Leiden, 1977. Reprinted by Global Publications, Binghamton, NY, 2002.

——, *The Mishnah: A New Translation*, Yale University Press, New Haven, CT, and London, UK, 1988.

——, *The Economics of the Mishnah*, Chicago University Press, Chicago, IL, and London, UK, 1990.

——, *Religious Belief and Economic Behavior*, Scholars Press, Atlanta, GA, 1999.

——, *The Hermeneutics of the Rabbinic Category-Formations: An Introduction*, University Press of America, Lanham, MD, 2000.

——, "Intentionality and Life Processes in the Law of Judaism: *Hallah* and *Makhsirin*," *The Review of Rabbinic Judaism IV.1*, Brill, Leiden and Boston, MA, 2001.

——, "The Religious Meaning of Halakhah," in: *The Halakhah: Historical and Religious Perspectives*, Brill, Leiden and Boston, MA, 2002.

——, Tamara Sonn, and Jonathan E. Brockopp, *Judaism and Islam in Practice*, Routledge, London, UK, and New York, NY, 1999.

Nock, A.D., *Conversion: The Old and the New in Religion from Alexander the Great to Augustine of Hippo*, Oxford University Press, Oxford, UK, 1961.

Otto, Rudolf, *The Idea of the Holy*, Oxford University Press, Oxford, UK, 1958.

Owen, Dennis E., "Ritual Studies as Ritual Practice: Catherine Bell's Challenge to Students of Ritual," *Religious Studies Review 24.1*, 1998.

Pannenberg, Wolfahrt, *Anthropologie in theologischer Perspective*, Vandenhoeck & Ruprecht, Göttingen, 1983.

Parpola, S. and R. M. Whiting, *Assyria 1995*, The Neo-Assyrian Text Corpus Project, Helsinki, 1997.

Pickering, W.S.F., "Mauss's Jewish Background: A Biographical Essay," in Wendy James and N.J. Allen (eds.), *Marcel Mauss: A Centenary Tribute*, Berghahn Books, New York, NY, and Oxford, UK, 1998.

Pines, Shlomo, "The Philosophical Purport of Maimonides' Works and the Purport of *The Guide for the Perplexed*", in: *Studies in the History of Jewish Thought*, The Magnes Press, Jerusalem, 1997.

Poland, Lynn, "The Idea of the Holy and the History of the Sublime," *The Journal of Religion*, vol. 72 (2), 1992.

Pongratz-Leisten, Beate, "The Other and the Enemy in the Mesopotamian Conception of the World," in: R.M. Whiting (ed.), *Mythology and Mythologies: Methodological Approaches to Intercultural Influences* (Melammu Symposia II), The Neo-Assyrian Text Corpus Project, Helsinki, 2001.

Poorthuis, M., and Ch. Safrai (eds.), *The Centrality of Jerusalem: Historical Perspectives*, Kok Pharos, Kampen, 1996.

Postgate, J.N., *Early Mesopotamia: Society and Economy at the Dawn of History*, Routledge, London, UK, and New York, NY, 1992.

Pritchard, James P., (ed.), *Ancient Near Eastern Texts Relating to the Old Testament* [third edition], Princeton University Press, Princeton, NJ, 1969.

Radcliffe-Brown, A.R., *Structure and Function in Primitive Society*, The Free Press, New York, NY, 1965.

Rappaport, Roy A., *Ritual and Religion in the Making of Humanity*, Cambridge University Press, Cambridge, UK, 1999.

Reynolds, Frank E. & David Tracy (eds.), *Myth and Philosophy*, Albany, NY, 1990.

Rice, Michael, *The Power of the Bull*, Routledge, London, UK, and New York, NY, 1998.

Robertson Smith, W., *The Religion of the Semites*, Meridian Books, New York, NY, 1956.

Sangren, P. Steven, *History and Magical Power in Chinese Community*, Stanford University Press, Stanford, CA, 1987.

Sawyer, John F.A. (ed.), *Reading Leviticus: A Conversation with Mary Douglas*, Sheffield Academic Press, Sheffield, UK, 1996.

Scarry, Elaine, *On Beauty and Being Just*, Princeton University Press, Princeton, NJ, 1999.

Segal, Alan F., *Paul the Convert*, Yale University Press, New Haven, CT, and London, UK, 1990.

Segal, Robert A., *Theorizing about Myth*, University of Massachusetts Press, Amherst, MA, 1999.

Silver, Morris, *Economic Structures of Antiquity*, Greenwood Press, Westport, CT, 1995.

Smart, Ninian, *The Science of Religion & the Sociology of Knowledge: Some Methodological Questions*, Princeton University Press, Princeton, NJ, 1973.

Smith, Jonathan Z., *Imagining Religion: From Babylon to Jonestown*, The University of Chicago Press, Chicago, IL, and London, UK, 1982.

———, *To Take Place: Toward Theory in Ritual*, The University of Chicago Press, Chicago, IL, and London, UK, 1987.

Snaith, Norman H., *The Distinctive Ideas of the Old Testament*, Schocken Books, New York, NY, 1964.

Soggin, J. Alberto, *Introduction to the Old Testament*, Westminster-John Knox Press, Louisville, KY, 1989.

Staal, Frits, *Rules Without Meaning: Ritual, Mantras, and the Human Sciences*, Peter Lang, New York, NY, 1990.

Strange, James S., "Reading Archaeological and Literary Evidence," in: Jacob Neusner (ed.), *Religion and the Political Order: Politics in Classical and Contemporary Christianity, Islam, and Judaism*, Scholars Press, Atlanta, GA, 1996.

Strathern, Andrew, "Witchcraft, Greed, Cannibalism, and Death: Some Related Themes from the New Guinea Highlands," in Maurice Bloch and Jonathan Parry (eds.), *Death and the Regeneration of Life*. Cambridge University Press, Cambridge, UK, 1989.

Sullivan, Lawrence E., *Ichanchu's Drum: An Orientation to Meaning in South American Religions*, Macmillan Publishing Company, New York, NY, 1988.

Talmon, Shemaryahu, *Literary Studies in the Hebrew Bible: Form and Content*: "The 'Navel of the Earth' and the Comparative Method", The Magnes Press and Brill, Jerusalem and Leiden, 1993.

Tambiah, Stanley J., *A Performative Approach to Ritual*, Proceedings of the British Academy, London, Volume LXV (1979), Oxford University Press, Oxford, UK, 1979.

Theissen, Gerd, *Social Reality and the Early Christians*, Fortress Press, Minneapolis, MN, 1992.

Trevor-Roper, Hugh, "The Invention of Tradition: The Highland Tradition of Scotland," in Eric Hobsbawm and Terence Ranger, *The Invention of Tradition*, Cambridge University Press, Cambridge, UK, 1983.

Turner, Victor, *Schism and Continuity in an African Society: A Study of Ndembu Village Life*, Manchester University Press, Manchester, 1957.

——, *The Forest of Symbols: Aspects of Ndembu Ritual*, Cornell University Press, Ithaca, NY, and London, UK, 1967.

——, *From Ritual to Theatre: The Human Seriousness of Play*, PAJ Publications, New York, NY, 1982.

——, *The Anthropology of Performance*, PAJ Publications: New York, NY, 1987.

Urbach, E.E., *The Sages: Their Concepts and Beliefs*, Harvard University Press, Cambridge, MA and London, UK, 1987.

Ware, Kallistos, "'My Helper and My Enemy': The Body in Greek Christianity" in Sarah Coakley (ed.), *Religion and the Body*, Cambridge University Press, Cambridge, UK, 1997.

Wattles, Jeffrey, *The Golden Rule*, Oxford University Press, Oxford, UK, 1996.

Weiss Halivni, David, *Midrash, Mishnah and Gemara: The Jewish Predilection for Justified Law*, Harvard University Press, Cambridge, MA, and London, UK, 1986.

——, *Derash and Peshat: Plain and Applied Meaning in Rabbinic Exegesis*, Oxford University Press, New York, NY, and Oxford, UK, 1991.

Winnicott, D.W., *Through Paediatrics to Psycho-Analysis*, New York, NY, 1975

——, *The Maturational Processes and the Facilitating Environment: Studies in the Theory of Emotional Development*, International Universities Press, Madison, CT, 1991.

Winter, Irene J., "Art in Empire: The Royal Image and the Visual Dimensions of Assyrian Ideology," in: S Parpola and R. M. Whiting, *Assyria 1995*, The Neo-Assyrian Text Corpus Project, Helsinki, 1997.

Wolkstein, Diane, and Samuel Noah Kramer, *Inanna, Queen of Heaven and Earth: Her Stories and Hymns from Sumer*, Harper and Row, New York, NY, 1983.

Yaphet, Sara, "Some Biblical Concepts of Sacral Place", in: Benjamin Z. Kedar and R.J. Zwi Werblowsky (eds.), *Sacred Space: Shrine, City, Land*, Macmillan and The Israel Academy of Sciences and Humanities, Houndmills, London, UK, and Jerusalem, 1998.

Yerushalmi, Yosef Hayim, *Zakhor: Jewish History and Jewish Memory*, University of Washington, Seattle, WA, and London, UK, 1982.

INDEX OF SCRIPTURE AND RABBINICAL WORKS

THE BRILL REFERENCE LIBRARY
OF
ANCIENT JUDAISM

The Brill Reference Library of Ancient Judaism *presents research on fundamental problems in the study of the authoritative texts, beliefs and practices, events and ideas, of the Judaic religious world from the sixth century B.C.E. to the sixth century C.E. Systematic accounts of principal phenomena, characteristics of Judaic life, works of a theoretical character, accounts of movements and trends, diverse expressions of the faith, new translations and commentaries of classical texts – all will find a place in the* Library.

1. Neusner, Jacob, *The Halakhah. An Encyclopaedia of the Law of Judaism.*
   5 Vols. 2000. ISBN 90 04 11617 6 (*set*)
   Vol. I. Between Israel and God. Part A. ISBN 90 04 11611 7
   Vol. II. Between Israel and God. Part B. Transcendent Transactions: Where Heaven and Earth Intersect. ISBN 90 04 11612 5
   Vol. III. Within Israel's Social Order. ISBN 90 04 11613 3
   Vol. IV. Inside the Walls of the Israelite Household. Part A. At the Meeting of Time and Space. ISBN 90 04 11614 1
   Vol. V. Inside the Walls of the Israelite Household. Part B. The Desacralization of the Household. ISBN 90 04 11616 8
2. Basser, Herbert W., *Studies in Exegesis.* Christian Critiques of Jewish Law and Rabbinic Responses 70-300 C.E. 2000. ISBN 90 04 11848 9
3. Neusner, Jacob, *Judaism's Story of Creation.* Scripture, Halakhah, Aggadah. 2000. ISBN 90 04 11899 3
4. Aaron, David H.; *Biblical Ambiguities.* Metaphor, Semantics and Divine Imagery. 2001. ISBN 90 04 12032 7
5. Neusner, Jacob, *The Reader's Guide to the Talmud.* 2001.
   ISBN 90 04 1287 0.
6. Neusner, Jacob, *The Theology of the Halakhah.* 2001. ISBN 90 04 12291 5.
7. Schwartz, Dov, *Faith at the Crossroads.* A Theological Profile of Religious Zionism. Translated by Batya Stein. 2002. ISBN 90 04 12461 6
8. Neusner, Jacob, *The Halakhah: Historical and Religious Perspectives.* 2002.
   ISBN 90 04 12219 2
9. Neusner, Jacob, *How the Talmud Works.* 2002. ISBN 90 04 12796 8
10. Gruenwald, Ithamar, *Rituals and Ritual Theory in Ancient Israel.* 2003.
    ISBN 90 04 12627 9

ISSN 1566-1237